in this series:

coming in this series:

A

The Punitive Society

Fo

MICHEL FOUCAULT

The Punitive Society

LECTURES AT THE COLLÈGE DE FRANCE

1972-1973

Edited by Bernard E. Harcourt
General Editors: François Ewald and Alessandro Fontana

English Series Editor: Arnold I. Davidson

TRANSLATED BY GRAHAM BURCHELL

palgrave
macmillan

THE PUNITIVE SOCIETY
© Éditions du Seuil/Gallimard 2013, edition established under the direction
of François Ewald and Alessandro Fontana, by Bernard E. Harcourt.
Translation © Graham Burchell, 2015

First published in France by Éditions du Seuil/Gallimard under the title
Punitive: Cours au Collège de France. 1972-1973.

English translation first published in hardcover 2015 by
PALGRAVE MACMILLAN

Palgrave Macmillan in the UK is an imprint of Macmillan Publishers Limited,
registered in England, company number 785998, of Houndmills, Basingstoke,
Hampshire, RG21 6XS.

Palgrave Macmillan in the US is a division of St Martin's Press LLC,
175 Fifth Avenue, New York, NY 10010.

Palgrave is the global academic imprint of the above companies and has
companies and representatives throughout the world.

Palgrave® and Macmillan® are registered trademarks in the United States,
the United Kingdom, Europe and other countries.

ISBN 978-1-4039-8660-3

Library of Congress Cataloging-in-Publication Data
Foucault, Michel, 1926-1984.
  [Société punitive. English]
  The punitive society : lectures at the Collège de France 1972-1973 /
    Bernard E. Harcourt ; translated by Graham Burchell.
      pages cm
  ISBN 978-1-4039-8660-3
  1. Social control--Philosophy. 2. Punishment--Philosophy. I. Harcourt,
    Bernard E., 1963- II. Burchell, Graham. III. Collège de France. IV. Title.
    V. Title: Michel Foucault the punitive society.
  B2430.F72113 2015
  303.3'3--dc23   2015003226

CONTENTS

possible the exercise of a power. The case of administrative survey (surveillance). *(II) Analysis of disciplinary power: normalization, habit, discipline.* ⌒ *Comparison of the use of the term "habit" in the philosophy of the eighteenth and nineteenth centuries. Comparison of power-sovereignty in the eighteenth century and power-normalization in the nineteenth century.* ⌒ *Sequestration produces the norm and produces normal individuals. New type of discourses: the human sciences.*

FOREWORD

MICHEL FOUCAULT TAUGHT AT the Collège de France from January 1971 until his death in June 1984 (with the exception of 1977 when he took a sabbatical year). The title of his chair was "The History of Systems of Thought."

On the proposal of Jules Vuillemin, the chair was created on 30 November 1969 by the general assembly of the professors of the Collège de France and replaced that of "The History of Philosophical Thought" held by Jean Hyppolite until his death. The same assembly elected Michel Foucault to the new chair on 12 April 1970.[1] He was 43 years old.

Michel Foucault's inaugural lecture was delivered on 2 December 1970.[2] Teaching at the Collège de France is governed by particular rules. Professors must provide 26 hours of teaching a year (with the possibility of a maximum of half this total being given in the form of seminars[3]). Each year they must present their original research and this obliges them to change the content of their teaching for each course. Courses and seminars are completely open; no enrolment or qualification is required and the professors do not award any qualifications.[4] In the terminology of the Collège de France, the professors do not have students but only auditors.

Michel Foucault's courses were held every Wednesday from January to March. The huge audience made up of students, teachers, researchers and the curious, including many who came from outside France, required two amphitheaters of the Collège de France. Foucault often complained about the distance between himself and his "public" and of how few exchanges the course made possible.[5] He would have liked a seminar in which real collective work could take place and made a number of attempts to bring this about. In the final years he devoted a long period to answering his auditors' questions at the end of each course.

This is how Gérard Petitjean, a journalist from *Le Nouvel Observateur*, described the atmosphere at Foucault's lectures in 1975:

When Foucault enters the amphitheater, brisk and dynamic like someone who plunges into the water, he steps over bodies to reach his chair, pushes away the cassette recorders so he can put down his papers, removes his jacket, lights a lamp and sets off at full speed. His voice is strong and effective, amplified by the loudspeakers that are the only concession to modernism in a hall that is barely lit by light spread from stucco bowls. The hall has three hundred places and there are five hundred people packed together, filling the smallest free space ... There is no oratorical effect. It is clear and terribly effective. There is absolutely no concession to improvisation. Foucault has twelve hours each year to explain in a public course the direction taken by his research in the year just ended. So everything is concentrated and he fills the margins like correspondents who have too much to say for the space available to them. At 19.15 Foucault stops. The students rush towards his desk; not to speak to him, but to stop their cassette recorders. There are no questions. In the pushing and shoving Foucault is alone. Foucault remarks: "It should be possible to discuss what I have put forward. Sometimes, when it has not been a good lecture, it would need very little, just one question, to put everything straight. However, this question never comes. The group effect in France makes any genuine discussion impossible. And as there is no feedback, the course is theatricalized. My relationship with the people there is like that of an actor or an acrobat. And when I have finished speaking, a sensation of total solitude ..."[6]

Foucault approached his teaching as a researcher: explorations for a future book as well as the opening up of fields of problematization were formulated as an invitation to possible future researchers. This is why the courses at the Collège de France do not duplicate the published books. They are not sketches for the books even though both books and courses share certain themes. They have their own status. They arise from a specific discursive regime within the set of Foucault's "philosophical activities." In particular they set out the program for a genealogy of knowledge/power relations, which are the terms in which he thinks of his work from the beginning of the 1970s, as opposed to the program of an archeology of discursive formations that previously orientated his work.[7]

The course also performed a role in contemporary reality. Those who followed his courses were not only held in thrall by the narrative that unfolded week by week and seduced by the rigorous exposition, they also found a perspective on contemporary reality. Michel Foucault's art consisted in using history to cut diagonally through contemporary reality. He could speak of Nietzsche or Aristotle, of expert psychiatric opinion or the Christian pastorate, but those who attended his lectures always took from what he said a perspective on the present and contemporary events. Foucault's specific strength in his courses was the subtle interplay between learned erudition, personal commitment, and work on the event.

♠

With their development and refinement in the 1970s, Foucault's desk was quickly invaded by cassette recorders. The courses—and some seminars—have thus been preserved.

This edition is based on the words delivered in public by Foucault. It gives a transcription of these words that is as literal as possible.[8] We would have liked to present it as such. However, the transition from an oral to a written presentation calls for editorial intervention: at the very least it requires the introduction of punctuation and division into paragraphs. Our principle has been always to remain as close as possible to the course actually delivered.

Summaries and repetitions have been removed whenever it seemed to be absolutely necessary. Interrupted sentences have been restored and faulty constructions corrected. Suspension points indicate that the recording is inaudible. When a sentence is obscure there is a conjectural integration or an addition between square brackets. An asterisk directing the reader to the bottom of the page indicates a significant divergence between the notes used by Foucault and the words actually uttered. Quotations have been checked and references to the texts used are indicated. The critical apparatus is limited to the elucidation of obscure points, the explanation of some allusions and the clarification of critical points. To make the lectures easier to read, each lecture is preceded by a brief summary that indicates its principal articulations.

For this year, 1972-1973, we do not have the recordings of Foucault's lectures made by Gilbert Burlet, but we do have a typescript produced by Jacqueline Germé. The text is based on this typescript and Foucault's preparatory manuscript. In the "Course Context," Bernard E. Harcourt explains the criteria employed to edit the text.[9]

The text of the course is followed by the summary published by the *Annuaire du Collège de France*. Foucault usually wrote these in June, some time after the end of the course. It was an opportunity for him to pick out retrospectively the intention and objectives of the course. It constitutes the best introduction to the course.

Each volume ends with a "context" for which the course editors are responsible. It seeks to provide the reader with elements of the biographical, ideological, and political context, situating the course within the published work and providing indications concerning its place within the corpus used in order to facilitate understanding and to avoid misinterpretations that might arise from a neglect of the circumstances in which each course was developed and delivered.

The Punitive Society, the course delivered in 1973, is edited by Bernard E. Harcourt.

♠

A new aspect of Michel Foucault's "œuvre" is published with this edition of the Collège de France courses.

Strictly speaking it is not a matter of unpublished work, since this edition reproduces words uttered publicly by Foucault. The written material Foucault used to support his lectures could be highly developed, as this volume attests.

This edition of the Collège de France courses was authorized by Michel Foucault's heirs who wanted to be able to satisfy the strong demand for their publication, in France as elsewhere, and to do this under indisputably responsible conditions. The editors have tried to be equal to the degree of confidence placed in them.

FRANÇOIS EWALD AND ALESSANDRO FONTANA

Alessandro Fontana died on 17 February 2013 before being able to complete the edition of Michel Foucault's lectures at the Collège de France, of which he was one of the initiators. Because it will maintain the style and rigor that he gave to it, the edition will continue to be published under his authority until its completion.—*F.E.*

1. Michel Foucault concluded a short document drawn up in support of his candidacy with these words: "We should undertake the history of systems of thought." "Titres et travaux," in *Dits et Écrits, 1954-1988*, four volumes, eds. Daniel Defert and François Ewald (Paris: Gallimard, 1994) vol. 1, p. 846; English translation by Robert Hurley, "Candidacy Presentation: Collège de France" in *The Essential Works of Michel Foucault, 1954-1984, vol. 1: Ethics: Subjectivity and Truth*, ed. Paul Rabinow (New York: The New Press, 1997) p. 9.

2. It was published by Gallimard in May 1971 with the title *L'Ordre du discours*, Paris, 1971. English translation by Ian McLeod, "The Order of Discourse," in Robert Young, ed., *Untying the Text* (London: Routledge and Kegan Paul, 1981).

3. This was Foucault's practice until the start of the 1980s.

4. Within the framework of the Collège de France.

5. In 1976, in the vain hope of reducing the size of the audience, Michel Foucault changed the time of his course from 17.45 to 9.00. See the beginning of the first lecture (7 January 1976) of *"Il faut défendre la société." Cours au Collège de France, 1976* (Paris: Gallimard/Seuil, 1997); English translation by David Macey, *"Society Must be Defended." Lectures at the Collège de France 1975-1976* (New York: Picador, 2003).

6. Gérard Petitjean, "Les Grands Prêtres de l'université française," *Le Nouvel Observateur*, 7 April 1975.

7. See especially, "Nietzsche, la généalogie, l'histoire," in *Dits et Écrits*, vol. 2, p. 137; English translation by Donald F. Brouchard and Sherry Simon, "Nietzsche, Genealogy, History" in *The Essential Works of Michel Foucault 1954-1984, vol. 2: Aesthetics, Method, and Epistemology*, ed. James Faubion (New York: The New Press, 1998) pp. 369-392.

8. We have made use of the recordings made by Gilbert Burlet and Jacques Lagrange in particular. These are deposited in the Collège de France and the Institut Mémoires de l'Édition Contemporaine.

9. See below pp. 299-300.

Translator's Note

The practices referred to by the French verb *surveiller* and the noun *surveillance* are, of course, fundamental and central in Foucault's analysis in these lectures, as also in *Surveiller et punir*. However, no single English verb or noun captures the range of meanings and family of practices covered by the French terms. The practices picked out by the French terms typically combine an epistemic with a coercive, goal-directed aspect. Depending on the context, the accent falls to a greater or lesser extent on one or other of these aspects, from watching, surveying, inspecting, and monitoring, to keeping watch over, surveillance, overseeing, and active supervision or superintendence (which is the term frequently used in English discussions of police in the eighteenth and early nineteenth centuries). To translate the French I have found it necessary to use a handful of different terms (surveillance, supervision, watching over, survey, and superintendence) depending on the context, including the French in brackets where I thought it necessary or useful.

The following abbreviations are used in the endnotes.

DE, I-IV   *Dits et* écrits, *1954-1988*, ed. D. Defert & F. Ewald avec la collaboration de Jacques Lagrange (Paris: Gallimard, 1994) 4 volumes.

"Quarto," I   *Dits et* écrits, *1954-1975*, ed. D. Defert & F. Ewald avec la collaboration de Jacques Lagrange (Paris: Gallimard, "Quarto," 2001).

"Quarto," II *Dits et* écrits, *1976-1988*, ed. D. Defert & F. Ewald avec la collaboration de Jacques Lagrange (Paris: Gallimard, "Quarto," 2001).

EW, 1   *The Essential Works of Foucault, 1954-1984. Volume 1: Ethics, Subjectivity and Truth*, ed. Paul Rabinow (New York: New Press, 1997).

EW, 2   *The Essential Works of Foucault, 1954-1984. Volume 2: Aesthetics, Method, and Epistemology*, ed. James D. Faubion (New York: New Press, 1998).

EW, 3   *The Essential Works of Foucault, 1954-1984. Volume 3: Power*, ed. James D. Faubion (New York: New Press, 2000).

one

3 JANUARY 1973

*Classification of societies: cremating and burying; assimilating
and excluding. Inadequacy of the notion of exclusion. The
psychiatric hospital. Inadequacy of the notion of transgression.
∽ Object of the lectures: critique of the notions of exclusion
and transgression, and analysis of the subtle tactics of
the sanction. (I) The four penal tactics: 1. exclusion;
2. compensation; 3. marking; 4. confinement. ∽ Initial
hypothesis: classification of societies of exclusion, redemption,
marking, or confinement. ∽ Possible objections and reply:
the same penalties have different functions in the four penal
tactics. Example of the fine. Example of the death penalty.
Damiens and the sovereign's power. Present day death penalty
as redoubled confinement. (II) Establishing the autonomy of
the level of penal tactics: 1. situating them within the sphere
of power; 2. examining political struggles and disputes around
power. ∽ Civil war as framework of power struggles: tactics
of struggle and penality; strategy of confinement.*

I WILL START WITH a somewhat playful hypothesis. You know that
in the nineteenth and twentieth centuries one entertained the idea of
classifying societies into two types according to the way in which they
dealt with their dead. Thus a distinction was made between cremating
and burying societies.[1] I wonder whether we could not attempt to
classify societies, not according to the fate they reserve for the dead,

but to the fate they reserve for those of the living whom they wish to be rid of, according to the way in which they bring those who seek to evade power under control, to how they react to those who in one way or another overstep, break, or get around the laws.*

There is a passage in *Tristes Tropiques* where Lévi-Strauss says that societies have ultimately found only two means for getting rid of a dangerous individual, of someone possessing a formidable and hostile force:[2] one consists in assimilating the very substance of this power, neutralizing whatever is dangerous, hostile in it; this is the anthropophagic solution in which absorption allows both assimilation and neutralization of this force.† The other consists in attempting to vanquish the hostility of this force, neutralizing whatever power it might possess; this is the opposite solution, consequently, that involves not assimilating, but neutralizing this force, not neutralizing the hostility, but vanquishing it and [ensuring] control of it. [It consists in] "ejecting dangerous individuals from the social body and keeping them temporarily or permanently in isolation, away from all contact with their fellows, in establishments specially intended for this purpose."[3] [Lévi-Strauss] calls this practice of exclusion "*anthropemy* (from the Greek *ēmein*, to vomit)":[4] mastering the dangerous forces in our society does not consist in assimilating them, but in excluding them.‡

I do not want to discuss this rather entertaining hypothesis. It may well be that such an opposition has a descriptive value when it is a matter of identifying or analyzing things like anthropophagy or the ritual of the scapegoat.[5] However, there are a number of reasons why I do not think it can be used if one wants to carry out a historical type of analysis.

To start with, this notion of *exclusion* seems to me to be too broad and, above all, composite and artificial. I am in a good position to say this, since I myself have used, and maybe abused it.[6] It has been used, in fact, to characterize, to designate rather vaguely the status given in our kind of society to delinquents, to ethnic, religious, and sexual minorities,

---

* Manuscript (fol. 1): "the rules."
† Manuscript (fol. 2) adds: "i.e.: eating it."
‡ Manuscript (fol. 2) adds: "Our society belongs to the second type, those that exclude the dangerous forces of madness or crime. And which exclude them by death, exile, or confinement."

to the mentally ill, and to individuals who fall outside the circuits of production or consumption, in short to all those who may be regarded as abnormal or deviant. I do not think that this notion has been useless; at a given moment it was able to perform a useful critical function inasmuch as it involved turning round those psychological, sociological, or psycho-sociological notions such as deviance, maladjustment, and abnormality, which had invaded the field of the human sciences and the psychological content of which hid a very precise function: to conceal the techniques, procedures, and apparatuses through which society excluded a number of individuals, so as then to pass them off as abnormal or deviant. To that extent, the critical function of the reversal of this notion of exclusion with regard to the psycho-sociological notions of deviance or maladjustment was important. But it seems to me that if one wants to pursue the analysis it becomes inadequate inasmuch as with the notion of exclusion the individual's* excluded status is basically given in the sphere of social representations. It is within the latter that the excluded appears as such: he no longer communicates with others at the level of the system of representations and it is in virtue of this that he appears, precisely, deviant. This notion of exclusion appears to me therefore to remain within the sphere of representations and does not take into account—is consequently unable to take into account—or analyze the [struggles], relations, and specific operations of power on the basis of which, precisely, exclusion takes place. Exclusion† would be the general effect in representation of a number of strategies and tactics of power that the very notion of exclusion itself is unable to get at. Moreover, this notion accords society in general responsibility for the mechanism by which the excluded is excluded. In other words, we not only lack the historical, political mechanism of power, but we risk being led astray regarding the instance that excludes, since exclusion [seems] to be referred to something like a social consensus of rejection, whereas behind this maybe there are a number of quite specific, and consequently definable, instances of power responsible for the mechanism of exclusion.

---

* Manuscript (fol. 3): "individual's (or group's) ..."
† Manuscript (fol. 4): "Exclusion is the general representative effect of much subtler strategies and tactics. These are what are to be determined."

The second reason why I cannot subscribe to Lévi-Strauss's hypothesis is that, basically, it opposes two supposedly quite different techniques, one of rejection and the other of assimilation. I wonder whether he has not been the victim of the digestive metaphor resulting from the notion of anthropophagy, because when we look closely at how these procedures of exclusion take place we see that they are not at all opposed to techniques of assimilation. There is no exile, no confinement[*] that does not include, along with what is generally described as expulsion, a transfer, a reactivation of the very power that imposes, constrains, and expels.

Thus, the psychiatric hospital is indeed the institutional site in and through which the expulsion of the mad person takes place; at the same time, and through the very operation of this expulsion, it is a center of the constitution and reconstitution[†] of a rationality that is imposed in an authoritarian way in the framework of relations of power within the hospital, and that will be reabsorbed outside the hospital itself in the form of a scientific discourse that circulates outside as knowledge about madness, for which the condition of possibility of it being rational is, precisely, the hospital.[‡] Inside the hospital, the mad person is the target of a certain relationship of authority that is articulated in decisions, orders, disciplines, and so on. This authority relationship is based on a certain power that is political through and through, but which is also justified and articulated on the basis of a number of so-called conditions of rationality, and this authority relationship exercised permanently over the mad person within the hospital is, through the very way in which the discourse and personage of the doctor function in the scientific community and society, converted into elements of rational information that are reinvested in the characteristic power relations of society. What functions as supervision (*surveillance*) in terms of the power relations inside the hospital, becomes scientific observation in the doctor's discourse, through the very fact that the doctor, on the one hand,

---

* The manuscript (fol. 4) adds: "or putting to death."

† The manuscript (fol. 4) adds: "permanent."

‡ Manuscript (fols. 4-5): "The power relationship (reason-madness) that reigns in confinement is shifted and turned round—outside confinement—as an object relation: mental illness is constituted here as an object of a rational knowledge. On the basis of this relation, non-madness can strengthen its power over madness."

occupies a position of power within the hospital, and, on the other, functions as someone delivering, and entitled to deliver, a scientific discourse outside the hospital. What was ordering, instructions, in terms of the authority relationship inside the hospital, is converted into diagnosis or prognosis, into nosography in the language of the doctor who, back outside the hospital, functions as the subject of a scientific discourse.

So that we see how a political relationship that structures the whole life of a psychiatric hospital is converted into a discourse of rationality, through which precisely the political authority—the basis on which the hospital is able to function—is strengthened. There is at once transfer from inside the hospital to outside and conversion of a power relationship into a relationship of knowledge. The patient appears within the hospital as the target of a relationship of political power but then becomes the object of a knowledge, of a scientific discourse in a system of general rationality that is strengthened by this very fact, since the rationality has thus acquired not only the power of knowing what happens in nature, in man, but also what happens in mad people. There is a sort of transfer and ingestion that really does make one think of what Lévi-Strauss calls anthropophagy: a process of ingestion for reinforcement.*

Thus, the lateral and constant aim of this course will be a critique of this notion of exclusion or, more precisely, its elaboration in terms of dimensions that make it possible both to break it down into its constituent elements and to find the relations of power that underlie it and make it possible.

In the same way, maybe we will need to undertake a critique of a notion whose success has been correlative to that of exclusion: *transgression*.[7] For a time the notion of transgression played [a role] roughly comparable to [that of] of exclusion. It too allowed a sort of critical reversal that was important inasmuch as it made it possible to circumvent notions like abnormality, fault, and law. It authorized a reversal of the negative into positive, of the positive into negative. It allowed all these notions

---

* The manuscript (fol. 5) adds: "But this anthropophagy appears only on condition of shifting the analysis; of not remaining at the general level of exclusion; and of identifying its underlying tactics of power."

to be ordered no longer by reference to the major notion of law, but to that of *limit*.*[8]

However, I think the notions of exclusion and transgression should now be considered as instruments that were important historically: for a given period they were critical reversers in the sphere of juridical, political, and moral representation; but these reversers remain pegged to the general system of representations against which they were turned. It seems to me that the directions indicated by the analyses conducted in terms of exclusion and transgression should be pursued in new dimensions in which it is no longer a question of the law, the rule, the representation, but of power rather than the law, of knowledge rather than representation.

*   *   *

I want to justify the title of the lectures and talk about this notion of *punishment*.[9] If I have taken precisely this dull, naive, weak, puerile notion, it is because I wanted to return to things at the level of their historical development, beginning with the analysis of what could be called the "subtle tactics of the sanction." I will start by picking out some of these. It seems to me that we can pick out four major forms of punitive tactics,[10] which I will define by verbs rather than nouns.

1. *To exclude.* The term is used here in the strict sense of driving, forcing out, and not in the sense of confining, as in the text by Lévi-Strauss. This punitive tactic involves prohibiting an individual's presence in communal or sacred places, removing or prohibiting all the laws of hospitality concerning him. It involves depriving him of his home, of suppressing even the reality of his home,[11] as when a banished person's home is burned down or—according to a Medieval law that persisted for a long time and even in revolutionary practices—[when one] sets

---

* The manuscript (fol. 6) adds: "To speak of transgression is not to designate the passage from the licit to the illicit (beyond the prohibition): it is to designate the passage to the limit, beyond the limit, the passage to what is without rule, and consequently without representation."

fire to the roof of the house of the person one wants to banish.* This was a highly favored tactic in archaic Greek penality.[†12]

2. *To organize a redemption, impose compensation.*[13] In this tactic, the breach of the rule, the infraction, gives rise to two moves: [on the one hand,] the emergence of an individual or a group who is constituted as victim of the damage and who, by virtue of this, is able to demand reparation; the offense, [on the other hand,] will create a number of obligations [for] the person considered to be the offender. Thus, there is not that void around the infraction, as in the first case, but the formation of a whole specific network of obligations, comparable to a debt to be repaid or damage to be redressed.[‡] The person who has contravened the rule is thus held forcibly within a set of constraining commitments.[§14] This tactic differs from the previous one: the first involves breaking all ties with the individual, all the ties by which he is held within power; this tactic, on the contrary, involves holding the offender to a network of obligations that are multiplied and intensified in comparison with the traditional network of obligations of his existence.

3. *To mark*: to scar, to leave a sign on the body, in short, to impose a virtual or visible reduction on the body, or, if one does not strike the individual's real body, to inflict a symbolic stain on his name, humiliate his character, damage his status. In any case, it involves leaving something like a trace on the visible or symbolic, physical or social, anatomical or statutory body. In this way, the individual who committed the infraction will be marked by an element of memory and recognition. In this system, the infraction is no longer something to be redressed, compensated for, rebalanced, and therefore, up to a certain point, erased, but rather something to be emphasized, something that must not fall into forgetfulness, that must remain fixed in a sort of

---

* The manuscript (fol. 8) adds: "in such a way that it is no more than a visible ruin: it involves escorting or pursuing him to the borders; it may also involve exposing him or entrusting him to the fate of a boat (like someone who no longer has any land, any place of shelter, food, or support to which he was entitled)."

† The manuscript (fol. 8) adds: "and still in the classical epoch."

‡ The manuscript (fol. 9) adds: "sometimes to a vengeance to be stopped, sometimes to a war to be prevented by a sort of redemption, sometimes to a liberty to be recovered by ransom."

§ The manuscript (fols. 9-10) adds: "at least so that he does not escape or commit a new infraction. This system of compensation and redemption seems to have been dominant in ancient Germanic societies."

monument, even if this is a scar, an amputation, or something involving shame or infamy;* faces exposed in the stocks, the amputated hands of thieves. In this system, the visible or social body must be the blazon of the penalties, and this blazon refers to two things: [on the one hand,] to the offense, of which it has to be the visible and immediately recognizable trace: I know full well that you are a thief because you no longer have hands; and, [on the other hand,] to the power that imposed the penalty and that, with this penalty, has left the mark of its sovereignty on the tortured body. It is not just the offense that is visible in the scar or amputation, it is the sovereign. This tactic of marking was preponderant in the West from the end of the High Middle Ages until the eighteenth century.

4. *To confine.* The tactic we practice and which was definitively established around the turn of the eighteenth and nineteenth centuries. We will talk about the political conditions of confinement taken in its most general form and of the knowledge effects of this confinement.

So, the initial hypothesis would be something like this: there are societies or penal practices of exclusion, redemption, marking, or confinement.[15] Is this first approach valid? I confess that I still have no idea. In any case, I would like to address some immediate objections that arise. For example: we have offered a rather general, abstract criticism of the notion of exclusion, reproaching it for operating at a level of generality that is too high for it to be employed at the historical level, but then we set about defining penal tactics that, after all, risk falling under the same criticism, since, whether it is marking, confinement, and so on, these are anyway schemas that are completely abstract with regard to the quite definite and, what's more, fairly constant corpus of real penalties. If we stick to the historical plane, we know that the alphabet of penalties is relatively limited and closed, and rather than introduce notions like those of confinement, marking, and so on, perhaps it would be much more reasonable to speak of real penalties that actually have been employed in societies: for example, the fine, putting to death.

Now, what I would like to show is that statutory and apparently constant penalties do not at all perform the same role, do not in fact correspond to the same economy of power in different systems. [Let us

---

* The manuscript (fol. 22) links "scar and shame," and then "amputation and infamy."

take first of all the case of] the fine. In all penal systems, whether or not exclusion, marking, or confinement is dominant, taking property is a constant penal practice. Now, I think we can see that the tactical function of this punishment varies in different systems.

What is the confiscation of property in the tactic of exclusion? It is a particular way of suppressing or compromising the right of residence, of thereby suspending the political privileges, the civil rights pertaining to the properties thus suppressed. It is a way of erasing the offender's citizenship. It is forcing him to look elsewhere for a place in the sun. It is preventing him from leaving behind any property after his departure or death.* Within the system of exclusion, the tactic of the fine performs the role of exile on the spot or of indirect exile.

We find the fine in a tactic of redemption, but with a completely different function; what is involved here is getting compensation from the offender for the damage caused, of getting him to pay a sort of ransom for the victim,† but also to put down a kind of indemnity or pledge with the person who judges, [who] performs the role of arbitrator,‡ thereby risking the power granted to him.[16] The fine thus has two functions in this system: compensation for the person presumed to be harmed and, at the same time, pledge given to the arbitrator.[17]

In the system of marking, the role of the fine differs from that of compensation; in fact, in this system it is very often symbolic and is not really a reduction of the individual's economic status. It does not compromise his citizenship rights. Rather, it has the symbolic function of designating the guilty, of marking him as such and, above all, of setting on him the visible mark of the sovereignty of power. To pay a fine in the system of marking is to bow before this power relationship that means that someone, an authority, can actually constrain you to give a sum of money, even§ if this is symbolic in comparison with the

---

* The manuscript (fol. 13) has: "a house, goods, a name."

† The manuscript (fol. 13) adds: "so that the victim does not start a private war too perilous for the offender."

‡ The manuscript (fol. 13) adds: "and whose verdict will allow the cycle of vengeance to be interrupted."

§ The manuscript sentence (fol. 14) states: "Even without pecuniary incidence on the condemned, it has a marking role in which the power exerted on the offender is manifested."

A supplementary paragraph (fol. 14) on confinement has: "Finally, in the system of confinement, the fine performs the role of an equivalent or of an attenuated form of confinement. Confinement

wealth you possess. So the fine does not exist as a penalty in the same way in different systems. It is a procedure whose tactical role is entirely different according to the punitive regimes within which it figures.

We could say the same about the death penalty, even if it seems that, in the end, there have not been many ways of dying. But in the framework of the procedures by which a power reacts to what challenges it, there are, precisely, many ways of dying. In a tactic of exclusion like that of archaic Greece, pure and simple execution, direct death, was ultimately rare and reserved for very specific offenses. There were specific procedures, in fact, which did not consist in putting to death, but rather in exposing someone to death, by driving them from the territory, abandoning them without goods, leaving them exposed to public condemnation, putting them in some way outside the law in such a way that anyone could kill them, even if no one was actually designated as the executioner.[18] There was also the way of killing that consisted in throwing someone into the sea from the top of a cliff, that is to say pushing them over to the other side of the limits of the territory, depriving them in the strict sense of the "maternal soil" and exposing them brutally, without any recourse or support, solely to the power of the gods. This was the abrupt form of exile.

In a redemption system,[*] death-punishment was basically repayment of the debt: it was the way in which a murder had to be paid for. And the best proof of this is that the murder could be punished by the death of a relative, rather than of the guilty person. The execution had to be equivalent to repayment of the debt, and not to a punishment of the supposedly guilty individual.[19]

It is easy to see how, in the practice of marking, death is a specific physical operation, a work on the body, a ritualized way of inscribing on the individual's body the marks of power, the individual's guilty status, or at least of inscribing the memory of the offense in the spectator's terror. If we see such a sumptuous variety of tortures (*supplices*) from the end of the Middle Ages until the eighteenth century, it is precisely because a whole series of variables had to be taken into account: the

---

is so many days of forced work, or so many days of work without pay. The fine is also so many days of work, or a fraction of that time. In both cases it is a matter of 'deprivation'."

* The manuscript (fol. 15) adds: "of old Germanic law."

status of the guilty person, for example, and we have beheading, which is death marked with the seal of nobility, and hanging, which is the death marking the villein. There is the stake for heretics, quartering for traitors, cutting ears off for thieves, piercing the tongue of blasphemers, and so on.[20]

We may recall one of the most tremendous scenes of this death by marking: the execution of Damiens in 1757.[21] Damiens was first condemned to make *amende honorable*, and then put on the wheel, his limbs broken by blows with an iron bar; his chest was torn open and molten wax poured into the wounds; he was then quartered and his joints severed; finally, he was incinerated and his ashes were thrown to the wind. In the imagination of the time, all this functioned as the final staging of that alphabet of tortures (*supplices*). The sovereign had been grazed by a visionary from the crowd. Political power responded to this act with the most complete display of its penal blazon. It exhibited the most atrocious and at the same time most ritual traces of its right of justice. The sovereign demonstrated what he could do with a man's body.*

If we still find death in our penality, which is essentially a penality of confinement, it is because death in this penality no longer has the role of displaying the marks of power on the human body, but that of the extreme and final, the perfect and unsurpassable form of confinement: those subject to this penalty—to this sort of redoubled confinement— are those one must be sure of having put away once and for all. Death,† is no longer torture, it is definitive closure, absolute security.[22]

I have tried to show the way in which death and the fine vary according to the four major punitive tactics because I have been trying to give autonomy to the level I would like to address, which is neither that of the great functions like exclusion or anthropophagy, nor that of penalties as defined by codes or customs, whose permanence conceals, I

---

* The manuscript (fol. 17) adds: "when he left on it the marks of his passage. The *supplice* of Damiens was the last great confrontation of the king and the people 'in person' on the stage of the scaffold, before that of 21 January [1793], where the confrontation takes place in the opposite direction: on the latter date, the king, stripped of all his sovereignty, was subjected to the mark of an egalitarian penalty, that beheading—which previously was the penalty for nobles and was now the penalty for all."

† The manuscript (fol. 17) adds: "is not the alternative to prison."

think, different roles. Between these general functions and the different roles exercised by penalties there is another level to be explored: that of penal tactics.*

I would like to note a number of things concerning these penal tactics. First, I have spoken about operations, I have tried to characterize them by terms such as to exclude, to confine, that is to say [as] operations situated between power and that on which it is exercised—they are operations carried out entirely within the sphere of power. By taking this as the primary level of analysis, I have not sought to deduce penal systems from a number of juridical or ethical representations of the offense or crime. So I will not pose the problem in the following terms: What idea of the evil or offense could one have had for one to respond to it in this or that way, with exile or confinement? I will pose the question differently. If I have spoken above all of these tactics it is because I would like to elucidate the following question: What forms of power are actually at work for power to respond to infractions that call its laws, rules, and exercise into question with tactics such as exclusion, marking, redemption, or confinement? If I fix on these tactics, and principally on confinement, it is not so as to attempt to reconstruct the set of juridical and moral representations that are supposed to support and justify these penal practices; it is because, starting from these tactics, I would like to define the relations of power actually brought into play through them.† In other words, I would like to approach these tactics as *analyzers* of power relations, and not as *revealers* of an ideology. Penality as analyzer of power; that is the theme of these lectures.

This means, secondly, that if it is true that the system of penal tactics may be envisaged as analyzer of power relations, then what is to be regarded as the central element is political struggle around and against power. It is the whole play of conflicts, of struggles between power as it is exercised in a society and the individuals or groups who seek in

---

* Manuscript (fol. 18): "that of penal operations, tactics, strategies."

† Manuscript (fols. 19-20): "That is to say, what will be in the forefront in this analysis are the forms of struggle between political power, as it is exercised in a society, and those—individuals or groups—who seek to escape this power, who challenge it locally or globally, who contravene its order or regulations."

The text that follows does not appear in the manuscript, which contains, however, four pages of notes (transcribed below p. 14) concerning the methodological consequences implied by this theoretical choice and the different impasses of sociological functionalism.

one way or another to escape this power, who challenge it locally or globally, who contravene its orders and its regulations. I do not mean that I will consider so-called common delinquency and political crime as absolutely equivalent. What I mean is that what has to be brought out first of all in the analysis of a penal system is the nature of the struggles that take place around power in a society.

So it is the notion of *civil war* that must be put at the heart of all these analyses of penality.[23] Civil war is, I think, philosophically, politically, and historically, a rather poorly developed notion. There are a number of reasons for this. It seems to me that the covering over, the disavowal of civil war, the assertion that civil war does not exist, is one of the first axioms of the exercise of power. This axiom has had huge theoretical repercussions since, whether we look to Hobbes or Rousseau, we see anyway that civil war is never seen as something positive, central, that can serve [in itself] as the starting point of an analysis. Either one speaks of the war of all against all as what exists before the social pact, and then it is no longer civil war, it is natural war; and once there is a contract, civil war can only be the monstrous continuation of the war of all against all in a social structure that should normally be governed by the pact. Or, on the contrary, civil war is conceived of as being nothing other than, as it were, the retroactive effect of an external war on the city itself, as the reflux of the war within the city's borders: so in this case it is the monstrous projection of external war on the State. In either case, civil war is the accident, the abnormality, and that which has to be avoided precisely to the extent that it is the theoretical-practical monstrosity.

Now I would like to conduct the analysis by considering, rather, that civil war is the permanent state on the basis of which a number of these tactics of struggle, of which penality is precisely a privileged example, can and should be understood. Civil war is the matrix of all struggles of power, of all strategies of power, and, consequently, it is also the matrix of all the struggles regarding and against power. It is the general matrix that enables us to understand the establishment and functioning of a particular strategy of penality: that of confinement. What I am going to try to show is the interplay, in nineteenth-century society, between a permanent civil war and the opposed tactics of power.[*]

---

* Four pages of notes at the end of the manuscript (fos. 20-23), which were not used in the course, contain the following:

"What will be foregrounded is therefore the struggle against, or with, or for power. Which implies, as methodological consequence, that it is necessary to shed sociological functionalism. To free oneself from the idea

- that it is society as a whole, en masse, in an obscure consensus, that reacts to the crime or offense;
- that this reaction is given form in rules, laws, customs that define the penality; and
- that power puts this penality to work in a more or less regular way (and at the price of a number of distortions, abuses, or privileges).

To shed this functionalism is to put power struggles, rather than social reactions, at the heart of penal practice.

To shed this sociological functionalism[24] is also to show how it took shape; how, at the beginning of the nineteenth century a very curious transfer of responsibility took place at the end of which

- society appeared as that which produced the crime (in accordance with a number of statistical constants and sociological laws);
- society appeared as that which was injured, wronged, damaged by the infraction. Society produces its own evil, it gives rise to its own enemy;
- society emerged as that which demanded that power punish crimes on the grounds of major moral options.

This transfer of responsibility concealed that it was not society that was in question in the crime, or at stake in its repression, but power.

It is translated at the level of penal theory in the idea that it is society that is greatly interested in the punishment, and that the latter's function must be the protection of society (Beccaria, Bentham).

It is translated at the level of practice by the generalization of the jury; it is not power or the representative of power who have to say whether society is injured, but society itself.

It is translated at the level of speculation by the constitution of a sociology of criminality or delinquency, i.e., the search for the social mechanisms that underpin both criminality and the requirements of its repression. This masking of power relations beneath social mechanisms is one of the characteristic phenomena of the way in which power is exercised in industrial capitalism. Let us take, as symbol of this masking, two scenes:

- that of the crowd at the execution of a culprit, i.e., at the deployment of the signs of power. It presses around the scaffold to see the display of the torture (*supplice*);
- that of the execution that takes place secretly at night, but where the exercise of power is concealed under an opinion survey.

In the same way we could show how the transition from torture to confinement corresponds to that shift from power relationship to social mechanism."

1. The classification of societies in terms of the way in which they deal with their dead is frequent in historical, anthropological, and archeological works from the 1830s to the 1960s, especially in the archeology of European prehistory. In particular, the article by Vere Gordon Childe, "Directional Changes in Funerary Practices during 50,000 years," published in 1945 in *Man*, vol. 45, pp. 13-19, can be consulted for information on the intersecting trajectories of burial and cremation societies (in his terminology, "*inhumationist*" and "*cremationist*" societies) in Europe. Foucault had already alluded to the classification of societies into cremating and burying in *Naissance de la clinique* (Paris: PUF, 1963) p. 170; English translation by A. M. Sheridan Smith, *The Birth of the Clinic. An Archaeology of Medical Perception* (London: Tavistock Publications, 1973) p. 166 (describing an important fact of civilization of the same "of the same order as ... the transformation from an incinerating to an inhuming culture"). In 1963 this reference served to signify the scale of the social transformation brought about by the invention of pathological anatomy and the medical gaze with regard to, on the one hand, the way in which doctors communicate with death (formerly through "the great myth of immortality," henceforth in the form of the medical gaze), and, on the other, the way in which cultures dispose of their dead (see ibid.).

2. See C. Lévi-Strauss, *Tristes Tropiques* (Paris: Plon, "Terre humaine," 1955) p. 448; English translation by John Weightman and Doreen Weightman, *Tristes Tropiques* (London: Penguin Classics, 2012) p. 388: "I am thinking, for instance, of our legal and prison systems. If we studied societies from the outside, it would be tempting to distinguish two contrasting types: those which practise cannibalism—that is, which regard the absorption of certain individuals possessing dangerous powers as the only means of neutralizing those powers and even of turning them to advantage—and those which, like our own society, adopt what might be called the practice of *anthropemy* (from the Greek, *ēmein*, to vomit); faced with the same problem, the latter type of society has chosen the opposite solution, which consists in ejecting dangerous individuals from the social body and keeping them temporarily or permanently in isolation, away from all contact with their fellows, in establishments specially intended for this purpose. Most of the societies which we call primitive would regard this custom with profound horror; it would make us, in their eyes, guilty of that same barbarity of which we are inclined to accuse them because of their symmetrically opposite behaviour."

    The anthropological analysis of cannibalism, linked to the classification of societies as assimilating or excluding, was developed by Alfred Métraux (1902-1963), in particular in: *La Religion des Tupinamba et ses rapports avec celle des autres tribus Tupi-Guarani* (Paris: Librairie Ernest Leroux, 1928) pp. 124-169, "L'anthropophagie rituelle des Tupinamba"; *Religions et Magies indiennes d'Amérique du Sud*, posthumous ed., Simone Dreyfus (Paris: Gallimard, "Bibliothèque des sciences humaines," 1967) pp. 45-78. The accounts referring to the practice of cannibalism on which Métraux based his views are, of course, clearly older. Thus we can cite the *Histoire d'un voyage fait en la terre du Brésil* (1578), by the Calvinist Jean de Léry (1534-1611), including his account of cannibalism in the Tupinamba (published in "Livre de poche," 1994, ch. XV: "Comment les Ameriquains traittent leurs prisonniers prins en guerre, et les ceremonies qu'ils observent tant à les tuer qu'a les manger," pp. 354-377); and the account by André Thevet (1516-1590), explorer and geographer, who traveled to Brazil in 1555-1556: *Histoire d'André Thevet, Angoumoisin, cosmographe du Roy, de deux voyages par luy faits aux Indes australes et occidentales* (Paris: Bibliothèque nationale de France, Fonds français, ms. no. 15454), reproduced in the collection "Les Classiques de la colonisation," Suzanne Lussagnet, ed., vol. II: *Les Français en Amérique pendant la deuxième moitié du XVIᵉ siècle* (Paris: PUF, 1953). See I. Combès, *La Tragédie cannibale chez les anciens Tupi-Guarani*, Preface by Pierre Chaunu (Paris: PUF, coll. "Histoire et décadence," 1994). Foucault will return to the notion of cannibalism in his analysis of the figure of the monster in *Les Anormaux. Cours au Collège de France, 1974-1975*, ed., V. Marchetti & A. Salomoni (Paris: Gallimard-

Seuil, "Hautes Études," 1999) lecture of 29 January 1975, pp. 94-97; English translation by Graham Burchell, *Abnormal. Lectures at the Collège de France 1974-1975*, English series editor, Arnold I. Davidson (New York: Picador, 2003) pp. 101-104, where he develops the double image of the cannibal monstrosity of the people and the incestuous monstrosity of the king; a discussion which will thus be linked to the two major figures of the criminal and criminality in the nineteenth century, at the intersection of psychiatry and penality.

3. C. Lévi-Strauss, *Tristes Tropiques*, Fr., p. 448; Eng., p. 388. Two years later, in his lecture of 29 January 1975, in *Les Anormaux*, p. 96; *Abnormal*, pp. 103-104, Foucault will maintain that although the structural linguistics approach of Lévi-Strauss is distinct from previous approaches like that of Lucien Lévy-Bruhl (see *La Mentalité primitive*, Paris: Alcan, "Travaux de l'Année sociologique, 1922; English translation by Lillian A. Clare, *Primitive Mentality*, London: George Allen & Unwin Ltd, 1923), and makes possible a "rehabilitation of the so-called savage," it ultimately comes up against the same cannibalism-incest dualism that we find in the different figures of the monster in the eighteenth century.

4. Lévi-Strauss, ibid.

5. Foucault is no doubt referring here to the works of René Girard, who had just published *La Violence et le Sacré* (Paris: Grasset, 1972); English translation by Patrick Gregory, *Violence and the Sacred* (Baltimore, MD: Johns Hopkins University Press, 1977) developing the notion of the "scapegoat" in both the Oedipal context, in which Foucault was interested (see below, note 11), and also that of the prisoner who is the victim of anthropophagy. On these two points, see *La Violence et le Sacré*, pp. 139-140, p. 139 n. 1; *Violence and the Sacred*, pp. 108-109, p. 130 n. 1: "A number of French scholars have detected in the Oedipus of both myth and tragedy a pharmakos and a 'scapegoat.' According to Marie Delcourt, the institution of the scapegoat explains the fate of the infant Oedipus, abandoned by his parents"; also, concerning the treatment of the prisoner in the Tupinamba people of Brazil, Fr., p. 381; Eng., p. 314: "the purpose of these indulgences was to transform the prisoner into a 'scapegoat.'" René Girard will develop these themes in *Le Bouc émissaire*, published ten years later (Paris: Grasset & Fasquelle, 1982); English translation by Yvonne Freccero, *The Scapegoat* (Baltimore, MD: Johns Hopkins University Press, 1989). At the beginning of the 1970s, Girard was teaching at the State University of New York at Buffalo; he was the intermediary between John Simon and Foucault for the latter's visit to Buffalo. Foucault gave some lectures there, in particular in March 1970; see D. Defert, "Chronologie" in *DE*, I, p. 35/"Quarto," I, p. 47. Foucault will use this reference in *Surveiller et Punir. Naissance de la prison* (Paris: Gallimard, "Bibliothèque des histoires," 1975), p. 263; English translation by Alan Sheridan, *Discipline and Punish. The Birth of the Prison* (London: Allen Lane, 1977) p. 259, when describing the chain-gang at the start of the nineteenth century.

6. Foucault had used the notion of exclusion previously; see his course at the Collège de France in 1972, "Penal Theories and Institutions," ninth lecture, ms. fol. 23 (comparison of Medieval penal practices of exchange and redemption with modern penal practices of exclusion); "Je perçois l'intolérable," (interview with G. Armleder in *Journal de Genève: Samedi littéraire*, "cahier 135," no. 170, 24-25 July 1971), *DE*, II, no. 94, p. 204/"Quarto" I, p. 1072: "Our society began to practice a system of exclusion and inclusion—confinement or imprisonment—against any individual who did not conform to those norms. Henceforth, people have been excluded from the circuit of the population and at the same time included in prisons"; "Le grand enfermement" (interview with N. Meienberg, *Tages Anzeiger Magazine*, no. 12, 25 March 1972, trans. J. Chavy), *DE*, II, no. 105, p. 306/"Quarto," I, 1174: "The problem is the following: to offer a critique of the system that explains the process by which present day society marginalizes a part of the population. That's it." In his inaugural lecture at the Collège de France, delivered on 2 December 1970 and published with the title *L'Ordre du discours* (Paris: Gallimard/nrf, 1971); English translation by Ian McLeod, "The Order of Discourse" in Robert Young, ed., *Untying the Text* (London: Routledge and Kegan Paul, 1981) from the

eleventh page (Eng., p. 52) Foucault employs the notion of exclusion extensively to designate "procedures whose role is to ward off its [discourse's] powers and dangers, to gain mastery over its chance events, to evade its ponderous, formidable materiality." Foucault pursues his aim by identifying three *"procedures of exclusion"* (emphasis in the French, p. 11; Eng., p. 52), alternatively defined as "principles of exclusion" (p. 11; p. 53) or "system of exclusion" (p. 12; p. 55), concerning prohibition (p. 11; p. 52), the opposition between madness and reason (p. 12; p. 53), and the division between true and false (p. 15; pp. 55-56). It might also be thought that the idea of exclusion—or, at least, of "expulsions" according to Foucault (see "Lettre de M. Michel Foucault," *DE*, II, no. 96, p. 210/"Quarto," I, p. 1078)—underlies his analysis of madness in the fourteenth and fifteenth centuries; see *Folie et Déraison. Histoire de la folie à l'âge classique* (Paris: Plon, 1961), pp. 10-13; English translation by Jonathan Murphy and Jean Khalfa, *History of Madness* (London and New York: Routledge, 2009) pp. 3-6.

The notion of exclusion is also fairly close to the concept of "repression" which Foucault developed the previous year in his course on "Penal Theories and Institutions" (see, for example, the beginning of the first lecture setting out his method: to situate penal theories and institutions "in their overall functioning, that is to say in systems of repression" (first folio); the fifth lecture concerning the fiscal apparatus of the State which "cannot function without being protected, doubled by a repressive apparatus" (fol. 10 bis); or the sixth lecture describing the setting up of a repressive State apparatus (fols. 18-20). In a similar way, Foucault will also distance himself from this notion of "repression" in the following years (see *Surveiller et Punir*, p. 28; *Discipline and Punish*, p. 23).

7. See M. Foucault, "Préface à la transgression" (*Critique*, 195-196: *Hommage à G. Bataille*, August-September 1963, pp. 751-769), *DE*, I, no. 13, pp. 233-250/"Quarto," I, pp. 261-278; English translation by Donald F. Bouchard and Sherry Simon (slightly amended), "A Preface to Transgression" in M. Foucault, *EW*, 2, pp. 69-87. Foucault had made considerable use of the notion of "transgression"; see, "Un problème m'interesse depuis longtemps, c'est celui du système pénal" (interview with J. Hafsia, *La Presse de Tunisie*, 12 August 1971, p. 5), *DE*, II, no. 95, p. 206/"Quarto," vol. I, p. 1074: "This is my concern: the problem of transgression of the law and the repression of illegality."

8. This notion of "limit" refers, of course, to the work of Georges Bataille on the limit experience; see "Préface à la transgression," pp. 236-239/pp. 264-267; "A Preface to Transgression," pp. 73-75 where, commenting on Bataille's œuvre, Foucault writes: "The limit and transgression depend on each other for whatever density of being they possess," p. 237/p. 265; p. 73. Moreover, in his "Présentation" in G. Bataille, *Œuvres complètes* (Paris: Gallimard/nrf, 1970) vol. I: *Premiers Écrits, 1922-1940*, p. 5; *DE*, II, no. 74, p. 25/"Quarto," I, p. 893, Foucault wrote that Bataille's *Somme athéologique* "introduced thought into the game—the risky game—of the limit, the extreme, the summit, the transgressive." Foucault readily acknowledged Bataille's influence: "the fourth reference point in my trajectory ... (I am thinking of writers like Blanchot, Artaud, and Bataille, who, I think, were extremely important for people of my generation)—was the question of limit experiences. Those forms of experiences that, instead of being considered central and positively valorized by society, were considered limit experiences, those borderline experiences that put into question the very things that were considered ordinarily acceptable": "Entretien avec André Berten" in M. Foucault, *Mal faire, dire vrai. Fonction de l'aveu en justice*, ed., F. Brion & B. E. Harcourt (Louvain: Presses universitaires de Louvain, 2012) p. 238; English translation by Stephen W. Sawyer, *Wrong-Doing, Truth-Telling. The Function of Avowal in Justice*, eds., Fabienne Brion & Bernard E. Harcourt (Chicago: University of Chicago Press, 2014) p. 238. In 1970, in his "Présentation," Foucault affirms again: "We know today: Bataille is one of the most important writers of his century."

9. According to Daniel Defert, many auditors had difficulty grasping the title of the course and understood "*The primitive society*" and not "*punitive*."

10. Some months later Foucault will put forward a slightly different version of the "four possible types of punishment" in his lectures at the Pontifical University of Rio de Janeiro, in May 1973, entitled "La vérité et les formes juridiques," *DE*, II, no. 139, pp. 538-562 (esp. pp. 590-591)/"Quarto," I, pp. 1406-1491 (esp. pp. 1458-1459); English translation by Robert Hurley, "Truth and Juridical Forms," M. Foucault, *EW*, 3, pp. 1-89 (esp. pp. 54-55): deportation, exclusion on the spot; compensation through forced labor; penalty of talion.

11. See Lévi-Strauss, *Tristes Tropiques*, Fr., p. 448; Eng., p. 338: "If a native had infringed the laws of the tribe, he was punished by having all his possessions destroyed, including his tent and horses."

12. The reference to exile in archaic Greek penality refers to Sophocles' *Oedipus the King*, which Foucault had already analyzed in his first course at the Collège de France: see *Leçons sur la volonté de savoir. Cours au Collège de France 1970-1971*, ed., Daniel Defert (Paris: Gallimard-Seuil, "Hautes Études," 2011) pp. 177-192; English translation by Graham Burchell, *Lectures on The Will to Know. Lectures at the Collège de France 1970-1971*, English series editor, Arnold I. Davidson (Basingstoke: Palgrave Macmillan, 2013) pp. 183-201. It is also analyzed in a lecture given at the State University of New York at Buffalo in March 1972, and then at Cornell University in October 1972: see *Le Savoir d'Œdipe*, ibid., pp. 223-253; *Oedipal Knowledge*, ibid., pp. 229-257. In the "Situation du cours," pp. 277-278; "Course Context," pp. 279-280, Daniel Defert notes that a total of seven different versions of the analysis of *Oedipus the King* can be found in the Foucault archive. Foucault develops one of these four months later in his lectures "La vérité et les formes juridiques," pp. 553-570/pp. 1421-1438; "Truth and Juridical Forms," pp. 16-32. He will return to it again in 1980, 1981, and 1983. See M. Foucault, *Mal faire, dire vrai*, p. 73 n. 1; *Wrong-doing, Truth-telling*, p. 82 n. 1.

13. These notions of redemption (*rachat*) and compensation—in this case: "reparation"—were developed in the 1970-1971 course in the context of Greek judicial practice; see *Leçons sur la volonté de savoir*, lecture of 3 February 1971, pp. 90-91; *Lectures on The Will to Know*, pp. 93-94. The themes are taken up again in "La vérité et les formes juridiques," pp. 572-574/ pp. 1440-1441; "Truth and Juridical Forms," p. 35.

    Concerning "medieval law" mentioned above, in the lectures of Joseph Strayer the reader will find the notion of a penal justice strictly linking the fine and the collection of revenue; see J. R. Strayer, *On the Medieval Origins of the Modern State* (Princeton, NJ: Princeton University Press, "Princeton Classics," 1970) p. 29: "The connection between the administration of justice and the collection of revenue remained close throughout the Middle Ages. Even when specialized groups of judges appeared, the judges were often used as revenue collectors and the old revenue collectors (sheriffs, *prévôts*, and the like) continued to hold court for petty offenses." Regarding the seventeenth century, see also, "Théories et Institutions pénales," fifth lecture (concerning the fiscal apparatus as a State apparatus, fol. 10).

14. See C. Lévi-Strauss, *Tristes Tropiques*, Fr., p. 448; Eng., p. 388: "This [reparation of the culprit for the losses sustained by his punishment] put him under an obligation to the group, and he had to show his gratitude to them by means of presents that the whole community ... helped him to assemble."

15. Foucault had already put forward some more rudimentary classifications of societies according to different types of penalties. In July 1971 he proposed classifying them into exiling societies, killing (or torturing or purifying) societies, and confining societies; see "Je perçois l'intolérable," *DE*, II, p. 203/"Quarto," I, p. 1071. In March 1972, Foucault proposed different "types of civilizations": "The civilizations which exile," those "which slaughter" or "torture," and then "societies that confine"; see "Le grand enfermement," *DE*, II, p. 297/"Quarto," I, p. 1165.

16. This theme of breaking the cycle of vengeance, more explicit in the manuscript, was introduced two years earlier in the *Leçons sur la volonté de savoir*, lecture of 3 February 1971, pp. 90-91; *Lectures on the Will to Know*, pp. 92-94, and will be taken up again in the present course: see below, lecture of 10 January 1973, p. 33; lecture of 7 February 1973, p. 114 (appendix). See also, on the appeasement of the spirits of vengeance, A. Métraux, *Religions et Magies indiennes d'Amérique du Sud*, p. 59: "The victim thus had the opportunity to assuage his anger and to take revenge to a certain extent on his torturers. This advantage conceded to the captive 'may have come from the desire to appease the victim's spirit.'"; p. 70: the purpose of the execution of the prisoner was to "appease the soul of a relative 'taken or eaten by the enemy'"; and pp. 73-78: all the precautions taken to avoid vengeance and to "protect oneself against the angry soul of one's victim."

17. The previous year Foucault dealt with the practice of the redemption and fine in Germanic law; see "Théories et Institutions pénales," eighth and ninth lectures; see the ninth lecture, manuscript fol. 12 (on *Wehrgeld* and *Fr[edus]*). In the ancient law of Germanic inspiration, the "*wergeld*" (*Whergeld*), in use among the Franks, constituted the legal pecuniary compensation due to the victim or victim's family in cases of wounding or murder, so as to avoid private vengeance. The amount of *wergeld* varies according to the social status of the victim; see F. Olivier-Martin, *Histoire du droit français des origines à la Révolution* (Paris: Éditions du CNRS, 1984 [1950]) p. 68. The "*fredus*," which represents a third of the *wergeld* is paid to the sovereign in order to reestablish peace; see, C. Debuyet, F. Digneffe, A. P. Pires, *Histoire des savoirs sur le crime et la peine* (Brussels: Larcier, "Crimen," 2008) vol. 2, p. 44.

18. This figure of the *homo sacer* in archaic law, "that figure of the man whom one can kill without committing murder, but that one cannot formally execute," will be studied by Giorgio Agemben in his *Homo sacer. Il potere sovrano e la nuda vita* (Torino: Einaudi, 1995); English translation by Daniel Heller-Roazen, *Homo Sacer. Sovereign Power and Bare Life* (Stanford, CA: Stanford University Press, 1998). Agemben's starting point in this text is Foucault's analysis of power in the 1980s and, more precisely, the intersection between, on the one hand, the study of the way in which the individual makes himself subject of an external control (the study of technologies of self) and, on the other hand, the study of State techniques through which life and population become target and concern—at the intersection of "techniques of subjective individualization and procedures of objective totalization" (It., p. 8; Eng., p. 11), precisely at the "hidden point of junction between the juridico-institutional and the biopolitical models of power" (It., p. 9; Eng., p. 11); a point of junction that, according to Agemben, remains "strangely unclear" (p. 8; p. 11) in Foucault's work, or "a blind spot to the eye of the researcher" (It., p. 9; Eng., p. 11). We could see in the present course, notably in this precise passage of this lecture of 3 January 1973—i.e., the analysis of the way in which punitive tactics (like the figure of the *homo sacer*) function in relations of power, or, Agemben will say, "the concrete ways in which power penetrates subjects' very bodies and forms of life" (p. 7; p. 10)—a text which is a precursor of the latter's work.

19. See M. Foucault, "Théories et Institution pénales," eighth and ninth lectures.

20. See *Surveiller et Punir*, p. 107; *Discipline and Punish*, p. 105. It is against this differentiation that Le Peletier de Saint-Fargeau will propose the equality of the guillotine: "an equal death for all" (ibid., Fr., p. 18; Eng., p. 12).

21. *Surveiller et Punir*, pp. 9-11; *Discipline and Punish*, pp. 3-6, begins with this scene.

22. In 1972, reacting to the rejection of the plea for clemency addressed to President Pompidou on behalf of Buffet and Bontemps, who had been condemned to death, Foucault had emphasized the continuity between the penalty of prison and the death penalty in, "Les deux morts de Pompidou," *Le Nouvel Observateur*, 421, 4-10 December, pp. 56-57; *DE*, II, no. 114, pp. 386-389/"Quarto," I, pp. 1254-1257; English translation by Robert Hurley, *EW*, 3, pp. 418-422: "[T]he guillotine is really just the visible and triumphant apex, the red and black tip, of a tall pyramid. The whole penal system is essentially pointed toward and governed by death." He

will repeat it on the occasion of the abolition of the death penalty in France in 1981, to mark the need to rethink the whole penal system, beyond the celebration of the disappearance of "the oldest penalty in the world"; see: "Le dossier 'peine de mort'. Ils ont écrit contre" in *Les Nouvelles littéraires*, 59th year, no. 2783, 16-23 April 1981, p. 17; *DE*, IV, no. 294, p. 168/"Quarto," II, p. 987; "Contre les peines de substitution" in *Libération*, no. 108, 18 September 1981, p. 5; *DE*, IV, no. 300, p. 206/"Quarto," II, p. 1025; English translation by Robert Hurley, "Against Replacement Penalties" in *EW*, 3, p. 459; On several occasions Foucault will stress the importance of the death penalty as mark of the sovereignty of justice, notably in "Le citron et le lait" in *Le Monde*, no. 10490, 21-22 October 1978, p. 14; *DE*, III, no. 246, pp. 695-698/"Quarto," vol. II, pp. 695-698; English translation by Robert Hurley, "Lemon and Milk" in *EW*, 3, pp. 435-438, and "Manières de justice" in *Le Nouvel Observateur*, no. 743, 5-11 February 1979, pp. 21-21; *DE*, III, no. 260, pp. 755-759/"Quarto," II, pp. 755-759. On this subject see also: "L'angoisse de juger" interview with R. Badinter and J. Laplanche, *Le Nouvel Observateur*, no. 655, 30 May—6 June 1977, pp. 92-96, 101, 104, 112, 120, 125-126; *DE*, III, no. 205, pp. 282-297/"Quarto," II, pp. 283-297; English translation by John Johnston, "The Anxiety of Judging" in M. Foucault, *Foucault Live*, ed., Sylvère Lotringer (New York: Semiotext(e), 1989) pp. 157-178; "Du bon usage du criminel" in *Le Nouvel Observateur*, no. 722, 11 September 1978, pp. 40-42; *DE*, III, no. 240, pp. 657-662/"Quarto," II, pp. 657-662; English translation by Robert Hurley, "The Proper Use of Criminals" in *EW*, 3, pp. 429-434; and "Punir est la chose la plus difficile qui soit," interview with A. Spire in *Témoignage chrétien*, no. 1942, 28 September 1981, p. 30; *DE*, IV, no. 301, pp. 208-210/"Quarto," II, pp. 1027-1029; English translation by Robert Hurley, "To Punish is the Most Difficult Thing There Is" in *EW*, 3, pp. 462-464.

In 1981, at the time of the abolition of the death penalty, Foucault will say: "The oldest penalty in the world is in the process of dying in France. This is cause for rejoicing, but not for self-congratulation." ("Contre les peines de substitution"; "Against Replacement Penalties," p. 459). For a presentation of Foucault's commitment against the death penalty, see A. Kiéfer, *Michel Foucault: le GIP, l'histoire et l'action*, philosophy thesis, November 2006, Université de Picardie Jules Verne d'Amiens, 2009, pp. 169-172.

23. Foucault will continue this analysis in the following years, in particular in the 1976 course, *"Il faut défendre la société". Cours au Collège de France 1975-1976*, ed., M. Bertani & A. Fontana (Paris: Gallimard-Seuil, "Hautes Études," 1997), lecture of 4 February 1976, p. 77 sq.; English translation by David Macey, *"Society Must Be Defended." Lectures at the Collège de France, 1975-1972*, English series editor, Arnold I. Davidson (New York: Picador, 1997), p. 89 sq.

24. On sociological functionalism, see also *Surveiller et Punir*, especially the criticism of Durkheim, p. 28; *Discipline and Punish*, p. 23.

two

10 JANUARY 1973

*The four elements of an analysis: 1. the constant, universal war internal to society; 2. a penal system that is neither universal nor univocal, but made by some for others; 3. the structure of universal superintendence (*surveillance*); 4. a system of confinement. (I) The content of the notion of civil war. (A) Civil war as resurgence of the war of all against all, according to Hobbes. (B) Distinction between civil war and war of all against all. New groups; examples of the* Nu-pieds *and the Luddite movement. (C) Politics as continuation of civil war. (II) The criminal's status as social enemy. ⌒ Knowledge effects: psychopathological or psychiatric hold on the criminal and deviance. ⌒ Epistemic effects: sociology of criminality as social pathology. The criminal as connector, transcriber, exchanger.*

I WOULD LIKE TO clarify the elements of this analysis.* First, during the period I will be dealing with, from 1825 to 1848, at the moment of

---

* The manuscript of the lecture begins (fols. 1-2) in the following way: "The point: to analyze penality at the level of its tactics, i.e., not

- what, in the name of what principle, and according to what scale of values it punishes, but:
- how it punishes; who punishes, who is punished, by what instruments.

Therefore:

- not to take as point of departure the great ethico-religious conceptions of fault, sin, impurity;
- nor to take major social functions such as exclusion, expulsion, rejection, but:
- to take as point of departure civil war, as general matrix of penal tactics."

the setting up and functioning of the great penal system to which the 1808 Code of criminal procedure (*Code d'instruction criminelle*) and the 1810 Penal Code had given the main lines, one thing is clear: we are in the midst of social war, which is not the war of all against all, but the war of rich against poor, of owners against those who have nothing, of bosses against proletarians.

Second element: the clear awareness, perfectly formulated in the discourse of the time, that social laws are made by people for whom they are not intended and applied to those who did not make them. In the minds of those who make it or discuss it, penal law has only apparent universality. Thus, [in his] intervention in the Chamber on 23 November 1831, when reform of the Penal Code and the creation of extenuating circumstances are being discussed, a deputy from the Var said: "The penal laws, intended for the most part for one class of society, are made by another. I acknowledge that they concern the whole of society—no one can be sure of always escaping their rigor—but it is true, nevertheless, that almost all crimes, and especially certain of them, are committed by the part of society to which the legislator does not belong. Now this part differs almost completely from the other in its mentality, mores, and its whole way of being. So to make suitable laws for it, it seems to me that the legislator should, above all, endeavor to forget what he is himself ... to look with care, not for the effect of a legal measure on himself, but on the quite differently disposed mind of the people for whom he works."[1] In the workers' literature we find the corresponding, but opposite assertion, that the penal law is not made to have a universal function.

Third point: the judicial, penal apparatus established at this time is governed entirely by the principle of universal and constant superintendence. We can refer to Julius, professor of criminal law at the University of Berlin who, [in 1827, says] in his "Lectures on prisons": "It is a fact worthy of the greatest interest, not only in the history of architecture, but in that of the human mind in general, that in the most distant times, I do not say of classical antiquity, but even of the East, genius conceived, and was pleased to decorate with all the treasures of human magnificence, buildings, such as temples, theaters, and amphitheaters, whose aim was to make accessible to a great multitude the spectacle and inspection of a small number of objects, where one watched the blood of men and animals flow."[2] In other words, an architecture, a civilization of the spectacle, where everyone gathered in a circle to look at something, a thing, a spectacle in the middle. And Julius continues: "while human imagination never appears to have applied itself to procuring for a small number, or even for a single individual, the instantaneous view of a great multitude of men or objects."[3]

Now this is precisely what takes place in the modern epoch: this inversion of the spectacle into surveillance.[4] We are in the process of inventing, Julius says, not just an architecture, an urbanism, but a whole mental disposition in general, such that, henceforth, men will be offered as a spectacle for a small number of people, even for a single individual charged with keeping watch over (*surveiller*) them. The spectacle is turned round into surveillance; the circle of citizens around a spectacle is reversed. We have a completely different structure in which individuals who are set out alongside each other in a flat space are watched from above by someone who is a kind of universal eye: "It was to modern times ..., to the ever increasing influence of the State and its ever deeper intervention into all the details and relations of social life, that the task fell of increasing and perfecting its guaranties by utilizing and directing towards this great aim the construction and distribution of buildings intended for keeping watch over a great multitude of individuals at the same time."[5]

We see that Julius attributes this kind of reversal of the spectacle into surveillance to the formation and growth of the State as the instance of superintendence, which makes it possible to control, observe, and intervene in the details of the relations of social life. Writing this, Julius only transcribes into his register what Napoleon himself said, or had said, since we find this in the introduction to the *Code d'instruction criminelle*: "you may consider that no part of the Empire to be without surveillance; that no crime, no offence, no contravention must go unprosecuted, and that the eye of the genius that can illuminate everything encompasses the whole of this vast machine, without the smallest detail escaping its attention."[6] And, speaking of the precise function of the prosecutor, the text continued: the prosecutor is "the eye of the public prosecutor, as the public prosecutor is the eye of the government. It is as a result of an active and faithful communication between the imperial prosecutor and the public prosecutor, and between the public prosecutor and His Majesty's minister, that the abuses that creep into the institutions, the half-heartedness that takes hold of persons, the lack of concern that may be forgiven in a private individual, but is a vice in a public official, can be known; and, if one were to suppose any slackening, any weakness, or disguise in communications between public and imperial prosecutors, evil would make immense progress before breaking out, and, without any crisis having occurred, we would suddenly find ourselves in a great state of languor and very close to decrepitude."[7] Thus, the theory of general surveillance developed by Julius exactly reflects what the imperial administration formulated in 1808.

The fourth element is confinement, imprisonment, of which Julius speaks moreover at the end of his text on surveillance: "the utility of this fundamental thought," that is to say of surveillance, is even greater with regard to prisons.[8]

We have, then, four points to mark out our analysis: the constant, universal war within society; a penal system that is neither universal nor univocal, but made by some for others; the structure of universal superintendence; and the system of confinement.

I would like to go back over the first point: the problem of civil war and the absence of any relation between this and the war of all against all. If in fact we accept these four elements, we see that the fundamental element is war. I would like to clarify a little this problem of the war of all against all and civil war and see how, for a time at least, the conception of criminality was related to these notions. [I will begin by looking more closely at the content] of the notion of civil war.

First of all, there is, I think, a certain tradition of political theory that equates civil war and the war of all against all, that establishes a direct, organic link between them. One of the most typical figures of this tradition is Hobbes.[*] Take the text where he says that civil war is a certain way of returning to the war of all against all or, anyway, that we must take the example of civil war if we want to have an idea of the war of all against all. After describing the relation of generalized war of individuals against each other, Hobbes writes: "It may peradventure be

---

* Manuscript (fol. 2): "Tradition that if Hobbes did not found, he at least formulated."

thought, there was never such a time, nor condition of warre as this" (of which I have just been speaking). "I believe it was never generally so, over all the world."[9] So the state of war of all against all is not a sort of absolutely primitive stage through which the whole of humanity would have passed and that it would have experienced in an [archaic] phase of its history; this war does not have a status of historical universality, but it remains nonetheless that for [Hobbes] there [exist] spatially limited and historically determinate examples [of it]: "there are many places, where they live so now," in this state of war; thus, "the savage people in many places of *America* ... Howsoever, it may be perceived what manner of life there would be, where there were no common Power to feare; by the manner of life, which men that have formerly lived under a peaceful government, use to degenerate into, in a Civil Warre."[10]

Civil war, then, is a historically determinate case of the resurgence of the war of all against all. It is a sort of epistemological model on the basis of which one should be able to decipher that state of war of all against all, and which is necessary for understanding the foundation and functioning of the sovereign. So, in Hobbes there is an example of the proximity of these two notions and it is moreover characteristic to see that precisely those who, in the following century, criticize the notion of the war of all against all, do not criticize this assimilation of civil war to the war of all against all. The existence of something like a war of all against all as an original or archaic state will be denied. Hobbes will be reproached for having made war a sort of model for the state of nature.[*]

Now, in contrast, I would like to show that this assimilation is not well founded, what its consequences have been, and what its context was. The impossibility of establishing continuity between, or of merging civil war and the war of all against all seems [clear][†] to me if we consider Hobbes's idea of the latter.

In the first place it is a natural, universal dimension of relations between individuals as individuals. The individual as such, in his relationship with others, is the bearer[‡] of this permanent possibility

---

[*] The manuscript (fol. 3) adds: "Not much criticism of the assimilation: civil war = war of all against all."

[†] Typescript (page 24): "to be blatant."

[‡] Manuscript (fol. 3): "of the possibility of civil war."

of the war of all against all. If there is in fact a war of all against all, it is first of all essentially because men are equal in the objects and ends they set their sights on, because they are equivalent in the means they possess for obtaining what they seek. They are, as it were, substitutable for each other, and that is precisely why they seek to replace each other and, when something is offered to the desire of one, the other may always substitute himself for the first, wanting to take his place and appropriate what he desires.[11] This substitutability, this convergence of desire characterizes this original competition.[12] Even if this competition were not to come into play, even if there were enough things in the world to satisfy both, even if someone were to seize hold of something in advance, one can never be sure that someone else won't come to replace him: all enjoyment, all possession is therefore precarious, precisely by virtue of this quasi-equality. Thus, there can never be property or enjoyment that does not include this dimension of distrust,[*] each individual knowing well that someone else may come to take his place.

With distrust added to competition, we have a second dimension of this war of all against all.[13] As a result, there is only one way to succeed in overcoming this distrust and halt this competition, which is that one of these perpetual combatants prevail over the others by something like an additional power, that is to say he appropriates not only an object of enjoyment, but, in addition, an instrument in order to capture this object, he increases consequently his own power in relation to the others and leaves the schematic status of equality given to individuals at the start; he has an additional power from which he expects precisely the effect that others will no longer seek to take his place and that he can peacefully enjoy what he has, that is to say, that he is respected.

The increase in power introduces men into the system of signs, of marks, and the additional power is basically meant to establish this visible mark [of the] power of [one of them][†] into the relationships between men. Hobbes calls this will to impose respect "glory": the ability, through external signs, to keep in awe those who might claim to take his place.[14]

---

* [In Hobbes, "diffidence," with the sense of distrust; G.B.]
† Typescript (p. 25): "of his power."

Glory, distrust, and competition are the three wholly individual dimensions that constitute the universal war of all individuals against all other individuals. Hobbes says so clearly: the war of all against all is "necessarily consequent ... to the natural Passions of men."[15] The state of war is therefore essential to the individual[*] and, if this is the case, it means that individuals will not escape war simply by grouping together; it needs much more than the group for this. Hobbes says that one may well have families, the family does not prevent the war of all against all continuing to operate within the family circle: "And in all places, where men have lived by small Families, to robbe and spoyle one another has been a Trade."[16] And even passing from a small to a big group will not suffice to avoid war: even though men be joined together in groups of a multitude of men, "yet if their actions be directed according to their particular judgements, and particular appetites, they can expect thereby no defence, nor protection, neither against a Common enemy, nor against the injuries of one another."[17] So it is not from the group effect, from a sort of transitory and mutual interest that men can expect something like the way out from war.[†]

Only the civil order, that is to say the appearance of a sovereign, will bring the war of all against all to an end. There has to have been that process by which the powers of all the individuals are transferred to a single individual, or to an assembly, and all wills are reduced to just one.[18] The war of all against all ceases only when the sovereign is effectively constituted by this transfer of power. If, conversely, the power slackens or breaks up, then one gradually returns to the state of war: "there is no farther protection of Subjects in their loyalty; then is the Common-wealth DISSOLVED, and every man at liberty to protect himself by such courses as his own discretion shall suggest to him."[19]

So civil war is, so to speak, the terminal state of the dissolution of the sovereign, just as the war of all against all is the initial state on the basis of which the sovereign can be constituted. So long as there is a sovereign

---

[*] Manuscript (fol. 4): "This state of war essential to the individual is in a relation of mutual exclusion with civil society. Wherever there is no civil society there is war of all against all. Small groups conduct themselves no differently than individuals ..."

[†] The manuscript (fol. 5) adds: "but the establishment of a new type of order."

there is no war of all against all and civil war can reappear only at the end of the day when the sovereign disappears.

Second, I think this conception of civil war, which would be a resurgence of the war of all against all, should be contrasted with a conception of civil war that, for a number of reasons, is very different from that of the war of all against all. In the first place, contrary to what we find in Hobbes, I do not think that civil war in any way brings into play an essential virtuality of relationships between individuals. In fact, there is no civil war that is not a confrontation between collective elements: kinship, clienteles, religions, ethnic groups, linguistic communities, classes, and so on. It is always through masses, through collective and plural elements that civil war is at once born, unfolds, and is carried on. So it is not at all the natural dimension of relationships between individuals qua individuals: the actors in civil war are always groups qua groups. Furthermore, civil war not only stages collective elements, it forms them. Far from being the process whereby we return from the commonwealth to individuality, from the sovereign to the state of nature, from the collective order to the war of all against all, civil war is the process through which and by which a number of new, previously unknown collective elements are formed. Thus, at the end of the Middle Ages, how was the peasantry constituted as an ideological community of interests, as a social class, if not through the processes of civil war, of popular uprisings that shook Europe from the fifteenth century until the middle of the eighteenth century and [formed] this peasant class whose unity was acquired through the process of civil war itself? In the same way, it was, on the one hand, the multiplicity, and, on the other, the political and economic evolution of the market riots that shook the eighteenth century—riots gradually transformed into wage riots, then into political insurrections—that gave cohesion to, and revealed as a unitary and collective force those people[*] that will be one of the essential protagonists of the Revolution: sans-culottism is effectively constituted through processes of civil war.

Civil war should not be seen as something that dissolves the collective component of the life of individuals and returns them to something like their original individuality. Civil war is rather a

---

[*] Manuscript (fol. 6): "the 'humble folk (*menu peuple*)': those who will be the *sans-culottes*."

process whose protagonists are collective and whose effects, moreover, are the emergence of new collective protagonists. Moreover, contrary to what political theory usually assumes, civil war is not prior to the constitution of power; no more than it is what necessarily marks its disappearance or weakening. Civil war is not a sort of antithesis of power, what exists before or reappears after it. Civil war and power are not mutually exclusive. Civil war takes place on the stage of power. There is civil war only in the element of constituted political power; it takes place in order to keep or conquer power, to confiscate or transform it. It is not that which is oblivious of or purely and simply destroys power, but always depends on elements of power.[*]

We could, moreover, attempt to describe some of the procedures peculiar to civil war, precisely in terms of the interplay it enters into with power. Thus, first point[†]: in civil war, a number of collective units, groups, seize certain fragments of power, not in order to abolish them and return to something like the war of all against all, but rather to reactivate them. [For example,] the market riots in the eighteenth century:[20] when an uprising was triggered by scarcity of grain, and so a rise in its price and in the price of bread, what took place was not a return to a confused and violent appropriation by individuals of what they could effectively lay their hands on. These riots conform to an almost constant schema. This involves the appropriation by certain people, not of corn directly, but of forms, processes, and rites of power. In England, the rioters reactivated the old regulations of the end of the sixteenth century, according to which grain could not be sold in the markets to the biggest buyers before first having been offered to the small buyers, who purchased at their price the amount they needed to

---

[*] Manuscript (fol. 7): "on elements, signs, instruments of power; it reconstitutes or gives rise to a power precisely inasmuch as it attacks another power. It multiplies power: it gives power a double, a reflection (in a sort of dangerous symmetry) or on the contrary it gives rise to an entirely different power."

[†] Manuscript (fol. 7), marginal notes:

  "1. It seizes hold of these fragments (market riots)
  2. It inverts their mechanism (justice)
  3. It reactivates their old forms
  4. It activates their symbols
  5. It effectuates their myth."

live. This priority of the small buyers was a regulatory form established by the English monarchy at the end of the sixteenth century.[21] The riot consisted in taking back this power and reactivating it. In the same way, during the riots, the grain inspections of bakers, millers, and farms, which should have been the work of the agents of political power, but which the latter did not assure for a number of reasons linked to relationships between political power and economic interests, were undertaken by the people themselves. A riot, therefore, consisted less in destroying the elements of power than in taking them over and using them.

We could also say—second point—that, in these uprisings, these power relationships are not only reactivated but reversed, that is to say exercised in a different direction. Thus, the September massacres during the French Revolution were a kind of reverse justice, that is to say the reconstitution of a tribunal.

Third point: we have the schema of reactivation, since it involves protesting against the inertia of the supposedly revolutionary tribunal that had been established in the previous weeks. There is reversal, since those that political decision intended to escape the tribunal are forced to appear before this popular tribunal. So those who were in prison precisely so as to escape the revolutionary tribunal—aristocrats, priests—are put on trial. So we have a schema of appropriation, reactivation, and reversal of the power relationship.

Fourth point: in the phenomena of uprising one can find what could be called the effectuation, the activation of the same symbols of power. Thus, the revolt of the *Nu-pieds*,[22] which covered Normandy, took for itself the explicit signs of the most legitimate power, since it had its seal, standard, and symbols and claimed to represent the legitimate monarchy.

In some cases—fifth point—there would even be the effectuation of a myth of power. There are cases where civil war takes place in an essentially collective mode, without centralization, without the organization of a single power. We often see these movements effectuate [their own] political centralization* at the level of myth. Thus, the *Nu-pieds*, a spontaneous movement without a single command, even though it spreads from village to village, invented a leader and a purely

---

* Typescript (p. 31): "the political centralization of their own movement."

mythical organization,* Jean Nu-Pieds along with counsellors around him, that functioned within the popular movement as myth, while the real initiators of the movement passed themselves off as no more than representatives of this mythical leader.[23] There is an identical schema in the Luddite movement,† at the beginning of the nineteenth century, in which we find again this effectuation of the myth of power.[24] This movement spread at the point where the worlds of workers and peasants met. Throughout this movement we find the myth of a character— Ludd—the supposed leader, the centralized power of the movement, a myth with a precise organizing function.[25] There is something like the staging of a power in abeyance, a mythical power, which ran through and at the same time elaborated this whole discourse.

Thus, civil war can in no way be seen as something external to power‡ or as interrupted by power, but as a matrix within which elements of power come to function, are reactivated, break up, but in the sense of parts breaking away from each other without thereby losing their activity, in which power is re-elaborated, taken up again in a mythical form of ancient forms. There is no civil war without the work of power and work on power.

Third, it will be said that there is at least one region where we can recognize an antithesis between power and civil war: this is the level of established power, which is indeed what expels all civil war. Civil war is, indeed, what threatens power from the outside.§ In fact, we could show that civil war is, rather, what haunts power, not in the sense of a fear, but inasmuch as civil war occupies, traverses, animates, and invests power through and through. We have the signs of this war precisely in the form of that surveillance, of that threat, of that possession of armed

---

* The manuscript (fol. 7) adds: "gave itself a 'quasi-king' with standard, seal, generals, decrees:

    - sometimes different King,

    - sometimes servant of the King."

† Manuscript (fol. 7): "Ex[ample] of the Luddites: two workers disguised as women who present themselves as the two wives of the 'mythical' John Ludd."

‡ Manuscript (fol. 7): "Civil war is neither prior nor external to power."

§ The manuscript (fol. 8) begins this paragraph in the following way: "Is it not antithetical to all established power? That which threatens it? Its formidable confrontation? What from the outside is in danger of happening to it as an absolute danger."

force, in short in the form of all the instruments of coercion that actually established power acquires in order to wage it. One should be able to study the daily exercise of power as a civil war: to exercise power is to conduct civil war in a certain way, and it ought to be possible to analyze all these instruments, tactics, and alliances that we can identify in terms of civil war.*

For an analysis of penality it is important to see that power is not what suppresses civil war, but what conducts and continues it. And, if it is true that external war is the continuation of politics, we must say, reciprocally, that politics is the continuation of civil war.[26] Consequently we have to reject the image Hobbes [proposed] in which, with the appearance of the exercise of sovereign [power], war is expelled from [the sovereign power's] space.†

*   *   *

[I would like now to move on from the content of the notion of civil war to the] status of the criminal. From the eighteenth century we see the formulation of the idea that crime is not just an offense, the category of offenses involving injury to another person, but that crime is what harms society, that is to say an action by which the individual breaks the social pact binding him to others and goes to war against his own

---

* The manuscript (fol. 8) adds: "in the form also of alliances between groups in power, or between beneficiaries of power."

† Foucault summarizes here a long passage of the manuscript (fol. 8-9) which states: "Hobbes's image (war, expelled from civil society, no longer reigns except on the frontiers as a sword raised against enemies of the State) is to be rejected.
Civil war is also conducted all around power (and its instruments), against it, in order to escape it or reverse it or confiscate it; in order to make use of it, the better to subjugate it, to make it more usable, to establish thereby a domination of which political power is only one aspect or instrument.
Leaving two problems aside for the moment:

- power/State;
- civil war/class [struggle];

What the project means: analyzing penality, not

- in terms of the war of all against all, but
- in terms of civil war."

society. The crime is an act that reactivates, provisionally no doubt, and momentarily, the war of all against all, that is to say, of one against all. The criminal is the social enemy[*] and consequently punishment must be neither reparation for the harm done to the other, nor punishment of the offense, but a measure of protection, of counter-war that society takes against the criminal.[27] We can refer to the theorists of the eighteenth century in whom we see a readjustment of the notion of crime around that of social hostility. Hence the notion of a penalty that is not to be measured by the gravity of the offense or harm, but by what is useful for society. It is important for society that its enemies be brought under control and do not multiply. It is necessary therefore to seize hold of them and prevent them from doing harm. This is what we find in Beccaria,[28] as in Paley, in England, who writes: "If the impunity of the delinquent were not dangerous for society, there would be no reason to punish."[29] So, punishment is established on the basis of a definition of the criminal as someone who wages war on society.[†]

Now this theoretical theme happens to be correlated with a whole judicial practice that is, in truth, much older.

In fact, if eighteenth-century theorists derive the definition of the criminal as someone who harms society from a coherent theoretical-political discourse, on the other hand, already from the Middle Ages we see the birth of a practice, through the institutions, that, in a way, anticipated this theoretical theme: public action—that is to say, the fact that a crime could be prosecuted by the representatives of authority, independently of the complaint brought by the victim—came to double, relay, and possibly replace the private action of vengeance or reparation that the victim could expect, such as the reparation prevalent, for example, in the Germanic system in the Middle Ages.[30] This public action is carried out by the institutional figure of the prosecutor or the King's counsel, figures who, in the name of the sovereign, call for a punishment because, from the Middle Ages, the sovereign no longer

---

* The manuscript (fol. 10) adds: "('foreign' but not external enemy)."

† The manuscript (fol. 11) adds: "Theme that is found shaped throughout penal theory [up to the] twentieth century. That this theme of crime as breach of the contract, of the criminal as [being] at war with society, as social enemy, was transcribed into the vocabulary of a political theory more or less derived from Hobbes, is true. Let us say, at any rate, that the statement that crime is an attack on civil society in its entirety can indeed be derived from a certain theory of the social contract."

appears on the scene of justice merely as the supreme dispenser of justice, the one to whom, in the last instance, one appeals, but as the one who is responsible for order, the one whose authority has been harmed precisely by the disorder or crime and who, as injured sovereign, can stand as accuser.[31] Thus for a long time in penal practice, the sovereign, replacing the criminal's private adversary, came face to face with the criminal. In the name of the order and peace he is supposed to maintain, he declares that the criminal has struck him, simply by virtue of the fact that he has put himself in a state of "savage" war with an individual by attacking him independently of the laws.*

We have, then, two processes that, at a certain level of analysis, can be picked out independently: first, a process of theoretical derivation from a Hobbesian kind of conception of the war of all against all, from the social contract to civil war and, finally, to the crime; second, an older process of institutional derivation, (from the sixteenth to the eighteenth century), that starts from the control of judicial disputes by monarchical power and leads to the institutionalization of certain legal figures and a number of legal rules that make the criminal function as the enemy of the sovereign of society.†

There is, moreover, a [sort] of "element"—the crime-social hostility, criminal-public enemy—that is neither a theoretical nor an institutional or practical element, but is the exchanger element, the connector element between these two series, one leading to the idea that the criminal is at war with society, and the other that is the confiscation of penal justice by monarchical power. This element functions as exchanger between the two series and is behind a whole series of theoretical, practical, and epistemological effects throughout the nineteenth century. From the end of the eighteenth century, we have in fact the organization of a whole series of institutions that will establish the figure of the criminal as a social enemy and define him practically as such:‡ the institutions of the

---

* The manuscript (fol. 12) adds: "He will therefore declare a both public and judicial war in the form of a public action in justice."
† The manuscript (fol. 13) adds: "Two derivations that encounter each other at a remarkable point. And their junction defines an 'element' that is neither purely institutional nor purely theoretical."
‡ The manuscript (fols. 13-14) clarifies:
"- the establishment of instruments that will permit the initiation of public action and support its unfolding
   so that public action does not simply follow private action.

public prosecutor's office, of criminal investigation, the prosecution, and the organization of a judicial police, which will make possible a duly considered initiation of public action; the jury, which already existed in England, for example, but which was originally the right to be judged by one's peers, whereas the jury we see at work in the nineteenth century is the institution that marks the right of society itself (or its representatives) to judge someone who has put themselves in conflict with it. To be judged by a jury is no longer to be judged by one's peers,* but to be judged in the name of society by its representatives.

We also have a whole series of knowledge effects grouped around the emergence of the criminal as an individual "estranged from society,"† irreducible to laws and general norms. Thus, from this connection, we see the constitution of the possibility‡ of a psychopathological or psychiatric hold on the criminal. The latter is actually someone who is irreducible to society, incapable of social adaptation, someone whose relationship with society is one of constant aggression, who is foreign to its norms and its values. Discourses and institutions like those organized under the name of the psychopathology of deviance will thus be able to arise in connection with the phenomena of criminality.§

In these epistemic effects, [again] we have the possibility of analysis, by society itself, of the production of its enemies:¶ how is it that a society arrives at a degree of crime, of decomposition, such that it produces so many people who are its enemies? We see how the possibility of a sociology of criminality as social pathology finds and fixes its place here.**

---

so that it can be effective;
hence essentially the organization of a police, or again
- the establishment of institutions like the jury."

* The manuscript (fol. 14) adds: "or by arbitrators."

† Manuscript (fol. 14): "individual breaking with society," "at war with society," "enemy of society."

‡ Manuscript (fol. 14): "the possibility of analyzing the criminal individual in terms of social maladjustment; of inferiority or exteriority in relation to the demands of social and collective rationality. The criminal as foreign to society, to its norms, values, and systems."

§ The manuscript (fol. 15) adds: "Thus emerges the possible hold on penality of the genre of discourses like psychopathology, psychiatry, the psychology of deviance."

¶ Manuscript (fol. 15): "Conversely (and correlated with this), analysis of a society's production of individuals who are both foreign to it and enemies of it."

** The manuscript (fol. 15) adds: "Crime social sickness, through which society decomposes, creates the very thing that is opposed to it, that is going to attack it. Or, on the contrary, the possibility

This kind of connector, which constitutes the criminal as social enemy, is in reality an instrument by which the class in power transfers to society, in the form of the jury, or to social consciousness, through the intermediary of all these epistemic relays, the function of rejecting the criminal. This exclusion, which I said I would not consider as a fundamental function, is what the class in power wants to be brought about by those to whom it has apparently transferred the function of judging or punishing. I want to make the critical analysis of this sociologization of the criminal as social enemy, a sociologization whose effects currently dominate penal practice, the psychopathology of delinquency, and the sociology of the criminal.*

---

of analyzing the level of criminality as indicating a very low threshold of the intolerable:[32] a very sharp sensibility."

* The typescript ends here. The manuscript contains five additional sheets (fols. 16-20) which contain the following:

"It is not a matter of showing that there was first of all a theory of the criminal as social enemy, as individual returning spontaneously to the war of all against all, and that, from this there followed as consequences new institutions, new laws, new codes, and new scientific or epistemic themes.

α - The criminal-enemy is not a theoretical principle, an axiom formulated by a discourse, or presupposed by a practice.

It is an element that cannot be localized exactly here or there.
But that circulates from one to the other, passes from one to the other.
It is not a theoretical axiom or a practical principle.
It is a transcriber, an *exchanger*.

Proof:
It is what permits an institution like public action (established for political and fiscal reasons) to be transposed into penal theory in the form of the principle: the crime injures not only the victim but society; society's interest is to be represented in the action of prosecution; and to have the right to initiate it.

It is that exchanger that in penal theory makes the prosecutor (agent of royal taxation) the representative of society.
It is again what makes the penalty defined by the codes a protective measure for society (in the terms of penal theory).
It is always the exchanger that makes it possible for the criminal (prosecuted by the representative of society and condemned in its name) to be described in (psychological, psychiatric) terms as an a-social individual.

It is what allows passage from one register to the other, from one system to the other; not the code of translation, but the element that allows the application of one code to another (from the practical code, to the theoretical code, to the epistemic code). It is what allows all the repercussions of these passages and transpositions. It is the universal intermediary.
β - Remarks regarding the exchanger.

1. M. Bernard, "Discours à la Chambre des députés," 23 November 1831, in *Archives parlementaires de 1787 à 1860. Recueil complet des débats législatifs et politiques des Chambres françaises,* deuxième série (Paris: Paul Dupont, 1889) vol. LXXII (from 23 November 1831 to 22 December 1831) p. 5. This passage reflects an important principle for Foucault, namely that there is no hidden ideology and that everything is always said by the actors themselves; see above, p. 36, footnote *. Foucault will return to this theme in his lecture of 28 February, in a criticism of the notions of the "unsaid (*non-dit*)" and "outside-text (*hors-texte*)"; see below, p. 165 and p. 166, note *.

2. N. H. Julius, *Vorselungen* über *die Gefängnisskunde* ..., (Berlin: Stuhr, 1828) 2 volumes; *Leçons sur les prisons, présentées en forme de cours au public de Berlin, en l'année 1827,* trans., (vol. I), H. Lagarmitte (Paris: F. G. Levrault, 1831) p. 384. Nicolaus Heinrich Julius (1783-1862), doctor in medicine, was a prison reformer and drew up the plans of the Insterburg penitentiary, built in 1830 in the Prussian kingdom. For study purposes he travelled to England, Wales, and Scotland in 1827, and to the United States 1834 to 1836, where he became a great admirer of the Philadelphia system, that is to say, in his own words, of the "*principle of uninterrupted solitude for the whole period of imprisonment*": N. H. Julius, *Nord-amerikas sittliche Zustände, nach eigenen Anschauungen in den Jahren 1834, 1835 und 1836* (Leipzig: F. A. Brockhaus, 1839); *Du système pénitentiaire américain in 1836,* trans., Victor Foucher (Paris: Joubert, 1837) p. 6, emphasis in original. Julius translated into German the work by G. de Beaumont & A. de

---

It is what is always said.

- Always said: it is said, and explicitly, in the texts, laws, and theories. It is presupposed in practices, decisions, and institutions. It is connoted in literary images. It is not the unsaid; it is the more-than-said. The excessively said.

- But in this excess, it is never fixed: it is not a principle from which the rest derives; it is not a conclusion. It plays now one role and now another: sometimes it is representation, sometimes it is a practical principle.

It is a permanent affirmation.

It is not an assertion that one can situate in a precise place in a discourse. The exchanger is what assures the coherence and relative systematicity of heterogeneous elements (for example):

• penal practice
• the theory of criminal law
• the codes
• psychiatric, sociological discourse

But these effects of reinforcement, stabilization are linked to mechanisms of limitation and closure. Thus: insofar as it will be possible (in terms of penal theory) to transcribe the figure of the prosecutor into representative of society, he can no longer be interpreted as the agent of a centralized power that seeks to make disputes subject to taxation to its advantage.
Nor can he be interpreted as the agent of a class holding power.
Likewise: inasmuch as the sociology of delinquency, in its vocabulary, describes the practice of public action on the basis of the exchanger (criminal-enemy), it is clear that whatever criticisms it may make of penal practice, psychological theory will never be able to re-evaluate it thoroughly. The exchanger therefore is
- the form taken by the intrinsic obscurity of a practice, its specific impermeability to the discourses that claim either to found it theoretically or to clarify it scientifically;
- the form taken by the powerlessness, ineffectiveness, inapplicability, in short the non-power of knowledge (*savoir*) and theory. Their state of break (*coupure*) and speculative inertia."

Tocqueville, *Du système pénitentiaire aux* États-Unis *et de son application en France, suivi d'un appendice sur les colonies pénales et de notes statistiques* (Paris: H. Fournier Jeune, 1833), 3rd edition expanded with the "Rapport de M. de Tocqueville sur le projet de loi de Réforme des prisons ..." (Paris: Librairie de Charles Gosselin, 1845); see A. Krebs, "Julius, Nikolaus Heinrich" in *Neue Deutsche Biographie*, Bd. 10, 1974, pp. 656-658.

Foucault will return to this extract from Julius and develop it in the chapter "Panopticism" in *Surveiller et Punir*, p. 218; *Discipline and Punish*, p. 216, where he writes: "A few years after Bentham, Julius gave this [disciplinary] society its birth certificate." Foucault also adds: "In his first version of the Panopticon, Bentham had also imagined an acoustic surveillance, operated by means of pipes leading from the cells to the central tower ... Julius tried to develop a system of dissymmetrical listening (Julius, *Leçons sur les prisons*, p. 18)" (Fr., p. 203 n. 2; Eng., p. 317 n. 3); see also, "La vérité et les formes juridques," *DE*, II, pp. 607-609/"Quarto," I, pp. 1475-1477; "Truth and Juridical Forms," *EW*, 3, pp. 71-73.

3. N. H. Julius, *Leçons sur les prisons*, pp. 384-385. It is interesting to identify here one of the two sources (Julius and Bentham) of one of the two origins (prison and hospital) of Foucault's interest in panopticism and generalized surveillance. He would have discovered the idea of panopticism at the time of his work on the origins of clinical medicine and on the clinical gaze; see, M. Foucault, "L'œil du pouvoir," interview with J.-P. Barou and M. Perrot, in J.-P. Barou, ed., *Le Panoptique* (Paris: Pierre Belfond, 1977) p. 9; *DE*, II, no. 195, p. 190/"Quarto," I, p. 190; English translation by Colin Gordon, "The Eye of Power" in M. Foucault, *Power/Knowledge. Selected Interviews and Other Writings 1972-1977*, ed., C. Gordon (Brighton: The Harvester Press, 1980) p. 146. Bruno Fortier, architect, teacher, and in charge of the Bibliothèque d'architecture, provided him with the architectural projects and plans for a circular hospital at the Hôtel-Dieu in the 1770s—radial plans which will be studied in Foucault's seminar on "the history of the hospital institution and of hospital architecture in the eighteenth century" at the Collège de France in 1972-1974: "Résumé du cours" in, *Le Pouvoir psychiatrique. Cours au Collège de France, 1973-1974*, ed., J. Lagrange (Paris: Gallimard-Seuil, "Hautes Études," 2003) p. 352; English translation by Graham Burchell, "Course Summary" in, *Psychiatric Power. Lectures at the Collège de France, 1973-1974*, English series editor, Arnold I. Davidson (Basingstoke: Palgrave Macmillan, 2006) p. 346. The seminar will result in the publication of B. Barret-Kriegel, A. Thalamy, F. Beguin, and B. Fortier, *Les Machines à guerir. Aux origines de l'hôpital moderne* (Brussels: Pierre Mardaga, "Architecture-Archives," 1979). As Fortier's documents show, the plans for an "immense radiating hospital" that would allow for "a constant and absolute surveillance" predate Bentham's Panopticon (see ibid., p. 48). On Bentham and the Panopticon, see below p. 77 note 16. In fact, Foucault traces the first models of "this isolating visibility" back to the dormitories of the Paris École militaire in 1751 (see "L'œil du pouvoir," p. 191/p. 191; "The Eye of Power," p. 147). Here, with Julius, the context is penality, of which Foucault says: "Then while studying the problems of the penal system, I noticed that all the great projects for re-organizing the prisons (which date, incidentally, from a slightly later period, the first half of the nineteenth century) take up this same theme, but accompanied this time by the almost invariable reference to Bentham. There was scarcely a text or a proposal about the prisons which didn't mention Bentham's 'device'—the 'Panopticon'" (ibid.).

4. See *Surveiller et Punir*, pp. 218-219; *Discipline and Punish*, pp. 216-217. Concerning Foucault's references to the "spectacle," see G. Debord, *La Société du spectacle* (Paris: Buchet/Chastel, 1967). One might even read here a criticism of Guy Debord, who put the notion of the spectacle at the center of the concept of modernity: according to Foucault, Julius emphasizes that the spectacle comes from Antiquity and that what marks the modern is not the appearance of the spectacle, but rather its eclipse, its reversal into surveillance. The previous passage from Julius articulates exactly this critique.

5. N. H. Julius, *Leçons sur les prisons*, p. 385.

6. J.-B. Treilhard, "Motifs du livre Ier, chapitres I à VIII, du *Code d'instruction criminelle*, présentés au corps législatif par MM. Treilhard, Réal et Faure, Conseillers d'État. Séance du 7 novembre 1808" in *Code d'instruction criminelle*, édition *conforme à l'édition originale du Bulletin des lois* (Paris: Le Prieur, 1811) pp. 5-32: p. 20. Foucault takes up this passage in his argument on the Panopticon in *Surveiller et Punir*, p. 219; *Discipline and Punish*, p. 217. See also, "La vérité et les formes juridiques," pp. 608-609/pp. 1476-1477; "Truth and Juridical Forms," pp. 72-73. The exposition of the purposes of the *Code d'instruction criminelle* is generally attributed to Jean-Baptiste, comte Treilhard (1742-1810), who was involved in drafting the Code. Treilhard, jurist and politician, was successively president of the *États généraux*, president of the National Constituent Assembly, president of the National Convention (from the trial of Louis XVI), member of the Committee of Public Safety, president of the Council of the Five Hundred, and member of the Directory. See Jean Treilhard, *Jean-Baptiste Treilhard, ministre plénipotentiaire de la République au Congrès de Rastadt* (Paris: Éd. Gaillon, 1939). Foucault returns to Treilhard in some interviews: see "À propos de l'enfermement pénitentiaire," interview with A. Krywin and F. Ringelheim, *Pro Justitia. Revue politique de droit*, vol. I, nos. 3-4: *La Prison*, October 1973, pp. 5-14; *DE*, II, no. 127, p. 437/"Quarto," I, p. 1305 (important role: Treilhard symbolizes the expansion of panopticism from an architectural form to a form of government: "Treilhard presents political power as a kind of Panopticon realized in the institutions"); see too *Surveiller et Punir*, p. 143, p. 219, p. 237; *Discipline and Punish*, p. 141, p. 217, p. 234.

7. J.-B. Treilhard, "Motifs" of the *Code d'instruction criminelle*, p. 23.

8. N. H. Julius, *Leçons sur les prisons*, p. 385. Julius remarks, pp. 385-386: "But the utility of this fundamental thought for any building, and the high degree of development of which it is susceptible, is manifested in no more rapid and fruitful manner than it is for prisons."

9. Thomas Hobbes, *Leviathan*, ed., C. B. Macpherson (Harmondsworth: Penguin Books, 1968) ch. xiii, p. 187. Foucault uses the French translation by François Tricaud, *Le Léviathan. Traité de la matière, de la forme et du pouvoir de la république ecclésiastique et civile* (Paris: Sirey, 1971) of the original edition "London, Printed for Andrew Crooke, at the Green Dragon in St. Pauls Church-yard, 1651." [There are three editions with this imprint. The English Penguin edition used here is based on the first, *Bear*, edition; G.B.] Foucault develops his analysis of Hobbes in "Il faut défendre la société," lecture of 14 January 1976, pp. 26-27, and especially of 4 February 1976, p. 77 sq.; "Society Must Be Defended," pp. 28-29, p. 89 sq.

10. Thomas Hobbes, *Leviathan*, p. 187, emphasis in original.

11. See ibid., pp. 183-184: "Nature hath made men so equall, in the faculties of body and mind ... From this equality of ability, ariseth equality of hope in the attaining of our Ends. And therefore if any two men desire the same thing, which neverthelesse they cannot both enjoy, they become enemies."

12. Ibid., p. 185: "So that in the nature of man, we find three principall causes of quarrell. First, Competition; Secondly, Diffidence; Thirdly, Glory."

13. Hobbes attributes the second cause of the war of all against all to "Diffidence" [*méfiance* (mistrust) in the French translation] (ibid., p. 185), after having discussed the "diffidence [*défiance* (distrust) in the French translation] of one another" (ibid., p. 184). In the manuscript, Foucault originally wrote "*méfiance*," but he changed the expression to "*défiance*." [In Hobbes, the English word in both cases is "diffidence"; G.B.].

14. Ibid., p. 185.

15. Ibid., ch. 17, p. 223.

16. Ibid., p. 224.

17. Ibid.

18. In the manuscript (fol. 5), Foucault here cites this passage: "And this civil order can be both established and preserved only by a power, i.e., by the transfer of the power of the

individuals, of 'all their power and strength upon one Man, or upon one Assembly of men, that may reduce all their Wills ... unto one Will'" (ibid., p. 227).

19. Ibid., ch. 29, p. 375.

20. The typescript (p. 29) gives this reference: "(cf. Thompson, in *Past and Present*, 1971)." Foucault is referring here to the famous article by the English Marxist historian, Edward P. Thompson, which had just been published: "The Moral Economy of the English Crowd in the Eighteenth Century," *Past and Present*, 50, February 1971, pp. 76-136. According to Daniel Defert, Foucault had a detailed knowledge of Thompson's work, especially, *The Making of the English Working Class* (London: Victor Gollancz, 1963), on the English artisans and working class between 1780 and 1832. With regard to these themes, Foucault also made use of the work of Paul Bois, especially, *Paysans de l'Ouest. Des structures économiques et sociales aux options politiques depuis l'époque révolutionnaire dans la Sarthe* (Le Mans: Mouton, 1960).

21. Foucault develops the question of the grain police as prototype of discipline in the French context. See *Sécurité, Territoire, Population. Cours au Collège de France, 1977-1978*, ed., Michel Senellart (Paris: Gallimard-Seuil, "Hautes Études," 2004) lectures of 18 January 1978, pp. 31-50; 29 March 1978, pp. 325-336; 5 April 1978, pp. 343-351; English translation by Graham Burchell, *Security, Territory, Population. Lectures at the Collège de France, 1977-1978*, English series editor, Arnold I. Davidson (Basingstoke: Palgrave Macmillan, 2007), pp. 29-49; pp. 318-328; pp. 335-343. The grain police that Foucault describes (ibid., pp. 33-34; Eng., pp. 31-32), "that great over-regulatory police" (ibid., 361; Eng., p. 353) will become synonymous with, or an illustration of, discipline and the antonym of "security." Describing the police regulations of grain collected by Delamare and Fréminville, Foucault says of them: "We are in the world of the regulation, the world of discipline" (ibid., p. 348; Eng., p. 340), and adds in the manuscript for this lecture: "And, in fact, the big practical treatises on police were collections of regulations" (ibid., footnote*).

22. The revolt of the "*Nu-pieds*" (sometimes called "Va-nu-pieds") broke out in the summer of 1639 in Normandy. Foucault devoted six lectures to this revolt in his course on "penal theories and institutions." It was a revolt against the fiscal and administrative system set off by the establishment of the *gabelle*—salt tax—under Louis XIII in different regions of the province, and was severely repressed in 1640. See B. Porchnev, *Les Soulèvements populaires en France de 1623 à 1648* (Paris: SEVPEN, "EPHE, VIᵉ section/CRH. Œuvres étrangers," 4, 1963) pp. 303-502. Foucault deals with peasant delinquency and lower class illegalism in *Surveiller et Punir*, p. 87; *Discipline and Punish*, p. 85 where he gives as references: O. Festy, *Les Délits ruraux et leur répression sous la Révolution et le Consulat. Étude d'histoire économique* (Paris: Librairie M. Riviere, "Bibliothèque d'histoire économique," 1956); M. Agulhon, *La Vie sociale en Provence intérieure au lendemain de la Révolution* (Paris: Société des études robespierristes, "Bibliothèque d'histoire révolutionnaire," 1970); Y.-M. Bercé, *Croquants et Nu-pieds. Les soulèvements paysans en France du XVIᵉ au XIXᵉ siècle* (Paris: Gallimard, "Archives," 55, 1974) p. 161. For a more recent work, see J.-L. Ménard, *La Révolte des Nu-Pieds en Normandie au XVIIᵉ siècle* (Paris: Éd. Dittmar, 2005).

23. The existence of "General Jean Nu-Pieds," the name under which a number of orders sent out in Normandy were signed, has been the subject of many debates, based on contradictory sources. Boris Porchnev, reviewing the different hypotheses, concludes: "We do not have sufficient evidence to be able to assert that Jean Nu-Pieds was an imaginary character." Real or imaginary, he was associated with a stamp—two bare feet set on a crescent—and a place of residence, at the base of the walls of Avranches. See B. Porchnev, *Les Soulèvements populaires en France de 1623 à 1638*, pp. 320-327.

24. The so-called "Luddite" revolt took the form of a movement of machine breaking—mainly looms—in the textile industry in the Midlands, Yorkshire, and Lancashire between 1811 and 1813. See E. P. Thompson, *The Making of the English Working Class*; E. J. Hobsbawm, "The Machine Breakers," *Past and Present*, 1, 1952, pp. 57-70. On the writings of the Luddite

movement, see K. Binfield, ed., *Writings of the Luddites* (Baltimore, MD: Johns Hopkins University Press, 2004).

25. The unity of the Luddite movement was to a large extent defined by the common claim, in different regions, of the figure of "General Ludd"—sometimes also described as king or captain—probably inspired by a regional idiom designating a machine breaker, in reference to a Ned Ludd who allegedly destroyed his master's loom in Leicester, 1779. See K. Navickas, "The Search for 'General Ludd': the Mythology of Luddism," *Social History*, vol. 30(3), 2005, pp. 281-295; P. Minard, "Le retour de Ned Ludd. Le luddisme et ses interprétations," *Revue d'histoire moderne et contemporaine*, vol. 54(1), January-March 2007, pp. 242-257.

26. See *Surveiller et Punir*, p. 170; *Discipline and Punish*, p. 168; "*Il faut défendre la société*," lectures of 7 January 1976, p. 16, and 21 January 1976, p. 41; "*Society Must Be Defended*," pp. 15-16, p. 48 [Either as a result of a slip or misprint, the English translation has: "the principle that war is a continuation of politics" where it should read "the principle that politics is a continuation of war"; G.B.]

27. See "La vérité et les formes juridiques," p. 590/p. 1458; "Truth and Juridical Forms," p. 54.

28. See C. Beccaria, *Dei delitti e delle pene* (Livorno: 1764); French translation by the abbé André Morellet, *Traité des délits et des peines, traduit de l'italien, d'après la troisième édition, revue, corrigée et augmentés par l'Auteur* (Lausanne, 1766); and by Maurice Chevallier, with a Preface by Robert Badinter, *Des délits et des peines* (Paris: Flammarion, 1991); English translation Richard Davies with Virginia Cox and Richard Bellamy, "On Crimes and Punishments" in *On Crimes and Punishments and Other Writings*, ed., Richard Bellamy (Cambridge: Cambridge University Press, 1995). The first French translation by Morellet changed the order of the chapters and the distribution of paragraphs fairly freely. The 1991 French edition is faithful to the order of the fifth and final edition provided directly by Beccaria. See B. E. Harcourt, "Beccaria, *Dei delitti e delle pene*" in *Dictionnaire des grandes œuvres juridiques*, ed., Olivier Cayl and Jean-Louis Halpérin (Paris: Dalloz, 2008) pp. 39-46. Foucault adds in the manuscript (fol. 10): "Beccaria: the penalty must be measured by what is useful for society (useful regarding its defense), // - in order that its enemy no longer starts again, is overcome; // - in order that other enemies are not incited." See C. Beccaria, *Des délits et des peines* (1991 translation) "Avis au lecteur," p. 57 (definition of the just and unjust in terms of "what is useful or harmful to society"); ch. II, pp. 63-65: "The sovereign's right to punish crimes is therefore founded on the necessity to defend the public safety entrusted to him from the usurpation of individuals"; ch. XII, pp. 86-87: "The end of punishments can only be, therefore, to prevent the guilty from causing further harm to his fellow citizens and to dissuade others from committing similar offenses"; *On Crimes and Punishments*, "To the Reader," p. 5: "the relationship between political justice and injustice, that is to say, what is socially useful and what is harmful"; Ch. 2, p. 10: "Here, then, is the foundation of the sovereign's right to punish crimes: the necessity of defending the repository of the public well-being from the usurpations of individuals; ch. 12, p. 31: "The purpose [of punishment], therefore, is nothing other than to prevent the offender from doing fresh harm to his fellows and to deter others from doing likewise."

29. W. Paley, "Of Crimes and Punishments," Book IV, ch. IX, in *The Principles of Moral and Political Philosophy* (London: R. Faulder, 1785) p. 526: "What would it be to the magistrate that offences went altogether unpunished, if the impunity of the offenders were followed by no danger or prejudice to the commonwealth?" William Paley (1743-1805), a British theologian, was a utilitarian theorist of penality, very close to Beccaria's theses and a precursor of Bentham in penal matters. Paley was known above all as author of *A View of the Evidence of Christianity* (London: 1794) and *Natural Theology* (London: 1802) developing the analogy of the world with a clock, necessarily governed by a watchmaker. After Paley's name in the manuscript, Foucault adds (fol. 11): "('rigorist')"; an allusion no doubt to the strict requirement that the penalty be measured on the scale of its utility for society, a doctrine

that Leon Radzinowicz has called "the doctrine of maximum severity"; see L. Radzinowicz, *A History of English Criminal Law and its Administration from 1750*, vol. 1: *The Movement for Reform* (London: Stevens and Sons, 1948) p. 231: "The Doctrine of Maximum Severity."

30. See above p. 19, note 17.

31. See J. R. Strayer, *On the Medieval Origins of the Modern State*, pp. 27-31. In the manuscript (fol. 12) Foucault adds: "the fact that the imposition and execution of the penalty are not assured or controlled by the injured party, but by the sole authority of the State." On the notion which in this epoch appears strictly associated with the execution of justice, see J. R. Strayer, pp. 36-44 and pp. 53-55.

32. The reference to a "very low threshold of the intolerable" echoes the inquiries: "*Intolérable*" of the Groupe d'information sur les prisons, of which Foucault was one of the co-founders in 1971. See P. Artières, L. Quéro, M. Zancarini-Fournel, eds., *Le Groupe d'information sur le prisons. Archives d'une lutte, 1970-1972* (Paris: Institut Mémoires de l'édition contemporaine/ IMEC, 2003); M. Foucault, "Je perçois l'intolérable," *DE*, II, p. 204/"Quarto," I, p. 1072.

three

17 JANUARY 1973

The appearance of the criminal as social enemy. Historical survey of first manifestations. (I) Economic analysis of delinquency in the eighteenth century by the physiocrats. Le Trosne, Mémoire sur les vagabonds (1764): More than a psychological propensity like idleness or a social phenomenon like begging, vagabondage is the matrix of crime and a scourge of the economy; it produces scarcity of labor, raises wages, and lowers production. ᗭ The laws inadequate; the measures recommended by Le Trosne: 1. enslavement; 2. outlawing; 3. peasant self-defense; 4. mass conscription. ᗭ Similarities of vagabonds and nobility. (II) The criminal-social enemy as literary theme. Gil Blas *and the beginning of the eighteenth century: the continuum and omnipresence of delinquency. Novels of terror at the end of the eighteenth century: localized and extra-social delinquency. Emergence of the dualities crime-innocence, evil-good.*

I WANTED TO EXPLAIN to you the kind of detachment of the criminal from the system of private obligations or disputes in which he was caught up in Medieval practices, and his emergence as a social enemy, as an individual opposed to the whole of society as such. We can symbolize this transformation with a text that was quite important institutionally and politically. It is a discourse delivered to the Constituent Assembly in October 1789, at the time of the reform of penal organization in

France, or more precisely, of a modification of the procedure of criminal investigation, in which the rapporteur of the project, Beaumetz,[1] describes what, according to him, is the mechanism and justification of criminal procedure in the Ancien Régime. In doing this he merely re-transcribes the practices of penal law in the Ancien Régime into the new vocabulary, which is, schematically, that of Beccaria, and, on the basis of that re-transcription in terms of public enemy, proposes a number of modifications to criminal procedure: "A crime is committed: the whole of society is injured in one of its members; hatred of the crime or private interest leads to a denunciation or motivates a complaint; the public prosecutor is informed by the injured party or roused by the general clamor, the crime is established, clues are gathered; its traces are confirmed. Public order must be avenged."[2] Beaumetz thus takes up again the elements of private and public prosecution according to the old rules of criminal procedure, which could in fact be initiated either by the complaint of an individual with a private interest, or by a denunciation, that is to say, by someone who is not involved in a private dispute with the offender, but who, in the name of the public interest, presents a statement of the crime to the prosecutor. The magistrate of the common interest then applies to the judge and asks to produce his witnesses, to present his evidence. The prosecutor is thus designated as the magistrate of the common interest. We have here the reinterpretation of the old penal practice in Beccaria's terms.

How does this "appearance" of the criminal as social enemy come about? I would like to begin by identifying some of the first manifestations of this theme and then to see what ensemble of political and economic processes finally ended up fixing the criminal at a certain level as social enemy, and what it is that conceals this operation that consists in describing, judging, and also excluding the criminal as social enemy.*

---

* The manuscript of the lecture (fol. 1) begins in this way:
"A massive phenomenon:

  - the detachment of the crime from the offense, the sin;
  - the detachment of the criminal from the game of private obligations and disputes; his emergence as a social enemy, an individual opposed to the whole of society, in a relationship of challenge, of hostility to the whole of society.

*   *   *

[So I will begin with] the analysis of some derivations. One of the most interesting manifestations of this appearance is provided by the first economic analyses of delinquency in the eighteenth century. There were, of course, already descriptions of the population of "thieves," and so on, and also an analysis of poverty and begging, as well as criticism of the means of assistance employed since the Middle Ages to relieve poverty, to reduce begging: private, ecclesiastical, or legislative measures. But this could not be called an analysis in terms of *political economy* in the strict sense. Now, [in the second half] of the eighteenth century, with the physiocrats, I think we see the first appearance of an analysis of delinquency conducted [in the form of] an analysis of economic processes.[3] What is particular about this analysis is that it fixes the position, role, and function of delinquency, not in relation to consumption, to the mass of goods available, but in relation to the mechanisms and processes of production; on the other hand, by virtue of them defining the delinquent [from the angle of] production, the physiocrats at the same time describe him as an enemy of society: it is the delinquent's position in relation to production that defines him as a public enemy.

A model of this kind of analysis is provided by the text by Le Trosne, *Mémoire sur les vagabonds et sur les mendiants* [published in] 1764.[4] In this work, vagabondage is given as the fundamental category of delinquency, which means, not that vagabondage is, as in earlier analyses, the, as it were, psychological point of departure of delinquency—Le Trosne does not mean that one wanders around and this vagabondage gradually leads to theft, and then to crime, but that vagabondage is the element on the basis of which other crimes are to be specified. It is the general matrix of crime that contains eminently all other forms of delinquency, not as potentialities, but as elements that constitute it and make it up.

Symbolize by → Beaumetz
Study:

  - some manifestations of this emergence,
  - the nature of this 'appearance'."

Now this thesis is opposed to two traditional types of analysis found at this time.

First, an analysis in which idleness is the mother of every vice and, thereby, of every crime.[5] Idleness is the psychological trait or fault from which every other form of deviation or crime derives. Now, in Le Trosne's type of analysis, vagabondage is not something like a fault or psychological propensity, it is in fact the set of vagabonds, that is to say a type of shared life, a social group that appears as a counter-society, unlike idleness, which, in the psychology of individuals, was something like an individual sin.[*]

Second, by presenting vagabondage as the general matrix of delinquency, Le Trosne is opposed to any analysis in which begging is the main element to be punished. In French legislation, vagabondage was not punished as such; the vagabond came under the penal system at the level of the action of asking someone else for one's subsistence without working. Now, for Le Trosne, vagabondage is the main thing to be punished; entry into the world of delinquency is the fact of travelling around, of not being settled on an estate, of not being defined by a job. Crime begins when one has no civil status, that is to say geographical location[†] within a definite community, when one is "disreputable (*sans aveu*)," according to the term taken up by the author, but precisely while changing its meaning.[6] Previously, in fact, to be "*sans aveu*," in the old law, was not being without a link with a fixed and established community, as in Le Trosne, but being without anyone to vouch for you, to stand surety for you before justice. So how does the fact of moving around, of being without territorial surety, constitute crime against the economy?

Le Trosne analyzes precisely the economic consequence of these constant movements. [First of all,] when one moves one causes a shortage of labor in the poorest regions, the effect of which is to raise wages, so that in an already less productive region the producer will be burdened with high wages; to poverty will be added [rising] prices and non-competition and, consequently, an even greater impoverishment. [Then,] by withdrawing from the place where they were the producers'

---

* Manuscript (fol. 3): "It is no longer a sin that entails all the others, it is a micro-society."
† The manuscript (fol. 3) adds the expression: "geographic pinning."

potential labor force, vagabonds lower production and prevent a certain level of productivity. [Furthermore,] when they move around they avoid all personal taxes (tallage, *corvée*), and, since these involve raising a fixed sum, this means that the total will have to be borne by fewer people; this increase in personal taxes will again reduce part of the revenue that normally could be capitalized to exploit the land. [Finally, vagabondage involves] people who, not marrying, randomly abandon their natural children and produce an idle population in the places through which they pass—which will take its share from overall consumption. If we stick to these first three effects of vagabondage, we see that the vagabond is no longer someone who takes a part of consumption without working, as he was in the Middle Ages. He is not so much someone who attacks the overall mass of things to be consumed, as someone who attacks the mechanisms of production, and at several levels: that of the number of workers, of the quantity of labor provided, and of the quantity of money returning to the land for its exploitation. The vagabond is therefore someone who disrupts production and not just a sterile consumer. He therefore occupies a position of constitutive hostility with regard to the normal mechanisms of production.

In this anti-productive function, how is it that vagabonds are not purely eliminated or forced back into the productive process? With regard to this Le Trosne rejects the thesis that where there is no work there are poor people who beg and have to move elsewhere; for him, in fact, one does not become a vagabond through the absence of work, for, if it is true that in some cases there is not enough subsistence, on the other hand, the possibility of work is never lacking: there is always enough work for everybody even though there is not enough subsistence for all. For the physiocrats, the generosity of the land is the work it provides, since it is only when it has been worked that it will produce enough; the first thing land supplies is work. The vagabond therefore is not someone who lacks subsistence and is thereby pushed outside, so much as someone who voluntarily refuses the work that the land so generously offers to us. He is not someone unemployed who, under duress, gradually starts to beg and travel around; he is someone who refuses to work. So there is a primary and fundamental identity between moving around and refusing work: for the physiocrats, this is where the vagabond's crime is to be found.

Now, how is it that society does not compel him? To account for this Le Trosne distinguishes himself from the criticism that, from the seventeenth to the beginning of the eighteenth century, was directed at wealthy and charitable people, at [those] who give; the multiplication of vagabonds was then attributed to that kind of economic error that consisted in giving a share of possible consumption without requiring a share of necessary work in return; now, if vagabonds subsist and multiply, it is not because one gives to them, but because they take. They establish a relationship of unrestrained power, outside the law, with the people of civil society in the midst of whom they live. Le Trosne thus analyzes the methods of establishing these violent relationships to which specific forms of crime, of delinquency, correspond. When they arrive in a village, [the vagabonds] begin by moving in and appropriating crops and animals, which is expressed as theft in the form of delinquency; [when] these spontaneous resources dry up, they enter the houses and make people give to them by threatening to burn down their houses or to kill them; with these resources they can even trade and go from village to village re-selling what they have been given; with this surplus they celebrate; they also procure money thanks to information from women and children, and if necessary by violence. In this way they are led from the first theft of plunder to arson or crime.[*]

So, to characterize the position of the delinquent in relation to society we have a sort of coupling of refusal to work and violence, which, to tell the truth, must no longer be concealed by the coupling of unemployment and request. Seventeenth-century analyses started from unemployment in order to account for begging and delinquency; for the physiocrats this couple no longer plays an organizing role. Criminals

---

[*] Manuscript (fols. 5-6): "Analysis of vagabond behavior:

   1. spontaneous appropriation;

   2. threatening to get people to give;

   3. they get people to give in order to trade (with bread rather than coins), they re-sell in the taverns;

   4. they feast and celebrate in the forest;

   5. they get people to give money with threats;

   6. they punish with fire, murder."

appear as social enemies through the violent power they exercise on the population and through the position they occupy in the process of production by their refusal to work. Le Trosne writes: "They are voracious insects that infect and devastate [the countryside], and daily devour the subsistence of the cultivators. They are literally enemy troops spread over the surface of the territory, living as they like, as in a conquered country, and collecting veritable taxes in the name of alms. These taxes exceed the tallage in the poorest countries ..."[7]; "They live in society without belonging to it; they live in society in the condition that men would be in if there were no law, police, or authority; in the condition that we suppose existed before the establishment of civil societies, but which, without ever having existed for a whole people, is, by a singular contradiction, realized in the middle of a policed society."[8] We see that the model of the war of all against all serves here as principle for the analysis of delinquency.

Why does civil society* find itself helpless before this enemy population? How is it that civil society does not react when, surrounded by the law, there are men outside the law? Le Trosne explains that men are helpless before this population precisely because they belong to civil society; reputable people, that is to say people with a place, civil status, an employer, have renounced the wild, free use of arms by virtue of the social contract; to be in society means precisely to agree to renounce the use of arms in one's immediate self-defense, for this right to defend oneself has been delegated to the sovereign. But this sovereign defends people by means of inadequate laws, and there are a number of reasons for this. First of all, due to a fundamental misinterpretation, the laws of the realm are not directed against vagabondage, but against begging. The laws let people circulate and only arrest them when they hold out their hands, although it is not serious to hold out one's hand in one's own village. What is serious is to leave it. And then the laws strike too late: begging is attacked and not vagabondage; but again, these laws are too lenient, since the most important penalty against begging is banishment, which consists in sending those from one's own province to another province—that is to say, transforming them into vagabonds. As a result, far from being the target of penality,

---

* Instead of "civil society," the manuscript (fol. 6) has: "men who work."

the vagabond is its effect. Finally, legislation is in error since it always starts from the postulate that vagabonds exist because there is no work and the vagabond is someone who has not had the opportunity to work; hence the practice of putting them in establishments of forced labor in which it was hoped they would acquire the habit of work. But, in fact, the vagabond is basically someone who refuses to work.

Le Trosne also puts forward four sorts of measures:

1. Slavery. To correct the vagabond we do not have to give back to him the opportunity to work; we have only to constrain him to the most forced work possible: "he is a ferocious beast that we cannot tame ...; we only succeed in subduing him by putting him in chains,"[9] that is to say, by forcing him to work performed under maximum supervision: the galleys, for example, but in perpetuity, since his refusal to work is essential. "We must regard them as having been acquired by the State by their sentencing, and as belonging to it like slaves to a master. There was never a more legitimate ground for establishing servitude. The State may therefore employ them in such work as it thinks fit, and treat them like its property."[10] And when the galleys are full, we will fill the mines.[11] And when there are too many in France, "we can also send them to the Colonies."*

2. Enslavement can be taken to its final consequences only on condition that it is accompanied by a juridical outlawing. Being condemned as a vagabond will mean falling outside any legal protection, and it is as such that one becomes a slave. And since slavery must not be evaded, the vagabond will be branded with the letter G on his brow or cheek, so that any slave who leaves his post may be arrested and executed by anyone. From the moment vagabonds are seized for the King, they are no longer part of the order of citizens; they no longer have civil status, the laws have nothing more to rule on regarding them and, in the places where they are held, penalties pronounced in order to prevent desertion or revolt are no longer part of the judicial order, they belong to the domain of military penalties.[12]

3. Self-defense of the peasant community. It is necessary to assure these procedures and for this to have a sufficient armed force. It is

---

* The manuscript (fol. 6) has, according to Le Trosne: "And when there are too many in France, 'we will sell them in North Africa and buy Christian slaves in return'."

therefore necessary to replace the insufficient forces of the gendarmerie and State police with the will of all: "The people of the countryside can supplement [the constabulary]; they are so abused and plagued by the vagabonds that we can assure the government that they are prepared to do anything to free themselves of them ...."[13] It is sufficient to authorize and arm them.

4. The hunt and mass conscription.[14] The text proposes a utopian procedure: that of an entire society at work with the right to kill on sight anyone who moves.* What is in fact recounted here, in a [sort] of furious reverie, a fictional anticipation,† is what the power operating in capitalist society did, by other means and by differently subtle tactics, in order to succeed in fixing to their work all those with the tendency to move. Le Trosne's dream was this great confinement to the place of work, in which he saw only this kind of great massacre where one could kill anyone who basically refused to be settled, this feudal, but already capitalist hunt. In its savagery and dreamlike quality, the text tells us what will happen meticulously when capitalist institutions and coercive measures are in place. The transition from hunt to *coercion*, transforming labor-power into productive force, is the penal system's condition for being able to function in our society.

But maybe this text is a puzzle. If one takes several of its elements—the description of vagabonds, the position assigned to them in relation to production, and so on—something else can be made out. For, after all, these characters who refuse to work, who evade taxes and thus place the whole of the fiscal burden on an increasingly restricted mass of people, who produce natural children, impose their subsistence levies, punish, and have a good time, are also all those who are the least itinerant, the nobles, the tax agents. That is to say, this text is surprising: we find in it complete historical exactness regarding both the mores of vagabonds and of other characters; it is the description of a vagabond counter-society as well as of the feudal society that the bourgeoisie wanted to get rid of. Read in this way, the text takes on an extraordinary violence: what is the rule of peasant self-defense if not a sort of call to insurrection? Thus, on one side the text says what will actually take place in the

---

* The manuscript (fol. 7) sums up: "Killing anyone who moves."

† The manuscript (fol. 7) sums up: "Utopia. Politics-fiction."

nineteenth century and, on the other, in code, it makes a real criticism
of the remnants of feudalism in eighteenth-century society: everyone
must belong to the State.*

So, with regard to their position in relation to the productive
system formed by the land, workers, and owners, this text establishes
a symmetry between vagabonds, on the one hand, and the remnants
of feudalism, on the other. There are, therefore, two ways of being
opposed to society: exercising a certain power, which is an obstacle to
production, and refusing to produce, thus exercising, but in a different
way, a counter-power opposed to production. The feudal and the
vagabond are two instances of anti-production, enemies of society. We
see what will be a fundamental assimilation being carried out here. In
fact, from the moment society is defined as the system of relationships
between individuals that makes production possible and permits its
maximization, one has a criterion that makes it possible to designate
the enemy of society: any person hostile or opposed to the rule of the
maximization of production.†

---

* Manuscript (fol. 8): "Should we see here a pamphlet in code whose decipherment would dispel
the apparent meaning?"
† The manuscript contains several pages (fols. 10-14) which Foucault did not take up in the
lecture:
"Some reference points of this emergence in juridical theory:
M[uyart] de Vouglans (*Institutes au droit criminel*, 1757)[15]
Traditional definition of the crime: "Crime is an act forbidden by the law by which one causes
harm to a third party by fraud or fault."

- "harm," "damage": central notions (and not by infraction, breach of authority);
- "third party": specified as private individual or public, but public enters into the category
of third party [fol. 10] and is affected in certain cases (scandal, disorder), which exist for
themselves, or which are added as circumstances to another harm affecting an individual.

Hence the idea that the crime creates obligation:

- while in the order of civil law there is obligation only by explicit and stated consent,
- in the criminal order, it is the act that creates obligation.

[*In the margin:*] Which permits retranscription, up to a point, in the vocabulary of sin, redemption,
punishment.
A strange idea for us, or rather an idea which is no longer found except in moral expressions: "to
pay one's debt"; but an idea to which the whole of the eighteenth-century problematic is opposed.
This practice is

- not: what is the nature and form of the obligation created by the crime,

*   *   *

We could have shown other signs of this emergence of the criminal as social enemy in juridical theory, literature, and so on. For example, alongside Le Trosne's text, let us put two literary texts: *Gil Blas*[17] and *Le Château des Pyrénées*.[18] At the beginning of the eighteenth century there is, in fact, a whole series of novels of movement in society. Thus, *Gil Blas*

- but: in what system of obligations am I caught up, what contract must I have entered into for one legitimately to punish me when I have broken a law? [fol. 11]

In classical thought, the crime is a quasi-contract; at any rate it has effects analogous to those of the contract. In modern thought, punishment rests on an ideal contract.

In any case, the formulation of the *Institutes* represents the old state of juridical thought. Now, in the *Lois criminelles de France* (1780),[16] we can single out another thread of discourse. The crime here is no longer defined solely by the harm but by the infraction. Or again the law appears to operate at two levels: on the one hand it prohibits or orders this or that, and, on the other, it prohibits one from breaching it.

It is always as law the object of prohibition: that which must not be transgressed, violated, scorned. It involves both a constraint with an external reference and a constraint referring to itself.

"Thus we see that its aim is not solely to forbid, but also to avenge the disregard of its authority by punishing those who violate its bans" ([*Lois criminelles de France*,] p. xxxiv). [fol. 12]

The constraint with external reference derives from the harm. (It is because an action must not be harmful that it is forbidden.)

The constraint self-referring to the law itself derives from sovereignty. If the law can punish by the sole fact that it has been violated, this is by virtue of the Prince's right "to have his law carried out."

The Imperium, the sovereignty that intrinsically inhabits the law.

We have here the theoretical expression of civil prosecution doubling private prosecution.

But in these same *Lois criminelles*, we have a third formulation which gets closer to Beccaria:

The crime is that which brings disorder to society

- by attacking society only,
- or by attacking society at the same time as one of its members,
- or by attacking only one of its members without attacking society in general.

Even if it is not *attacked*, society is *disturbed*. [fol. 13]

With the consequence that punishment has two ends:

- to compensate the private individual as much as possible;
- to render the criminal (but also those who might imitate him) harmless.

With regard to the first formulation, society has come to occupy the place of the injured third party (of the third party of whom it was said that it could be an individual or the public).

The emergence of the criminal as adversary of society is made out in these different texts that are superimposed and entangled in one and the same work." (fol. 14)

is a kind of representation of social mobility, of movement in society and its connections with delinquency. In *Gil Blas* it is geographical movement, but also [mobility] through social strata.[19] Now Gil Blas constantly encounters delinquency in the course of these movements, but a very particular delinquency. It is always graduated, since, by small successive touches, it passes continuously from adultery to theft, to leaving without paying for food or lodgings, and highway robbery: all this is mixed together in the landscapes through which Gil Blas passes.* It surrounds every profession, every social status with a sort of shadow, a mist of possibilities. There is no rank that does not have its margin of possible delinquency: there is the delinquency connected to the innkeeper, the delinquency of the physician, of the noble, of the magistrate, and so on. Each has its margin of delinquency in which it is caught up, trapped, or else is its resource, its possibility. Every character is thus completely reversible: honest from one point of view, dishonest from another, and, in this sense, the character of the valet or secretary is utterly typical of this reversibility of the delinquent-non-delinquent character. The valet who robs his master is a commendable thief inasmuch as if he steals, in one sense, in another sense he gives money that had been badly employed to people who need it. He is a man of the uncertain margins, the exchanger type between delinquency and non-delinquency, and [with regard to] financial as well as sexual honesty. Such is the delinquency that runs throughout society, courses through its veins, as it were, from high to low, and is the very game of society.†

---

* The manuscript (fol. 15) adds: "From womanizer to galley slave; continuity, rapidity of transition."
† The manuscript (fols. 16-17) adds: "It (delinquency) animates it

- it changes it, since this is how men who are nothing become powerful; and the powerful perish. But at the same time
- it leaves it the same: the actors may change, the roles remain; the masks drop, the identities remain.

Delinquency is a kind of permanent social function.
If it is its wrong side, it is, as one says, the other side of the coin, the verso of a sheet of paper.
It is rather the game of society:

- the fact that it has some play, some free space, inactive zones, regions of turbulence.
- it is also risk, good luck and bad luck; the opposition being taken/not being taken.

At the end of the eighteenth century we pass on to the novels of terror, [like those of] Ann Radcliffe.[20] Criminality has changed its form and appearance: it is no longer something continuous, graduated, and ambiguous; it is no longer the potentiality that each carries around with [himself]; it is not intertwined with social relationships: it is localized and outside society. We no longer find crime in the middle of society, but in extra-social sites: convents, castles, underground passages, a mountain hollowed out like a fortress. Within this geography peculiar to crime we have a sort of entirely closed society, with its initiations, rites, values, and hierarchy; in this society we do not find any ambiguous character, for the passage to criminality is made all at once, en bloc, once and for all: one is either wicked by nature because one came into the world with a negative mark and is the incarnation of evil, or one passed into criminality because in one's life one committed an inexpiable offense (betrayal, crime) that plunged one into evil. In comparison to this perfectly situated, isolated counter-society, there can be only the world of innocents and victims; between the two worlds there can be only hatred, war, and fundamental hostility on the criminal side, and only relationships in the form of capture and imprisonment on the other side.

Whereas in *Gil Blas* the central figure is theft and ambiguous forms of honesty-dishonesty, the central figure in the novels of terror is war, death, for which this counter-society is the metaphor: to cross into the latter is to cross over to the side of death and to pass through this counter-society and survive, as happens to some privileged heroes, is to return to life. All the massive oppositions: life/death, innocence/crime, good/evil, characterize the form of delinquency that we see appear in this genre of narrative. Between *Gil Blas* and *Le Château*, Le Trosne's text marks the point where the figure of delinquency tips over.[*]

Theft, appropriation, redistribution (much more than murder and death) are at the center of these accounts or fictions.

But forty years later we see the appearance of a completely different type of narrative. *Château des Pyrénées.*"

[*] The manuscript includes two other sheets (fols. 19 and 20) which Foucault did not draw on in the lecture of 17 January 1973: "Many other facts could testify to this appearance—or constitution—of the criminal as enemy. For example: in penal practices, the transition from deportation (essentially with the form of banishment) to the penitentiary colony

America ≠ Botany Bay

1. Bon-Albert Briois de Beaumetz (1759-1801) was elected deputy to the General Estates in 1789 by the Artois nobility. He was on the center left and called for the abolition of torture prior to the judicial procedure. He is known for trying to curb revolutionary violence. See J. Tulard, J.-F. Fayard, and A. Fierro, *Histoire et Dictionnaire de la Révolution française, 1789-1799* (Paris: Robert Laffont, "Bouquins," 1987) p. 571. Beaumetz was part of the committee set up by the Constituent Assembly to propose "a project of declaration on some provisional changes in the criminal ordinance," and submitted a report to the Constituent on 29 September 1789. See *Archives parlementaires de 1787 à 1860. Recueil complet des débats législatifs et politiques des Chambres françaises*, first series (1789 to 1799), (Paris: Librairie administrative de Paul Dupont, 1877) vol. IX, 16 September 1789 to 11 November 1789, pp. 213-217.

2. B. A. Briois de Beaumetz, in *Archives parlementaires 1787-1860*, vol. IX, p. 214, col. 2.

3. Foucault analyzed physiocratic thought in *Les Mots et les Choses* (Paris: Gallimard, "Bibliothèque des sciences humaines, 1966) pp. 204-214 ("La formation de la valeur") and pp. 268-269 (on the notion of scarcity); English translation by A. Sheridan, *The Order of Things. An Archaeology of the Human Sciences* (London: Tavistock, 1970) pp. 189-200 ("The creation of value") and p. 256. In *Folie et Déraison. Histoire de la folie à l'âge classique*, pp. 494-498; *History of Madness*, pp. 406-410, Foucault studied the role of population as a factor of wealth in the physiocrats. In *Sécurité, Territoire, Population*, esp., pp. 35-50, pp. 71-81, and pp. 349-365; *Security, Territory, Population*, pp. 33-49, pp. 69-79, and pp. 341-357, Foucault again deals with the physiocrats, their ideas concerning the installation of "security" apparatuses being essential; see p. 36; Eng., p. 34: "thanks to the relay, the support of the physiocrats and their theory, [there] was in reality a complete change, or rather a phase in a major change in the techniques of government and an element in the deployment of what I will call apparatuses of security." See, too, the analysis of neo-liberalism in *Naissance de la biopolitique. Cours au Collège de France, 1978-1979*, ed., M. Senellart (Paris: Gallimard-Seuil, "Hautes Études," 2004) pp. 55-57, pp. 62-67, and pp. 296-300; English translation by Graham Burchell, *The Birth of Biopolitics. Lectures at the Collège de France, 1978-1979*, English

---

But we should wonder less about the bundle of elements that signal this appearance, than about its status. Insofar as this appearance will serve as starting point, and this is what is to be analyzed.

- What is going on behind this sociologization of crime, this establishment of the criminal as enemy of society, behind this reinterpretation of the forms of penality in terms of a social mechanics or reaction, behind this emergence of society (and not just of the sovereign, or of political power) as essential character on the judicial stage?
- Behind the formation of a knowledge of criminality that no longer puts the old question of the inquiry "who did what?" but the new question "what then is needed to be a criminal?"; "what must society be for crime to be possible in it?"

Questions that are no longer pegged to the fact, but to nature and the norm. Questions that no longer come under a discursive practice of the *inquiry*, but from a discursive practice of the *examination*.
What is going on behind all this?
What is this process, or this event described as "appearance," "emergence"? What does it mean to assert that the criminal *appears* as public enemy, that crime is defined as, functions as, and serves as breach of the social bond?

- Is it a question of the organization of a dominant representation or of a system of dominant representation: the criminal *represented* as enemy?"

series editor, Arnold I. Davidson (Basingstoke: Palgrave Macmillan, 2008) pp. 53-55, pp. 63-68, and pp. 292-296. The physiocrats, also known as the "economists," were a group of thinkers in favor of free exchange, of free trade in grain, and of economic liberalism generally. Their name is a neologism, the symbol of their ideological basis, that expresses the idea of a reign (*-crat*) of the natural order (*physio*). It comes from the collection published by Pierre-Samuel du Pont de Nemours in 1768, *Physiocratie ou Constitution naturelle du gouvernement le plus avantageux au genre humain* (Leyde-Paris: Merlin, 1768).

François Quesnay (1694-1774), royal surgeon and physician of Madame de Pompadour, gave birth to the movement in 1756 with his first writings on the economy—two entries in the *Encyclopedia* ("Fermiers" in 1756 and "Grains" in 1757)—and wrote on questions of political economy until 1767, when he published his *Despotisme de la Chine*. See F. Quesnay, *Œuvres économiques complètes et autres textes*, ed., Christine Théré, Loïc Charles, and Jean-Claude Perrot (Paris: Institut national d'études démographiques/INED, 2005) 2 volumes. The group contained other illustrious members, notably: Victor Riqueti, marquis de Mirabeau (1715-1789), author of *L'Ami des hommes, ou Traité de la population* (Avignon: 1756); Guillaume-François Le Trosne (1728-1780), jurist and author, as we will see, of *Mémoire sur les vagabonds et sur les mendiants* (Paris: P. G. Simon, 1764); Pierre-Paul Le Mercier de La Rivière (1719-1801), intendant of Martinique and author of *L'Ordre naturel et essentiel des sociétés politiques* (Paris: Desaint, 1767); and Pierre-Samuel du Pont de Nemours (1739-1817), businessman, economist, and, later, American diplomat, editor of several of the works of the physiocrats as well as of their review, Éphémérides *du citoyen, ou Bibliothèque raisonée des sciences morales et politiques*. Du Pont de Nemours gives a clear account of physiocrat thought in his note "Sur les Économistes" in *Œuvres de Mr. Turgot, Ministre d'État, Précédées et accompagnées de Mémoires et de Notes sur sa Vie, son Administration et ses Ouvrages*, ed., P.-S. Du Pont de Nemours (Paris: impr. Delance, 1808) 3 volumes. The reference works on the physiocrats are those of G. Weulersse, *Le Mouvement physiocratique en France de 1756 à 1770* (Paris: Félix Alcan, 1910) 2 volumes. For a more recent analysis, see B. E. Harcourt, *The Illusion of Free Markets* (Cambridge, MA: Harvard University Press, 2011) pp. 78-102.

4. G.-F. Le Trosne, *Mémoire sur les vagabonds et sur les mendiants*. Le Trosne set himself up as the King's lawyer in the presidial court of Orléans. From 1763 to 1767 he wrote several small works on agriculture and commerce, especially in the review, *Éphémérides du citoyen*, cited above. In 1764, alongside the appearance of his *Mémoire*, he published his *Discours sur l'état actuel de la magistrature et sur les causes de sa décadence*, in which he militates in particular for freedom of export; the following year, he drafted a text pleading for *La Liberté du commerce des grains toujours utile & jamais nuisible* (Paris: 1765). In *Surveiller et Punir*, p. 90; *Discipline and Punish*, p. 88, Foucault identifies him as "the physiocrat who was councilor at the presidial court of Orléans," and in the same work (p. 79, p. 84, p. 87, pp. 90-91; Eng., pp. 76-77, p. 81, p. 84, and p. 88) in which he refers to the *Mémoire* as well as a later work by Le Trosne, *Vues sur la justice criminelle* (Paris: Debure Frères, 1777), he writes: "For Le Trosne, as for so many others at that time, the struggle for the delimitation of the power to punish was articulated directly on the need to subject popular illegalism to a stricter and more constant control" (p. 91; Eng., p. 88 [trans. slightly modified; G.B]).

5. This theme was well established and even consecrated in proverbs of the time. See *Dictionnaire de l'Académie françoise, L-Z* (Paris: 1765) vol. II, p. 171: "Idleness is the mother of every vice."

6. See G.-F. Le Trosne, *Mémoire sur les vagabonds et sur les mendicants*, p. 18: "the crimes committed by vagabonds and dishonorable people (*Gens sans aveu*)"; and p. 42, n. 1.

7. Ibid., p. 4. Foucault quotes this passage in *Surveiller et Punir*, p. 79; *Discipline and Punish*, pp. 76-77.

8. Le Trosne, *Mémoire sur les vagabonds*, p. 8.

9. Ibid., pp. 46-47.

10. Ibid., p. 54.

11. See also, ibid., p. 56: "This means, as simple as it is legitimate, ensures the execution of judgments in the most precise manner, and allows galley slaves to be employed wherever one likes outside the Marine Départements without fear of desertion. They can be used to develop mines, create harbors, construct canals so as to bring circulation and life to certain Provinces."

12. Ibid., p. 54: "The most important thing is to prevent their escape, and there is a sure means which will dispense with having to guard them at such expense. It only involves branding them on the brow or cheek with the letter G, instead of branding them on the shoulder, and ordering the death penalty for anyone found away from his post, allowing anyone to arrest them, and prescribing the procedure to be followed to establish desertion and apply the penalty. The investigation must be very short and very simple, like that followed for condemning deserters to death."

13. Ibid., p. 59.

14. See ibid., p. 63: "The inhabitants of one or several parishes will be brought together, and each will be obliged to provide one man, and the woods will be surrounded in order to conduct a beat and a thorough search. It will be easy for the government to purge the countryside of vagabonds in a few days." See too, ibid., p. 2: "Third, we will establish the sole means for suppressing vagabonds." The expression "the sole means" is repeated twice and underlined in the manuscript (fol. 7).

15. See p. 74, note 2.

16. See [P.-F. Muyart de Vouglans,] Les Loix criminelles de France, dans leur ordre naturel. Dédiées au Roi, par Muyart de Vouglans, Conseiller au Grand-Conseil (Paris: Merigot le Jeune, 1780).

17. A.-R. Lesage, L'Histoire de Gil Blas de Santillane, 1715-1735, 12 volumes. Lesage's novel recounts the irregular adventures of the young student, then valet and servant, through every stratum of society, and, according to Jules Romains, "Lesage et le roman moderne," The French Review, 21(2), December 1947, p. 97, represents "the last masterpiece of the so-called 'picaresque' novel." For Foucault, the figure of Gil Blas will come to symbolize an old form of illegalism and a more adventurer kind of delinquency in comparison with the professionalization and disciplinary formation more typical of the delinquent "network" in the carceral milieu from the nineteenth century. In Surveiller et Punir, p. 307; Discipline and Punish, p. 300, Foucault describes the "domain of adventure that Gil Blas, Sheppard or Mandrin, each in his own way, explored in detail" as an "uncertain space that was for criminality a training ground and a region of refuge, [where,] in dangerous comings and goings, poverty, unemployment, hounded innocence, cunning, struggle against the powerful, the refusal of obligations and laws, and organized crime came together" [translation modified; G.B.]. Gil Blas represents "a man of the old illegalisms" (p. 288; Eng., p. 282 [translation slightly amended; G.B.]). On the "literature of crime" ("aesthetic rewriting" and "detective novel"), see p. 72 and p. 292; Eng., pp. 68-69 and p. 286.

18. A. Radcliffe [apocryphal], Les Visions du château des Pyrénées, trans., Germain Garnier and Mme. Zimmermann [from] the edition printed in London by G. and J. Robinson, 1803 (Paris: Lecointe et Durey, 1821) 4 volumes; new edition translated by Yves Tessier (Paris: Éditions B.I.E.N., 1946). The English writer Ann Radcliffe (1764-1823) is considered one of the pioneers of the Gothic novel, a literary genre that used the supernatural and the macabre, the most famous and latest example of which is Mary Shelley's Frankenstein (1818). Her most well-known works include The Romance of the Forest (London: T. Hookham & Carpenter, 1791) 3 volumes; The Mysteries of Udolpho (London: G. & J. Robinson, 1794) 4 volumes; and The Italian, or the Confessional of the Black Penitents (London: T. Cadell Junior and W. Davies, Successors to Mr. Cadell, in the Strand, 1797) 3 volumes. According to Foucault, the apocryphal novel, Les Visions du château des Pyrénées, symbolizes a fear that "haunted the latter half of the eighteenth century: the fear of darkened spaces, of the pall of gloom which

prevents the full visibility of things, men and truths"; "L'œil du pouvoir," p. 196/p. 196; "The Eye of Power," p. 153.

The surrealist painter René Magritte shared with Foucault a certain fascination for *Le Château des Pyrénées*, which he depicted in oil on canvas in 1959. Magritte writes regarding this canvas that "*Le Château des Pyrénées* ... will have the character of an apparition, which Ann Radcliffe would have loved, if her book *Le Château des Pyrénées* really lets us know what she loved"; letter to Torczyner, 20 April 1959, in H. Torczyner, *L'Ami Magritte. Correspondance et souvenirs* (Anvers: fonds Mercador, 1992) p. 118. Foucault asked Harry Torczyner, international lawyer and Magritte's representative in the United States, if he could see the canvas, which he did, visiting Torczyner in New York in 1975.

It is interesting to note here that one of the major exhibitions of Magritte in New York, at the Sidney Janis gallery in 1954, was entitled: "*Les Mots et les Choses.*" Following the publication of Foucault's book in 1966, Magritte sent him a "few reflections relative to my reading of your book *Les Mots et les Choses*," letter of 23 May 1966, in M. Foucault, *Ceci n'est pas une pipe* (Montpellier: Fata Morgana, 1973), p. 83; *DE*, I, no. 53, pp. 636-650/"Quarto," I, pp. 636-650; English translation by James Harkness, *This Is Not a Pipe. With Illustrations and Letters by René Magritte* (Berkeley: University of California Press, 1983) p. 57.

19. We find here some reflections developed by Louis Chevalier in his analysis of the evolution of the representation of criminality in the work of Balzac, *Classes laborieuses et Classes dangereuses à Paris pendant la première moitié du XIXe siècle* (Paris: Perrin, "Pour l'histoire," 2002 [Plon, 1958]) p. 55: "as for all the representatives of old style criminality, criminal society is a closed society, including proletariat and aristocracy, low and high underworld." However, he adds, in later novels, like *Cousin Bette*: "criminality is described, although in an incidental way, and often without regard to the rest of the work, as no longer attaching itself only to those giants of crime to whom Balzac will mainly devote his attention, but as emanating from the totality of the popular masses: no longer exceptional but general and truly social" (p. 70).

20. Foucault was interested in the novels of terror and returned quite often to the works of Ann Radcliffe. In 1963, in "Le langage à l'infini," *Tel Quel*, Autumn 1963, no. 15, pp. 44-53; *DE*, I, no. 14, pp. 250-261/"Quarto," I, pp. 278-289; English translation by Donald F. Bouchard and Sherry Simon, slightly amended by editors, "Language to Infinity" in *EW*, 2, pp. 89-101, he situates the novels of terror, as well as the work of the Marquis du Sade, at the origin of literary modernity: "Perhaps what we should rigorously define as "literature" came into existence at precisely the moment, at the end of the eighteenth century, when a language appeared that appropriates and consumes all other languages in its lightning flash, giving birth to an obscure but dominant figure where death, the mirror and the double, and the wavelike succession of words to infinity enact their roles" (p. 260/p. 288; Eng., p. 100). See also, "Un 'nouveau roman' de terreur," *France-Observateur*, 14th year, no. 710, 12 December 1963, p. 14; *DE*, I, no. 18, pp. 285-287/"Quarto," I, pp. 313-315.

In "Qu'est-ce que'un auteur?" *Bulletin de la Société française de philosophie*, 1969, no. 3, pp. 73-104; *DE*, I, no. 69, pp. 789-821/"Quarto," I, pp. 817-837; English translation by Josué V. Harari, slightly amended by editors, "What is an author?" in, *EW*, 2, pp. 205-222, Foucault claims that Ann Radcliffe "made possible the appearance of the Gothic horror novel at the beginning of the nineteenth century": "Ann Radcliffe's texts opened the way for a certain number of resemblances and analogies which have their model or principle in her work. The latter contains characteristic signs, figures, relationships, and structures that could be reused by others. In other words, to say that Ann Radcliffe founded the Gothic horror novel means that in the nineteenth-century Gothic novel one will find, as in Ann Radcliffe's works, the theme of the heroine caught in the trap of her own innocence, the hidden castle, the character of the black, cursed hero devoted to making the world expiate the evil done to him, and all the rest of it" (p. 805/p. 833; Eng., pp. 217-218). In the 1977 interview, "L'œil du pouvoir," p. 196/p.196; "The Eye of Power," p. 154, Foucault suggests that Ann Radcliffe's novels form a "negative (*contre-figure*)" to the transparency of Bentham's Panopticon: "During the Revolutionary period the Gothic novels develop a whole fantasy-world of stone walls, darkness, hideouts and dungeons which harbor, in significant complicity, brigands and aristocrats, monks and traitors. The landscapes of Ann Radcliffe's novels are composed of mountains and forests, caves, ruined castles and terrifyingly dark and silent convents. Now these imaginary spaces are like the negative (*"contre-figure"*) of the transparency and visibility which it is aimed to establish" (p. 197/p. 197; Eng., pp. 153-154). On the figures of monsters in Ann Radcliffe's novels, see *Les anormaux*, lecture of 29 January 1975, pp. 92-97; *Abnormal*, pp. 100-104.

For a more detailed analysis and an intersecting reading of Foucault, Ann Radcliffe, and Jeremy Bentham, see C. Wrobel, "Gothique et Panoptique: lecture croisée des œuvres de Jeremy Bentham (1748-1832) et Ann Radcliffe (1764-1823)," doctoral thesis in English and Anglo-Saxon language and literature, University of Paris X, 2009 http://www.theses.fr/2009PA100110; ibid., "Gothique, Réforme et Panoptique," *Revue d'études benthamiennes*, no. 7, 2010 http://etudes-benthamiennes.revues.org/214.

four

24 JANUARY 1973

(III) Other signs of the emergence of the criminal-social enemy. Debate on the death penalty in 1791. (IV) Relationship between the theoretical-political effects of a discourse and punitive tactics in the same period. Main system of punishment: in England, organization of penitentiary system in 1790-1800; in France, 1791-1821. Heterogeneity of criminal-social enemy and the prison: rift between the penal and the penitentiary. ⌢ According to penal theory, punishment as social defense; hence these four principles: relativity; gradation; continuous supervision (surveillance); publicity and infallibility;* and three models of punishment: infamy, talion, slavery. ⌢ In prison: time the only graduated variable. The prison-form and the wage-form: twin historical forms. Capitalist power and system of penality: power's hold on time.*

WE COULD ALSO HAVE cited other signs of this emergence of the criminal as social enemy,[†] for example, the debate on the death penalty

---

* [The French has here *"surveillance, publique et infaillible,"* but this is misleading. In the lecture "continuous supervision" during punishment is the third principle, while "publicity and infallibility" of the penalty is the fourth principle; see below pp. 67-68; G.B.]

† The manuscript (fol. 1) begins in the following way:

"1. The criminal "appears" as "enemy" of society.

   Society "appears" as injured, wounded by the crime.

   Punishment "appears" as protection, defense of society.

   Phenomenon which is opposed

in May 1791 when Le Peletier de Saint-Fargeau presented his draft
Penal Code.[1] The arguments actually started from the principle that
everyone considered to be fundamental: crime is an attack on society
and the criminal is a social enemy.[2] Thus, faced with those who evoked
the principle formulated by Rousseau in the *Social Contract*—since
the criminal is the enemy of society, he must be exiled or killed[3]—
Robespierre, in an apparently anti-Rousseauist manner yet from the
same theoretical basis, objected that inasmuch as the criminal is an
enemy of society, the latter precisely does not have the right to kill him,
because once it has seized hold of a criminal the battle is over; society
is faced with an enemy prisoner, as it were, and it would be as barbaric
for society to kill an enemy it has already vanquished as it would for a
warrior to kill his captive or an adult to kill a child: the society that
kills the criminal it has judged is like an adult who would kill a child.[4]
Such a debate allows us to study the theoretical-political effect of this
principle of the criminal-social enemy. It also provides a reference for
the analysis of a theoretical-political discussion. This analysis would,
for example, have to take into account what Marx wrote regarding the
discussion of the theft of wood,[5] and what Blanqui, fifteen years later,
wrote on what took place regarding rights over wine.[6] Starting from
these models, we could maybe see how to analyze political discussions,
oppositions, and struggles of discourse within a given political situation.

*   *   *

Let us return to this setting up of the appearance of the criminal as
social enemy. This term "appearance" is certainly unsatisfactory. Where
does the latter appear as such? To whom? Is it a matter of the formation
of an ideology, of the organization of a type of discourse, of a pattern of
behavior? This notion, left empty for the moment, remains at least the
index of a problem to be posed.[*] I want now to analyze the event that

---

- to the old conception of crime as injury. Modality of dispute;
- to the classical conception of crime as attack on sovereignty. Modality of State crime.

See in Muyart de Vouglans these three conceptions which are entangled.
See the discussion of the death penalty in 1791."
* Manuscript (fol.2):

took place then. To do this, I will shift the analysis by no longer taking penal theory and practice as the target, but the relationship between the latter and the effective tactic of punishment in the same period. Now we observe a remarkable phenomenon: in the same period as the principle of the criminal-social enemy is formulated and put into practice within penal institutions, a new punitive tactic appears: imprisonment.

A new tactic, prison, despite appearances, is in fact not a very old punishment whose fortune has grown continuously over the centuries. Until the end of the eighteenth century it was never really a punishment within the penal system. The introduction of the prison [into the system] dates from the end of the eighteenth century, as is testified by the *Criminal Code* drafted by Serpillon in 1767: "Prison is not regarded as a penalty, according to our civil law,"[7] that is to say, secular as opposed to canon law; "although princes are sometimes inclined to inflict this penalty for reasons of State, they are exceptional executive measures, ordinary justice makes no use of this kind of sentence."[8] Now let us look at some texts [from] around fifty years later,* like that of the great debate of 1831,[9] which marks an important moment inasmuch as it concerns the first major revision of the penal system after the *Code d'instruction criminelle* of 1808 and the Penal Code of 1810. At the beginning of the July monarchy, part of the Penal Code is subject to revision. This, for example, is what Rémusat declares on the first of December 1831: "What is the system of penality allowed by the new law? It is incarceration in all its forms. Indeed, compare the four principal penalties which remain in the Penal Code"[10]—which, strangely, does not include the death penalty, as if this was a penalty on the borders of the system of punishment: "Forced labor for life or for

---

"2. What is the process or event designated or hidden by the word "appear"?
  - The formation of an ideology, or of an ideological element? The crime "represented" as hostility, the criminal "represented" as enemy?
  - In fact, it is a matter of something else that takes place at a different level. And the mechanisms of which are different.
It is a matter of the effective constitution of a state of hostility between criminals and the totality of a political body; the designation of a war front; a whole enterprise of segregation by which criminals on one side, and society on the other, find themselves facing each other.
And that is where we encounter confinement."
* Manuscript (fol. 3): "Now, some sixty years later, the deprivation of liberty and confinement are considered to be the most natural and most frequent penalty."

a fixed time is a form of incarceration. The penal colony is an open-air prison. Detention, reclusion, and correctional imprisonment are, in a way, merely different names for one and the same punishment."[11]

Thus, between these two texts, imprisonment has taken hold as a system of punishment. Some reference points: in 1799, as a result of the War of American Independence,[*] England has to review its punitive tactic.[12] After Howard's inquiry into European prisons,[13] Howard and Blackstone propose a draft law in which incarceration appears as an explicit penalty: "many individuals convicted of crimes previously punished with deportation, could well, if subjected to solitary detention, not only inspire terror in those who might be tempted to imitate them, but even themselves acquire the habit of work and thus be corrected."[14] In fact, we have to wait until 1790-1800 for the penitentiary system to be established in England.[15] In 1793 Bentham produces his plan of the Panopticon, which will become the architectural matrix for European prisons. The project was inspired by his naval engineer brother who had constructed ports and docks for Catherine II of Russia and conceived for that purpose a plan of generalized superintendence of the port.[16]

In France there is a gap. We have to wait until 1791 for the theoretical formulation of the principle of incarceration as a general schema of punishment. The first text to give what is perhaps its most radical formulation is that of Duport, on 31 May 1791, in the discussion of the Penal Code.[17] He declares in fact: "If we now ask what the universal and constant feeling is on which we can establish a system of repression and penalties, every sentient being will answer you in concert: it is the love of liberty; liberty, the good without which life itself becomes a veritable torture; liberty, the burning desire for which has developed so many and such courageous efforts; liberty, finally, the loss of which, to which may be added the deprivation of all the enjoyments of nature, can alone become a real, repressive, and durable penalty, which does not at all alter the mores of the people, which makes the price of a conduct conforming to the laws more perceptible to citizens; a penalty, moreover, which can be graduated in such a way as to be applied to different crimes, allowing one to observe that proportion between them that is so important and required by different degrees of perversity and harmfulness."[18] This text,

---

[*] Manuscript (fol. 4): "1799: War of Independence prevents deportation."

therefore, theorizes loss of liberty as that which should serve as common denominator of the whole punitive system and, moreover, this is indeed what the draft Penal Code presented by Le Peletier proposes.[19] Up to the 1810 Code, the whole system of incarceration is organized; very quickly, from 1791, we see the appearance of *maisons d'arrêt* for those charged with an offense, *maisons de justice* for those accused, and prisons for those sentenced. Under the Empire a whole hierarchy of prisons is set up, from the *maisons de justice* found in the cantons, the *maisons d'arrêt* in the arrondissements, departmental *maisons de détention, maisons centrales*, and the military penal colonies (*bagnes*) of Brest, Rochefort, and Toulon. From the statistical point of view this represents: in 1818, 44,484 prisoners, of which 10,000 are those charged and 9,700 colonists, that is one in 662 in a population of 29.5 million inhabitants;[20] in 1822, 41,000 prisoners, of which 10,400 colonists, or one in 778 inhabitants;[21] [whereas presently we have] 30,000 [prisoners for a population of] 50 million [inhabitants], or one in 1,500.[22]

So the problem is this: on the one hand, at the end of the eighteenth century we see a whole reorganization of the system of penalties around incarceration, and, on the other hand, this reorganization is contemporary with the emergence[23] of the criminal-social enemy. Now if it is true that the two phenomena are probably correlated, we can say nonetheless that the system of incarceration does not derive from the reorganization of penal theory and practice around the theme of the criminal-social enemy. In other words, the insertion of the prison in the system of penalties is a phenomenon that will intersect the latter, but the reorganization of penal theory and practice around the theme of the criminal-social enemy did not bring about, either as logical consequence or direct historical consequence, the exclusive use of the prison as punitive instrument. The two processes of, on the one hand, the discursive derivation leading to the formulation of the principle of the criminal as social enemy and, on the other, punishment, are heterogeneous. So that between the penal, organized around the principle of the criminal, and the penitentiary,* organized around

---

* The manuscript (fol. 6) adds: "between the 'to punish' and the punishment."

the prison, [we see] a rift the historical appearance of which we must now delimit.*

Now this rift is not merely the result of an internal contradiction of the system or of an initial heterogeneity, that is to say, something like the effect of diverse historical sedimentations, but can be analyzed in terms of a general tactic. Certainly, there are conflicts and contradictions between the penal and the penitentiary.[24] We see them confront each other, giving rise to discourses that do not interpenetrate, but intertwine: the discourse of penal law and the discourse of what from 1820-1830 is called the "science of prisons," which presents itself as an autonomous discourse, distinct from the discourse of law, and which gives rise, after some transformations, to criminology.[25] But this opposition at the level of discourses, of types of knowledge authorized by the practice of law on the one hand, and of confinement on the other, only relays the interplay found at the level of institutions: the never ending attempt by the penitentiary system to escape penetration by the juridical and the law, and the judicial system's effort to control the penitentiary system, which is heterogeneous to it. In this regard, we can refer to a text of the Duke Decazes, Minister of the Interior in 1818, who writes to Louis XVIII: "The trouble is that the law does not penetrate the prison."[26],†

Thus, imprisonment cannot be derived as a practical and discursive consequence of penal theory or judicial practice. Certainly, something like prisons already existed in judicial practice, but in reality the penal prison was not used to punish, but in order to have a guarantee on the person. It was a matter of having a physical guarantee, like the status that was given to prisoners of war, preventive custody, or remand.‡ In 1768, Le Trosne said: "Prison by itself is not at all a penalty. The detention of the accused is a necessary precaution in order to secure his

---

* The manuscript (fol. 7) adds: "and which has its consequences and its effects until now."

† The manuscript (fol. 7) adds: "But what has to be shown is what takes place in, what takes place through this discrepancy, the play of power carried out in it."

‡ The manuscript (fol. 8) clarifies: "Doubtless prison existed, and since the M[iddle] A[ges]. But it was not a punishment, but having a surety; a guarantee on the person; a physical and bodily guarantee. Hence its three usages: war, debt, preventive custody."

person, and to have him at one's disposal."[27] Thus, one does not punish someone when one puts him in prison; one secures him.*

Similarly, we cannot derive the system of imprisonment from a sort of theoretical model based on the penal theory of criminal-social enemy. We can refer to the texts of Beccaria, Brissot, *[Théorie] des lois criminelles* [1781], or of Le Peletier de Saint-Fargeau.[28] How in fact do the latter deduce a system of actual punishments from the principle of the criminal-social enemy? If it is true, as Brissot says, that "crime is only an *attack on order, on the social interest*,"[29] what should the punishment be? Punishment then is not something [to do with] reparation or vengeance. Neither does it have anything to do with chastisement or penance. It is solely the defense and protection of society.

Hence four principles of penalties. This means, first, that every society can modulate the scale of its penalties according to its needs, since the penalty no longer derives intrinsically from the gravity of the offense, but only from social utility. The weaker a society, the more easily it is endangered by crime, and so penal practice will be more severe; an ordered society not seriously affected by a crime may be content with a relatively light system of penalties.[30] So, as first principle we have the relativity of penalties, which is not ordered by reference to the individual himself, but to the state of society. This condition means that there cannot be any universal model of penalties. On the other hand, if the penalty is a penance, the possibility of it being too strong basically hardly matters when it is a question of saving the individual's soul or of reconciling him; but if the penalty is a reaction and defense of society, it becomes an abuse of power if it exceeds the measure. Therefore, and this is the second principle, there needs to be a fine gradation of counter-attacks commensurate with the attacks on society. The aim of punishment is to disarm the enemy, which can take two forms: render him incapable of doing harm or reintroduce him into the social contract. Hence, the third principle of this system of penality: the principle of supervising the individual throughout his punishment

---

* Manuscript (fol. 8): "The prison-penalty does not derive from the prison-surety. Effort rather to separate them. There was even the idea of creating *maisons d'arrêt* and *maisons de justice* that would not confine those sentenced."

and re-education.* Fourth principle: if the penalty must be protection of society, then it must aim to prevent the creation of new enemies; it must therefore be exemplary and dissuade those who might arise as enemies. It must therefore take place in a public and infallible manner.†

Now these general principles lead towards three models of actual punishment, which figure in all the discourses of the jurists wanting to reform the penal system and none of which is the prison.

1. *The model of infamy*, ideal model of punishment.[31] The shame that marks the guilty person is first of all a reaction of the whole of society; furthermore, society has no need here to delegate its right to judge to any authority; it judges immediately by its own reaction. It is a justice that does not need to pass through the judicial power. There is a penal utopia in this in which judgment in the juridical sense of the term would be entirely reduced to judgment in the psychological sense; the judgment will be nothing other than the totality of the individual judgments of the citizens. The dissolution of judicial power into the collective judgment of individuals is the ideal judgment, the model that will be reactivated in the theme of popular justice.[32] In short, it is an ideal penalty inasmuch as it varies from society to society; each society establishes the intensity of infamy to be allocated to each crime. Thus, there is no need for court or code. One does not have to say in advance that this act will be allocated this penalty. Infamy corresponds at every moment point by point to each crime. Finally, it is revocable; it allows for reconciliation, leaving only a memory and not traces, unlike corporal penalties. It is therefore the only punishment in which the system of penalties accords exactly with the penal principle of the criminal-social enemy. It is a transparent punishment: only the gaze and murmur, the instantaneous and possibly constant judgment of each and all constitutes this kind of permanent court [Brissot will write:] "The triumph of a good legislation is when public opinion is strong enough to punish only the crimes that offend against public morals, or the national spirit, or even those that undermine public security ... Happy the people in

---

* Manuscript (fol. 10): "Therefore, principle of supervision; principle of reeducation."

† Manuscript (fols. 10-11): "It must therefore be certain, fearful, and public ... Towards what real and concrete punishments is this certain, visible, disarming rather than punishing, and quantitatively and qualitatively graduated penality linked to the needs of social protection, oriented?"

which the feeling of honor can be the sole law! It has almost no need of legislation: infamy, there is its penal code."[33]

2. *The model of talion:*[34] its resurgence in the eighteenth century is in line with the derivation of principles. In effect it is a penalty that, in its nature and strength, is exactly correlative with the offense itself; through it, society succeeds in turning the attack made on it back against the criminal. In this way one is sure that the penalty is really graduated according to the act and there will be no abuse of power, since society does not respond by anything other than what has actually been done to it: it is a pure and simple social counter-attack. "Attacks on persons," Beccaria says, "must incontestably be punished with corporal penalties."[35] "Personal offenses, contrary to honor ... must be punished with infamy."[36] "A theft which is not accompanied by violence should be punished with a pecuniary sanction."[37] Similarly, Brissot explains how each crime must have its specific penalty;[*] and Le Peletier lays down the principle of talion on 23 May 1791: "Physical pains will punish attacks whose source was ferocity; hard labor will be imposed on the convict whose crime was the product of laziness; infamy will punish actions inspired only by an abject and degraded soul."[39] Now at the very moment at which Le Peletier lays down the principle of talion in this way, the penalties that will actually be adopted are no longer founded on this principle, but homogenized around incarceration.

3. *The model of slavery:*[40] that is to say, hard and public labor. This is not as pure as infamy, or as controlled as talion, but it allows society to receive reparation; [it is] the pact of the individual's reformation as a member of society; it is the forced re-edition of the social contract between the criminal and society. This penalty has the advantage of being graduated and of producing fear, more than being fearsome.

---

[*] Concerning the reference to Brissot, the manuscript (fol. 12) adds:
"Public offenses:

civil, political crimes → civil, pecuniary, fiscal, work penalties
religious crimes → religious penalties

Private offenses

against life → corporal punishments
against property → pecuniary and corporal punishments
against honor → moral penalties."[38]

When one thinks of slavery, one imagines "all the wretched moments of the slave's life in one point,"[41] and by synthesizing them thus in one's imagination, one can represent to oneself "the sum of all the wretched moments" of the slave's life,[42] whereas the latter "is distracted by the feeling of his present misery from the idea of his future misery."[*]

Thus, from a few theoretical principles we see a certain number of models of punishment emerging, none of which are homogeneous with the prison. Now, the necessity of the prison asserts itself with such force that the very ones who claimed in their plans to establish such a penal system, proposed in fact a system of imprisonment.[44] So what happened for the discourse to be suddenly cut off at the point where its thread led quite naturally to the definition of penalties modeled on infamy, talion, or slavery, and for a completely different model to be imposed from a different side: confinement? The prison, in fact, is not a collective system like infamy, not graduated in its nature like talion, or reforming like forced labor. It is an abstract, monotonous, rigid punitive system[†] that came to be imposed not only in reality, in the passage to realization, but in discourse. At the point when those who were producing their projects were obliged to formulate their penal theory in actual draft laws, the game was already over: the models deducible from penal theory were replaced by this monotonous system.

Now there is only one variable in such a model that can introduce the modulations that are so important for the theoreticians: time. Prison is the system in which the variable of time replaces all the variables envisaged by the other models. We see a form appearing here that is completely different from that suggested by the new penal theory, and a form that is not at all of a juridical or punitive order: the wage-form. Just as the wage rewards the time for which labor-power has been purchased from someone, the penalty corresponds to the infraction, not in terms of reparation or exact adjustment, but in terms of quantity of time of liberty.

---

[*] In his manuscript, sheets 13, 14, 15, Foucault adds three references to Beccaria, Brissot, and Brillat-Savarin.[43]

[†] Manuscript [fols. 15-16]: "In comparison with the immediate and collective character of infamy, the graduated and necessarily measured character of talion, and the utilitarian and reforming character of Public Works or Forced Labor, the prison presents an abstract, general, monotonous, rigid character. 'Loss of liberty' (as loss of the good that everyone values and everyone possesses)."

The system of punishments reveals the *prison-form* as sanction for the crime, which cannot be derived from the theory and is related to the *wage-form*: just as a wage is given for a period of labor, so a period of liberty is taken as the price of an infraction.[45] Time being the only good possessed, it is purchased for labor or taken for an infraction. The wage serves to pay for the period of labor; the period of liberty will serve to pay for the infraction.

There is something here that puts us on the track of a number of problems, but it is not the solution of the problem. I do not mean that the wage imposed its form; that the socio-economic model was taken up by penal practice. Nothing in the history of the institutions or in the texts allows us to say that this model was transferred into the penal system. I mean simply that the prison-form and the wage-form are historically twin forms, without us being able to say yet what their exact relationships are.

But this parallel is not just a metaphor, as is shown by certain points. First of all, [in the] nineteenth-century penal systems, the continuity and overlap established between the penalties of the fine and prison: when one cannot pay a fine, one goes to prison. The fine appears as substitute for the day's labor, prison representing the equivalent of a certain quantity of money. [Then,] we see the appearance of a whole ideology of the penalty as debt, which reactivates the old notions of Germanic law that Christianity and classical law had erased. Now, there is nothing more remote from the theory than this principle of the penalty as debt; on the contrary, everything indicates that the penalty is a precaution and social defense.* This resurgence of payment of the debt to erase the crime derives in fact from this interpenetration of the wage and prison forms. [Finally,] there is a curious proximity and at the same time opposition between labor and prison:† prison is, in a way, very close to something like a wage, but at the same time it is the opposite of a wage. Hence, there is the feeling that prison should be like free labor that the prisoner gives to society in place of a wage, and that therefore it excludes the actual wage. Hence the tendency to organize the prison like a factory and, at the same time, the ideological

---

* The manuscript (fol. 18) adds: "but the 'truth' is precisely in these 'ideological' discourses."
† The manuscript (fol. 18) adds: "analogy and irreducibility."

and institutional impossibility of accepting that the prisoner receive a wage during his time in prison, since the latter is like the wage that he pays back to society.

Thus, the introduction inside the prison of the general principles governing the economics and politics of work [outside] contradicts all of the penal system's previous functioning. What we see appearing through these two forms is the introduction of *time* into the capitalist system of power and into the system of penality.[46] Into the system of penality: for the first time in the history of penal systems, one no longer punishes through the body or through goods, but through time to live. What society will appropriate to punish the individual is the time left to live. Time is exchanged against power. [And] behind the wage-form, the objective of the form of power put to work by capitalist society is essentially for it to be exercised on people's time: the organization of the worker's time [in] the workshop, the distribution and calculation of this time in the wage, the control of leisure, of the worker's life, saving, pensions, and so on.[47] The way in which power framed time so as to be able to control it from start to finish made possible, historically and [in terms of] relations of power, the existence of the wage-form. It needed this overall hold of power on time.[*] Thus, what allows us to analyze the punitive regime of crimes and the disciplinary regime of labor as of a piece is the relationship of the time of life to political power: that repression of time and repression through time, that kind of continuity between workshop clock, production line stopwatch, and prison calendar.[†]

---

[*] The manuscript (fol. 19) adds: "from the workshop clock to the pension fund, capitalist power clings to time, seizes hold of it, makes it purchasable and utilizable."

[†] In the manuscript there follow four sheets numbered 20 to 23 (see similar themes in the following lecture of 31 January):

"*Objections*—The religious 'model' which links prison to sin.

Distinguish:

(α) Ecclesiastical imprisonment. Prison as canonical penalty. And which in fact tends to disappear. (For example in France, the law of 1629).

Canonical imprisonment disappeared when penal imprisonment was definitively established.

(β) Monastic organization. It has often been invoked; ... it is a matter here of the transposition, into monastic life, of rules and forms of life of a certain work confinement, which is of secular origin. [fol. 20]

We could say rather that the monastic system transferred an exogenous form into its punitive practices.

The cellular arrangement: which allowed prison architecture to utilize it as it was? In fact it is

1. The debate of the National Constituent Assembly "on the whole of the draft Penal Code and in particular on the question of whether the death penalty is or is not to be conserved" took place in May and June 1791. See *Archives parlementaires de 1787 à 1860*, first series (1787 to 1799) [see above, p. 56, note 1], vol. XXVI (12 May to 5 June 1791) p. 618, col. 2. Louis-Michel Le Peletier de Saint-Fargeau (1760-1793) was the rapporteur for the draft Penal Code and presented it in the name of the Constitution and criminal legislation Committees on 30 May 1791; see ibid., p. 617. Le Peletier de Saint-Fargeau appears frequently

---

much rather the insertion of the Protestant, Quaker model, arranged around the examination of conscience, soul searching, dialogue with God.

The convent cell transformed into prison cell did not impose on the latter its form of life, its ethic, its conception of penance. The convent cell that has become prison cell is defined at the point of intersection of a morality of life (of essentially Protestant inspiration) and a new space of confinement.

The penitentiary cell is the place of Calvinist, Quaker conscience, fixed by the tactic of internment in a Gothic architecture. [fol. 21]

It is in the Quakers that we find the theory of punishment by forced confinement.

History that goes back to W[illiam] Penn: his attempt to construct a penal code without death penalty. The English prevent him.

- With Independence, attenuation of the death penalty; and organization of a penality in which death is limited (murder, arson, and treason), in which imprisonment figures alongside public works, flogging, and mutilation.
- In [17]90, suppression of public works owing to scandal.

Organization of a system in which punishment is confinement: loss of liberty, breaking contacts with the world outside; and isolation, at least for a period, in cells measuring eight by six feet, maize for food, no reading.

According to L[a] R[ochefoucauld-]Liancourt[48] it is a matter of:

- 'getting the prisoners to forget all their old habits';
- bringing about 'a change ... of diet,' which, 'renewing his blood entirely, softening it, refreshing it, softens his soul and inclines it to the mildness that brings him to repent.' [fol. 22]

'In this abandon[ment] ... of every living being, he is [more] inclined to descend into himself, to reflect on his faults, the pain of which he feels so bitterly.'

And after this soul-searching, in which he discovers the depth of his fall, he can receive words of exhortation.

'The inspectors ... talk with [the prisoners], seek to know them, exhort them, console them, encourage them, reconcile them with themselves. These conversations are not frequent, they would have less effect in that case; their faces are always calm, never cheerful.'

Respect, coldness, sadness, and calm.

If there is a religious model of the prison, it is indeed in Calvinist theology or morality, and not in the monastic institution.

Emphasize this because it allows us to limit fairly strictly a historical analysis through the model, its transfer, or its reactivation.

If this model of such a distant origin, so foreign in its spirit to a great part of Europe, was able in this way to universalize itself in nineteenth-century society, it is not at all [through] its intrinsic strength." [fol. 23]

in these lectures, as in *Surveiller et Punir, Discipline and Punish*. He was elected to the Estates-General by the Paris nobility, and then elected to the Convention, and developed a plan of public education, voted after his death—assassinated on the eve of the execution of Louis XVI, 20 January 1793, by a royalist who reproached him for having voted in favor of the King's death. See J. Tulard, J.-F. Fayard, and A. Fierro, *Histoire et Dictionnaire de la Révolution française*, pp. 946-947. The complete debates of 1791 in the National Constituent Assembly, as well as the "Report of the draft Penal Code" presented by Le Peletier de Saint-Fargeau, are reproduced *in extenso* on the site of the National Assembly http://www.assemblee-nationale. fr/histoire/peinedemort/debat_1791.asp.

2. This new notion of the criminal-social enemy is opposed, as the manuscript (fol. 1) indicates, on the one hand, "to the old conception of injury" and to the "modality of the dispute," and on the other hand, "to the classical conception of the crime as attack on sovereignty" and to the "modality of the State crime" (see above, p. 62, footnote *). In Pierre-François Muyart de Vouglans (1713-1791), lawyer at the Paris Parlement, then of the Grand Council, we find this notion of criminal-social enemy; thus, in his *Réfutation des principes hasardés dans le* Traité des délits et peines, *traduit de l'italien* (Paris: Desaint, 1767) p. 7, Vouglans accuses Beccaria of having written "a plea in favor of that unhappy portion of humanity, which is its scourge, which dishonors it, and which sometimes is even its destroyer." The conception of crime as injury is, moreover, present in the very definition that Vouglans gives of it in his *Institutes au droit criminel, ou Principes généraux en ces matières* (Paris: Le Breton, 1757) p. 2: crime "is an act forbidden by the law by which one causes harm to a third party by fraud or fault; *factum jure prohibitum, quo quis dolo vel culpâ facientis læditur.*" See too his conception of crime as being a direct "attack" on "the sovereignty of the King" or an "attack especially on the State" (ibid., p. 449). In the Course Summary (below, p. 250), Foucault refers to the *Institutes* of Vouglans as one of the "great monuments of classical criminal law." Vouglans is referred to frequently in *Surveiller et Punir*, p. 50, pp. 51-52, p. 77, and p. 306; *Discipline and Punish*, p. 36, pp. 47-48, p. 75, and p. 325 n. 3).

3. See J.-J. Rousseau, *Du contrat social, ou Principes du droit publique*, Book II, ch. 5: "Du droit de vie et de mort" in *Œuvres complètes* (Paris: Gallimard, 1964), vol. 3, pp. 376-377; English translation by G. D. H. Cole, *The Social Contract*, in *The Social Contract and Discourses*, ed., G. D. H. Cole, revised and augmented by J. H. Brumfitt and John C. Hall (London: J. M. Dent & Sons, 1973), "The Right of Life and Death," p. 190: "Again, every malefactor, by attacking social rights, becomes on forfeit a rebel and a traitor to his country; by violating its laws he ceases to be a member of it; he even makes war upon it. In such a case the preservation of the State is inconsistent with his own, and one or other must perish; in putting the guilty to death, we slay not so much the citizen as an enemy. The trial and the judgment are the proofs that he has broken the social treaty, and is in consequence no longer a member of the State. Since, then, he has recognized himself to be such by living there, he must be removed by exile as a violator of the compact, or by death as a public enemy; so such an enemy is not a moral person but merely a man; and in such a case the right of war is to kill the vanquished." Foucault takes up this analysis of the general theory of the contract in *Surveiller et Punir*, pp. 92-93; *Discipline and Punish*, p. 90.

4. See M. de Robespierre, "Discours à l'Assemblée nationale," 30 May 1791, *Archives parlementaires 1787-1860*, first series, vol. XXVI, p. 622, col. 1: "A victor who puts to death his captive enemies is called barbaric! (*Murmurings*) A mature man who cuts the throat of a child whom he could disarm and punish seems a monster! (*Murmurings*). An accused condemned by society is for that society at the most no more than a defeated enemy, before it he is weaker than a child before a mature man."

5. Foucault is referring here to a series of five articles which appeared on 25, 27, and 30 October and 1 and 3 November, 1942 in the *Rheinische Zeitung*, of which Marx was an editor. These texts analyze the debates of the Sixth Rhine Province Assembly on the "law relative to the

theft of wood." Foucault had annotated Marx's texts concerning this law. See K. Marx, *Karl Marx, Collected Works*, Volume 1 (New York: International Publishers, 1975). The law relative to the theft of wood provided for punishment of any "appropriation of wood from someone else," whether it be the gathering up of branches or cutting and theft of green wood; see ibid., p. 226. The articles denounce the law as serving the interests of the forest owners, and in this way sketches a definition "of bourgeois juridical ideology" (P. Lascoumes and H. Zander, *Marx: du "vol de bois" à la critique du droit*, Paris: PUF, 1984, p. 241). Marx's text also includes appeals to a *"customary right* ... which is ... a customary right of the poor in all countries," (p. 230) which have been widely commented upon. Edward P. Thompson also analyzes these writings of Marx in his theorization of "new definitions of property"; see E. P. Thompson, "Modes de domination et révolution en Angleterre," *Actes de la recherche en sciences sociales*, vol. 2 (2-3), 1976, especially p. 139. On this subject, see also, below, "Course Context," pp. 285-286.

6. Despite a gap of only seven years from Marx's texts on the "theft of wood," this probably refers to L.-A. Blanqui, "Impôt des boissons" in *La Critique sociale* (Paris: Félix Alcan, 1885) 2 volumes, vol. 2: "Fragments and notes" pp. 188-224. This text, written in December 1849, offers a caustic and detailed commentary on the parliamentary discussions regarding establishing a "progressive tax in the opposite direction to wealth" (p. 189). Blanqui denounces "the greedy egoism of the people of finance and ... the servility of all governments towards this caste, whose interests, requirements, and cupidity are the only regulator, the sole compass of all the interests of power" (ibid.). Louis-Auguste Blanqui (1805-1881) was a French theorist and politician whose tireless commitment in favor of a revolution through arms meant that he spent a large part of his life in prison. In December 1849 he was incarcerated for having organized a popular *coup de force* against the Assembly in favor of Poland; see M. Mourre, *Dictionnaire encyclopédique d'histoire* (Paris: Bordas, 1978) 7 volumes, vol. 1, pp. 576-577.

7. F. Serpillon, *Code criminel, ou Commentaire sur l'ordonnance de 1670* (Lyon: Périsse, 1767), vol. 2, third part, title XXV: "Des sentences, jugements et arrêts," art. XIII, §33, p. 105. This passage will be taken up in the "Course Summary" below, p. 249, as well as in *Surveiller et Punir*, p. 120; *Discipline and Punish*, p. 118. Serpillon's *Traité des matières criminelles*, published in 1767, was one of the last treatises of the penal law of the Ancien Régime. François Serpillon (1695-1772), jurist, was Lieutenant general of Autun; see H. Richard, "Un criminaliste bourguignon: François Serpillon, 1695-1772" in *Histoire et Criminalité de l'Antiquité au XXe siècle: nouvelles approches. Actes du colloque de Dijon-Chenove, 3-5 octobre 1991* (Dijon: Éditions universitaires de Dijon, 1992) pp. 439-448. Serpillon reappears in *Surveiller et Punir; Discipline and Punish* as a figure of penal severity: "jurists like Serpillon or Blackstone were insisting in the middle of the eighteenth century that a failure on the part of the executioner did not mean that the condemned man's life was spared" (p. 56; Eng., p. 52).

8. F. Serpillon, *Code criminel*, vol. 2, p. 106. Serpillon paraphrases here the arguments of the jurisconsult, magistrate, and historian, Jean Bouhier (1673-1746), which can be found in [J. Bouhier], *Œuvres de jurisprudence de M. Bouhier* (Dijon: Louis-Nicolas Frantin, 1788) vol. 2, ch. LV, § LXIV, p. 451: "Does condemnation to perpetual prison replace confiscation of goods?" Serpillon writes: "M. the President Bouhier, ch. 65, n. 66, vol. 2, p. 149, puts forward the question of whether condemnation to perpetual prison replaces confiscation: he says that it may appear extraordinary" (*Code criminel*). Foucault clarifies this reference to Bouhier in the manuscript. See too *Surveiller et Punir*, p. 121; *Discipline and Punish*, p. 119: "And this imprisonment came to be rejected by both classical jurists and reformers. Prisons are the work of princes, said a traditionalist like Serpillon, who sheltered behind the authority of Judge Bouhier: 'Although, for reasons of State, princes are sometimes inclined to inflict this penalty, ordinary justice makes no use of this kind of sentence'."

9. See "Discussion du projet de loi tendant à introduire des réformes dans le Code pénal," *Archives parlementaires, 1787-1860*, second series, vol. LXXI (from 21 October 1831 to 22 November 1831) p. 759 sq.; and "Suite de la discussion du projet relatif à des réformes à introduire dans le lois pénales," *Archives parlementaires, 1787-1860*, second series, vol. LXXII, p. 2 sq.

10. C. de Rémusat, "Discussion du projet de loi relatif à des réformes dans la législation pénale," Chamber of Deputies, 1 December 1831, *Archives parlementaires, 1787-1860*, second series, vol. LXXII, p. 185, col. 2. Charles de Rémusat (1797-1875), politician, writer, and philosopher, was a close relative of Adolphe Thiers and was elected to the Chamber of Deputies in October 1830 after the July revolution. The quotation is taken up in *Surveiller et Punir*, p. 117; *Discipline and Punish*, p. 115. See also below, "Course summary," p. 250, where the passage is augmented with a discourse of Pierre-François Van Meenen (1772-1858), lawyer, philosopher, and professor at the Free University of Brussels, at the opening in 1847 of the International Penitentiary Congress of Brussels (see, too, *Surveiller et Punir*, p. 16; *Discipline and Punish*, p. 10).

11. C. de Rémusat, "Discussion," see previous note.

12. See *Surveiller et Punir*, pp. 125-126; *Discipline and Punish*, p. 123.

13. See J. Howard, *The State of the Prisons in England and Wales with Preliminary Observations and an Account of some Foreign Prisons and Hospitals* (London: J. Johnson, C. Dilly, and T. Cadell, m dcc xcii, 4th edition); translation of the English 1777 and 1784 editions, Christian Cartier and Jacques-Guy Petit, *L'État des prisons, des hôpitaux et des maisons de force en Europe au XVIIIᵉ siècle*, trans. (Paris: Éditions de l'Atelier, 1994). John Howard (1726-1790) conducted inquiries into the prisons of England and the Continent (Germany, Belgium, Denmark, Spain, Flanders, France, Holland, Italy, Poland, Portugal, Russia, Siberia, Sweden, and Switzerland, among others) from 1773 to 1790, and published texts on prisons from 1777 to 1784. Foucault refers here to Julius, *Leçons sur les prisons*, pp. 299-301, dealing with events in England and "obstacles to deportation to America" (p. 300), as well as to the works of Howard and to Sir William Blackstone's (1723-1780) and John Howard's drafting of laws relating to penitentiary establishments; on the description of places of confinement, see *Surveiller et Punir*, esp., pp. 197-206; *Discipline and Punish*, pp. 231-235. For more recent research see J.-G. Petit, "Obscurité des Lumières: les prisons d'Europe, d'après John Howard, autour 1780," *Criminologie*, vol. 28 (1), 1995, pp. 5-22.

14. Foucault here quotes a passage from the preamble to a law promulgated in 1779 and drawn up by Blackstone with Howard's help. See Great Britain, *The Statutes at large, from the Sixteenth Year of the Reign of King George the Third to the Twentieth Year of the Reign of King George the Third, inclusive* (London: Charles Eyre & William Strahan, 1780 [19 Geo. III, c. 74]) vol. 13, section V, p. 487: "And whereas, if many Offenders, convicted of Crimes for which Transportation hath been usually inflicted, were ordered to solitary Imprisonment, accompanied by well-regulated Labor, and religious Instruction, it might be the Means, under Providence, not only of deterring others from the Commission of the like Crimes, but also of reforming the Individuals, and inuring them to Habits of Industry." This passage is cited by Julius in his *Leçons sur les prisons* (pp. 300-301): "Many individuals convicted of crimes which were commonly punished by deportation, could, with God's help, if subjected to solitary detention, to regular work and the influence of religious instruction, not only inspire terror in those who might be tempted to imitate them, but even correct themselves and acquire the habit of work." See also *Surveiller et Punir*, pp. 125-126; *Discipline and Punish*, p. 123 on the "triple function" of "individual imprisonment"—as "example to be feared, instrument of conversion, and condition for an apprenticeship"—and on the birth of the penitentiary (*pénitencier*) in England. Foucault will again refer to William Blackstone's *Commentaries on the Laws of England* (Oxford: The Clarendon Press, 1758) on the theme of the individual as enemy of society. Blackstone figures, alongside the great reformers, as a

herald of the new principle according to which the crime constitutes an offense to the King's sovereignty; see below, "Course summary," p. 253.

15. See *Surveiller et Punir*, p. 20; *Discipline and Punish*, p. 14.

16. J. Bentham, *Panopticon, or the Inspection-House*, in *The Works of Jeremy Bentham*, ed., John Bowring (Edinburgh: William Tait, 1791) vol. IV, pp. 37-173, republished in, *The Panopticon Writings*, ed., Miran Božovič (London: Verso, 1995). In 1786-1787, Jeremy Bentham traveled in Russia to join his brother who was responsible for the superintendence (*surveillance*) of ports, factories, and workshops of Prince Potemkin; see A. Stanziani, "The Traveling Panopticon: Labor Institutions and Labor Practices in Russia and Britain in the Eighteenth and Nineteenth Centuries," *Comparative Studies in Society and History*, vol. 51 (4), October 2009, pp. 715-741. Bentham outlined his reflections on the panoptic principle applied within the penitentiary framework, encompassing factories, asylums, hospitals, *maisons de force*, and schools, in a series of letters sent from Russia in 1787 and published by order of the National Assembly in France. The notion of social panopticism, generalized surveillance of the whole of society, will mark Foucault's thought in the years 1973-1976, and this lecture allows us to follow its emergence. At the origin of this interest for the *Panopticon* there is the hospital and the prison; see above, p. 38, note 3. The centrality of social panopticism will be developed in the following year's lectures, *Le Pouvoir psychiatrique*; *Psychiatric Power*, in which Foucault declares in the third lecture that Bentham's *Panopticon*, as symbol, represents the culminating point, the moment "when disciplinary power becomes an absolutely generalized social form ... which provides the most general political and technical formula of disciplinary power" (p. 43; Eng., p. 41; see also pp. 75-81; Eng., pp. 73-79). On this theme, see again, "La vérité et les formes juridiques," p. 606/p. 1474; "Truth and Juridical Forms," p. 70: "Panopticism is one of the characteristic traits of our society ... Today we live in a society programmed basically by Bentham, a panoptic society, a society where panopticism reigns"; and "À propos de l'enfermement pénitentiaire," *DE*, II, p. 437/"Quarto," I, p. 1305: "What seems to me even more fundamental [for explaining the profound changes in the real practice of penality], is the putting under surveillance of the plebian, lower class, working class, and peasant population. Placing under general, continuous surveillance by new forms of political power. The real problem is the police. I will say, if you like, that what was invented at the end of the eighteenth and the beginning of the nineteenth century is panopticism"; see, too, *Surveiller et Punir*, pp. 201-206; *Discipline and Punish*, pp. 195-200.

17. A. Duport, "Discours à l'Assemblée nationale constituante," 31 May 1791, *Archives parlementaires, 1787-1860*, first series, vol. XXVI, pp. 646-650. Adrien Duport (1759-1798), lawyer elected to the Estates-General by the Paris nobility, founded the Club des Feuillants with Barnave and Alexandre de Lameth and had a great influence on the establishment of the new judicial system during the Revolution. See J. Tulard, F.-J. Fayard, and A. Fierro, *Histoire et Dictionnaire de la Révolution française*, pp. 782-783.

18. A. Duport, *Archives parlementaires 1787-1860*, vol. XXVI, p. 648, col. 1; taken up in *Surveiller et Punir*, p. 234; *Discipline and Punish*, p. 232 ("universal and constant"). Foucault adds in the manuscript (fols. 4-5): "Chabroud criticizes moreover this standardization of the penalty: '... if I have betrayed my country, I am imprisoned; if I have killed my father, I am imprisoned; every imaginable offense is punished in the same uniform way ... It seems to me like seeing a physician who has the same remedy for every ill'." This extract from Chabroud's discourse of 30 May 1791, which appeared in *Archives parlementaires, 1787-1860*, vol. XXVI, p. 618, col. 1, is taken up in *Surveiller et Punir*, p. 119; *Discipline and Punish*, p. 117. Charles Chabroud (1750-1816) was deputy for the Dauphiné at the National Assembly.

19. See L.-M. Le Peletier de Saint-Fargeau, discourse to the National Assembly "on the whole of the draft Penal Code," *Archives parlementaires, 1787-1860*, first series, vol. XXVI, p. 618, col. 2.

20. In the manuscript (fol. 5), Foucault gives this reference: "Villermé (prisons as they are)." See L.-R. Villermé, *Des prisons telles qu'elles sont et telles qu'elles devreaient* être (Paris: Méquignon-Marvis, 1820) p. 137: "On 1 July 1818 ... 44,484 [prisoners]. Assuming the population of the realm to be 29,448,408 individuals, one prisoner for 662"; of which 9,925 "in the penal colonies."

21. In the manuscript (fol. 5), Foucault gives this reference: "Julius. 1822." See N. H. Julius, *Leçons sur les prisons*, p. 27: "the number of individuals held in French prisons during 1822 ... amounted to 41,307, that is to say *one prisoner in seven hundred and seventy eight inhabitants*" (underlined in the text).

22. See N.-D. Barré, "130 années de statistique pénitentiaire en France," *Déviance et Société*, vol. 10 (2), 1986, pp. 107-128, esp., p. 115 (in 1973 the metropolitan carceral population rose to 30,306 men and women).

23. Here, and in many places, the manuscript uses and puts the terms "appearance" or "appears" in quotation marks, whereas the typescript has the word "emergence"; see above, p. 61 footnote † and p. 62. It would seem that Foucault put this notion of "appearance" at arm's length when he gave his lectures. He does not seem to have returned to the expression "'appearance' of the criminal-enemy," and he does not use the term "appear" in *Surveiller et Punir, Discipline and Punish*.

24. See *Surveiller et Punir*, pp. 251-255; *Discipline and Punish*, pp. 248-252.

25. The "science of prisons" dates from the end of the nineteenth century. It is strongly linked to Charles Lucas (1803-1899), one of the founders of the Société générale des prisons established in 1877, two years after the law on cellular imprisonment (1875), for overseeing the application of which he is given responsibility. The Society, made up mainly of jurists, takes on the mission of, among other things, promoting penitentiary science in Europe, assisted notably by a review that it publishes from 1877. Charles Lucas, liberal lawyer of the Restoration and eventually Inspector General of prisons, expressed himself very early on in favor of the improvement of prison conditions and abolition of the death penalty. See C. Lucas, *Du système pénitentiaire en Europe et aux États-Unis*, vol. I (Paris: Bossange, 1828), vol. II (Paris: Dehay, 1830); *Conclusion générale de l'ouvrage sur le système pénitentiaire en Europe et aux États-Unis* (Paris: Béchet, 1834); *De la réforme des prisons, ou de la théorie de l'emprisonnement, de ses principes, de ses moyens et de ses conditions pratiques* (Paris: Legrand et Bergounioux, 1836-1838) 3 volumes (cited in the "Course summary," below, p. 264, note 7). In his writings and practice, Lucas recommends a rationalist science of prisons. Foucault places him alongside Julius as partisan of the "old project" of "founding a science of prisons" able to provide architectural, administrative, and pedagogical principles for an institution which "corrects" (ibid., p. 252). Lucas will play a central role in *Surveiller et Punir, Discipline and Punish*, in particular in the fourth part: "Prison," pp. 239-256; Eng., pp. 231-256.

26. Élie Louis Decazes, Count and then Duke Decazes (1780-1860), was Minister Secretary of State at the Department of the Interior under Louis XVIII in 1819 and drafted an important *Rapport au Roi sur les prisons et pièces à l'appui du rapport*, 21 December 1819; see R. Langeron, *Decazes, ministre du Roi* (Paris: Hachette, 1960). In this report, Decazes utters an assertion similar to the one we have just read: "it [the law] must follow him into the prison where it has sent him" (Decazes, "Rapport au Roi," *Le Moniteur universel*, No. 100, Paris, Mme. Vve. Agasse, Saturday 10 April, 1819, p. 424. It is interesting to note here the remark of Vidocq (see *Surveiller et Punir*, pp. 288-289; *Discipline and Punish*, pp. 282-284) in *Supplément aux Mémoires de Vidocq* (Paris: Les Marchands de nouveautés, 2nd edition, 1831) vol. 2, p. 10: "the law does not penetrate the prisons." Decazes is referred to several times in *Surveiller et Punir, Discipline and Punish* with reference to his inquiry carried out in 1819 on different places of detention (see p. 118 and p. 236; Eng., p. 116 and p. 234); on his *Rapport*, see ibid., p. 251; Eng., p. 248: "the penalty must be nothing more than the deprivation of liberty; like our present rulers, Decazes said it, but with the brilliance of his language: 'The law must follow

the convicted man into the prison where it has sent him'." The theme is taken up by the G.I.P., which sheds light on the articulation both of the G.I.P. and Foucault's genealogical research in *Surveiller et Punir; Discipline and Punish.*

27. G.-F. Le Trosne, *Vues sur la justice criminelle*, p. 41 n.a. Foucault will compare this text with that of 1764 on vagabondage, in *Surveiller et Punir*, p. 91; *Discipline and Punish*, p. 88: "A penal system must be conceived as a mechanism intended to administer illegalisms differentially, not to eliminate them all" [translation slightly amended; G.B.].

28. See: C. Beccaria, *Des délits et des peines; On Crimes and Punishments*; J. P. Brissot de Warville, *Théorie des loix criminelles* (Berlin: [s.n.], 1781) 2 volumes; L.-M. Le Peletier de Saint-Fargeau, "Rapport sur le projet du Code pénal" at the National Assembly, 23 May 1791, *Archives parlementaires 1787-1860*, first series, vol. XXVI, pp. 319-345.

29. J. P. Brissot de Warville, *Théorie des loix criminelles*, vol. 1, p. 101 (emphasis in the original). Jacques Pierre Brissot de Warville (1754-1793), a writer on a variety of subjects, was imprisoned for a while in the Bastille, was then a member of the Convention, a member and leader of the Girondins, and died on the guillotine 31 October 1793. His *Théorie des loix criminelles* is one of his first publications, which could be described as a work of his youth and in the tradition of the *philosophes*, written at a time when he was a clerk of a prosecutor and preparing for a career in law. Brissot addresses his work to Voltaire: "It is to you, sublime Voltaire, who blowing the fire of your genius on your century, have created it, given it life; it is to you that the universe owes the pure light which enlightens it" (ibid., p. 8). Foucault places Brissot alongside Beccaria among the great reformers and quotes him frequently in *Surveiller et Punir* (p. 98, pp. 108-110, p. 114, p. 121); *Discipline and Punish* (p. 95, pp. 106-108, pp. 111-112, p. 119) as illustrative of the envisaging of penal reform in the eighteenth century.

30. Compare this with the passage in the second essay of *On the Genealogy of Morality* where Nietzsche writes: "As the power and self-confidence of a community grows, its penal law becomes more lenient ... It is not impossible to imagine a society *so conscious of its power* that it could allow itself the noblest luxury available to it—that of letting its malefactors go *unpunished*. 'What do I care about my parasites', it could say, 'let them live and flourish: I am strong enough for all that!'" Friedrich Nietzsche, *On the Genealogy of Morality*, trans. Carol Diethe, ed. Keith Ansell-Pearson (Cambridge: Cambridge University Press, 1994) 2, 10, p. 51.

31. Foucault refers here mainly to Brissot, who on several occasions elaborates on the advantages of the effects of public opinion as a punitive technique; *Théorie des loix criminelles*, vol. 1, pp. 187-190, p. 223, p. 242, p. 340. See below, "Course summary," p. 253. Beccaria also looks into the question of infamy and devotes a whole chapter to it: "De l'infamie," *Traité des délits et des peines*, 1766, ch. XVIII, pp. 121-125; *Des délits et des peines*, 1991, ch. XXII, pp. 114-116; *On Crimes and Punishments*, ch. 23, "Public disgrace."

32. This reference to popular justice refers to a wider debate in the context of the events of 1970-1972 in which Foucault was opposed to popular tribunals. See M. Foucault, "Sur la justice populaire. Débat avec les maos" (interview with [Benny Lévy] and [André Glucksmann]), 5 February 1972, *Les Temps modernes*, no. 310 bis, June 1972, pp. 355-366; *DE*, II, no. 108, pp. 340-369/"Quarto," I, 1208-1237; English translation by John Mepham, "On Popular Justice: A Discussion with Maoists" in Michel Foucault: *Power/Knowledge. Selected Interviews and Other Writings 1972-1977*, ed., Colin Gordon (Brighton: The Harvester Press, 1980); "Les intellectuels et le pouvoir" (interview with Gilles Deleuze), 4 March 1972, *L'Arc*, no. 49: *Gilles Deleuze*, 2nd quarter, 1972, pp. 3-10; *DE*, II, no. 106, pp. 306-315/"Quarto," I, pp. 1174-1183; English translation by Donald F. Bouchard and Sherry Simon, "Intellectuals and Power" in M. Foucault, *Language, Counter-Memory, Practice. Selected Essays and Interviews*, ed., Donald F. Bouchard (Oxford: Basil Blackwell, 1977).

In 1970, Jean-Paul Sartre presided, in the role of prosecutor, over a popular tribunal on the State's responsibility in the death of several miners at the coalmines of Fouquièreslez-Lens, following which Daniel Defert proposed to Foucault that he run a commission of inquiry into prisons. Foucault was opposed to the popular model and launched instead the Groupe d'information sur les prisons/G.I.P, a social movement whose aim was to let the prisoners speak, to give truth to the discourse and experience of the incarcerated, to create a field in which a certain truth of the prison could emerge. Foucault turned away therefore from the model and personalization of popular justice, explaining his choice in the following way: "the G.I.P. means: no organization, no leader, we truly do everything so that it remains an anonymous movement that only exists through the three letters of its name. Everyone can speak. Whoever speaks does not do so because he has a title or a name, but because he has something to say. The only slogan of the G.I.P is: 'Let the prisoners speak! (*La parole aux détenus*)'"; "Le grand enfermement," p. 304/p. 1172 (see above, p. 16, note 6). For a detailed analysis of these events, see "Situation du cours" in M. Foucault, *Mal faire, dire vrai*, pp. 267-271; *Wrong-doing, Truth-telling*, pp. 274-277.

33. J. P. Brissot de Warville, *Théorie des loix criminelles*, vol. 1, pp. 187-188.

34. Foucault refers here mainly to Beccaria's *Traité des délits et des peines*; *On Crimes and Punishment*, and to Le Peletier de Saint-Fargeau, "Rapport sur le projet du Code pénal"; see below, "Course summary," p. 255.

35. C. Beccaria, *Traité des délits et des peines*, 1766, ch. XXXVII, p. 159; *Des délits et des peines*, 1991, ch. XX, p. 110; *On Crimes and Punishments*, ch. 20, p. 50: "Some crimes are assaults on persons, others are offenses against goods. The former should always be punished with corporal punishment."

36. Ibid., 1766, ch. XVIII, p. 174; 1991, ch. XXIII, p. 114; Eng., ch. 23, p. 54: "Personal injuries which damage honor ... ought to be punished with public disgrace."

37. Ibid., 1766, ch. XXX, p. 174; 1991, ch. XXII, p. 113; Eng., ch. 22, p. 53: "Thefts without violence should be punished with fines."

38. The table is found in J. P. Brissot de Warville, *Théorie des loix criminelles*, vol. 1, p. 127: "Double corresponding scale of crimes and penalties, against the general interest."

39. L.-M. Le Peletier de Saint-Fargeau, "Rapport sur le projet du Code pénal," p. 322, col. 1.

40. Foucault refers here mainly to the works of Beccaria, *Traité des délits et des peines*, 1766, ch. XXX, pp. 105-106; *Des délits et des peines*, 1991, ch. XXII, p. 130; *On Crimes and Punishments*, ch. 22, p. 53; and Brissot, *Théorie des loix criminelles*, vol. 1, p. 147.

41. V. Beccaria, *Traité des délits et des peines*, 1766, ch. XVI, pp. 105-106; *Des délits et des peines*, 1991, ch. XXVIII, p. 130; *On Crimes and Punishments*, ch. 28, p. 69: "if we add up all the unhappy moments of slavery, perhaps it is even more [cruel than death], but the [moments of slavery] are spread out over an entire life, whereas [death] exerts its force only at a single moment. And this is an advantage of penal servitude, because it frightens those who see it more than those who undergo it. For the former thinks about the sum of unhappy moments, whereas the latter is distracted from present unhappiness by the prospect of future pain."

42. Ibid.

43. Foucault quotes the following extracts:
(α) - [fol. 13] "Beccaria: regarding a particular case (the poor who steal and who cannot pay) he lays down the general principle that 'the most appropriate punishment will be the only sort of slavery that can be called just, the temporary slavery of work and the person to society, in order to compensate it with complete and personal dependence for the unjust and despotic power he has encroached on the social pact.'
It can be graduated
It is absolute, terrible (no man in the world can choose deliberately to wholly and definitively lose his own liberty).
His example: through the play of the duration perceived by others, felt by himself."
Traité des délits et des peines, 1776, ch. XXX, p. 175; *Des délits et des peines*, ch. XXII, pp. 113-114; *On Crimes and Punishments*, ch. 22, p. 53: "the most fitting punishment shall be the only sort of

slavery which can be called just, namely the temporary enslavement of the labor and person of the criminal to society, so that he may redress his unjust despotism against the social contract by a period of complete personal subjection."

(β) - [fol. 14] "Brissot: 'But what to substitute for the death penalty ...? Slavery, which makes the guilty unable to harm society, work which makes him useful, lengthy and permanent pain, which frightens those who might be tempted to imitate him. Useful tortures are called for! Do not France and England have their colonies? Sweden and Poland their mines of Coperberg and Wieliska; Russia its Siberian deserts; Spain the mines of Potosi and California, Italy its marshes, its galleys, all the countries of deserts to populate, moors to clear, manufactories to develop, buildings and public highways to construct? Replace these wretched Negroes who are guilty only of having woolly heads ... with the guilty you will have judged worthy of being deprived of a liberty harmful to the human race'." J. P. Brissot de Warville, *Théorie des loix criminelles*, vol. 1, pp. 147-148.

"For murderers, perpetual slavery: 'he will not even have the dreadful consolation of resting his head on the scaffold'." Ibid., p. 149.

"Get the young and adults to visit [the mines and works]:
'These patriotic pilgrimages would be much more useful than those the Turks make to Mecca'." Ibid., p. 150.

"Not talion: 'make him useful to the country whose laws he has violated'." Ibid., p. 154.

(γ) - [fol. 15] "Brillat-Savarin (2 June 91—Discussion of draft Penal Code);
'while the ports offer you works which call for large number of arms, while you still have vast moors to be cleared, while you have canals to be opened and marshes to be drained'." J. A. Brillat-Savarin, "Suite de la discussion sur le Code pénal et adoption du principe de la peine des travaux forcés," 2 June 1791, *Archives parlementaires, 1787-1860*, first series, vol. XXVI, p. 712, col. 1.

44. In the manuscript (fol. 15) Foucault indicates this reference: "See Chabroud's text [cited above, note 18] as criticism of Le Peletier's project." See *Archives parlementaires, 1787-1860*, first series, vol. XXVI, p. 618, col. 1.

45. See *Surveiller et Punir*, pp. 234-235; *Discipline and Punish*, pp. 232-233.

46. The central role of the control of time, of the individual's life and body, will be taken up in "La vérité et les formes juridiques," pp. 616-617/pp. 1484-1485; "Truth and Juridical Forms," pp. 80-81; in *Le Pouvoir psychiatrique*, pp. 48-49; *Psychiatric Power*, pp. 46-47; then in *Surveiller et Punir*, pp. 137-171; *Discipline and Punish*, Part Three, ch. 1, "Docile bodies," pp. 135-169. In *Surveiller et Punir, Discipline and Punish*, the conception of time will be joined to reflections relating to the "duration" of penalties, and in this context Foucault will note that those who were opposed to the death penalty—a punishment of short duration—very often envisaged definitive penalties; see ibid., p. 110 n. 1; Eng., p. 108 and p. 312 n. 1 referring to: "J. P. Brissot, *Théorie des lois criminelles*, 1781, pp. 29-30; C. E. Dufriche de Valazé, *Des lois pénales*, 1784, p. 344." Foucault notes "perpetual imprisonment for those who have been judged 'irremediably wicked'."

47. The discipline of the workshop and the workshop-prison analogy will be an important theme not only in this course, see below, lecture of 21 March, but also in the following year's course; see *Le Pouvoir psychiatrique*, lecture of 21 November 1973, pp. 53-54, and lecture of 28 November, pp. 72-75 (on the workshop discipline of the Gobelins), and p. 95; *Psychiatric Power*, pp. 51-52, pp. 70-73, and p. 93.

48. See below, lecture of 31 January, pp. 88-89 and pp. 97-98, notes 18-21.

five

31 JANUARY 1973

The prison-form and the wage-form (continuation). Power's hold on time: condition of possibility of the capitalist system and of imprisonment. ⌒ From archeology to genealogy. ⌒ Objections of the religious model and replies. (A) The monastic cell: to exclude the world, and not to punish. (B) The Quakers: rejection of the English penal code and of the death penalty. ⌒ Opposition to Beccaria concerning infraction and wrongdoing; the conception of sin. (C) Organization of the prison of Philadelphia and of Walnut Street: first mention of the "penitentiary (pénitentier)". (D) Consequences: 1. grafting of Christian morality on criminal justice; 2. knowledge (connaissance) of the prisoner: a form of knowledge (savoir) becomes possible; 3. religion invests the prison. Progressive re-Christianization of crime.

A NUMBER OF PUNITIVE models can be derived from the re-centering of penal theory and practice around the principle of the criminal-social enemy.* Now these models, perfectly derivable from the theory and practice, are precisely not those that are implemented when one passes from plan to legislation, from the statement of principles to real organization. There is a moment, in discourse and practice, when

---

* The manuscript (fol. 1) draws up the list already referred to in the previous lecture: "infamy; talion, slavery."

something else is substituted for what was derivable, as we see in Le Peletier de Saint-Fargeau.* This something else is the prison-form.

I have tried to show that the prison-form can be brought together with the wage-form as the introduction of a certain quantity of time into a system of equivalences: wage against so much time of labor, prison against this or that offense. I have emphasized this kinship, but without saying that the model of the wage was transferred into penality. I have said only that the same form is found in the wage and in prison: on the one hand, the time of life becomes an exchangeable material; on the other hand, the measure of time allows the quantification of the exchange, through the relation established either between a quantity of labor and a quantity of money, or between a quantity of time and the gravity of the offense. The form refers to the essential phenomenon, which is the introduction of the quantity of time as measure, and not only as economic measure in the capitalist system, but also as moral measure. Behind this introduction, for the quantity of time to become material and measure of exchange, power must have a hold on time, [not as an] ideological abstraction, but as a real extraction of time from people's lives: real condition of possibility of the functioning of the wages system and the system of imprisonment.

There is a real process here that one should be able to analyze on the basis of the power relationships that ensure this real extraction of time. It is at this level of power that prison and wage communicate. This is not because the wage would have served as the representative model for the prison, but because prison and wage connect up, each at its own level and in its own way, to the apparatus of power that ensures the real extraction of time and introduces this into a system of exchanges and measures. The problem is precisely to find this apparatus of power and to see how the prison-form could effectively be inserted and become an instrument in power relations. Until now, we have been studying the threads of possible derivations: for example, how ideas and

---

* The manuscript (fols. 1-2) clarifies: "Example: Le Peletier [de] Saint-Fargeau, in 1971, lays down the principle of punishments focused around the talion (with lateral interventions from other models). In fact, he proposes a confinement.

Another example: Howard, Blackstone, and Fothergill around 1779—and what actually this became in England.

Derivability is not carried out. Lateral intervention. Something else is substituted."[1]

institutions join up with each other within the theoretical and practical penal system. Now it is a matter of finding the power relationships that made the historical emergence of something like the prison possible. After an archeological type of analysis, it is a matter of undertaking a dynastic, genealogical type of analysis, focusing on filiations on the basis of power relations.[2]

*   *   *

So, the prison is introduced laterally into the derivative network of theories and practices, and unexpectedly, forcibly. So where does this form come from? For, although it cuts laterally across the network of derivation of the penal system, it is not formed at the moment of this intrusion.

I would like to begin this analysis by considering an objection:[*] is it not perilous to say that the prison arises suddenly within the penal system towards the end of the eighteenth century, when we have lived in a society that has been familiar with monastic enclosure, a convent-form for centuries? Would it not be more reasonable to see if we could trace the genealogy of the prison-form from a certain monastic form of community? Thus, in France, prisons are housed in monasteries: the cellular confinement of prisons found its point of fixation in the monastic space.

But this filiation comes up against an objection of a general kind: we should not forget what the function of monastic seclusion was. Actually, on what side is the permeability? What is involved here is not preventing someone's access to the outside world, not preventing them from leaving, but protecting places, bodies, and souls from the outside world: seclusion closes off the inside from all the possible assaults of the outside; it is one of those holy places into which there is no way one can enter. So seclusion does not confine someone's liberty within a place he cannot leave and in relation to which the outside is inaccessible; it defines a protected internal space that must become inaccessible to the outside. It is the world that is kept outside, and not the individual

---

* Manuscript (fol. 3): "The problem will be elucidated by studying two objections: religious confinement and political confinement."

inside. It is the world that is confined to the outside. So punitive confinement and monastic seclusion are fundamentally heterogeneous.[3] Certainly, the retreat is linked to sin; but even when motivated by sin it is not in itself a punishment. It appears as the *condition* of repentance, of remorse, as the place that, through its sacralized solitude, is right for enabling chastisement (fasting, flagellation, and so on) to become acts of penance and for reconciling the individual with God. The retreat does not ensure penance in itself, but ensures that the chastisements one imposes on oneself have real value as penance for the redemption of the soul and the reconciliation of the person, so that the sign of true repentance lies in love of the retreat.

If, at a certain point, we find a recurrence of the theme of the Christian retreat regarding prisons, it is later, in the nineteenth century, with the reappearance of the Christian theme supported and codified by the medical theme of therapeutic isolation and [the] sociological [theme] of a break with the delinquent milieu.[4] But this is only a secondary adjustment grafted onto a medical and sociological codification of the prison, for the prison does not originally appear in strict descent from the monastic institution, as its final blossoming.* Certainly, the Church practiced a punitive confinement to a certain degree—but, precisely, to what degree? In three very particular cases, in fact. First, like the whole of the penal system of the time, the Church practiced non-punitive confinement, that is to say as security, before bringing someone to trial, during inquisitorial confinement, or before handing them over to temporal justice, for example.[5] In the second case, we do find a form of punitive confinement, but this is when it is a question of shielding the clergy from temporal justice; confinement is indeed then a canonical penalty found in different versions of canon law, but this punishment diminished considerably from the end of the Middle Ages, and in France canonical confinement by the Church was prohibited in 1629.[6] In the third case we find a religious and punitive confinement, but when clergy or laymen are confined as punishment in places like monasteries.[7] This is the case with the *lettres di cachet*, for example.[8] But anyway, we see that punitive confinement cannot be considered as a general ecclesiastical practice; it existed for the clergy only in the Middle

---

* The manuscript (fol. 5) adds: "No talk of a monastic model of the prison."

Ages, and, apart from them, prisoners were confined by the secular power. So I do not think we can say that confinement is a laicized form of a Catholic penalty. Prison is not the monastery or convent of the industrial period.[9]

However, having said that, it is true that punitive confinement is indeed born within religious milieus, but milieus that are not only foreign but completely hostile to the monastic form. We find it in fact, [in] its nascent form, in non-Catholic communities like those of the Anglo-Saxon Protestant Dissenters, from the seventeenth up to the end of the eighteenth century.[10] I will take the example of one of these communities, which was certainly the most precocious, the most vigilant in the organization of this new punitive form of the prison: the American society of the Quakers.[11] Historically, the dissident communities were hostile to the English penal system for a number of mainly de facto reasons: the question for them was that of preventing Anglican power from encroaching onto their own system of morality; each group thus had to give itself its law and a system of punishment as the sanction of its law.

More precisely, from the seventeenth [up to the end of the eighteenth] century, the English penal code was extraordinarily severe—in correlation with the revolutionary movements of this period—to such an extent that the death penalty sanctioned around two hundred kinds of infraction. Now some of these communities were hostile to the death penalty. Also, when the Quakers became established in America, they wanted to escape the English penal system and develop a new penal code without the death penalty. They came up against the refusal of the English administrators and there was a muted struggle with the English administration up until Independence. With the independence of Pennsylvania, the first measure was to limit the death penalty and establish a new punitive armory in which the prison appears alongside mutilations, flogging, and public works. In 1790, the death penalty was no longer applied except for one or two cases, and prison became the basic penalty.*

---

* The manuscript (fol. 7) adds: "Then, in [17]90, suppression of public works, which is replaced by the prison."[12]

So if it is true that the prison-form, as institution and practice, cannot be derived from the penal theories of Beccaria, Brissot, and so on, it can be derived from the Quaker conception of religion, morality, and power. For the Quakers, in fact, if political power functioned normally, it should have no other end or raison d'être than to practice moral divisions: power is fitted to its true vocation only on condition of being nothing other than a force of coercion and morality. Power must be moral, and any politics beyond this morality of power is to be excluded. As Burroughs says, the government must "punish and suppress the malefactors," it must praise and reward "those who do good"; it must "protect the person and property of men against the violence and wrongdoing of the wicked."[13] The fundamental notion justifying power is that of evil:* it is only because there is evil and wicked people that power is justified in suppressing them and, in the final analysis, when it has succeeded in suppressing the wicked, it must suppress itself; there will then remain only the community of the just, who can communicate between themselves and spontaneously do good together. The central character of evil† with regard to political organization is one of the foundations of the Quaker conception of politics. Now, we have here a definition of crime, of the infraction, that is the opposite of that found in Beccaria or Brissot: for these reformers, the problem was one of making a [clear] distinction between infraction and moral wrongdoing and to define the former in relation to society, whatever religion or natural law imposed on man; the infraction cannot therefore be superimposed on moral wrongdoing or sin, it is not a moral infraction but an infraction of the law as formulated by the sovereign and justified by social utility.[14] For the Quakers, on the contrary, it is above all evil, as morally and religiously defined, that is punishable.

The problem that arises then is this: if it is true that evil exists and that a power really is needed in order to try to curb it, with what right can human power claim such a gigantic task as that of suppressing evil? Is it not God himself, who has permitted evil to exist, who must

---

* Manuscript (fol. 7): "Moral conception of power." Marginal addition: "It is the existence of evil that founds power."

† The manuscript (fol. 7) adds: "central character of the notion of *evil (evil men, evil doers)*" [words in italics in English in the manuscript; G.B.].

suppress it? If it is true that evil is universal, it is also true that the ways of salvation are open everywhere and at every moment. No one is damned in advance. As Fox says "the ocean of darkness and death" is universal, yet "the ocean of light and love" is also universal and will prevail;[15] "every man was enlightened ... and I saw [the divine Light] shine through all."[16] Thus, God has not withdrawn from anyone, and each may therefore find him; and, if there is good in every man, it is up to everyone to take in hand the task of bringing out this light and making it shine. The relationship to God therefore has no need to be mediated by objects and rites. Piety has nothing to do with sacred places or privileged moments; every man may encounter God at any moment and in any place, in the depths of solitude or within the community. Two conditions are necessary for grasping this light in oneself: the rectitude of a mind undisturbed by the passions and images of the world, and, therefore, the retreat. But one can help each to find the light within them; hence the importance of solitude, the retreat, but also dialogue, teaching, the search in common.[*]

Now, we can derive from this the organization of the Philadelphia prison,[17] which is described in a text by La Rochefoucauld-Liancourt, *Des prisons de Philadelphie* (1796). It was actually a Quaker society that, from 1780-1790, took [responsibility for] the organization and administration of penality in Pennsylvania. Here are some of its principles, according to La Rochefoucauld: it is a matter of "getting the prisoners to forget all their old habits,"[18] of erasing from them everything that may comprise old passions, images deposited in the mind. In effect, the mind must become empty and pure again so that the inner divine light shines out anew. Furthermore, one must bring about in the prisoner an "absolute change in the quality and kind of diet," which, "renewing his blood entirely, softening it, and refreshing it, softens his soul and inclines it to the mildness that brings him to repent."[19] This is the phase of cellular confinement; the prisoner is isolated, without information concerning the outside world, and

---

[*] The manuscript (fol. 9) adds: "But if God is present in every man, if each man brings with him some light, we can encounter God in him (on condition that he has not extinguished the light in himself): we also help him to encounter the light. Hence the importance of teaching, testimony, the search in common for the light."

without communication. Then, "in this total abandonment of every living being, he is more inclined to descend into himself, to reflect on his sins, the pain of which he feels so bitterly."[20] After this re-descent into himself, he can hear the word anew: prisoners will not be entitled to hear anything from anyone apart from the inspectors who talk "with them, seek to know them, exhort them, console them, encourage them, reconcile them with themselves. These conversations are not frequent, in which case they would have less effect; their faces are always calm, never cheerful."[21] Respect, coldness, sadness, and calm must reign in the prison.*

It is with regard to this institution that the term "penitentiary (*pénitentier*)" is used. An incredible term. How, in fact, can we speak of penance at a time when the theory of society, the practico-theoretical ensemble of penality, implies that there can be crime only if society is injured, punishment only inasmuch as society has to defend itself, and where there cannot be any fundamental relationship between sin and crime, penalty and penance? How can we explain the emergence of this term *penitentiary* (*pénitentier*) to designate an institution that will be used by a penal system for its punishments? There is heterogeneity here: on one side we have a judicial principle of punishment as the consequence of an infraction and protection of society, and, on the other, a moral principle of a punishment that will be a process of penance as a result of a moral wrongdoing. This entails a number of consequences.

First, this would be the first real transplant of Christian morality into the criminal justice system, because hitherto criminal justice in the Christian world had not been Christianized. It seems to me that Christianity and the penal system were always impermeable to each other. In the period when crime is defined by the dispute and the problem is precisely liquidation of the dispute and reparation for the infraction, we have a penal system that in itself is not homogeneous with the Christian system. In a later period, at the end of the Middle Ages, when we see the emergence of the sovereign as the one who is always injured along with the victim of the dispute, we have a practice

---

* The manuscript (fol. 10) adds: "The establishment of Walnut Street prison corresponds to this regime. [The organization here consists in] cells, each of which opens onto a small garden; [a] central court which allows supervision; [and] individual work for each prisoner."

of criminal law that returns to the Roman conception of the *crimen maiestatis* and not a penetration of law by Christianity.[22] The real process that led from the German law of reparation of disputes to the law of the seventeenth century is not one of Christianization: it is the problem of the tax levy throughout the penal procedure that induced a number of transformations, like the quasi-State takeover of justice in France, without Christianity having anything to say about it.[23] The old German law was fiscalized.*

Moreover, it is difficult to see why the Church as such would have sought to confiscate lay justice for itself when it had its own instances of control, its own mechanisms of repression and punishment, and its own fiscal procedures. Its interest, both as institution and as ideological unit, excluded seeking to merge with the secular mechanisms of punishment, to confuse judicial penalty and religious penance in one and the same punishment. But this confusion is brought about in the eighteenth century at a moment of supposed de-Christianization. And this first meshing of Christian morality with judicial practice does not take place at the level of principles. Christian conscience does not break into the penal system as a result of an ideological penetration. It does so[†] from the bottom, at the final stage of the penal process: prison, punishment. Christian conscience penetrates the juridical through the penitentiary's invasion of the whole of the penal and the juridical. The site of the possible confusion between crime and sin, which is never quite, but always on the point of being made, is the prison.[‡] Thus that culpabilization of crime takes place whose effects will be felt in other domains: psychiatry, criminology.

Second, if it is true that the prison does function on the basis of this Pennsylvanian model, knowledge of the prisoner as such becomes a central problem. In this system, the function of the prison is actually not purely and simply to assure that the punishment is inflicted and has been fully carried out, but at the same time to double the whole unfolding of the punishment with a supervision (*surveillance*) focusing

---

* Manuscript (fol. 11), in margin: "Fiscalization of criminal justice rather than Christianization of Germanic or Roman law."

† The manuscript (fol. 11) adds: "its strange location." In margin: "the rise of the penitentiary comes from the base."

‡ Manuscript (fol. 11): "This is what explains the *cellular* character of the prison."

not only on its completion, but also on the inner transformations of the prisoner during his penalty. Punishment is not just an act that is carried out, it is an unfolding process whose effects on the person who is its object must be monitored: "The constable who brings the prisoner gives the inspectors a succinct account of his crime, of the circumstances that may aggravate or mitigate it, of those of his trial, of the offenses or crimes of which he may have been previously accused, in short of the known character of this man in his earlier life. This account sent by the court that pronounced the sentence allows the inspectors to form a first opinion of the new prisoner, and of the greater or lesser supervisory attention he is to be given."[24]

In this program of the knowledge (*connaissance*) of the prisoner that must be acquired, of the criminal as object of knowledge (*savoir*), a number of elements stand out that will have great historical importance: the need for a judicial record, a dossier, of a biography, of an observation of the man's character, of inspectors whose attentions are supervisory, that is to say the penal control and supervision of the medical and religious transformation. This institution thus opens up a whole field of possible knowledge. Now, it in this same period that the hospital structure appears, which gives rise to the institutional space in which man as body will be known. Thus, the foundations both for what will become the anatomical-physiological science of man and for something like psychopathology, criminology, and sociology arise at the same time: what the hospital is for the body, the prison is for the soul.

Finally, third, we can see how the prominent presence in the prison of the man of religion is understandable. It is actually a new phenomenon for religion to accompany punishment in this way. It is because the penalty becomes penance and the penal system is being Christianized. It is new, because this is no longer the situation of the priest's presence at the death penalty; in that case he is present to play a double role: to assure the condemned of the possibility of salvation of his soul by giving him the last rites, and to save the person who condemned him from the certainty of committing a mortal sin by sending someone to their death who could not be saved. Now, in the new penal system, we have a priest who accompanies the penalty throughout its course, inasmuch as it must be a penance. The priest has to be witness, guarantor, and instrument of the transformation that the penalty must induce. Thus, the priest's [presence in] the prison is an absolutely constitutive figure of the process: the place of the culpabilization of crime is prison, the priest is its instrument. Whereas the prison was basically foreign to the Church, we see it become its privileged object; in the movement [of Christianization], prison, along with the asylum, will be a privileged place. The prison will be the space within which a knowledge becomes possible and, at the same time and for the same reasons, a place invested by religion.

This also explains the impression of the prison's antiquity from which it is so difficult to free oneself: if it appears to be so deeply rooted in our culture, this is precisely because it was born weighed down with a Christian morality that gives it a historical depth it does not possess. At the confluence of this Christian morality, with its millenary thickness, and a knowledge, which in reality only arises from the prison but whose function is to justify it, to rationalize it, the prison appears ineradicable, held in a sort of "obviousness"; in this way it is endlessly revived.

So we cannot say that prison reproduces an old religious model of the monastery, but that a new form of juridical-religious connection is established through it. At the time, this notion of the *penitentiary* was quite surprising although for us it has lost that sharpness. But in 1830, those who, like Julius,[25] reflect on this, say that the great invention of modern penality is this kind of "penitentiary" element; and their problem is precisely one of reviewing all penal institutions from the point of view [of] penitentiary science. The problem then is how this small model, born on the other side of the Atlantic, can be found in the European world about the same time. What is the economic, political, and social background that made this emergence of the penitentiary, this progressive re-Christianization of crime, possible?*

---

* The manuscript (fol. 13) has two further paragraphs:

"Remarks.

(α) We presently find if not the architectural form, at least the penitentiary model of Walnut Street in modern prisons. Isolation, the ethico-psychological interview, breaking with the milieu, the use of tranquilizers, the relative individualization of the penalty according to penal behavior, all derive directly from this little kernel.

(β) The architectural form of Walnut Street gives rise

1. Le Peletier de Saint-Fargeau's speech to which Foucault is referring is found in his "Rapport sur le projet du Code pénal" to the National Assembly, 23 May 1791, *Archives parlementaires de 1787 à 1860*, first series, vol. XXVI (12 May to 5 June 1791) pp. 319-345, see p. 322, col. 1; passage referred to in the "Course summary," below p. 255. The reference to Blackstone, Howard, and Fothergill is to their draft law, promulgated in 1799 (see above, p. 76, n. 14).

2. These lines offer a revealing juxtaposition of the archeological method and the genealogical method (study of filiations). Foucault still employs the terms "genealogical" and "dynastic" here as equivalents; see "Théories et Institutions pénales," thirteenth lecture. The archeological method was developed some years earlier in *L'Archéologie du savoir* (Paris: Gallimard, 1969); English translation by A. Sheridan, *The Archaeology of Knowledge* (London: Tavistock and New York: Pantheon, 1972). Here we are at a turning point where Foucault develops the genealogical method he had already evoked and announced in his inaugural lecture at the Collège de France in 1970, *L'Ordre du discours*; "The Order of Discourse," and which he will apply two years after these lectures on "the punitive society" in *Surveiller et Punir*, *Discipline and Punish*. The first method is founded on the study of derivations; see this example: "the penal ensemble, characterized by prohibition and sanction, the law [and which] ... brings with it a certain theory of the infraction as act of hostility towards society ... is deduced, in an archeologically correct way, from the State institutionalization of justice, which means that, from the Middle Ages, we have a practice of justice ordered in terms of the exercise of sovereign political power" (lecture of 7 February, below, p. 111). The second is founded on an analysis of the productive effects of power relationships. Here, the genealogical question is clearly stated (above, pp. 83-84, see p. 83): "what are the power relationships that made the historical emergence of something like the prison possible"?

    Foucault takes up this distinction between "archeology" and the "dynastic" in an interview with S. Hasumi in September 1972, "De l'archéologie à la dynastique," *DE*, II, no. 119, p. 406/"Quarto," p. 1274: "I am changing level: after analyzing types of discourse, I am trying to see how these types of discourse were able to be formed historically and on what historical realities they are articulated. What I call the 'archeology of knowledge' is precisely the marking out and description of types of discourse and what I call the 'dynastics of knowledge' is the relation existing between these great types of discourse observable in a culture and the historical conditions, the economic conditions, the political conditions of their appearance and formation. So, *Les Mots et les Choses*; *The Order of Things* became *L'Archéologie du savoir*; *The Archaeology of Knowledge*, and what I am now undertaking is at the level of the dynastics of knowledge"; an analysis continued in *Surveiller et Punir*, p. 27; *Discipline and Punish*, p. 23: "The objective of this book: ... a genealogy of the present scientifico-legal complex from which the power to punish derives its bases, justifications, and rules, from which it extends its effects and by which it masks its exorbitant singularity."

    Foucault will continue to develop this contrast the following year in his 1973-1974 lectures, *Le Pouvoir psychiatrique*; *Psychiatric Power*. There, carrying out a critical return to the *Histoire de la folie*; *The History of Madness*, Foucault develops what could be called a genealogy of knowledge or discourse—a study of the way in which relations of power give rise to discursive practices: "in comparison with what I call archeology, the discursive analysis of power would operate at a level—I am not very happy with the word "fundamental"—let's say at a level

---

- to workers' cities (individual accommodation + small garden with individualizing functions
→ inhibition of group effects)
- to the big prisons for which Bentham provides the first model.

M[onastic] F[orm] + a workers' city → Walnut Street."

that would enable discursive practice to be grasped at precisely the point where it is formed" (*Le Pouvoir psychiatrique*, lecture of 7 November 1973, p. 14; *Psychiatric Power*, p. 13). See, too, "La vérité et les formes juridiques," p. 554/p. 1422 and pp. 643-644/pp. 1511-1512; "Truth and Juridical Forms," p. 17; "Dialogue on Power," interview with Los Angeles students, recording May 1975, in S. Wade, ed., *Chez Foucault* (Los Angeles: Circabook, 1978) pp. 4-22; *"Il faut défendre la société,"* lecture of 7 January 1976, p. 11; *"Society Must Be Defended,"* p. 10: "Compared to the attempt to inscribe knowledges in the power-hierarchy typical of science, genealogy is, then, a sort of attempt to desubjugate historical knowledges, to set them free"; "Structuralism and Post-Structuralism," interview with G. Raulet, *Telos*, vol. XVI, no. 55, Spring 1983, pp. 194-211.

For a more recent discussion, see A. Davidson, "On Epistemology and Archeology: From Canguilhem to Foucault" in A. Davidson, *The Emergence of Sexuality: Historical Epistemology and the Formation of Concepts* (Cambridge, MA: Harvard University Press, 2004) pp. 192-206.

3. This comment could be read as a criticism of the work of Erving Goffman on so-called "total institutions," among which Goffman included monasteries, convents, and cloisters, religious establishments in short, which he described as "establishments designed as retreats from the world," E. Goffman, *Asylums: Essays on the Social Situation of Mental Patients and Other Inmates* (New York: Doubleday, "Anchor Books," 1961) p. 5. According to Daniel Defert, the practice of the G.I.P. led to a theoretical rejection of Goffman's analyses at the very heart of the group. Foucault's analysis here, on the nature of the relations between the inside and the outside—a central theme in Goffman—seems to indicate a dialogue on these points; see also, below, "Course context," pp. 273-276.

4. Relative to the medical theme of therapeutic isolation, in *Histoire de la folie*; *History of Madness*, Part Three, ch. 4, "Birth of the asylum," Foucault traces the origin of psychiatric internment in the theory of "moral treatment" of the insane developed in France by Philippe Pinel (1745-1826), and then by Jean-Étienne Esquirol (1772-1840), and links it to Quaker practices. It is on the basis of comparable principles that in 1796 the Quaker, William Tuke (1732-1822) founded the Retreat in York, England, where the insane lived according to religious principles, isolated from the outside world. As Foucault notes, Tuke observed that: "To encourage the influence of religious principles over the mind of the insane, is considered of great consequence, as a means of cure" (Samuel Tuke [1784-1857], *Description of the Retreat, an Institution near York for insane persons*, 1813, pp. 160-161, quoted by Foucault in *Histoire de la folie*, p. 580; *History of Madness*, p. 482). Foucault gives a detailed commentary on the Retreat (ibid., pp. 559-590; Eng., pp. 471-491), a "complementary figure" (p. 590; Eng., p. 491) to Pinel's practices.

Relative to the sociological theme of the break with the delinquent milieu, we could refer to the debates relative to the "cellularist" law of 1875, in which we find a synthesis of the sociological theory of the social milieu (see Gabriel Tarde, *La Criminalité comparée* [1886]; *Les Lois de l'imitation* [1890]) and of the Christian notion of expiation through spiritual retreat to a cell. The debates regarding the law on individual cellular confinement in 1875, in continuity with sociological theories of social degeneration, present cellularism as a means of blocking delinquent contagion. At the National Assembly, the viscount d'Haussonville defends his proposed law by inserting it in the perspective of the moral recovery of France: "our plan comes from an analogous concern. The commission (the parliamentary commission of inquiry concerning penitentiary establishments, under M. le vicomte d'Houssonville) was inspired by lofty, moral and Christian thinking" (Session of 20 May 1875, *Annales de l'Assemblée nationale*, quoted in R. Badinter, *La Prison républicaine (1871-1914)*, Paris: Fayard, 1992, p. 68). Foucault returns to this parallel with the moral dimension of the Christian retreat, *Surveiller et Punir*, p. 241; *Discipline and Punish*, p. 238: "'Alone in his cell, the convict is handed over to himself; in the silence of his passions and of the world that surrounds him, he descends into his conscience, he questions it and feels awakening within him the moral feeling that never entirely perishes in the heart of man' (*Journal des* économistes, II, 1842)."

5. Used very early on by the Church, the practice of preventive detention developed considerably with the establishment of the Inquisition in the twelfth century, and functioned in close connection with the secular power. It then became, apart from a security measure, a privileged means of pressure for obtaining confessions. On this theme, see J. Giraud, *Histoire de l'Inquisition au Moyen Âge* (Paris: A. Picard, 1935-1938) 2 volumes; J.-G. Petit, N. Castan, C. Faugeron, M. Faugeron, M. Pierre, and A. Zysberg, *Histoire des galères, bagnes et prisons. Introduction à l'histoire pénale de la France*, Preface by Michèle Perrot (Toulouse: Privat, "Bibliothèque historique Privat," 1991, pp. 26-28; J. B. Given, "Dans l'ombre de la prison. La prison de l'Inquisition dans la société languedocienne" in Isabelle Heullant-Donat, Julie Claustre, and Élisabeth Lusset, ed., *Enfermements. Le cloître et la prison (VIᵉ-XVIIIᵉ siècle)*, (Paris: Publications de la Sorbonne, 2011) pp. 305-320. Furthermore, the Church refusing to shed blood, the condemned are handed over to the secular arm when capital punishment is pronounced by an ecclesiastical court; see J.-G. Petit *et al.*, *Histoire des galères, bagnes et prisons*, p. 27.

6. The role of Catholic jurisdictions continued to diminish from the sixteenth century, as their competence is claimed by royal justice; see B. Garnot, *Justice et Société en France aux XVIᵉ, XVIIᵉ et XVIIIᵉ siècles* (Gap-Paris, Éd. Ophrys, "Synthèse histoire," 2000) p. 120. On 20 July 1629, by the Nîmes Edict of Grace, or Peace of Alais, Louis XIII marked the end of the Protestant revolts by confirming respect for the Protestant religion guaranteed by the Edict of Nantes (1598). The Edict also restores freedom of Catholic worship in regions where Protestants are dominant and regulates the organization of the Church there. It seems in particular to exclude the presence of laymen in monasteries as well as monks not observing the principles regulating their life within an order: "We order nonetheless, that in all the monasteries of these towns restored to obedience to us, no monks can be placed or established there other than those living in exact observation of their Rule, according to the letters that they will obtain from us" (C. Bergeal and A. Durrleman, *Protestantisme et Libertés en France au XVIIᵉ siècle. De l'édit de Nantes à sa révocation 1598-1685* (Carrières-sous-Poissy: La Clause, "Textes d'histoire protestante," 2001, p. 71). See *Journal de la France et des Français. Chronologie politique, culturelle et religieuse de Clovis à 2000* (Paris: Gallimard, "Quarto," 2001); F.-O. Touati, ed., "Règle" in *Vocabulaire historique du Moyen Âge* (Paris: La Boutique de l'Histoire, 2000 [1995, 1997]).

7. Attested from the fourth century (see E. Lusset, "Entre les murs. L'enfermement punitif des religieux criminels au sein du cloître (XXIᵉ-XVᵉ siècle)" in I. Heullant-Donat, J. Claustre, and E. Lusset, eds., *Enfermements*, pp. 153-167) punitive confinement within monastic establishments developed from the sixth century (see J. Hillner, "L'enfermement monastique au VIᵉ siècle," pp. 39-56, esp., pp. 40-42) for both laymen and monks, and is generalized in the twelfth century with the formation of the religious order. This confinement, varying from a few days to perpetuity, sanctioned different offenses according to different periods and regions. We can cite here, avoiding the confession of one's sins (see J.-G. Petit *et al.*, *Histoire des galères, bagnes et prisons*, p. 26), disobeying the secular power (see P. Hatlie, *The Monks and Monasteries of Constantinople, ca. 350-850*, Cambridge: Cambridge University Press, 2007, p. 165, cited by J. Hillner, "L'enfermement monastique," p. 41), or the perpetration of "serious crimes" (see: C. Vogel, "Les sanctions infligées aux laïques et aux clercs par les conciles gallo-romains et mérovingiens," *Revue de droit canonique*, vol. 2, 1952, pp. 186-188; A. Lefebvre-Teillard, "Les officialités à la veille du concile de Trente," *Revue internationale de droit comparé*, vol. 25 (4), 1973, p. 85, cited by Véronique Beaulande-Barraud, "Prison pénale, prison pénitentielle dans les sentences d'officialité" in I. Heullant-Donat *et al.*, *Enfermements*, p. 290).

8. Exceptional during the Middle Ages, confinement of laymen in religious communities was practiced by the royal power from the end of the seventeenth century, mainly due to the presence of religious establishments throughout the realm. According to a historian: "Between 1778 and 1784, these [religious] communities confined 30.9% of those detained by *lettres de cachet*" (C. Quétel, *De Par le Roy. Essai sur les lettres de cachet*, Toulouse: Privat, 1981, pp. 174-175, and C. Quétel, "En maison de force au siècle des Lumières," *Cahiers des Annales de Normandie*, no. 13, 1981, pp. 43-79). Studying the *lettres de cachet* in Paris, Frantz Funck-Brentano draws up thus a list of "castles, forts, religious establishments, and particular houses in Paris that receive residents by order of the King" in the second half of the eighteenth century; see Frantz Funck-Brentano, *Les Lettres de cachet à Paris. Étude suivie d'une liste des prisonniers de la Bastille (1659-1789)* (Paris: Imprimerie nationale, 1903, pp. xxxvii-xxxviii). Among the numerous convents, religious establishments, and Christian schools, the author dwells on the case of the convent of the Mathurines of the rue de la Poste: "The regime of the residents was regulated by the Archbishop of Paris. All the details of the internal administration came under his jurisdiction. The inmates lived in common, went out accompanied by an extern sister, and the superior constantly received letters written by husbands irritated by the excessive liberty allowed their loose wives" (ibid., p. xxxviii).

9. On the question of the laicization of confinement—from canonical to penal confinement—see: A. Porteau-Bitker, "L'emprisonnement dans le droit laïque au Moyen Âge," *Revue historique de droit français et étranger*, no. 46, 1968, pp. 211-245 and pp. 389-428; J. Leclercq, "Le cloître est-il une prison?" *Revue d'ascétique et de mystique*, vol. 47, no. 188, Oct.-Dec. 1971, pp. 407-420.

10. Dissenters is a generic term designating believers who separate from an established Church. More specifically it designates the Protestant communities formed in opposition to the doctrine and power of the Anglican Church. See, B. R. White, *The English Separatist Tradition: From the Marian Martyrs to the Pilgrim Fathers* (London: Oxford University Press, 1971); M. R. Watts, *The Dissenters* (Oxford: The Clarendon Press, 1978), 2 volumes.

11. The religious Society of Friends was formed in the 1640s under the notable influence of George Fox (1624-1691); its adherents, the Quakers, were persecuted in England during the second half of the seventeenth century, at least until the Toleration Act of 1689. A number of them emigrated at this time to the province of Pennsylvania, founded in 1681 by the Quaker William Penn. See: W. C. Braithwaite, *The Beginnings of Quakerism* (London: Macmillan and Co., 1912); W. C. Braithwaite, *The Second Period of Quakerism* (London: Macmillan and Co., 1919); H. H. Brinton, *Friends for 300 Years: The History and Beliefs of the Society of Friends since George Fox started the Quaker Movement* (New York: Harper, 1952); P. Brodin, *Les Quakers en Amérique du Nord: au XVIIe siècle et au début du XVIIIe* (Paris: Dervy-Livres, 1985). Foucault had already studied the history of the Quakers, the thought and writings of Samuel Tuke, George Fox, and the Society of Friends, in the context of the birth of the asylum. See *Folie et Déraison*, pp. 557-590; *History of Madness*, pp. 467-511; the theme is taken up in "La vérité et les formes juridiques," p. 596 sq./p. 1464 sq.; "Truth and Juridical Forms," p. 60 sq., and of course in *Surveiller et Punir*, *Discipline and Punish*.

12. Despite the attempt by Michel Le Peletier de Saint-Fargeau to abolish the death penalty, the French Penal Code adopted by the Constituent Assembly in 1791 held that it could be applied for "thirty-four crimes of a political nature as well as for murder, poisoning, parricide, and arson"; J.-L. Halpérin, *Histoire des droits en Europe de 1750 à nos jours* (Paris: Flammarion, 2004) p. 62. Contrary to what Foucault asserts, the Penal Code of 1791 provided for a "punishment of irons (*peine de fers*)," a central measure of its repressive arsenal, defined in article 6 as consisting in: "forced labor, for the State, in *maisons de force*, or in ports and arsenals, or in mines, or for draining marshes, or finally for any other hard works which, on the request of *départements*, can be determined by the legislative body, and replaced by forced labor in the penal colonies"; quoted in P. Lascoumes, P. Poncela, and P. Lenoël, *Au nom de*

l'ordre. Une histoire politique du code pénal (Paris: Hachette, 1989) p. 357. From 1972 this *peine de fers* is replaced by forced labor in the penal colonies; see ibid., pp. 67-69; J.-L. Halpérin, *Histoire des droits en Europe.*

13. In the manuscript Foucault gives this reference: "Burroughs (Works, p. 247-248)." See E. Burroughs, *The Memorable Works of a Son of Thunder and Consolation: Namely That True Prophet and Faithful Servant of God, and Sufferer for the Testimony of Jesus, Edward Burroughs, Who Dyed a Prisoner for the Word of God in the City of London, the Fourteenth of the Twelfth Month, 1662* (London: Ellis Hookes, 1672, ch. x, "Concerning Governours, and Governments, and Subjection to them, this testimony I give to the World [1657]"), p. 247: "Governours, Rulers, and Magistrates ... such as be a terrour to all evil in their Government, and that fears God and hates covetousness, and delights in Equity, in Justice, and true Judgment, and gives diligent heed to try the cause of the poor, and will judge justly, without respect of men, who justifies the good, and gives praise to the Well-doer; such Government and Governours we reverence, where Sin and Iniquity is kept under, Drunkenness, Swearing, Murther, Quarrelling, and all the ways and works of the flesh are terrified, and a Well-doer praised and justified; this Government of men reaches to the witness of God in every man, and that answers to the justice and righteousness of all such Governours and Government, and these witness that they are of God." Edward Burroughs (1634-1663) was one of the founders of the Quaker movement; see P. Brodin, *Les Quakers en Amérique du Nord.*

14. M. Foucault, "La vérité et les formes juridiques," pp. 589-590/pp. 1457-1458, esp. p. 590/p. 1458; "Truth and Juridical Forms," p. 53: "A penal law must simply represent what is useful for society."

15. George Fox (1624-1691, founder of the Society of Friends) *An Autobiography,* ed., Rufus M. Jones (Philadelphia: Ferris and Leach, 1904) p. 87: "I saw also, that there was an ocean of darkness and death, but an infinite ocean of light and love, which flowed over the ocean of darkness. In that also I saw the infinite love of God, and I had great openings"; and p. 88: "For I had been brought through the very ocean of darkness and death, and through and over the power of Satan, by the eternal, glorious power of Christ."

16. Ibid., p. 101: "Now the Lord God opened to me by His invisible power that every man was enlightened by the divine Light of Christ, and I saw it shine through all." Foucault cites this passage also in *Surveiller et Punir,* p. 241 n. 4; *Discipline and Punish,* p. 318 n. 7, and links it directly to the emergence of the prison in New England: "'Every man', said Fox, 'is illuminated by the divine light and I have seen it shine through every man.' It was in the spirit of the Quakers and of Walnut Street that the prisons of Pennsylvania, Pittsburgh and Cherry Hill were organized from 1820."

17. Foucault develops this analysis of the prison and of the Philadelphia model in *Surveiller et Punir,* pp. 126-127; *Discipline and Punish,* pp. 123-125. His approach is based on several texts: *Visite à la prison de Philadelphie, ou* Énoncé *exact de la sage administration qui a lieu dans les divers departements de cette maison. Ouvrage où l'on trouve l'histoire successive de la réformation des loix pénales de la Pen[n]sylvanie, avec des observations sur l'impolitique et l'injustice des peines capitales, en forme de lettre à un ami, par Robert J. Turnbull. Traduit de l'anglais et augmenté d'un plan qui en offre les différentes parties, par le D. Petit-Radel* (Paris: Gabon, 1799 [Year VIII]); N. K. Teeters, *The Cradle of the Penitentiary: The Walnut Street Jail at Philadelphia, 1773-1835,* sponsored by the Pennsylvania Prison Society, 1955; J. T. Sellin, *Pioneering in Penology: The Amsterdam Houses of Correction in the Sixteenth and Seventeeth Centuries* (Philadelphia: University of Pennsylvania Press, 1944).

18. F.-A.-F de La Rochefoucauld-Liancourt, *Des Prisons de Philadelphie, par un Européen* (Paris: Du Pont, 1796 ["Year V of the Republic"]), p. 11. François-Alexandre-Frédéric, duc de La Rochefoucauld-Liancourt (1747-1827), educator and reformer, founded the École nationale supérieure des arts et métiers at Châlons. A royalist, La Rochefoucauld-Liancourt emigrates in 1792, first to England and then to the United States where he writes this book on prisons.

From his return to France in 1799, he engages in politics, becomes a member of the Society of Christian Morality, supporter of the abolition of slavery, and takes part in a commission of inquiry into the prisons.

19. Ibid., p. 14. See too above, p. 73 (footnote †, p, 72).

20. Ibid.

21. Ibid., p. 27.

22. See *Surveiller et Punir*, pp. 51-52; *Discipline and Punish*, pp. 47-48. Under the Roman Republic, the crime of *crimen maiestatis*, which will become the crime of lese majesty, designated any attack on the magistrates of the Roman people, and then, under the Empire, and especially with the development of the imperial cult under Tiberius, the notion also sanctions impiety towards the emperor. Fallen into disuse at the beginning of the Middle Ages, the notion of *crimen maiestatis* is reinvested by royal power with the rediscovery of Roman law, but maintains a certain fuzziness. At the end of the Middle Ages it underwent a considerable expansion characterized by its depersonalization: "it is the king's status that is in question and not the sovereign's person itself that is to be protected by an extensive definition of lese majesty"; J. Hoareau-Dodineau, *Die et le Roi. La répression du blasphème et de l'injure au roi à la fin du Moyen Âge* (Limoges: Presses universitaires de Limoges, 2002) pp. 169-211, see p. 205. See: Y. Thomas, "L'Institution de la Majesté," *Revue de synthèse*, 1991, nos. 3-4, pp. 331-386; J. Chiffoleau, "Sur le crime de majesté médiéval" in *Genèse de l'État moderne en Méditerranée. Approches historique et anthropologique des pratiques et des représentations* (Rome: "Collection de l'École française de Rome," 1993) pp. 183-213.

23. See J. R. Strayer, *On the Medieval Origins of the Modern State*, pp. 29-30.

24. F.-A.-F. de La Rochefoucauld-Liancourt, *Des prisons de Philadelphie, par un Européen*, pp. 15-16.

25. See N. H. Julius, *Leçons sur les prisons*. In the manuscript (fol. 13) Foucault refers not only to Julius, but also to "Charles Lucas"; see above, p. 78 note 25.

six

7 FEBRUARY 1973

*The penitentiary, dimension of all the contemporary social
controls. (I) The generalization and conditions of acceptability
of the prison-form. (A) England. Spontaneous groups for
ensuring order: 1. Quakers and Methodists; 2. Societies for the
suppression of vice; 3. Self-defense groups; 4. Private police.* ⌒
*New system of control: inculcate conduct, moralize and control
the* lower classes.[*] *Colquhoun,* A Treatise on the Police
of the Metropolis *(1797). Three principles: 1. Morality
as foundation of the penal system; 2. Need for State-police;
3. Police target the lower classes.* ⌒ *Conclusions: 1. State as
agent of morality; 2. Links with the development of capitalism;
3. The coercive as prison's condition of acceptability.* ⌒
*Present movements of moral dissidence: dissolving the penality-
morality link.*

[†]I HAVE STRESSED THE fact that the prison was born in the element
of the penitentiary because of the tendency of some historians to say that
the prison existed for a long time as an empty form in which individuals
were shut up, with the prison having no other function than to soak up
this population that one wanted to be rid of, and that it was after negative

---

[*] [In English in original; G.B.]

[†] The manuscript (fol. 1) has the title: "Generalization of the prison." The first sentence states:
"Generalization is not the right word."
Then: "Quaker imprisonment is not a practice that would be widely imitated ... Walnut Street is
more the contemporary, than the first, of a series of events of the same type."

experience and research that the penitentiary was [added] to the prison in order to rectify its effects, to reform it, as a way of adapting it to social requirements that appear later. The penitentiary element would thus be what corrected the prison. Now, there are two operations behind this reading: first, making it seem that the development of a penitentiary system and of something one is not afraid to call penitentiary science corrects the prison; that penitentiary knowledge constitutes a domain of experience sufficiently independent of the prison for it to be able to influence and rectify it. Now, precisely inasmuch as the penitentiary is not an element added on to the prison, but an element within which the prison is born, any development of knowledge arising in this dimension can only consolidate the prison. Everything formulated in the domain of the experience of penitentiary knowledge and theory belongs already to the element that gave rise to the prison. The second operation is the masking of the fact that the penitentiary is in reality a much broader phenomenon than imprisonment, that what is involved is a general dimension of all the social controls that characterize societies like ours. The penitentiary element, of which the prison is only one expression, is a feature of the whole of society. The penitentiary is therefore the prison's associated field.

I would like to show how this prison-form was generalized. To tell the truth, generalization is not a very good notion, because I do not think that the prison was a form born on the other side of the Atlantic and then widely copied, losing the features of its original location and religious origin. I think, rather, that the Quaker prison is contemporary with a series of events of the same type; let us recall the whole network of exchanges that took place very early on between America and Europe regarding prisons.* We would also need to see when it was, no doubt around [1780], that the prison visit appeared in travel accounts (those of John Howard for example[2]), [in] the economic, social, and demographic inquiries that were made then and were one of the great

---

* The manuscript (fol. 1) adds:

   "- between England and America, religious sects and societies were agents of diffusion;
   - between France and America, a whole series of more political exchanges before and during the Revolution. // L[a] R[ochefoucauld-]Liancourt (1796): *Prisons de Philadelphie*."[1]

instruments of the formation of social knowledge. This is the network that served as support to the generalization of the model.

Actually, in a domain like the history of ideas it has to be recognized that influence can never be considered a cause.* It is only ever a determinate phenomenon, that is to say, there is transfer from one domain to another, from one time to another, only where there is, of course, a network of communication, but also where there is the possibility of *extracting* the model, and of what could be called *acceptability* where it is received.† How does it come about that something can in actual fact be inserted and accepted within a field? That is to say, all the problems of influence are in fact governed by the more fundamental problem of acceptability. So what was it that made [the prison-form] acceptable in countries like France and England, and even in countries as remote from Quaker thought as Austria, where, in 1787, Joseph II published a code in which the prison is the general form of punishment?[3] How did this transplant of the prison into juridical, religious, social, and political systems that were so foreign to it come about? I will take two reference points, England and France, to study the conditions of acceptability that made possible the generalization of the prison-form and the penitentiary domain in the eighteenth century.‡

---

* Manuscript (fol. 2): "Rather we should look for the conditions on which these transfers and exchanges were possible."
† The manuscript (fol. 2) adds: "The fact of influence requires, as prior determination, definition of

- the vehicle and trajectory of the transfer;
- the constant elements that form the model;
- the conditions that make extracting the model possible and, at its point of arrival, its insertion and acceptance.

Influences: these are the local and limited effects of general conditions of *extraction* and *acceptability*."
‡ Manuscript (fols. 2-3): "In the case of the prison and penitentiary system, how, in a few years, could the punitive prototype formed in a Quaker milieu in America be accepted

- in England, despite a fairly widespread distrust of the Quakers;
- in France, to which these religious forms were foreign;
- and finally in the whole of Europe. The 1787 Code in Austria.

Two examples of the process that assured the acceptability of the "penitentiary" in European society; its transplant into juridical and religious systems that were heterogeneous to it; and its effects of reorganization of the whole penal system.
The invasion and complete redistribution of the penal by the penitentiary.

$*$ $*$ $*$

[I will begin with England.] From the end of the seventeenth century, there were other groups alongside the Quakers that explicitly adopted the aim of supervision, control, and punishment. They were groups[*] that were not organized from above and that took on the task of maintaining *order* or, anyway, of defining new types of order and seeking the appropriate instruments for ensuring this order. We can define four major types. First, the dissident religious communities. Among these, in the forefront, were the Quakers and the Methodists.[4] These groups had a double function of order; on the one hand, to ensure a number of tasks of repression and moral sanction within the group. Thus, the Methodist groups led by Wesley[5] in the second half of the eighteenth century received regular visits from inspectors of morality who examined all the cases of disorder—adultery, refusal to work, drunkenness—and imposed sanctions. It was an endogenous collective control of individual morality. On the other hand, to ensure an external control, inasmuch as there was the question of providing for the needs of all the equivocal, shifting elements that could circulate on the fringes of groups: the unemployed, destitute, disabled, mad (we may recall that the first clinic in England was opened near York by the Society of Friends).[6]

Second, societies more indirectly attached to religious communities. Thus, the "Society for the Reformation of Manners," which, before its disappearance in 1737, had more than 100 affiliates; it resumed its activities in 1760 under the influence of Wesley and the Methodists.[†] It set itself a number of objectives: Sunday observance, that is to say preventing popular entertainments, going to the tavern, meeting there, and spending money; preventing gambling and drunkenness, sources of spending and obstacles to work; suppressing prostitution and anything that may threaten the family; repressing bad language. In 1763, Wesley said to one of his groups that the main task of the

---

How these little men [in] black, who did not take off their hats, can be seen as ancestors in the genealogy of our morality."

[*] Manuscript (fol. 4): "spontaneous groups (at any rate, not organized from above)."

[†] The manuscript (fol. 5) refers to the "Society for the reformation of manners (1692-1737)." It adds that it had "100 branches at the time of the death of William III; of which ten in Dublin" and that the society "started up again around 1755."[7]

association was to prevent "the lowest and vilest class of society from seizing on young inexperienced men and extorting money from them."[8] These societies multiply at the end of the eighteenth century. In 1787, William Wilberforce[9] urges the King to make a famous "Proclamation for the Encouragement of Piety and Virtue; and for the Preventing of Vice, Profaneness and Immorality." Following this, Wilberforce creates the "Proclamation Society," transformed in 1802 into the "Society for the Suppression of Vice," which lasts until 1820.[*] It aimed to impose Lord's Day observance, to prevent the publication of licentious books, and to close gambling houses and brothels. These societies were different from the first in that, not being religious societies, they were not concerned with establishing the reign of an endogenous discipline. Their members are, by definition, statutorily virtuous. Controls are exercised solely over external elements, and in two ways: on the one hand, by a number of interventions, pressures, and threats; and on the other, if the former fail, by moving on to a second kind of intervention in the courts: denunciation, prosecution. Here we have an intervention that focuses essentially on morality, the first form of which is in the realm of moral advice, exhortation, but the second is purely juridical, as if the aim of these societies was to force the hand of judicial power so as to ensure the suture between the domains of morality and legality.

Third, paramilitary self-defense groups, which appear late around 1799, at a time when England begins to be shaken by a number of popular movements.[†] Thus, around 1780, the inhabitants of areas of London organized themselves into patrols and ensured superintendence and moral order; they were recruited essentially from notables and the high bourgeoisie.[‡] In parallel, there is a whole literature

---

[*] The manuscript (fol. 5) refers to the "*Proclamation Society*" and to the "*Society for the Suppression of Vice*" (which had up to 600 members)."[10]

[†] The manuscript (fol. 6) adds:

"- after the great economic, religious, and political riots of the end of the century (*Gordon Riots*) - and to struggle against Jacobin influence."[11]

[‡] The manuscript (fol. 6) gives several examples:

"- After the Gordon Riots (1780) the inhabitants [*"principals"*] of St. Leonard organize into patrols of 10-14. They ask to arm themselves. The government encourages all *"persons of note"*; - City Association, Horse and Men. Light Horse Volunt[eer]s, London Military Foot Association, London Artillery Company;

that encourages these societies. We should note that, twenty years later, these notables will have found a quite different formula: using precisely the poorest people to carry out these tasks; they will then have invented the police.

Finally, fourth, groups of a primarily economic character: a sort of private police charged with superintending bourgeois wealth in the new forms in which it is exposed at the height of a period of economic development (warehouses, docks, roads). Thus, at the end of the eighteenth century, the shipping companies create a kind of police superintendence of the port in London.

To what does this proliferation of moral kinds of societies correspond? It is a period of economic development, that is to say, first of all, of population movements. Economic development disrupts the old territorial organizations—market towns, justices of the peace, parishes—by emptying them of their population. And, in some of the big towns, on the other hand, groups of unorganized individuals attach themselves to an urban center that cannot frame them within its own organizations or assimilate them. Now, not only are people displaced, but at the same time wealth is fixed differently: increasingly capital is invested in machinery and stock. The division of labor means that the circulation of goods in large quantities and at successive stages of elaboration and transformation results in them being located at increasingly massive points—warehouses, docks—so that, at the very moment that the capitalist mode of production is developing, capital is exposed to a number of risks that previously were much more controllable. Capital is exposed not only to armed robbery and plunder, as before, but to daily depredation by those who live on it, alongside it.* Depredation by those who handle this wealth thus exposed in a new way, due to the division of labor and the extent of markets and stocks, is one of the reasons why it will be necessary to establish a different order, a different way of controlling populations and preventing the practice of the transfer of

---

- Hanway (in a book of 1775 republished in 1780) proposes militia of 23 persons, *'opulent and of the community'*." [words in italics in English in manuscript; G.B.].[12]

* The manuscript (fol. 7) adds: "The organization of these circuits with important storage points and the treatment of large quantities entails the organization of a new apparatus of control."

property. The problem is one of the moral training of populations: their manners must be reformed so as to reduce the risks to bourgeois wealth.

Now the English regime does not offer such guarantees. Due to the weakness of the central power, there is, on the one hand, a micro-territoriality of judicial bodies and instruments of penality that cannot move around and follow the movements of wealth, and, on the other, an extremely strict penal code,* established in the seventeenth century when royal power tried to recapture its power by increasing the severity of the laws, and which, operating in terms of all or nothing, is completely unsuitable and eludes the grasp of precisely those who want to make use of it.[13] Thus courts, employing the technique of pious perjury, often avoid applying the penalty by disqualifying the crime.[14] Also, when accumulation is exposing wealth to new risks, a whole series of remedial organisms are needed, and these are, precisely, these associations.

So, there is at this time a search for, and organization of, a new system of control with the following general characteristics. In the first place, it is a system situated on the borders of morality and penality. The primary function of these societies is not so much to detect and punish crime as first to attack moral faults, and, even before this, psychological propensities, habits, manners, and behavior such as idleness, gambling, and debauchery. It [also] involves attacking the conditions and instruments that facilitate these faults, like drinking dens, gambling, lotteries, and brothels. Finally, it involves not only producing something like a penal sanction, but something much more positive and continuous. It involves teaching, inculcating conduct, as Burke said at the end of the eighteenth century: "Patience, labor, sobriety, frugality, and religion are what should be taught."[15] Similarly, in an essay of 1804, Boadman writes: "The difficulty is, how to prevail upon a people, who have been long accustomed to a life of idleness, extravagance, and dissipation, to overcome its allurements, and to lead with steadiness and perseverance a life of temperance, moderation, and virtue: this, indeed, is difficult, but absolutely necessary."[16]

Now when we consider the objectives of these societies and the way in which they operated, what is interesting is that we see a kind of "re-

---

* The manuscript (fol. 8) adds: "(a 'bloody chaos')."

moralization" arising "from below," in petit bourgeois groups.* And this enterprise shifts considerably, and at an accelerated pace, in the second half of the eighteenth century. First of all, it shifts through these societies' recruitment, so at the level of their social insertion. At the beginning of the century, their recruitment is, above all, petit bourgeois; at the end of the century, as in the "Proclamation Society" or that "for the Suppression of Vice," it is great notables, Lords, and representatives of the Anglican Church. [It is] as if, through the aristocracy, these societies were increasingly getting closer to power itself, to the State apparatus, as if they were beginning to be taken charge of by those who held State power. Then, [it shifts] through the way these groups act. In effect, if, to start with, Quaker and Methodist groups practice a sort of moral control over themselves or their immediate neighborhood, this is because the first and most important question for them is escaping the application of such a heavy penal system. When you think about it, the self-defense of these groups is quite ambiguous: it involves repressing wrongdoing so that power does not encroach upon them. The Quakers try therefore to introduce not just a religious, but almost a penal, judicial dissidence. Now at the end of the eighteenth century the objective of these societies is modified at the same time as their social recruitment changes: they campaign for new decrees, new laws, for the intervention of judicial power as such.† They act as pressure groups on power, and no longer [as] groups of self-defense against power.

Finally, [they shift] at the level of their object: at the beginning of the century, these groups were basically concerned with controlling marginal, dubious, restless, wandering elements, and so on; at the end of the century, those designated as having to be the object of moral control are the "lower classes" as such. Let us complete Burke's sentence: "Patience, labor, sobriety, frugality, and religion are what should be taught," this is what "should be recommended to the laboring poor."[17] At the start of the century one would have spoken only of the poor, those who do not work (the idle, the unemployed); now it is a matter of the

---

* Typescript (p. 89): "in groups like the Quakers, the Methodists." Given the context, which refers to security associations in England, and not only to the previous religious groups, we quote the manuscript (fol. 9).

† The manuscript (fol. 10) adds two examples: "for a law for Sunday" and "for the organization of a docks police."

developing working class. And, in 1804, the Bishop Watson, preaching before the Society for the Suppression of Vice said: "The laws are good: but they are eluded by the *lower classes*; and the *higher classes* hold them for nothing (*for nought*)."[18],* Now there is a difference between these classes in the sense that Watson wants the upper classes to observe the laws also; not because the laws are general, but because having to bear mainly upon the lower classes, the example of their observance by the higher classes is the instrument by which one will be able to get the lowest classes to observe them also.[19] The obedience of the Great is not in itself an end;† their immorality is not in itself a problem—it is in danger of becoming one insofar as their example may be an excuse for the *lower classes*‡ not to obey the laws.[20] Things are even clearer in a public address of the Society for the Suppression of Vice, in 1802: it is not just a question of controlling the low and laboring classes morally, but of controlling them politically, in terms of the dangers of revolt.§

We have, then, a double movement: on the one hand, through these groups of control and superintendence, there is a junction of the moral and the penal. Now in the theory of criminal law that appears at the end of the eighteenth century with Beccaria and Bentham, there is a break between moral wrongdoing and infraction. All the theorists of penal law separate the two: for them, laws do not have to punish the moral conduct of people; they are concerned only with the utility of society and not individual morality. Now, at the same time, we have all this practice of spontaneous superintendence organized by groups and, finally, by one class of another, a whole practice of superintendence that attempts to re-moralize penality and invest it in a kind of moral atmosphere, in short, that seeks to establish continuity between moral control and repression on the one hand, and the penal sanction on the other. So what we see is a moralization of the penal system, despite the practice and discourse of this system. All this movement allows penality

---

* [Words in italics in English in original; G.B.]

† The manuscript (fol. 10) adds: "it is an instrument so that the inferiors obey."

‡ [English in original; G.B.]

§ The manuscript (fols. 10-11) presents this passage in the form of a quotation: "In a public address of the Society for the Suppression of Vice (1802): 'All cases of sedition, or others of a political nature, should such occasionally be disclosed by their vigilance, they will transmit to the Magistrates, or to the officers of government, whose peculiar duty it is, to take cognizance of offences committed against the state'."[21]

to spread widely into everyday life. On the other hand, and at the same time, we have a second, very important movement by which the demand for moralization shifts towards the State: a movement of takeover by the State. The upper classes, insofar as they control power, are the bearers of this demand, whereas the laboring and lower classes become the point of application of the moralization of penality. The State sees itself called upon to become the instrument* of the moralization of these classes.

In short, we have a moralization of penality; a distribution of the classes on both sides of this penal morality; and State control of the instruments of the latter. We have an example of this movement in the figure of Colquhoun,[22] in whose work we see the appearance of what will determine Western morality—unfortunately, when we teach morality, when we study the history of morals, we always analyze the *Groundwork of the Metaphysics of Morals*[23] and do not read this character who is fundamental for our morality. The inventor of the English police, this Glasgow merchant, returns after a period in Virginia and becomes President of the Chamber of Commerce; he then settles in London where, in 1792, shipping companies ask him to solve the problem of superintendence of the docks and protection of bourgeois wealth. [This is a] basic problem, [as we shall see with] Bentham's brother;[24] to understand a society's system of morality we have to ask the question: Where is the wealth? The history of morality should be organized entirely by this question of the location and movement of wealth.

In 1795, Colquhoun writes his *A Treatise on the Police of the Metropolis*,[25] in which the guiding principles of these societies are theorized and systematized.† The first principle is that the foundation of a penal system must be morality. Precisely when Beccaria, Brissot, and others‡ are saying that there is no relationship between morality and law, Colquhoun writes: "Nothing contributes in a greater degree to deprave the minds of the people, than the little regard which Laws pay to Morality; by inflicting more severe punishments on offenders who commit, what may be termed, *Political Crimes*, and crimes against property, than on those

---

* The manuscript (fol. 12) adds: "(by the laws it defines, or the police it introduces)."
† The manuscript (fol. 12) notes that Colquhoun is "linked to the religious sects" and "responsible in a semi-private capacity with the dock police, which he completely reorganizes."
‡ The manuscript (fol. 13) adds here Bentham's name: "Direct opposition to Bentham, Beccaria."

who violate religion and virtue."[26] And Colquhoun, just when he is contradicting the theory of penal law, turns its propositions around, for he adds that the law is useful to society precisely to the extent that it takes morality into consideration*.[27] Where Beccaria says that the law does not deal with morality inasmuch as it is concerned only with the interest of society, Colquhoun says that the law deals with social interest to the extent that it sanctions morality: "Those men are easily seduced from their Loyalty who are apostates from private virtue";[28] "The Laws are armed against the *powers* of Rebellion, but are not calculated to oppose its *principle*."[29]

Second principle: if the law must be especially concerned with morality, and if it is essential to the safety of the State and the exercise of its sovereignty, an authority is needed to superintend, not the application of the laws, but, well before that, the morality of individuals. The laws are then no more than that which gives such superintending bodies the possibility of intervening and acting at the level of morality:[†] "Wherever proper police attaches, good order and security will prevail; where it does not, confusion, irregularity, outrages, and crimes must be expected."[30] It needs "*an active principle, calculated to concentrate and connect the whole Police[‡] of the Metropolis and the nation; and to reduce the general management to system and method, by the interposition of a superintending agency, composed of able, intelligent, and indefatigable men.*"[31]

Third principle: the specific target of this agency will be the *lower classes*:[§] "wherever great bodies of aquatic laborers are collected together, risk of danger from turbulent behavior, will be greater in proportion to the number of depraved characters, who, from being collected in one spot, may hatch mischief, and carry it into effect much easier in Docks than on the River."[32] Political conspiracies, the concentration of workers in the factory, in the workers' cities, we have here all the themes of the police in the nineteenth century. As Colquhoun adds, police "is quite a new science in political œconomy."[33]

---

* The manuscript (fol. 13-14) states: "the principle that control of morality is even the best possible protection for the State."

† Manuscript (fol. 14): "A State body is needed to control morality. This is the police."

‡ According to the typescript (p. 94), Foucault says: "the surveillance" instead of "the police," which is the word used in the manuscript (fol. 14) and the translation cited.

§ [English in original; G.B.]

We can draw a number of [conclusions] from this. First, we have here a process of the superimposition of ethical and penal codes that takes place in the course of the eighteenth century. Its agents are more or less spontaneous groups, but which, gradually expanding and drawing close to the upper classes, and so to power, end up transferring to the State itself and to a specific body—the police—the task of exercising a whole set of controls of everyday life. In this way the State becomes the basic agent of morality, of ethical-juridical supervision and control. Second, we can sense the links between these movements and the development of capitalism:* the progressive application of this control solely to the lower classes and, finally, to the workers; the links between this process and the struggle against the new forms of depredation linked to the new risks to wealth being capitalized.† Third, we should also note that, behind these specifically legal prohibitions, there is the development of a range of everyday constraints that focus on behavior, manners, and habits, and the effect of which is not to sanction something like an infraction, but to act on individuals positively, to transform them morally, to bring about a correction. Thus, what is installed is not just an ethical-juridical control, a State control to the advantage of a class, it is something like the *coercive* factor. We are dealing with a form of coercion that differs from the penal sanction, an everyday coercion that focuses on ways of being and seeks to bring about a certain correction of individuals. The coercive is what establishes a connection between morality and penality. Its target is not just the infractions of individuals, but their nature, their character. It must have permanent and fundamental supervision (*surveillance*) as its instrument.‡ Now the coercive is very close to and homogeneous with what I have called the penitentiary. The penitentiary, which is spread throughout the prisons, is basically like the extension, the "natural" sanction [of the] coercive. When the latter comes up against its limit and has to pass from pedagogy to punishment, it produces the penitentiary, which takes over the functions of the coercive, but by getting them to operate within a

---

* The manuscript (fol. 16) adds: "more exactly the establishment of the political instruments of capitalism."

† The manuscript (fol. 16) adds: "all this will suffice to prove it. But it needs to be analyzed in more detail."

‡ Manuscript (fol. 16): "permanent and total."

punitive system of the prison.* Prison is the place where the general principles of coercion, the forms, theses, and conditions of coercion, are concentrated for use on those who sought to escape coercion. Prison is the intensification, in the form of the penitentiary, of the system of coercion.

Thus we can begin to answer the question: How was the prison, with its penitentiary horizon, which arose in such a singular and localized religious community, able to spread [in this way] and acquire the institutional scale we are familiar with? The *coercive* is precisely the condition of the prison's acceptability.† If the prison, with its geographical and religious features, was able to insert itself into the penal system, it is because capitalism utilized coercion in setting up its specific forms of political power. We have therefore two ensembles: the penal ensemble, characterized by the prohibition and the sanction, the law; and the punitive ensemble, characterized by the coercive penitentiary system. The first ensemble brings with it a certain theory of the infraction as an act of hostility towards society; the second brings with it the practice of confinement. The first is deduced, in an archeologically correct fashion, from the State institutionalization of justice, which means that, from the Middle Ages, we have a practice of justice organized by reference to the exercise of sovereign political power: this gives procedures of inquisition, the intervention of someone like the prosecutor, and so on. A theory of the infraction as act of hostility towards the sovereign was derived from this whole practical ensemble. The other ensemble is formed in a movement of development, not of the State itself, but of the capitalist mode of production; in this second system, we see this mode of production provide itself with the instruments of a political power,‡ but also of a moral power. The genealogical problem then, is how these two ensembles, of different origin, came to be added to each other and function within a single tactic.[34]

Fourth, there were groups within which the connection of the punitive and the penal was carried out.§ These are those non-conformist

---

* Manuscript (fol. 17): "The transition from the coercive to its regime of punishment gives the penitentiary."
† The manuscript (fol. 17) adds: "(and of the penitentiary system connected to it)."
‡ The manuscript (fol. 17) adds: "new."
§ Manuscript (fol. 18): "Importance of these groups through which the connection of the punitive

and religious groups* that imposed this connection on the State from outside, that demanded that the State assure it. They set out to moralize society regardless of the State,† or at any rate, with its help if it agreed, and, when they wished to moralize society, it turned out that in fact they had brought morality under State control and made the State the principal agent of moralization.

*   *   *

There is a kind of historical symmetry between this eighteenth-century dissidence and the present-day movement of "moral dissidence" in Europe and the United States. Thus, the [movements] that struggle for the right to abortion, to the formation of non-familial sexual groups, to idleness‡—that is to say all those who struggle for the de-culpabilization of penal infractions and against the actual functioning of the penal system—are, in a sense, doing the symmetrical and opposite of those in the eighteenth century who devoted themselves to the task of linking together morality, capitalist production, and State apparatus.[35] The function of present-day groups is to undo this. This is what distinguishes them from the "non-conformists," from those who, in the name of transgression, ignore the law or wish to consider it unreal. The point of attack of the former is where there is an intrication of a morality, certain power relationships peculiar to capitalist society, and instruments of control assured by the State.§ To struggle against coercion is not the same as breaking the taboo, and one cannot take the place of the other. To practice transgression is for a person, in a place, for a moment, to render the law unreal and powerless;[36] to engage in dissidence¶ is to attack this connection, this coercion.

---

and the penal, of the coercive and the prohibition, of penance and the sanction, was carried out."
* Manuscript (fol. 18) adds: "(at least in England)."
† Manuscript (fol. 18) adds: "or, at least, the sovereign."
‡ The manuscript (fol. 18) adds: "the right to homosexuality" and "the right to drugs."
§ The manuscript (fol. 19) adds: "It is a matter of undoing what the "dissidents" of the eighteenth century tied together (morality, defense of capitalist production, State control). Undoing that by which the capitalist mode of production was organized into a system of power."
¶ Manuscript (fol. 19): "'To engage in moral dissidence' is then not at all 'to practice transgression': the one cannot take the place of the other. Similarly, 'to struggle against coercion' is not at all 'to break the taboo.' In one case it is a matter of rendering the law unreal and powerless for

Think of the demonstration by abortion doctors and of the response of the Minister, Foyer, who made this quite extraordinary statement: it is altogether regrettable that the doctors' manifesto appeared during the election, because the problem of abortion is a problem of legislation and so must be dealt with in calm and reflection; since it is a problem of legislation, it cannot be raised during the election.[37] So we have the following: a minister who, in a regime in which the deputies are no more than legislators and elected, does not want the problem to be addressed by those who elect the legislators. The deputies must be elected without their electors having raised the question with them. This is precisely because a moral distance is introduced regarding abortion: what the government means when it says that only elected deputies are able to take care of the issue, but not those who elect them, is that the ethical-juridical problem of abortion is not a matter for the explicit choice of individuals, not a matter for the national will itself. This is because the law prohibiting abortion is a basic law that cannot be tampered with by the elector, whereas the Constitution may at least be modified by referendum; so it is like a natural law, since the elector cannot tamper with it, but it is not like a natural law, since it can be changed, but without electors demanding that their deputies do so. To say that the deputies can change the law without their electors having any control over this, is to say that the change can be a matter only for power and those elected, not as representatives of a real national will, but as agents of a power that precisely exceeds their mandate, since it cannot be fixed by electoral mandate. So it is only at the level of the exercise of power that something like abortion legislation can be modified.

This reveals the way in which the system of morality and the actual exercise of power have been tied to each other since the nineteenth century. The conclusion to be drawn from this is that morality does not exist in people's heads; it is inscribed in power relations and only the modification of these power relations can bring about the modification of morality.*

---

a moment. In the other case (engaging in dissidence), it is a matter of attacking, undoing the connection: morality-capitalist power-the State. Illegality has to be an instrument in the anti-coercive struggle."

* The last sheet of the manuscript (fol. 21) adds: "All in all: a whole coercive-penitentiary system very broadly typical of our society, and in which the prison figures as an important component

APPENDIX

The manuscript of the sixth lecture ends with five unnumbered sheets which contain the following:
"- State takeover of penal justice.
- Constitution of a disciplinary society that also gives rise to certain types of knowledge (*savoir*).
This formation is characterized by two apparently contradictory facts. Or rather one fact: the reform of the penal system, which has two strongly contradictory aspects.

A. A new penal theory
Beccaria, Bentham, Le Peletier [de] Saint-Fargeau
1. No relationship between crime and moral wrongdoing
- there is wrongdoing in relation to a moral, natural, religious law;
- there is crime only in relation to a civil law, once the law is formulated.
And this civil law defines what is useful to society.
Crime, social nuisance; disorder, trouble.
The criminal is the social enemy. Breach of the social pact.

2. The law that punishes must in any case install:
• a vengeance
• a redemption

3. Punishment must therefore be calculated so that injury to society is made up for or so that no one has an interest in imposing a similar injury
Hence four types of punishment
• transportation
• forced labor
• talion
• shame

B. Now in fact we see something entirely different appear

(both instrument and historical model). An accepted model. The coercive, condition of acceptability of the penitentiary."

A prison system that does not correspond
- completely to an exclusion,
- or to social reparation,
- or to talion.

Legislation increasingly focused
- not on social utility,
- but on the individual.

A penality that increasingly proposes both
- control of individuals,
- and their reform.

And which thereby, instead of sanctioning only infractions, sanctions individuals, potentialities, qualities.
Dangerous individual.

And thereby, instead of coming under an autonomous judicial power, penality [passes] through a whole network of institutions
- of surveillance-police
- of correction: pedagogical, psychological, psychiatric, medical.
Social orthopedics.
Social controls.

Panopticism: the different uses of the Panopticon
- universal surveillance,
- constant correction.
The Panopticon as utopia.

Panopticism as form of power, but also
type of knowledge
the Examination.
Inquiry: knowing events—according to witnesses, according to observation criteria.
Examination: knowing individuals according to observation by power-holders and criteria of normality.

Reasons for the growth and State takeover of controls:
- a new demographic state, but especially
- a new form of the materiality of wealth
• industrial
• landed.
Illegalisms."

1. See F.-A.-F. de La Rochefoucauld-Liancourt, *Des prisons de Philadelphie, par un Européen*; see also, J.-G. Petit *et al.*, *Histoire de galères, bagnes et prisons*, p. 134.

2. In 1773, the English philanthropist, John Howard (see above, p. 76 notes 13 and 14) became the High Sheriff of Bedfordshire and, in this capacity, discovered the conditions of local prisons. In particular he found that many prisoners, declared innocent by their judges, were still incarcerated due to their inability to pay the sum owed to their jailers. He tried to convince the county Justices of Peace of the need to raise a tax to pay the jailers, a request that was rejected on the grounds of the absence of a precedent. From 1773 until his death in 1790, Howard undertook many journeys in the British Isles and the rest of Europe visiting their prisons. See J. Howard, *The State of the Prisons in England and Wales etc.*, 1777, augmented edition 1784. His work had considerable influence in the United Kingdom and Europe, resulting in particular in the adoption of several reforms by the British Parliament, including the remuneration of jailers through taxation. See C. Carlier and J.-G. Petit, "Avant-propos" to J. Howard, *L'État des prisons, des hôpitaux et des maisons de force en Europe au XVIIIᵉ siècle*, new translation and critical edition by Christian Carlier and Jacques-Guy Petit (Paris: Les Éditions de l'Atelier/Éditions ouvrièrs, 1994) pp. 9-66; J. Aikin, *A View of the Life, Travels and Philanthropic Labours of the Late John Howard, Esq., L.L.D., F.R.S.*, (Boston, MA: Maning & Moring, 1794); F. Gaëtan de La Rochefoucauld-Liancourt, *Vie de John Howard* (Paris: Dondey-Dupré, 1840); A. Rivière, "Howard. Sa vie, son œuvre," *Revue pénitentiaire*, 1891, pp. 651-680; L. Baumgartner, *John Howard (1726-1790), Hospital and Prison Reformer: A Bibliography* (Baltimore, MD: The Johns Hopkins Press, 1939).

   In England, the practice of travel accounts is part more generally of the "rage for travel [which] seized on Englishmen," particularly with the practice of the "Grand Tour," an educational journey across Europe—mainly in Italy and France—by wealthy young aristocrats in the seventeenth and eighteenth centuries: see G. M. Trevalyan, *English Social History. A Survey of Six Centuries: Chaucer to Queen Victoria* (London: Pelican Books, 1967) p. 399. In this vein, between 1724 and 1726 Daniel Defoe published *A Tour Through the Whole Island of Great Britain* (London: J. M. Dent and Co., 1927), an account of his travels in the British Isles which is focused on the economy but describes, "by the way," the prisons of London, in which the author had briefly been an inmate. John Howard's writings are on the fringes of this tradition insofar as their subject matter is restricted to penitentiary matters.

3. Influenced by Beccaria's *On Crimes and Punishments* (1764), the Austrian Penal Code, promulgated by Joseph II in 1787, is marked by a softening of the repressive arsenal. The principles of legality and proportionality of penalties are affirmed. The imperial code established a strict distinction between criminal and political offences, and the death penalty is limited solely to the "crime of sedition judged by a war council"; J.-L. Halpérin, *Histoire des droits en Europe de 1750 à nos jours*, p. 62; see *Surveiller et Punir*, p. 119; *Discipline and Punish*, p. 117. Detention—alone, with irons, or with public labor—was one of the pillars of the sanction of criminal offences; see Y. Cartuyvels, *D'où vient le code pénal? Une approche généalogique des premiers codes pénaux absolutistes au XVIIIᵉ siècle* (Paris-Brussels: De Boeck, 1996) pp. 264-300.

4. Founded under the influence of John Wesley (1703-1791), the Methodist societies were the most important non-conformist movement in the eighteenth century. When Wesley died in 1791 these societies had 72,000 members, which increased to a million and a half in 1850. See J. Cannon, ed., *The Oxford Companion to British History* (Oxford: Oxford University Press, 1997) p. 339. Theologically, the Methodist movement is characterized by its emphasis on personal conversion and salvation through faith, as well as a certain doctrinal flexibility. See E. P. Thompson, *The Making of the English Working Class*, pp. 37-38. A largely working-class movement, the various Methodist churches played an important social role—although sometimes overestimated (see ibid., pp. 41-46)—in the formation of the workers'

movement in the eighteenth century, particularly through the education of the poor and their integration in the Church organization. See R. Southey, *Life of Wesley and the Rise and Progress of Methodism* (London: Harper and Brothers, 1890 [1846]) 3 volumes; W. E. H. Lecky, *History of the English People in the 18th Century* (New York: D. Appleton & Co., 1891) vol. III; J. Kent, *The Age of Disunity* (London: Epworth Press, 1966).

5. John Wesley (1703-1791) was the founder of Methodism. Ordained in the Anglican Church, from 1729 he gathered around himself in Oxford a group of Christians whose strict observance of the rules of life and study fixed by the Church gave them the name of "methodists." In 1738, after a short activity as missionary in Georgia, Wesley undertook to evangelize England, preaching not only in churches, but also in the open and in local religious societies. He was always opposed to the independence of Methodism vis-à-vis the Anglican Church, a break that occurred shortly after his death, in 1791. See R. Southey, *Life of Wesley and the Rise of Methodism*; M. Lelière, *John Wesley: sa vie, son œuvre* (Paris: Chapelle Malesherbes, 1922 [Librairie évangélique, 1883]); M. L. Edwards, *John Wesley and the Eighteenth Century* (New York: Abingdon Press, 1933); J. H. Whiteley, *Wesley's England: A Survey of XVIIIth Century Social and Cultural Conditions* (London: Epworth Press, 1938); J. Kent, *Wesley and the Wesleyans* (Cambridge: Cambridge University Press, 2002).

6. The Society of Friends is the official name of the Quaker movement; see above, p. 96, note 11.

7. John Pollock points out that the project of Wilberforce to found the Proclamation Society was inspired by the Societies for the Reformation of Manners, created, "for the encouragement of Piety and Virtue; and for the Preventing of Vice, Profaneness and Immorality," echoing the 1692 proclamation of William and Mary (publication having been delayed for three years from the beginning of the reign)—an act traditionally marking the accession to the throne of a new sovereign; see J. Pollock, *Wilberforce* (London: Constable, 1977) p. 59 (the author notes that the proclamations are available in *Handlist of Proclamations 1714-1800*, Bibliotheca Lindesiana, 1913). These societies are implanted in Ireland from 1693, where they are used to consolidate the power of the Anglicans against the Catholics. See D. W. R. Bahlman, *The Moral Revolution of 1688* (New Haven, CT: Yale University Press, 1957); J. Innes, "Politics and Morals: The Reformation of Manners Movement in Later Eighteenth-Century England" in Eckhart Hellmuth, ed., *The Transformation of Political Culture: England and Germany in the Late Eighteenth Century* (Oxford: Oxford University Press, 1990); T. C. Barnard, "Reforming Irish Manners: The Religious Societies in Dublin during the 1690s," *The Historical Journal*, vol. 35 (4), December 1992, pp. 805-838; A. Hunt, *Governing Morals: A Social History of Moral Regulation* (Cambridge: Cambridge University Press, 1999). On Wilberforce, see below, note 9.

8. [J. Wesley,] *The Works of the Reverend John Wesley, A.M., Sometime Fellow of Lincoln College, Oxford* (New York: J. Emory and B. Waugh, 1831) 7 volumes: vol. I, Sermon LII (preached before the Society for Reformation of Manners, on Sunday, January 30, 1763, at the Chapel in West Street, Seven Dials), p. 460: "Some of these were of the lowest and vilest class commonly called gamblers; who make a trade of seizing on young and inexperienced men, and tricking them out of all their money: and after they have beggared them, they frequently teach them the same mystery of iniquity." Foucault will come back to this passage some months later, in May 1973, in "La vérité et les formes juridiques," pp. 596-597/pp. 1464-1465; "Truth and Juridical Forms," p. 61.

9. English Protestant evangelist and politician, William Wilberforce (1759-1833) is better known for his commitment to the abolition of slavery, which he defended notably as Member of Parliament. Very conservative in his internal political commitments, he took part in the foundation of several evangelical societies including the Proclamation Society to Prosecute Blasphemy and Vice (1787) and the Society for Bettering the Condition of the Poor (1796). See: R. I. Wilberforce and S. Wilberforce, *The Life of William Wilberforce by his sons Robert Isaac Wilberforce and Samuel Wilberforce* (Cambridge: Cambridge University Press, 2011 [1838]); R.

Coupland, *Wilberforce: A Narrative* (Oxford: Clarendon Press, 1923); and more recently, W. Hague, *William Wilberforce: The Life of the Great Anti-slave Campaigner* (London, New York, Toronto: Harper Perennial, 2008).

10. See in particular: Society for the Suppression of Vice, *The Constable's Assistant: Being a Compendium of the Duties and Powers of Constables and Other Police Officers*, 1808 (augmented editions: 3rd ed., 1818, 4th ed., 1831); see "La vérité et les formes juridiques," p. 597/p. 1465; "Truth and Juridical Forms," p. 61.

11. In June 1780, the Gordon Riots broke out in London following the rejection by the House of Commons of a petition opposing concessions granted to Catholics, and particularly to admission to Parliament. Numerous acts of violence, directed essentially against rich Catholics and representatives of power, broke out in the following days. The London authorities of Wilkes, in conflict with royal power, only intervene late, when the rioters attack the Bank of England. The name of the riots comes from that of Lord George Gordon, president of the Protestant association which submitted the petition to the House, and to whose harangues a heavy responsibility in unleashing the violence was attributed. See: E. P. Thompson, *The Making of the English Working Class*, pp. 71-72; G. Rudé, "The Gordon Riots: A Study of the Rioters and their Victims," *Transactions of the Royal Historical Society*, 5th series, no. 6, 1956, pp. 3-114; C. Hibbert, *King Mob: The Story of Lord George Gordon and the Riots of 1780* (Stroud: Sutton Publishing, 2004 [1958]). Foucault refers again to the Gordon Riots in *Surveiller et Punir*, p. 18; *Discipline and Punish*, p. 12; see, too, "La vérité et les formes juridiques," pp. 597-598/pp. 1465-1466; "Truth and Juridical Forms," pp. 61-62.

12. See J. Hanway, *The Defects of Police. The Cause of Immorality and the Continual Robberies Committed: Particularly in and about the Metropolis* (London: J. Dodsley, 1775), cited in *Surveiller et Punir*, p. 125 and p. 130; *Discipline and Punish*, p. 123 and p. 314, n. 13.

13. On the severity of the law in England in the eighteenth century and the problems arising from this, see: D. Hay, "Property, Authority and the Criminal Law" in Douglas Hay, Peter Linebaugh, and E. P. Thompson, *Albion's Fatal Tree: Crime and Society in Eighteenth Century England* (New York: Pantheon Books, 1975); J. H. Langbein, "Albion's Fatal Flaws," *Past and Present*, no. 98 (1), pp. 96-120, republished in David Sugarman, ed., *Law in History: Histories of Law and Society* (New York: New York University Press, 1996) vol. 1.

14. The expression "pious perjury" seems to come from William Blackstone, who uses it to describe the practice of English juries of undervaluing on oath the monetary value of a theft so as not to have to apply a penalty they consider to be too severe; see W. Blackstone, *Commentaries on the Laws of England (1765-1769)* (London: A. Strahan, 1825) 4 volumes: vol. 4, p. 237. Bentham also reports that, the law providing for the death penalty in cases of theft exceeding a value of thirty-nine shillings, juries affirm on oath that two gold coins are worth less than that sum: "Take two pieces of gold coins, each of full weight, and, under the eye of an approving judge, to change the prisoner's doom from death to transportation, the two-and-forty shillings'-worth of coin be valued by twelve jurymen, speaking upon their oaths, and nine-and-thirty shillings, and no more"; J. Bentham, *Rationale of Judicial Evidence, Specially Applied to English Practice from the manuscripts of Jeremy Bentham*, in *Works*, ed., John Stuart Mill (London: Hunt and Clark, 1827) 5 volumes: vol. 5, p. 418.

15. E. Burke, "Thoughts and Details on Scarcity, Originally Presented to the Right Hon. William Pitt, in the Month of November, 1795" in *The Works of Edmund Burke* (Boston, MA: Charles C. Little and James Brown, 1839) 9 volumes: vol. 4, pp. 250-280, spec. p. 253: "Patience, labor, sobriety, frugality and religion, should be recommended to them [the laborers]; all the rest is downright *fraud*. It is horrible to call them 'The *once happy* laborer'."

16. A. Boadman, "On Population," "Essay XXV" in *Georgical Essays*, ed., Alexander Hunter (York: T. Wilson and R. Spence, 1804) vol. V, p. 398.

17. E. Burke, "Thoughts and Details on Scarcity," p. 253. Foucault plays on Burke's words, who wrote this passage precisely *against* the language "of the laboring poor." At the time, in 1795,

in a period of scarcity, Burke was engaged in a debate with William Pitt on the subject of the role of government and intellectuals—and more precisely, of the language of intellectuals and politicians—with regard to workers: "Nothing can be so base and so wicked as the political canting language, 'The laboring *poor.*' Let compassion be shewn in action, the more the better, according to every man's ability, but let there be no lamentation of their condition. It is no relief to their miserable circumstances; it is only an insult to their miserable understandings" (ibid., p. 252). In 1963, the Marxist historian, E. P. Thompson, linked Burke's remarks with the works of Patrick Colquhoun, particularly concerning his analysis of the question of delinquency and societies for the suppression of vice; see E. P. Thompson, "Satan's Strongholds" in *The Making of the English Working Class,* pp. 56-57.

18. R. Watson, "Sermon VII. Let Us Not Be Weary in Well-doing" in *Miscellaneous Tracts on Religious, Political, and Agricultural Subjects* (London: T. Cadell and W. Davies, 1815) 2 volumes, vol. 1, p. 537: "The laws are good: but they are eluded by the lower classes, and set at nought by the higher." Richard Watson (1737-1816), Bishop of Llandaff, read this sermon at Society for the Suppression of Vice at the parish church; see "A Sermon preached before the Society for the Suppression of Vice, in the Parish Church of St. George, Hanover Square, on Thursday the 3rd of May 1804; to which are added the Plan of the society, a summary of its proceedings, and a list of its members" (London: T. Woodfall, 1804); see, too, M. Foucault, "La vérité et les formes juridiques," p. 599/p. 1467; "Truth and Juridical Forms," pp. 63-64.

19. See R. Watson, "Sermon VII," pp. 537-538: "I would be ashamed to recommend from this place the Suppression of Vice amongst some, if I did not recommend its suppression amongst all; being sensible that the good example of their superiors would be of more efficacy in suppressing the Vices of the lower orders, than the very best execution of the very best laws even can be."

20. See ibid., pp. 539-540: "The suppression of Vice, though it may through your perseverance, when assisted by others who shall concur with you, be very extensive; yet it is not the only good which will be derived from your Association. The very circumstances of near a thousand persons become 'in the midst of a crooked and perverse generation, shining lights,' to conduct men ...—to conduct such unhappy, comfortless, benighted travellers into the narrow path which leads to Heaven; this is of itself a proof that Religion has not yet left the land ..."

21. Society for the Suppression of Vice, "Part the first, of an address to the public, from the Society for the Suppression of Vice, instituted in London, 1802: setting forth, with a list of the members, the utility and necessity of such an institution, and its claim to public support," (London: printed for the Society, 1803) p. 58 n.*.

22. Patrick Colquhoun (1745-1820) founded, in collaboration with Jeremy Bentham, the first regular police in England, the Thames River Police, responsible for protecting the goods of the merchants of the Port of London on the Thames. Thus he is considered as one of the inventors of the modern police in England, having laid the foundations of what will become, under the impetus of Robert Peel thirty years later, the new police of London. Colquhoun is the author, in 1797, of the text on which Foucault bases himself here: *A Treatise on the Police of the Metropolis* (London: H. Fry, 1797).

23. I. Kant, *Grundlegung zur Metaphysik der Sitten* (1785).

24. See above, p. 77, note 16.

25. P. Colquhoun, *Traité sur la police de Londres, contenant le détail des crimes et délits que se commettent dans cette capitale, et indiquant les moyens de les prévenir,* translated from the sixth English edition by L.C.D.B. (Paris: Léopold Collin, 1807) 2 volumes; P. Colquhoun, *A Treatise on the Police of the Metropolis; containing a detail of the Various Crimes and Misdemeanors By which Public and Private Property and Security are, at present, Injured and Endangered: and suggesting Remedies for their Prevention* (London: H. Baldwin, 1800, sixth edition). Foucault does not appear to return to the moral aspect of Colquhoun in *Surveiller et Punir,* although he cites the work at

several points (see p. 88, p. 119, and p. 291; *Discipline and Punish*, pp. 85-86, p. 313 n. 3, and p. 323 n. 21.

26. *A Treatise on the Police of the Metropolis*, p. 34.

27. See ibid., p. 36: "The only means, therefore, of securing the peace of Society, and of preventing more atrocious crimes, is, to enforce by lesser punishments, the observance of religious and moral duties: Without this, Laws are but weak Guardians either of the State, or the persons or property of the Subject."

28. Ibid., p. 37. In the manuscript (fol. 13) Foucault gives another quotation, which is not used in the lecture: "A man of pure morals always makes the best Subject of every State; and few have suffered punishment as public delinquents, who have not long remained unpunished as private offenders" (p. 36).

29. Ibid., p. 37.

30. Ibid., p. 218, footnote.

31. Ibid., p. 25 (emphasis in the original).

32. Ibid., p. 218, footnote.

33. Ibid.

34. On this juxtaposition of archeology and genealogy, see above, pp. 93-94, note 2.

35. As a member of the Groupe d'information sur la santé, Foucault will be involved in these questions of the right to abortion; see "Convoqués à la P.J.," the text signed by M. Foucault, A. Landau, and J. Y. Petit, *Le Nouvel Observateur*, no. 468, 29 October-4 November 1973, p. 53; *DE*, II, no. 128, pp. 445-447/"Quarto," 1, pp. 1313-1315.

36. On the notion of transgression, see above, p. 6 footnote *.

37. Foucault is reacting here to the remarks made the day before, 6 February 1973, by the Minister of Health, Jean Foyer, an ardent Catholic and resolute opponent of any liberalization of abortion. In response to the manifesto of 330 doctors declaring, in *Le Nouvel Observateur* of 5 February, and taken up in *Le Monde* of 6 February, "to practice abortions or helping them to be realized according to their means outside of any financial dealing." Foyer actually declared: "It is deplorable that a political operation be launched on such a serious problem during an election" (quoted by *L'Express* of 12 February 1973). On 9 January 1973, Georges Pompidou had already adopted a similar position vis-à-vis debates on the de-penalization of abortion (ibid.). The manifesto of the "330" echoed that of April 1971, signed by 343 women affirming that they had had an abortion. See J.-Y. Le Naour and C. Valenti, *Histoire de l'avortement, XIXe-XXe siècle* (Paris: Seuil, 2003) pp. 240-242; see also "Convoqués à la P.J."

seven

14 FEBRUARY 1973

(A) England (continued). The great rise of virtues. (B) France. Appearance of new techniques of removal and confinement. In France, investment of State apparatus by lateral social interest: lettres de cachet, a means of social control that produces moralization and psychologization of the penalty in the nineteenth century. Capillary counter-investment of associations, families, and corporations. ∽ Field of knowledge, biographical archives: influence of psychiatric, sociological, and criminological knowledge in the nineteenth century. ∽ Replacement of lettres de cachet by centralized State bodies: the big reformatories.

*WE HAVE SEEN THE establishment of a process of control [in England] made necessary by both the movement of individuals and the new system of location of wealth. We have seen that, as the nineteenth century approaches, the promoters of this control are no longer those religious groups of basically petit-bourgeois composition, but people connected to power: merchants, aristocrats. The target likewise changes: it is no longer marginal or irregular individuals so much as the class of workers, so that at the end of the eighteenth century we have a set-up which means that one social class exercises overall control over the other.†

---

* The manuscript (fol. 1) has the title: "The great rise of virtues in England," which makes the link with the previous lecture.

† The manuscript (fols. 1-2) continues:

*   *   *

In France, the modality of the process is different. Actually, in France, the great economic depression of the seventeenth century and the social crises that punctuated it did not lead to a bourgeois revolution like in England, but to a monarchy* that was [confronted with] specific problems of control. Faced with the scale of the popular movements at the end of the seventeenth century, power had only two instruments of control and repression available to it: the army and justice. Now, from the end of the Middle Ages to the seventeenth century, the judicial apparatus was the object of a process of private appropriation, since judicial offices had become part of the system of venality, with the result that they were passed on through inheritance. Thus, those who had to apply justice had certain interests in common with landowners, so that, faced with the growth of royal taxation and economic depression, the group responsible for dispensing justice was as restive in the face of royal power as the majority of the population. Thus, royal power saw justice evade its demands for repression. As for the army, on several occasions it did intervene; but it is a heavy and costly instrument, not only for the State, but also for the populations [in which] it was installed, so that those who called upon it suffered from it at least as much as the movements against which they wished to be defended.†

"These controls were:

- assured first of all from 'below': by groups which escaped the penal system by carrying out their own control;
- gradually transferred to the same classes which exercise power; and this under the pressure
  • of popular political movements
  • and the formation of the proletariat.

The State as agent, or essential support of the moralization of the poor classes.
We arrive at the following:

- we have studied the system of sanctions and discovered the heterogeneity of the punitive in relation to the penal;
- the punitive, studied in turn, in its American prototype, manifested a whole mechanics of not so much the sanction as of penance;
- and this penitentiary element, studied in turn, turned out to be only one component in a play of coercion, of positive constraints: obligation of the good."

* Manuscript (fol. 4): "an absolute monarchy."
† The manuscript (fol. 5) contains the following list, regarding "the eighteenth century situation":

Hence the need to call upon a different apparatus: this was the invention that consisted in replacing repression with a technique of removal from the population.[1] Instead of sending an army, it was economically less costly and politically more sensible to remove in advance the elements of population that risked being dangerous; it was in this way that confinement replaced the technique of the control of populations by justice and the army. At the same time power provided itself with two apparatuses that were to be the instruments of this close cover and control;[2] on the one hand, an apparatus that is both administrative and parajudicial: the intendants of justice, police, and finance; on the other hand, a police apparatus, directly in the king's hands, and relayed by the police lieutenants.[*] Now these two apparatuses have the distinctive feature of straddling the judicial and the non-judicial; on the one hand, the police lieutenants and intendants have the right, in at least some cases, to intervene instead of the ordinary judicial apparatus and to take certain properly judicial decisions on behalf of the judicial system; thus, the provost marshal, the intendant of police have the right to judge judicially in cases of vagabondage. On the other hand, the lieutenants, the intendants have parajudicial powers in that, without observing any of the forms of justice and without taking decisions that are judicial in themselves, they have the right to take administrative measures: extradition, banishment, imprisonment.[†] This system lasted for a relatively long time and had a certain success since some, like Colquhoun, wanted to see it adopted in England. Furthermore, despite the system being dismantled at the time of the

---

"α. feudalization and private appropriation of justice through the purchase of offices;

β. alliance between this feudalized justice and other strata of population against State taxation;

γ. popular movements, in the face of which this justice is powerless if not semi-complicit;

δ. general intolerance of the population; armed intervention; repeated consequence of this 'armed justice';

ε. development of the technique: removal/confinement."

[*] The manuscript (fol. 4) adds: "With the lieutenant general of police. Mounted police force. Provost of the marshals." In the margin: "general surveillance; interventionism."

[†] The manuscript (fols. 4-5) adds: "without going through any of the forms of police. And this in two very precise types of case:

- either when the undesirable conduct does not fall under the law,

- or when there is an infraction, but the offender is in this way given the possibility of escaping justice."

Revolution, it was broadly restored very quickly after Thermidor. This system, less costly and less obtrusive than armed intervention, was still burdensome. It is, in effect, and for all classes of society, an instrument of tax levy. Finally, it is an apparatus that dispossesses a large number of people of their judicial and therefore political power, notably the remaining feudal elements and parliamentarians.[*]

So why was this system tolerated? Its strength and subtlety derive from it being, despite appearances, a double entry system. Actually, it seems to me that for a repressive State apparatus really to function, it must be tolerated. Now, two great mechanisms make this toleration possible. First of all, there is the schema of the Second Empire or of fascism.[†] In this case there is a process of transfer from the repressive State apparatus to marginalized strata of the population. The police apparatus of Napoleon III relied upon a certain number of civilians, that of German fascism on the black or brown shirts, the S.A.,[‡] that is to say on social categories formed by the *Lumpenproletariat*, the unemployed proletariat, or elements of a ruined petite bourgeoisie. It is to these economically and politically marginalized elements that these tasks of control and repression are entrusted. The advantage of this system of transfer is to give this apparatus a spontaneous, autochthonous look. In fact, this police is assured by a significant number of people. It has extra-institutional[§] possibilities of intervention and a sort of controlled freedom within a very precise ideology: nationalism, racism, and so on. Thus social control is exercised both from outside, since it is a marginalized stratum that receives certain functions delegated to it by the State apparatus, and from inside, inasmuch as this control is exercised by a supposedly common ideology.[¶]

---

[*] The manuscript (fol. 3) adds: "In fact, the system held up for a fairly long time. It was even keenly desired in England. And despite the Revolution, it was finally restored (or rather integrated into a new system) and not suppressed.

[*Addition between the lines*] → precondition of toleration of a repressive apparatus.

If it was able to hold up, it was because it was a double entry system."

[†] Manuscript (fol. 6): "Or the example of fascism or Nazism."

[‡] The manuscript (fol. 6) adds: "S.S., responsible for immediate, violent, extrajudicial repression."

[§] Manuscript (fol. 6) in the margin: "and extra-legal."

[¶] The manuscript (fol. 6) adds: "Coupling between: transfer of police power and injection, reinforcement of an ideology that assures, guides the use of this power."

The other schema consists in this: instead of transferring it, the State apparatus* is kept in the hands of a limited number of people, subject to the central power, but one sees to it that this apparatus, while serving the interest of the dominant class can, at the same time, in a lateral manner, serve certain local and particular interests. This involves creating sorts of circuits of diversion so that, at different points of the State apparatus, certain individuals, who do not necessarily belong to the ruling class or have the same interests, can locally [divert] a fraction of power and use it on their own account. These groups thus strengthen power, finally, since they exercise the power passed on to them by the dominant class in line with this State apparatus—which allows certain individuals, who have no direct interests in supporting power, to adhere to it.† In this way, in the same State apparatus, the interest of the dominant class holding power is intertwined with a lateral social "use" that enables this apparatus to be masked‡ and made tolerable. We have here a phenomenon of "investment and counter-investment" of the State apparatus by the dominant "class interest" and lateral interests,§ and not a phenomenon of splitting and transfer of the apparatus.

Now what characterizes the very strange State apparatus organized by the monarchy in the seventeenth-eighteenth centuries? The *parajudicial, para-Statist* apparatus of the Ancien Regime was tolerated for so long because it conformed to the second schema. What, then, ensures the counter-investment of this apparatus? What permits its social use at a capillary level?¶ It is the *lettres de cachet*, the mobile element that allows this apparatus, corresponding to an overall class interest, to be used

---

* The manuscript (fol. 6) adds: "(in part, and for one side only of its functioning)".

† The manuscript (fols. 6-7) adds: "It is a matter of allowing a marginal use, *rather* a micro-use, a capillary use, at the lowest level, *from below*, of an apparatus that is otherwise governed by a class interest."
In the margin (fol. 7): "Lateral utility," then "synaptic loop, circuit of diversion, makes it possible for some individuals, groups, and interests (different from those of the dominant class) to divert a part of power for themselves. Adhering to the class in power—not through class interest—but through the homogeneity of power."

‡ Manuscript (fol. 7): "to mask this class interest." Above the expression "social 'use'" the word "capillary" is added.

§ Instead of the opposition: class interest/lateral interests, the manuscript (fol. 7) has: "'class interest-social use'."

¶ Manuscript (fol. 8): "How, in the 'police' or rather *parajudicial and Statist* system of the Ancien Regime, was this use, this counter-investment assured—rendering the whole acceptable."

laterally by a number of individuals who certainly do not share the political and economic interests of the class in power.[3]

*   *   *

In the historiography of the nineteenth century, the *lettre de cachet* is regarded as a symbol of arbitrary, autocratic power:[4] it is the presence of the king himself and his power in the everyday life of individuals; it is that by which the signs of the monarchy penetrate people's everyday life. Now, it seems to me that the letters have a completely different function and that their movement is not from the top down. What actually is the administrative mechanism[*] of the *lettre de cachet*? It involves a decision by the king bearing on an individual case, and which therefore cannot have universal validity. And, if we except a limited number sent of his own accord by the king himself to get rid of characters deemed dangerous, the mass of letters are solicited by individuals, families, religious groups, notables, legal people (notaries, and so on), and corporations. So a number of letters often come from a low level in the social scale: lawyers, village residents, tradespeople, craftsmen. In the province one requests the letter from the intendant, in Paris from the lieutenant of police. It is forwarded to them by sub-delegates. Without even informing the King's Household, the lieutenant and intendant generally conduct an inquiry into the situation of the person making the request[†] in the circle of those around him. So the decision is reached at the level of a particular domain of public opinion; once the inquiry has been made, and if it confirms the legitimacy of the request, [then] application is made to the King's Household, which grants the signature.[‡]

Thus, [in terms of the] administrative circuit, the letter is a process which comes from below and is authenticated below. What is requested[§] is only an act of power, which in such a centralized monarchy can come only from above and carry the mark of the king. The intervention of a

---

[*] Manuscript (fol. 8): "their, if not 'judicial,' at least administrative mechanism."

[†] The manuscript (fol. 9) adds: "by the subdelegate who makes enquiries among the people around the supplicant (his neighbors, his curate, people of note of the place, the corporation)."

[‡] The manuscript (fol. 9) adds: "and the letter (never really signed by the King himself) is sent."

[§] Manuscript (fol. 10): "one requests the King's *mark*, as mark of a power, of a sovereignty fully present in the King."

sovereign power is requested in order to appropriate it temporarily, so as to get power to extend to oneself and allow one, by this diversion, to exert a kind of sovereign power in the king's name through which one obtains the exile or imprisonment of one's neighbor, one's relative, and so on. It is, in a way, a temporary appropriation of royal power, with its signs and marks, at the level of local powers, groups, and individuals. The sign that the *lettre de cachet* is not something like the lightning expression of royal power traversing society and falling on an individual, but a circular process going from the people to the people, is that generally it is the person requesting the letter, and not the king, who pays the board and lodging of the person confined; similarly, if a letter is revoked, it is rarely on the king's initiative, but through the intervention of the intendant or lieutenant, who take care to consult whoever it was that requested the letter. So there is no more arbitrary decision of the king in freeing than there is in confining.

Now, when a letter concerns a punishment, for what is it requested? Basically, it is a matter of parapenal sanctions regarding certain forms of behavior that are not defined as infractions by the Penal Code, but that are unacceptable to private individuals, local micro-powers (parishes, corporations, and so on): conjugal infidelity, debauchery, squandering a patrimony, a dissolute life, agitation, that is to say the two great categories of disorderliness and violence.[5] It is also a matter of parajudicial punishment of cases subject to the law, but to which one is not keen on the law being applied: witchcraft, for example, raises so many problems for the exercise of justice that most sorcerers* are the object of *lettres de cachet* and confined. Finally, there are cases where the letters are used because no jurisdiction or jurisprudence yet exists for dealing with them. This is the case for the first labor conflicts, which are settled by letters. These conflicts, like the printers' strike in Paris, appear with the economic recovery around 1724-1725: around 1723, the master printers had adopted the practice of bringing in workers from Germany who were paid less than French workers, leading to a strike led notably by a young printer, Thouinet.[6] In 1724, the master printers, quite outside the rules of corporative jurisprudence, appeal to the

---

* The manuscript (fol. 10) notes that the severity of the law is also applied to "sodomites" as well as "witches."

police lieutenant to confine Thouinet. Set free quite quickly, Thouinet, who is exiled forty leagues from Paris, asks the lieutenant to be allowed to return to Paris so that he can practice his profession. The police lieutenant asks the master printers for their views, and they refuse to annul the *lettre de cachet*. Similarly, a number of clock workers, who are prized abroad, are arrested by means of *lettres de cachet* to prevent them from leaving their country.

Thus, the *lettre de cachet*, coming from below, serves to take control of all that the traditional penal system allows to escape. In practice it produces confinement:[*] eight out of ten call for this punishment. Now this confinement is not carried out in prisons, but half in religious establishments to a large extent intended for this role, and in secular establishments, some of which are the *hôpitaux générales*, others private boarding houses or *maisons de force*.[7] We have here the historical filiation of the psychiatric clinic. Actually, the first clinics for nervous diseases, which we see appearing at the end of the eighteenth century, are geographically and institutionally linked to these. Furthermore, this confinement does not function as a penalty: it does not sanction an offense and its duration is not fixed in advance; it must last until a certain change has taken place in the individual, until the latter has demonstrated his remorse and changed his tendencies. This is, moreover, the justification given by the person requesting the letter, and similarly, when he asks for the letter to be lifted, the inmate invokes the correction that has taken place in him.[†]

This is the outline of what will be a crucial change. In fact, in the classical economy of the penal system, the aim of the penalty is indeed to change something, but where and in what? To change something in the tendencies of others, for example. In the classical system, the penalty must have its effect on those who have not yet committed the crime. The preventative function of the penalty is basically directed at others, by way of example. Here, on the contrary, the idea arises of an internment

---

* The manuscript (fol. 11) adds: "(sometimes also movement, or prohibition to go to a place)."
† Manuscript (fols. 11-12): "It is in general the justification given by the person requesting the letter. He may indicate how long he supposes the length of time of resipiscence.

- when the person confined claims his freedom, he emphasizes that he is corrected;
- freedom is accorded after inquiry has been made or opinion given on this improvement."

that must remain in force until the tendencies, not of others, but of those who committed the offense, are changed. This new orientation of the punitive system moves away from the mechanism of the penal system. All the nineteenth-century moralization and psychologization of the penalty will enter through this orientation.

Thus, what is expressed through the *lettre de cachet* is not so much the intervention of an absolute power as a certain *moral consensus* located in families, in localities. Hence the polymorphous, ambiguous character of what is rejected and condemned by these regional forms of consensus, which means that these letters designate and cast out a whole category of individuals into a vast confusion and wealth: the agitated, the sick, those who have committed offenses. Here, for example, is a letter from the police lieutenant addressed to the minister of the Royal Household at the end of the eighteenth century: "Yesterday the wife of a prosecutor of the jurisdiction of the consuls, named Bertrand, was taken to the Châtelet. This woman, after having got it into her head that she was saintly, received communion every day for more than six months, without any preparation and even after having eaten. This conduct could merit the most extreme torture, according to the provisions of the laws, but, as there is more madness than evil intent, and because we could not make the punishment of this sort of crime public without harming religion and arousing the evil discourses of libertines and badly converted protestants, it seems to me that the most suitable solution would be to oblige the husband to pay for his wife's board ..."[8] In this case it is the police lieutenant who suggests that the husband request a *lettre de cachet* because the penal system is too unwieldy to make use of it, and for reasons of propriety (scandal) and circumstances (the Protestants and libertines). The woman is to be placed in a convent because, he says, "I do not doubt that the good examples of a regular community, together with a charitable attention, will re-establish both her spirit and health in a few months."[9] So there is a reference here to resipiscence, which is as much remorse in the moral sense as return to health; a reference, also, to the instrument of a regular life, to a regularity of social life as well as of a monastic rule observed within a community.[*]

---

[*] The manuscript (fol. 12) adds: "The other essential element is not arbitrariness, it is *correction*. With all the possible ambiguities of this word, which designates a pedagogy, a cure, a religious repentance, and a moral conversion."[10]

This enables us to see that, while being part of this pyramid rising up to the king,* the *lettre de cachet* operates in an opposite direction to that of royal arbitrariness. The letter, which is the instrument of a sort of capillary and marginal counter-investment, rises back up the "parajudicial" State apparatus. It should be noted that the points at which these counter-investments by the *lettre de cachet* take place are, in a way, socially important places in that they become relays and diversions of power: we see these letters requested and authenticated at the level of communities like the parish—an administrative, fiscal, and religious unit, and, at the same time, the site of the formation of a sort of consensus that asks power to respect its morality, order, and regularity— the family, the corporation. These sites are exchangers between power from above and power from below.

It should also be stressed that a whole field of knowledge is formed confusedly through this system of exchanges between appeal, inquiry, and response, between denunciation and supervision; a whole biographical archive is formed. In fact, prior to the *lettres de cachet*, people are noted, they enter the written archive only through their genealogy or the infamy of their crime; wealth, the heroic deed, the name, the crime are the elements by which individuals enter the system of writing. Henceforth, through these letters, we see the description, at the level of the everyday and of life, of series of biographical banalities that begin to become the object of a form of knowledge, still infra-epistemological at this time, but that will be precisely the basis on which the great clinical psychiatric and sociological knowledge of the nineteenth century will be able to be constructed. And, at the same time,† this banality of the everyday, all that does not have the brilliance of the noble deed, the name, the crime, the wealth, all that barely irregular colorlessness will be described in terms of a certain code. In the *lettres de cachet* we find the socially accepted and recognized signs of individual irregularity; there is thus a whole series of categories at work whose distribution and evolution should be studied: debauchery, dissipation, violence, extravagance, self-delusion, plotting, and so on. Now, these elements do not exactly constitute the psychological characteristics of individuals

---

* Manuscript (fol. 13): "while being an intrinsic part of the 'parajudicial' police apparatus."
† Manuscript (fol. 14): "At the same time a codified description of deviance."

that enable them to be classified; nor are they symptoms like those of a disease; they are not signs. In reality they are *marks*, that is to say the features by which a power bringing itself to bear on an individual places that individual in a situation of subjugation from which certain measures may follow: exclusion, confinement, and so on.

Finally, as well as this function of the mark, we find narrative devices in the letters, since the life is recounted with silences, causal chains, and so on. All of this gives a sort of perpetual biography of infamy, a sort of anti-Plutarch: the life of infamous men.* Here, for example, is a letter from d'Argenson to Pontchartrain of 4 March 1709: "The woman named Drouet, to whom is rightly imputed the wandering and disorderly life of the young lady de Cavaus, is certainly a very dangerous adventuress, who has roamed the provinces of the realm and followed the armies; offered to work as a spy for generals; given them usually false advice, and deceived, perhaps, both sides. I know that M. de Vendôme lived to regret it more than once, and that having been chased away from the Flanders army on his orders, she returned to Paris where the young lady de Cavaus surrendered completely to her guidance. They were together in Béarn and Languedoc, where they sought out some dupes, sharing expenses, without going to great effort in the choice of means. Returned to Paris, they kept a poor inn or cheap eating-house, which was the meeting place for the lackeys of the quarter. But, what is most odd, is that these lackeys often passed the night there, in shameful discussions, and that the two persons increased further these abominations by public expressions of a monstrous passion, which still seems to continue. I think therefore that this unfortunate woman must be confined in the Hôpital général, at the same time as the young lady de Cavaus will be taken to the Refuge, in execution of the King's order that it pleased you to send me, and the correction of one of the two will not have much effect if the other were to remain free."[12] This hidden integration of biography into knowledge, from the angle of irregularity, is probably one of the fundamental phenomena of our knowledge, and it will have immense importance, not only when the penal system is reorganized, but when psychiatric, sociological, and criminal knowledge are formed. These will be formed on the basis of this slow and obscure

---

* Manuscript (fol. 15), adds between the lines: "against La Bruyère."[11]

accumulation of a police knowledge that apprehends people through the political marks that have been set on them and have thereby delineated their irregularity. An entire history could be written of the knowledge of sexuality, showing how, from this continuous and century-old inquiry into people's dissoluteness, a knowledge was formed that is taken over by psychiatry at the beginning of the nineteenth century, when that famous debauchery became the, as it were, natural context for the genesis of mental illness, and that is also taken over by organic medicine around 1824, when general paralysis, with its syphilitic, and hence debauched origin, appeared in knowledge. This same heritage will be codified differently around 1840, when hysteria makes its entrée. This knowledge of dissoluteness will produce, but no doubt as one of its phases, psychoanalysis and the present theory of desire, which is its passing figure. It is this formidable knowledge of dissoluteness that has given successively these diverse figures of knowledge.

*   *   *

With regard to the relations between the English and French systems, we can say that in England a movement of social control is gradually imposed on the State on the basis of a religious irredentism, while in France we have the opposite figure, since the movement relies on an extremely centralized State apparatus. Consequently, in England the essential instruments of social control are measures and sanctions like exhortation, exclusion from the group,* whereas in France the key instrument is confinement.† But, apart from these differences, we can grasp a fundamental analogy: with completely different supports, they both involve, in fact, the same movement of constraint and the same elements to be controlled. The denunciations are the same in both places.‡ This control has, in short, the same initiators and relays: family, religious or work community. Moreover, in both cases we can observe

---

* The manuscript (fol. 15) also has, regarding England: "isolation" and "exile."

† The manuscript (fol. 15) has, for the French case: "the instruments of control are less moral and more 'physical': confinement."

‡ The manuscript (fol. 16) notes that "what is denounced to the police lieutenant and what Wesley wants to rebuke in the course of his inspection, is the same thing."

the same movement of a shift towards the State.* It is true that, up to a point, the *lettre de cachet* falls into disuse in the eighteenth century; but this in no way signifies, as might be thought, a dismantling of royal power. Thus, in 1784, Breteuil regulates it[13] in such a way that it is no longer very usable;† and we see the appearance of really centralized State bodies: the big reformatories (*maisons de correction*), which aim to confine and correct beggars, vagabonds, and the poor who cannot work. In place of the *lettre de cachet*, we have therefore a strongly centralized apparatus, with the class in power, on the one hand, and the class on which power is exercised, on the other.‡ This integration of the moral order, of public order within the State apparatus is indicated in a text of 1790 by Duport, the great judicial theoretician of the Constituent: "It is false that public order is different from justice; this is a mark of despotism."§ He believes that public order was really ensured arbitrarily by the king, alongside justice; in fact, when he denounces despotism, he denounces a

---

* Manuscript (fol. 16): "In England, shift towards the State and the upper classes of a control that becomes increasingly clearly social. In France, tendency to use *lettres de cachet* less and less; general hostility to confinement."

† The manuscript (fol. 16) adds:

"- keep 'those whose mind is alienated';

A - keep only one out of two [of] those who indulge in excess: 'Families sometimes exaggerate the wrongs of the subjects whose detention they have requested.' If one let them, 'it would no longer be a correction, but a real penalty'."[14]

‡ The manuscript (fol. 17) adds: "Now this resistance to the *lettres de cachet*, which ends up with their almost unanimous suppression, is accompanied by the setting up of a system that is more really centralizing and more socially polarized than the *lettres de cachet*:

- the organization of the reformatories at the end of the Ancien Régime → prison;
- and the decisions of the Constituent concerning the nationalization of hospital goods and all assistance funds;
- assignation to a chosen few of a task of both the distribution of aid and moral control.

In the *Troisième rapport du Comité de mendicité* (15 January 1791), it would be necessary to create a committee 'in order to govern exceptionally the reformatories, homes, to know the offenses or good conduct of those detained in them; to pronounce on the punishments or clemency ... that they may deserve.'

- The central importance of work. The main control will be obtained by putting everyone to work. The government must favor, not aid, but the means of work: 'Open some works, open workshops, facilitate sales outlets for labor ...' It is necessary 'to encourage' those 'who will put to work at their own expense the greatest number of workers: for that is truly ... the most useful for the country' (*Troisième rapport du Comité de mendicité*)."[15]

§
   "1. Public order is not by nature different from justice.
   2. Police must be nothing other than the inevitability of justice."[16]

duality that existed between the two—and, demanding the integration of public order in justice, he put responsibility for the maintenance of public order, which was previously secured by these mechanisms from below,[*] in the hands of the State apparatus, and so of the ruling class.

---

[*] The manuscript (fols. 18-20) ends in the following way:
"The suppression of the police lieutenant, of *lettres de cachet*, and of practices of confinement do correspond to the dismantling of monarchical power; but in fact it was a matter—with another starting point and in other ways—of a process that (in France as in England) was going in the direction of the integration of mechanisms of penance and correction into the apparatus of justice and the penal system.
Adding yet another difference:

- In England: the depredation of financial and economic capital (with industrial development, the division of labor) was one factor in the acceleration of the process.
- In France: it is rather peasant property, the redistribution of rights in the framework of individual property, which brought about a depredation. [fol. 18]

Conclusion. The *rapprochement* of the English and French processes allow us to see how it was possible to integrate the prison institution (with the penitentiary, corrective element that accompanies it) into a penal theory and penal practice previously unknown and even foreign to it.
We can straightaway indicate some of the effects of this junction.

1. A culpabilization of the penal infraction, which it is very important to note is not a residual effect of Christianity.
   Secular culpabilization of the infraction, which then allowed penality and the prison to be invested by Christianity in the nineteenth century:
   - Christian philanthropy;
   - the priest as prison functionary;
   - 'Christian morality' as normative ideology;
   - codification of this morality in the language of psychology. [fol. 19]
2. A redefinition of the role of the penalty.
   Certainly, for a long time there had been a refusal to see the penalty as a pure and simple sanction of the offence. In particular, the penalty had to prevent new crimes. In this sense, it was held to be a deterrent, but it was above all a matter of preventing others.
   The role of the penalty now is to bring about an internal transformation in the very one who committed an offence.
3. This use of the prison and this new role of the penalty are linked to mechanisms of 'moral' control: there is no penitentiary system without general surveillance; no penal confinement without control of the population. No prison without police. Prison and police are chronological twins. In fact, the judicial and penal institution comes to be framed between these two other institutions, which do not seem to communicate directly with each other. [fol. 20]
   We can even say that it was the legislator's great concern → 1808, there cannot be any imprisonment without judicial intervention.
   But historically, they are linked; and far from being solely instruments of justice, they have completely covered it and given it a completely different mode of functioning.
4. The formation of a double field of knowledge.
   (α) The knowledge of permanent surveillance.
   The dossiers of surveillance.

1. See M. Foucault, "Théories et Institutions pénales," sixth lecture, fols. 18-19 (in the seventeenth century "removal from the dangerous population" is introduced: "To remove, or threaten to remove a part of the population does not have the economic disadvantages of invasion"); seventh lecture, fol. 2.

2. See M. Foucault, "La vérité et les formes juridiques," pp. 600-601/pp. 1468-1469; "Truth and Juridical Forms," pp. 64-65.

3. Foucault was interested in the *lettres de cachet* very early on and, more generally, in the archives of confinement of the Hôpital général and the Bastille—from the 1950s when he was writing *Folie et Déraison. Histoire de la folie*, pp. 156-158 and p. 508; *History of Madness*, pp. 125-126, p. 446. The themes taken up in this lecture date from that period: the *lettre de cachet* as a "popular practice," "demanded from below," and so reflecting "a process going from below to above" and not an arbitrary exercise of monarchical power; nine years later he will describe "the extraordinary beauty of these texts" ("À propos des lettres de cachet" with Arlette Farge, Michelle Perrot, André Béjin, and Michel Foucault, *Les lundis de l'histoire*, France Culture, 27 November 1982). See *Le Désordre des familles. Lettres de cachet des Archives de la Bastille*, presented by A. Farge and M. Foucault (Paris: Gallimard, 1982) where these themes are developed and documented; see p. 10: "Reading these dossiers has put us on the track less of the sovereign's anger than of the passions of humble folk, at the center of which we find family relations—husbands and wives, parents and children." This focus of interest forms part of the broader framework of archive works: the documentation collected on Pierre Rivière in 1973; the project of an "anthology of existence" on "La vie des hommes infâmes" in 1977 in *Les Cahiers du chemin*, 29, 15 January 1977, pp. 12-29; *DE*, III, no. 198, pp. 237-253/"Quarto," II, pp. 237-253; English translation by Robert Hurley, "Lives of Infamous Men" in *EW*, 3; the collection created by Éditions Gallimard in 1978 entitled "Les vies parallèles," in which the memoirs of Herculine Barbin, a character taxed at the time with "masculine hermaphroditism," appeared: *Herculine Barbin, dite Alexina B.*; English translation by Richard McDougall, *Herculine Barbin. Being the Recently Discovered Memoirs of a Nineteenth-Century French Hermaphrodite* (Brighton: The Harvester Press, 1980); as well as, in 1979, the cryptographic manuscripts (BnF) of Henry Legrand, *Le Cercle amoureux*, translated and presented by Jean-Paul Dumont and Paul-Ursin Dumont.

4. Foucault takes up this analysis in *Surveiller et punir*, p. 216; *Discipline and Punish*, p. 214.

5. See *Folie et Déraison. Histoire de la folie*, p. 157; *History of Madness*, p. 125 (family, neighbor, entourage, parish priest makes the request on the basis of grievances or apprehensions of

---

Statistics.

(β) Individual, clinical knowledge (*savoir*) of transformation.

It is necessary to know (*connaître*) individuals.

We have here a coupling—statistical knowledge-knowledge of the individual—which we find again in medical knowledge at the same time (at the time of the birth of the clinic) and a bit later at the time of the birth of evolutionism (with *Lyell* and Darwin). [fol. 21]

Now we should note:

(1) that the language that will allow general observations to be transcribed in terms of individual analysis, and conversely, the language that will allow 'police' observations to be transcribed in 'theoretical' terms, the ethical-religious in scientific terms, is medical language. Medical language is the general transcriber;

(2) that what we have here, taking place in judicial practice, is a type of knowledge which is radically different from the *inquiry*.

And this is the *examination*." [fol. 22]

*

disorderliness, scandal, madness, or crime); "La vie des hommes infâmes," p. 246/p. 246; "The Lives of Infamous Men," p. 167 (the *lettres de cachet* concern obscure histories of violence and family disorder): "rejected or abused spouses, a squandered fortune, conflicts of interest, disobedient young people, knavery or carousing, and all the little disorders of conduct"; and the inquiry which followed "needed to establish whether the debauchery or drunken spree, the violence or the libertinage, called for an internment, and under what conditions and for how long—a job for the police, who would collect statements by witnesses, information from spies, and all the haze of doubtful rumor that forms around each individual"; A. Farge and M. Foucault, *Le Désordre des familles*, p. 9: "We were also struck by the fact that in many cases these requests were formulated with regard to family and completely private affairs: minor conflicts between parents and children, domestic disputes, loose living of spouses, a boy's or girl's disorderliness."

6. In his study, *La Grande Industrie en France sous le règne de Louis XV* (Paris: Albert Fontemoing, 1900), pp. 323-324, Germain Martin recounts: "The *lettres de cachet* will help maintain order. Some years later [after similar petitions in 1720], it is necessary to deal ruthlessly with Thouinet, a young printer. Does he not dare to rouse all the other skilled workers and get them to leave their masters rather than see their wages reduced? The bosses apply to the Minister of Justice who demands that 'the young printer be arrested, to set an example.' He is incarcerated on 16 November, and on 4 February 1725 he is banished to forty leagues from Paris for 6 months. But the agent of the book trade demanded that he be completely prohibited from staying in the capital. This journeyman 'was conspiring' and furthermore 'was distributing very bad books to the public'." Martin cites "*Arch. de la Bastille*, 10858" and Franz Funck-Brentano, *La Question ouvrière sous l'Ancien Régime d'après les dossiers provenant des prisonniers par lettres de cachet* (Paris: 1802) p. 2 sq. The name "Thouinet" does not appear however in F. Funck-Brentano, *Les Lettres de cachet à Paris. Étude suivie d'une liste des prisonniers de la Bastille (1659-1789)* (Paris: Imprimerie nationale, 1903).

7. See above, p. 96 note 8.

8. In the margin (fol. 8), Foucault adds in crayon this reference: "p. 452, photocopy." See the collection of letters and police reports edited by Pierre Clément, *La Police sous Louis XIV* (Paris: Didier et Cie, 1866), in which this quotation is found exactly (pp. 452-453) in a letter of the Minister of State and Lieutenant General of police, Marc-René d'Argenson, to the comte de Pontchartrain, Secretary of State to the Maison du Roi, written in Paris, 20 June 1699 (document no. 33, which at the time was conserved at the Bibliothèque impériale with the classification mark: "Ms. Fr. 8, 122, fol. 437," ibid., p. 453).

9. Ibid.

10. In the margin (fol. 12), in crayon, Foucault adds this reference: "pp. 460-461." It would appear that, here too, he consulted the collection of Pierre Clément in which, on pages 460-461, we find several of the themes touched on here, concerning the affair of a young lady Leviston who wanted to strangle herself. Mademoiselle Leviston had been transferred from the Madeleine convent to the Hôpital général and asked to be returned to the Madeleine. The theme of resipiscence is present in a letter from d'Argenson to Pontchartrain (no. 39): it is noted that the young lady "really promises to be more sensible and restrained there" (ibid., p. 461). Moral consensus, through the opinions of the nuns, also appears very important (ibid.: "The nuns of the hôpital, who have inspected her conduct, seem fairly happy with it"), the notion of cure also, since the health of the young lady remains central (ibid.: "her health is very delicate, and I am doubtful that the hospital diet is suited to her temperament").

11. Quite obviously, there is a play on words here with reference to the titles of well-known works: Plutarch, *Parallel Lives* (Cambridge, MA: Harvard University Press) 11 volumes; and Jean de La Bruyère, *Les Caractères, ou les Mœurs de ce siècle*, in *Œuvres complètes* (Paris: Gallimard, 1935 [1688]). Four years later, in 1977, Foucault will write a text borrowing this exact expression: "La vie des hommes infâmes"; "The Lives of Infamous Men." Foucault

presented this text as a preface to a forthcoming book that was to be "an anthology of existences," collecting archives of confinement from the Hôpital générale and the Bastille: "I wanted to assemble a few rudiments for a legend of obscure men, out of the discourses that, in sorrow or in rage, they exchanged with power" (p. 241; p. 162). The same intention could be found in the project for "Les vies parallèles" as in this collection.

12. Letter from d'Argenson to Pontchartrain, no. 41, 4 March 1709, in P. Clément, *La Police sous Louis XIV*, pp. 462-463.

13. See "Circular letter from Mr. the Baron de Breteuil, Minister of State, to MM. the Intendants of the Provinces of his Department on the subject of Lettres de Cachet & Detention Orders," Versailles, 25 October, 1784 http://psychiatrie.histoire.free.fr/psyhist/1780/breteuil.htm.

14. Ibid.

15. See F.-A.-F. de La Rochefoucauld-Liancourt, *Troisième rapport du Comité de Mendicité. Bases constitutionelles du Système général de la Législation et de l'administration de Secours* (Paris: Imprimerie nationale, 15 January 1791) p. 28 and p. 34.

16. Foucault will come back to the importance of this theme in Duport's thought. With regard to the kinship that Duport sees between the criminal and the tyrant, see *Les Anormaux*, lecture of 29 January 1975, p. 86; *Abnormal*, p. 93: "In 1790, precisely when the new Penal Code is under discussion, Duport, who is far from representing an extreme position, says: 'The despot and the malefactor both disturb public order. In our eyes, an arbitrary order and a murder are equal'."

eight

21 FEBRUARY 1973

*(B) France (continued). Recapitulation and outcome: the punitive society. Mechanism: control of lower-class or popular illegalism (*illégalisme populaire*). 1. Popular illegalism in the eighteenth century. The case of the Maine weavers. Merchants and weavers circumvent the regulations. The positive functioning of illegalisms. 2. Reversal at the end of the eighteenth century. The bourgeoisie seizes the judicial apparatus in order to get rid of lower-class illegalism now become "depredation." Worker depredation; plunder by workers in the Port of London. 3. Organization of the penal and penitentiary system. Instruments: the notion of social enemy; moralization of the working class; prison, colony, army, police.* ∽ *In the nineteenth century, worker illegalism, target of the whole repressive system of the bourgeoisie.*

I HAVE TRIED TO show the rise of a coercive system that in its nature and functioning was heterogeneous to the eighteenth-century penal system. We see this system operating in societies of moralization and in the game of *lettres de cachet*. This coercive system was gradually shifted in its points of application and instruments, and was taken over by the State apparatus at the end of the eighteenth century, and we can say that at the end of the first twenty years of the nineteenth century the State apparatus had, for the most part, taken over responsibility for the coercive system, which was in turn grafted onto the penal system, so that for the first time we have a penal system that is a penitentiary system. In short, we are dealing with something that I call the punitive society, that is to say a society in which the judicial State apparatus makes additional use of corrective and penitentiary functions. Such is the point of outcome.*

[The question] we have to ask is: Why did this slow shift towards the State apparatus accelerate, and why did we finally end up with this unified system? This problem, seemingly very simple to solve, is, in reality, rather more complicated. Simple, because for some time I thought it could be solved in a few words: at the end of the eighteenth century, in which the growth and installation of the capitalist mode of production provoked a number of political crises, the political surveillance of a populace (*une plèbe*) that is becoming a proletariat involves the organization of a new repressive apparatus.[1] In short, corresponding to the rise of capitalism there would have been a whole series of movements of lower-class sedition to which the power of the bourgeoisie responded with a new judicial and penitentiary system. Now I am not sure I am right in using the term "seditious mobs (*plèbe séditieuse*)."[2] Actually, it seems to me that the mechanism that brought about the formation of this punitive system is, in a sense, deeper and broader than that of the simple control of the seditious mobs. What had to be controlled, what the bourgeoisie demanded that the State apparatus control through the penitentiary system,† is a deeper and more constant phenomenon of which sedition is only a particular case: *lower-class or popular illegalism (illégalisme populaire)*.[3] It seems to me that until the end of the eighteenth century a certain lower-class illegalism was not only *compatible* with, but *useful* to the development of the bourgeois economy; a point arrived when this illegalism functionally

---

* The manuscript (fol. 1 bis) adds: "But this is not an explanation. Or rather, there is still:

- the problem of why this slow process of transfer. Why not a binary system?
- the problem of why it succeeded so abruptly. Why was justice penitentiarized? Why did the State itself become the great 'penitentiary (*pénitentier*)'?" [the sense of "penitentiary" here is not so much "prison," as rather the office or function of administering "penance" (like the office of a priest as "penitentiary" in the Catholic Church); G.B.]

† Manuscript (fol. 2): "by the police and penal system, by that kind of supervision, moralization, coercion."

enmeshed in the development of the economy, became incompatible with it.*

*   *   *

What do we mean by lower-class illegalism? Let us take the example of the Maine weavers from the book by [Paul] Bois on the *Paysans de l'Ouest.*[4] It is an interesting example since it concerns a profession that very quickly enters into the capitalist system and is still practiced in the eighteenth century on the border of town and country, and it has the particular advantage for us of having been one of the freest professions: there was neither corporation nor *jurande*, but only regulations issued by the general inspector of finances, who had organized the profession in the seventeenth century, resulting in the regulation of 1748.[5] These weavers are therefore craftsmen who together possess skills and produce cloth marketed at another level by the merchants who distribute and export it. Control was carried out through ordinances, like that of 1748; now the latter, although relatively less strict than corporative rules, was, even so, constraining: it defined the quality of different kinds of cloth, the required length of pieces, the artisan's mark, deposited in an office, and so on.[†] All this was supervised by a number of people: sworn guards who belonged to the place, received payment, and got around half of the proceeds from fines. Moreover, all these operations—measurement, marking, market—entail the loss of certain rights.[‡] Hence, to escape these constraints, which were not all unfavorable to the artisans[§] and protected them against the competition of the merchants, a partly double illegalism was established. The merchant, who had to market the cloth, as well as the weaver, who had to produce it, came to an agreement outside the regulations so as to try to evade them. They entered into contracts in advance, outside the official market. Thanks to this direct understanding, the two parties were in direct contact and established

---

* Manuscript (fol. 2): "this lower class illegalism was an obstacle; more, a danger."

† The manuscript (fol. 2) notes that the 1748 ordinance also concerned "the market, its occurrence, [and] prices."

‡ The manuscript (fol. 3) adds: "if there is a dispute and if one of the two parties demands a check."

§ The manuscript (fol. 3) adds: "who often could not read, had no measuring instruments."

a certain number of commercial relationships that were, in a sense, the laws of the market.* Finally, the merchant could advance money to the weaver who was thus able to acquire new instruments of production. Thus, gradually, the capitalist mode of production is injected, inserted into an artisanal system thanks to this practice of double illegalism.

Now, this form of illegalism is important for several reasons. First, it is a "functional" illegalism: far from being an obstacle, from acting as a deduction from the profit of capital being industrialized, it allows a capitalist kind of profit relationship to become clear. What this illegalism is opposed to is not at all merchant profit, it is the feudal levy, either the direct levy of the lord, or the indirect and State-controlled levy. It is opposed to a whole series of levies through the interplay of rights and fines. It is not then an attack against material property; it is an attack against rights. It is not theft; it is anti-feudal *fraud*, which serves the bourgeoisie. It is a sort of front in the struggle of the bourgeoisie for a new legality.

Second, it is a systematic illegalism, inasmuch as it is almost a mode of functioning of the whole of society. We have in fact this coupling of lower-class illegalism with that of the merchants, the illegalism of business. On the other hand, we also have the illegalism of the privileged, who evade the law through status, tolerance, or exception. There are a certain number of relations, some antagonistic, between this illegalism of the privileged and lower-class illegalism. In fact, lower-class illegalism reduces proportionally feudal revenue or, indirectly, State levies. But, on the other hand, this is not a radical antagonism and finds a number of compromises. Thus, for a part of the seventeenth century, neither the nobility nor the big landowners exerted great pressure for their rights to be respected. They preferred to obtain certain privileges directly from the court: tax exemptions, pensions, material advantages, and so on. Thus, their own illegalism compensated for and adapted to the illegalism of those for whom they were lords. This introduced new contradictions at a different level since, for the State to be able to pay these incomes, to accord these advantages, rights could not be excessively short-circuited at the level of State revenues.

---

* The manuscript (fol. 3) adds: "they avoided marking, judged the quality, quantity, and price between them."

So in the seventeenth century we have three types of illegalism playing off against each other: lower-class, business, privileged. To which a fourth must be added, which gets the system to work: that of government (*le pouvoir*).* The direct representatives of power—intendants, sub-delegates, police lieutenants—have often been seen as the agents of arbitrary power, but in fact, rather than agents of arbitrariness or strict legality, they were arbitrators of illegalism. Thus, in the very many convictions of artisans the representatives of royal power often intervened to reduce the fines.† Bois cites the case of fines of 100 *livres* reduced to one *livre* or a few *sols*.⁶ Thus power intervened as a regulator of these illegalisms, playing each off against the others.‡

Third, [this illegalism] is both economic and political.§ Certainly, when a law is got round, when a market relationship is established that escapes the regulatory system, it could be said that there is nothing political in this, that it is solely a matter of economic interests. It remains nonetheless that whenever a law is by-passed, or a regulation is violated, what is attacked is less the things themselves than the levy on them, the operation of power exercised on them, the regulatory authority. Thus, there is a continuum between specifically economic illegalism and the quasi-political violation of power's authority, and it is difficult to separate the two in eighteenth-century lower-class illegalism.¶ We can see its two extremities moreover. There is a point, in fact, at which this illegalism turns into what is well and truly the delinquency of common law: imprisonment for a fine leading to smuggling, vagrancy, begging, and so on. At the other pole, this illegalism tends towards strictly political struggle when it takes collective forms against new measures [linked to] economic decline: tax strikes, looting of tax collections,

---

* The manuscript (fol. 5) adds: "if this term has a meaning in an absolute monarchy without a legislative body in the strict sense."

† The manuscript (fol. 5) adds: "according to interests, pressures, dangers of agitation."

‡ The manuscript (fol. 5) adds: "This power, which will be given up later as an arbitrariness clashing with legality, was rather an arbitration between illegalisms. Illegalisms that functioned positively in the development of society and the economy."

§ Manuscript (fol. 6): "We can see, this illegalism is neither completely of the order of common law, nor of the order of politics."

¶ The manuscript (fol. 6) adds: "It is true that in their individual or even collective manifestations (where there was a general refusal to apply a regulation, settle a right, pay a tax), there was no political confrontation (against the regime, the king). It remains nonetheless that all these attacks were not directed at things, but at powers, regulatory authorities."

sedition.[7] The bourgeoisie occupies an ambiguous position behind all this: it supports these anti-legal struggles insofar as they serve it; it drops them when they fall into common law criminality or take the form of political struggles. It accepts smuggling and rejects banditry; it accepts tax refusal but rejects highway robbery.[*]

Fourth, [this illegalism] is oscillating. It is not a matter of a definitive decision to cross over to the other side of the law and practice illegality. In fact, there is a whole interplay between popular illegalism and the law. It could almost be said that respect for legality is only a strategy in this game of illegalism.[†] When a conflict occurs in this partly double illegalism and the lower strata realize that the bourgeoisie is exploiting them, they abandon the terrain of this illegalism and ask those who guarantee legality, the agents of royal power, for protection.[‡] However, whereas legality does not fail the bourgeoisie or the privileged when they need to resort to it, when the play of illegalisms leads the bourgeoisie to call for its intervention, the judicial apparatus not being controlled by the lower strata, most of the time it does not respond to their demands; hence their need to reactivate these forms of legality with their own means. Thus, in the eighteenth century we see phenomena like market riots.[9] When the old market regulations have been abandoned for some years, it turns out that the rise in prices prevents smaller buyers from buying and they ask for the regulations to be put back in force; in a sort of mixture of theater and violence, they take it upon themselves to reconstitute the judicial apparatus which failed them when they needed it. They re-establish market laws and taxation. At the extreme end of this reactivation we find the popular court,[10] a way of reactivating, within illegalism, the strategically needed legality.[§]

---

* The manuscript (fols. 6-7) refers here to: "Mandrin. This illegalism holds firmly both ends of the chain: from banditry to sedition. It accompanies the battle of the bourgeoisie while overflowing it at the two extremes."[8]

† Manuscript (fol. 7): "[Lower-class illegalism] constitutes above all a complex interplay with other illegalisms. In particular with that to which it is linked: bourgeois or business illegalism."

‡ The manuscript (fol. 7) adds: "[in this] they act no differently than the other social classes which also appeal to justice and send in the prosecutor or arresting police officer."

§ The manuscript (fols. 7-8) adds: "This reactivation of justice by the popular masses does not express an innate taste, a profound sense in the masses for the correct functioning of judicial institutions. The masses do not long for the court; and they do not love the judges with a love disappointed for too long. The resort to legality is part of the game of illegalism that they conduct, in their alliance and conflict with the other social classes."

All in all, there is a massive practice of illegalism in the lower strata, which corresponds to other illegalisms; and we cannot understand the operation of a penal system, a system of laws and prohibitions, if we do not examine the positive functioning of illegalisms. It is an intellectual prejudice that first there are prohibitions and then transgressions, [or] to think that there is incestuous desire and then the prohibition of incest; in fact, if a prohibition has to be understood and analyzed in relation to what it prohibits, it should also be analyzed in terms of those who prohibit and those on whom the prohibition weighs. But I think also that we cannot analyze something like a law and a prohibition without situating it within the real field of illegalism within which it functions. A law functions, it is applied only within a field of illegalism* that is actually practiced and, in a way, supports it. Take the case of abortion, for example: it is obvious that the law can function only insofar as there is a field of illegal practices that allow it to be applied. Linking the positive functioning of illegalism to the existence of the law is one of the conditions for understanding its functioning that is unfortunately too often forgotten.[11]

Basically, by relying sometimes on an illegalism of the privileged, from whom it tried to get itself granted privileges, and sometimes on a lower-class illegalism, which was like its combat vanguard, the bourgeoisie succeeded in overturning the juridical forms.† Taking a broader view, we could say the following: since the Middle Ages, the bourgeoisie invented three means to control the juridical apparatus of the State. First, appropriation of the judicial apparatus: this was venality, the purchase of offices.[12] Second, working its way into the State apparatus and governing it. Third, promoting the practice of illegalism:

---

* Manuscript (fol. 8):

"- on the one hand, this illegalism made the breaches, opened the channels, knocked down the doors through which new relations of production could be established;
- on the other, it was controlled, managed, induced by that whole parajudicial apparatus (intendants, police lieutenants) comprising the correctional apparatus."

In the margin: "method: positive functions of illegalism."
† The manuscript (fol. 9) adds: "which previously had been able to protect it (and from which it had lived, by appropriating offices). To control the law, individual appropriation had failed: concerted illegalism succeeded → Revolution."

letting other social strata practice it so as to be able to practice it itself in a functional system of combined illegalisms and, thanks to this, to overturn the legality that had served it but was becoming too burdensome. The 1789 Revolution is the outcome of this lengthy process of combined illegalisms thanks to which the bourgeois economy was able to open up its way.

We can now better define the problem: at the end of the eighteenth century, this administrative, police apparatus of extra-judicial superintendence, which we have seen does not function so much as representative of legality but as instance of arbitration of illegalisms, will be transformed by the bourgeoisie into a judicial apparatus charged precisely with getting rid of popular illegalism. Taking power, the bourgeoisie will take hold of this apparatus, which was mixed with the general system of illegalisms, and make it responsible for getting its legality applied. This is how the penitentiary element, which I think functioned in the network of the non-legal, is taken over and integrated into the system of justice, precisely when the bourgeoisie is no longer able to tolerate popular illegalism.*

Hence the question: In this complicity of illegalisms, why was there a point at which bourgeois illegalism could no longer tolerate the operation of lower-class illegalism? Let us again take the case of the weaver, who in the middle of the eighteenth century possessed his

---

* The manuscript (fols. 9-10) has here: "But it is not enough to say: having established its own legality, the bourgeoisie strived to get it respected.
Worker depredation.
The whole series of measures from Turgot to the beginning of the Revolution demolishes:

- the set of rights that weigh on production;
- the set of regulations that limit its forms, the development of production.

Lower-class illegalism no longer has a hold.
But at the same time there are established

- on the one hand, a juridically simplified form of property;
- on the other, a mode of production in which all the means of production are brought together in the hands of one social class.

As a result, the popular masses are no longer faced with the hostility of the laws, rules, and rights that weigh on [them] (and against which [they] may struggle with the help of others): [they] have to deal with things, things that do not belong to them, that belong to others."

skill, tools, raw material, and housing.* Compare this with the Port of London worker in the second half of the eighteenth century: nothing belongs to him, [but] on the other hand, he has right in front of him, on the boats, in the docks, a wealth estimated by Colquhoun to equal 70 million pounds a year.† This fortune is there, before being marketed, before its transformation, in direct contact with the Port workers. Under these conditions, the depredation of this fortune thus displayed becomes inevitable: all this is "exposed to depredations, not only from the criminal habits of many of the aquatic laborers and others who are employed, but from the temptations to plunder, arising from the confusion unavoidable in a crowded port, and the facilities afforded in the disposal of stolen properties."[14]

Now, with regard to the operation of this depredation, it should be noted that it does not take place from the outside, that is to say it is not unemployed workers, vagabonds who, passing by, seize upon the wealth; the channel of this depredation is the agents responsible for handling this wealth. It is a system of internal complicity and not an external assault. Out of the nine categories of robbery in the Port distinguished by Colquhoun, seven involve the collusion of Port workers.[15] We have here a system very close to the classical smuggling of the seventeenth and eighteenth centuries, which involved the collusion of customs agents. This system also has its circuits of receiving and marketing.[16] This system of theft, linked to the presence of wealth, is comparable to that of smuggling. More than the quantity of wealth stolen, it is perhaps the form that is remarkable and disturbing: there is here, in effect, a whole coherent, underground, and parasitic economic activity. And we get the impression that lower-class illegalism, the old form of which was tolerated by the bourgeoisie, rather than attacking rights and the power that maintains them, as previously, now attacks the actual material forms of bourgeoisie wealth. And it is even forced to batten on it: leaving craft industry, the worker is no longer in contact with the law, but with things regulated solely by the principle: "this is not yours."

---

* The manuscript (fol. 10) adds: "All that he touched, he possessed."

† The manuscript (fol. 11) notes: "Colquhoun estimated it at 70,000,000. 13,500 ships load or unload; 31 million import; 29 million export; 9 million rigging. To which must be added the depredations in the Royal Marine warehouses."[13]

In the system of craft industry the worker was in contact with things, a large part of which belonged to him, and through these he dealt with a regulatory world of power, which he could try to evade precisely by practicing illegalism, but when the worker is faced only with a wealth, the only way of practicing illegalism is depredation.

In this way, by force of circumstance, through the installation of the base of the capitalist economy, these lower strata, shifted from craft industry to wage labor, are at the same time obliged to shift from fraud to theft. Now, in the same period, by the same mechanism, the privileged also find themselves systematically shifted from (fiscal, judicial, seigniorial) exaction to fraud. It is these who now claim the exclusive privilege of being able to get round the law, to escape regulation, and they give themselves this right twice over: first, availing themselves of the possibility of not falling under the blow of penal law thanks to certain social privileges; second, by giving themselves the power to make and dismantle the law. Practicing fraud, escaping the law will therefore have two new forms: making the law and, by status, escaping it. Legislative power is thus profoundly linked, in the bourgeoisie, to the practice of illegalism.[*]

We have here a process that will govern from a distance the whole organization and functioning of the penal and penitentiary system and bring about the split between the two justices. Starting from this, certain phenomena appear that are important for the setting up of this penal system. We can say that, with proletarianization, the populace transferred to bourgeois property the techniques and forms of illegalism it had developed throughout the eighteenth century in collusion with the bourgeoisie. Consequently, when the bourgeoisie registers the transfer of this illegalism onto its property, and dreads its effects, it will need to repress it.[†]

---

[*] The manuscript (fol. 15) adds: "We see emerging the two great types of delinquency, which have a very different judicial status: theft, as illegalism of someone who produces on the basis of a materiality that does not belong to him; [and] fraud, as illegalism of someone for whom wealth is linked to the law. Not that it is subject to the law, but it gives access to the possibility of making and dismantling, of imposing and getting around the law. Politics ↔ swindling."

[†] The manuscript (fol. 15) adds: "The bourgeoisie had not yet escaped feudal predation than it came up against depredation."

Hence, a number of consequences. First, the denunciation of all those socialized forms of illegalism [and the denunciation] of anyone who practices them as a social enemy. While the eighteenth-century delinquent who practiced fraud and smuggling was not a social enemy, inasmuch as he enabled the system to function, the delinquent at the end of the century is defined as a social enemy. Thus, we see the theoretical notion of the criminal as someone who breaks the social contract reallocated to the interior of this tactic of the bourgeoisie. Second, at the start of the nineteenth century, the systematic use of infiltration, spies, and informers to break up group illegality.* Certainly, the informer existed in the seventeenth century and served mainly for keeping watch; henceforth, the bourgeoisie infiltrates delinquent groups with its own agents.† Third, the bourgeoisie wanted to insert something more than just the negative law of "this is not yours" between the worker and the production apparatus he had in his hands. A supplementary code was needed that complements this law and gets it to work: the worker himself had to be moralized. When he is told: "You are only your labor-power and I have paid the market price for it,"‡ and when so much wealth is put in his hands, it is necessary to inject into the relationship between the worker and what he is working on a whole series of obligations and constraints that overlay the law of wages, which is apparently the simple law of the market.§ The wage contract must be accompanied by a coercion that is like its validity clause: the working class must be "regenerated," "moralized." Thus the transfer of the penitentiary takes place with one social class applying it to another: it is in this class relationship between the bourgeoisie and the proletariat that the condensed and remodeled penitentiary system begins to function; it will be a political instrument of the control and maintenance of relations of production. Fourth, something more is needed for this supplementary code to function effectively and for the

---

* The manuscript (fol. 16) adds: "(who is no longer the '*mouche*' of the eighteenth century)."[17]

† The manuscript (fol. 16) adds: "an institution which corresponds exactly to these 'smuggler' forms of depredation ... Just as depredation relies on elements within the apparatus of production, repression will rely on elements within the apparatus of depredation. Police-thieves collusion will take up in a different form the collusion between agents and those practicing fraud."

‡ The manuscript (fol. 16) adds: "even if you starve."

§ The manuscript (fol. 17) adds: "which is its indispensable complement."

delinquent actually to appear as a social enemy: the actual separation of delinquents from non-delinquents within those lower strata practicing illegalism. The great continuous mass of economico-political illegalism, going from common law crime to political revolt, must be broken up and the purely delinquent must be placed on one side, and those free of delinquency, who may be called non-delinquent, on the other.

Thus, the bourgeoisie has no great wish to suppress delinquency.[18] The main objective of the penal system is breaking this continuum of lower-class illegalism and the organization of a world of delinquency. There are two instruments for this. On the one hand, an ideological instrument: the theory of the delinquent as social enemy. This is no longer someone who struggles against the law, who wishes to evade power, but someone who is at war with every member of society. And the suddenly monstrous face the criminal assumes at the end of the eighteenth century, in literature and in penal theorists, corresponds to this need to break lower-class illegalism in two. On the other hand, practical instruments. How will the bourgeoisie substantivize delinquency, isolate it?

The first means is the prison. Its institution has scarcely been defined, the first establishments opened, than already its property of taking back into prison those who have left it is known. The great cycle of recidivism was seen and acknowledged straight away; a closed circuit of delinquency needed to be established for the latter to stand out against the great background of lower-class illegalism. Thus, the prison's locking away has to be understood in two senses: the prison is where one locks up delinquents, but it is also the system by which delinquency is sealed off as a kind of autonomous, clear-cut social phenomenon in itself. The other means consists in pitting delinquents and non-delinquents against each other. This is how prison work was presented as in competition with the worker's work. In nineteenth-century prisons, the prisoners' material conditions were no worse than workers' housing conditions and subsistence: this kind of competition in poverty was also one of the factors of this break. Finally, the main means was to establish the reign of real hostile relationships between delinquents and non-delinquents. Hence the fact that delinquents were a privileged source of recruits for the police, and that, since Napoleon, the army had been a way of soaking up delinquency in society and of using those who refused the work ethic that one was trying to inculcate in workers against the workers themselves in situations of strikes and political revolts.

Prison, colonies, army, police:[*] these were all so many means for breaking up lower-class illegalism and preventing the application of its techniques to bourgeois property. Of course, these means did not entirely eradicate economic illegalism (machine breaking), social illegalism (formation of associations), civil illegalism (rejection of marriage),[†] and political illegalism (riots). Thus the problem of illegalism remained fully on the agenda in the history of the working class in the nineteenth century, but it is a different history from that of the eighteenth century. In the eighteenth century, illegalism functions in a complex relationship with bourgeois illegalism; on the other hand, in the nineteenth century, workers' illegalism is the major target of the whole repressive system of the bourgeoisie. And we can say that the strength of anarchist ideology is linked to the persistence and rigor of this illegalist consciousness and practice in the working class—a persistence and rigor that neither parliamentary nor trade union legality succeed in absorbing.

---

[*] Manuscript (fol. 17): "Prison, colonies, army, police: refusal of the work ethic."
[†] Manuscript (fol. 18) adds: "moral illegalism."

1. See M. Foucault, "Théories et Institutions pénales," seventh lecture, fol. 2: "all the major phases of development of the penal system, of the repressive system, are ways of responding to forms of popular struggles"; fol. 3: "The couple penal system-delinquency is an effect of the couple repressive system-seditious [system]. An effect in the sense that it is a product, a condition of preservation, a displacement, and an occultation."

2. Foucault will put forward an analysis of illegalisms (see the following note and "Course context" below, pp. 281-283) more precise than the reference to the notion of "seditious mobs," which was used and keenly debated at the time. See E. P. Thompson, *The Making of the English Working Class*, p. 62: "Too often historians have used the term ['mobs'] lazily, to evade further analysis, or ... as a gesture of prejudice." For Foucault, the penal system is not the result of a fear aroused by the "seditious mobs," but rather by the industrialization of bourgeois fortune that will display its wealth before the lower classes, and therefore make it available to it; see "Course context" below, p. 278. In an interview given a few months later, Foucault "corrects" his own use of the term "seditious mobs": "In fact I do not think it is so much the problem of the seditious mobs that is essential, but the fact that bourgeois wealth, by the very necessities of economic development, is invested in such a way that it is in the hands of those who were responsible for production. Every worker was a possible predator. And every creation of surplus value was at the same time the opportunity, or anyway the possibility, of a possible purloining": M. Foucault, "À propos de l'enfermement pénitentiaire," *DE*, II, p. 438/"Quarto," I, p. 1306.

3. This analysis of popular illegalism—and of illegalism more generally—will become a fundamental theme in Foucault's thought concerning the penal system and will be developed over the following months and in *Surveiller et Punir; Discipline and Punish*. Foucault develops the theme in several interviews at this time. See "À propos de l'enfermement pénitentiaire," pp. 435-436/pp. 1303-1304: "... in any regime, the different social groups, the different classes, the different castes each have their illegalism. In the Ancien Régime, these illegalisms had reached a state of relative adjustment ... All these illegalisms, obviously, were played off against each other ... The bourgeoisie had, in a sense, need of popular illegalism. A kind of *modus vivendi* was established therefore. And what I think happened is that when the bourgeoisie had taken political power and was able to adapt the structures of the exercise of power to its economic interests, the popular illegalism that it had tolerated, and that, as it were, had found a kind of possible space of existence in the Ancien Régime, became intolerable for it; it absolutely had to muzzle it. And I think that the penal system, and especially the general system of surveillance that was developed at the end of the eighteenth and beginning of the nineteenth century in all the countries of Europe, is the sanction of this new fact: that the old popular illegalism, which was tolerated in some of its forms under the Ancien Régime, became literally impossible: all the lower strata effectively had to be placed under surveillance." See also *Surveiller et Punir*, pp. 84-91 and pp. 277-282; *Discipline and Punish*, pp. 82-89 and pp. 275-280.

4. The book in question is the doctoral thesis of Paul Bois, *Paysans de l'Ouest. Des structures économiques et sociales aux options politiques depuis l'époque révolutionnaire dans la Sarthe* (see above, p. 40 note 20). Foucault bases himself on the analysis in chapter XI of the second book: "Les tisserands. Étude sociale," pp. 415-543.

5. The general regulation of 1748 sets out, in particular, the modes of fabrication. See R. Musset, *Le Bas-Maine. Étude géographique* (Paris: Armand Colin, "Bibliothèque

de la Foundation Thiers," 1917); H. E. Sée, *Les Origines du capitalisme moderne* (Paris: A. Colin, "Collection Armand Colin: Section d'histoire et sciences économiques" 79, 1926) pp. 102-114; F. Dornic, *L'Industrie textile dans le Maine et ses débouchés internationaux (1650-1815)* (Le Mans: Pierre-Belon, 1955); P. Bois, *Paysans de l'Ouest*, p. 518 sq. For a more recent publication, see R. Plessix, "Les tisserands du Haut-Maine à la fin du XVIIIe siècle," *Annales de Bretagne et des pays de l'Ouest*, vol. 97 (3), 1990, pp. 193-205: "Les industries textiles dans l'Ouest, XVIIIe-XXe siècles."

6. See P. Bois, *Paysans de l'Ouest*, pp. 528-529.
7. See E. P. Thompson, "The Moral Economy of the English Crowd" (see above, p. 40 note 20).
8. This reference to the great bandit in the tradition of Robin Hood is taken up in *Surveiller et Punir*, p. 86; *Discipline and Punish*, p. 84 in the context of a discussion of lower-class illegalisms.
9. See E. P. Thompson, "The Moral Economy of the English Crowd."
10. On the question of popular courts, see above, p. 79 note 32.
11. Theme taken up in *Surveiller et Punir*, p. 23 [This theme is not taken up here. Illegalism is discussed by Foucault in Part Four, Chapter 2 "Illégalismes et délinquance"; "Illegalities and delinquency." See in particular *Discipline and Punish*, pp. 271-272; G.B.]
12. See ibid., pp. 82-83; pp. 80-81 and pp. 220-221; pp. 213-214.
13. See P. Colquhoun, *A Treatise on the Police of the Metropolis*: "Value of Merchandize imported £.30,957,421"; "Value of Merchandize exported 29,640,568"; "Value of the Hull, Tackle, Apparel and Stores ... 8,825,000"; "General Total 70,267,989"; "Commerce of a Single River ... where 13,444 ships and vessels ..."; ibid., p. 604: "above 13,000 vessels ... arrive at, and depart from, the Port of London, with merchandize, in the course of a year ... bringing and carrying away property, estimated at above *Seventy Millions Sterling*" (emphasis in original).
14. Ibid., p. 217. In the manuscript (fols. 11-12) Foucault adds two other quotations from Colquhoun: "Now, says Colquhoun, how will the worker react to this situation: 'The analogy between actual pillage and smuggling in the conception of the nautical labourers, and the uncontrolled habit of plunder which too long existed, trained up myriads of delinquents who affixed in their minds no degree of moral turpitude'" (p. 323); and "'plunder must have been excessive, especially where from its analogy to smuggling, at least in the conceptions of those who were implicated; and from its gradual increase, the culprits seldom were restrained by a sense of the moral turpitude of the offence'" (p. 217). Foucault continues: "No difference therefore between attack on the regulation and attack on property; between violating the law and stealing things. But this is not just a confusion at the level of perception. It is the transfer of a whole system of behavior" (fol. 12).
15. In the manuscript Foucault gives two examples of these forms of robbery that presuppose collusion or are the direct work of seamen or Port employees. The first example is that of the "Mud-Larks [who], on the pretext of searching for old bits of iron, get their hands on some produce" (fol. 13). Colquhoun describes this type of robbery as resulting from a lucrative arrangement between Port employees, coopers in particular, who handed over "small bags of sugar, coffee, pimento, ginger" to these *"Mud-Larks"* who pretended to search in the mud for old ropes and iron, and who "received a share of the booty" (*Treatise*, pp. 230-231).
   The second example is that of the "Light-Horsemen [who], on the pretense of selling 'sweepings' (of sugar), claimed as a perquisite, provided themselves with great quantities of it" (fol. 13). Colquhoun's description (ibid., pp. 223-226) of

these *Light-Horsemen* brings out the connivance of the two parties in the perpetration of this illegalism, which has its source in "a connection which was formed between the Mates of West India ships and the criminal Receivers, residing near the river, who were accustomed to assail them under the pretence of purchasing what is called *sweepings*, or in other words, the spillings or drainings of sugars, which remained in the hold and between the decks after the cargo was discharged. These sweepings were claimed as a perquisite by a certain proportion of the Mates, contrary to the repeated and express rules established by the Committee of Merchants" (p. 223).

16. In the manuscript, on the subject of the circuits of marketing smuggled goods, Foucault points out that they operate at two levels: "- the receivers of retail articles. Purchase directly varied objects. A third of the price.// - the receivers of wholesale (specialized) who resell either to retailers, or to entrepreneurs, or to the State.// - barrows which make the collection around London" (fol. 13). Colquhoun describes this "class" of Dealers (p. 75) in the third chapter of his work (p. 74 sq.). He divides them into two classes, "*Wholesale* and *Retail Dealers*" (p. 75), and points out that "these pests of Society ... [have] increased, from about 300 to 3000, in the course of the last twenty years, in the Metropolis alone!" (p. 12).

Foucault adds: "This contraband has its language but it has above all its currency. F[orged] M[oney] // 40 to 50 counterfeiters in England // One of the counterfeiters has produced 200,000 pounds in seven years. // Circuits interfering with those of receivers ('the Jews'). // Colquhoun estimates a 0.75% the value of depredations in relation to the value of the wealth exposed to danger. If the profit is 10% this would make a depredation of 7.5%" (fols. 13-14). Colquhoun describes the details of this 'enormous evil' and the coinage of counterfeit money in chapter VII (ibid., p. 171 sq.) after having given a more general description in the first chapter (ibid., pp. 15-20). Colquhoun associates 'Jews' (as well as the 'Irish') with counterfeit money: 'The lower ranks among the Irish, and the German Jews, are the chief supporters of the trade of circulating base money in London' (ibid., p. 189). With regard to the value of depredations, Colquhoun writes: 'when by calculation it is also found, that the whole amount of the aggregate plunder, great and extensive as it appears to be, does not much exceed *three quarters per cent.* on the value of the whole property exposed to danger: the Reader will be reconciled to an estimate, which from the elucidations contained in this chapter, will ultimately appear to be by no means exaggerated" (ibid., p. 215).

17. Foucault returns to the role of delinquents as informers (*mouchards*) and *agents provocateurs* in the eighteenth and nineteenth centuries in *Surveiller et Punir*, p. 285 and n. 2; *Discipline and Punish*, p. 280 and p. 322 n. 17.

18. See M. Foucault, *"Il faut défendre la société"*, lecture of 14 January 1976, pp. 28-30, see p. 30; *"Society Must Be Defended"*, pp. 31-33, p. 33: "The bourgeoisie does not give a damn about delinquents, or about how they are punished or rehabilitated, as that is of no great economic interest. On the other hand, the set of mechanisms whereby delinquents are controlled, kept track of, punished, and reformed does generate a bourgeois interest that functions within the economico-political system as a whole."

nine

28 FEBRUARY 1973

(B) France (continued). Pinning the moral on the penal.
4. Peasant depredation: in the eighteenth century, illegalism
as functional element of peasant life; end of eighteenth
century, abolition of feudal rights; nineteenth century, tighter
exploitation. The case of the exploitation of forests. New
illegalism against the contract; challenge and civil dispute.
5. Consequences: (i) the army as source and exchanger of
illegalisms; (ii) illegalism as the stake of the Revolution;
(iii) a massive and programmed bourgeois response: the
"lower class" as "degenerate class." The new character of the
delinquent: wild, immoral, but can be regenerated by superin-
tendence. ∽ Reflections: the intelligence of the bourgeoisie; the
stupidity of intellectuals; the seriousness of the struggle.

I HAVE TRIED TO answer the question of the transfer of the
penitentiary element into the penal apparatus by showing that the
notion of "seditious mobs" was not sufficient to resolve the problems.
In its place I have introduced the more operational notion of lower-class
illegalism (*illégalisme populaire*). Now, it seems to me that under the
Ancien Régime this illegalism formed a system with the illegalisms of
the other social classes and that, coupled more precisely and closely
with bourgeois illegalism, it contributed to the development of capitalist
society. Finally, at a certain point, this illegalism was no longer tolerable
to the class that had just taken power, because wealth, in its materiality,

is spatialized in new forms[1] and runs the risk of being attacked frontally by a lower-class illegalism that, henceforth, would not clash with the system of the laws and regulations of power, but with its goods themselves in their material existence.*

The lower strata transfer the techniques of the old illegalism to the very body of wealth and can reply to the bourgeoisie: did we not violate the law, plunder wealth together? To which, the bourgeoisie replies that what was attacked under the Ancien Régime were rules, laws, and unjustifiable abuses, and it was a question of power, and so of politics; whereas now things, property, and so common law, natural law is being attacked. Previously, abuses of power were attacked; now violating the law displays a lack of morality.† It is at this point that the pinning of the system of moral correction on the penal system takes place. Thus, Colquhoun says: "It is however ardently to be hoped, that the period is fast approaching when ... the suggestions offered in subsequent chapters, may tend to accelerate the renovation of this forlorn and miserable class of outcasts [criminals], by means of an appropriate *Penitentiary System*."[2]

A possible objection to this analysis is that the example chosen is limited and the fact that the only link that the urban population has with bourgeois wealth is the law of property: "this does not belong to you." To tell the truth, this stratum of population is very limited in relation to the demographic whole of the eighteenth century. Can we explain a phenomenon as general as the establishment of a new penality on the basis of the sole example of this embryo of the working class? Is this not to attribute a process that took place in the eighteenth century to a "great fear," which is actually a phenomenon of the nineteenth century?

I will refer then to an example of rural illegalism and put as an epigraph to this analysis a text appearing in an anonymous pamphlet: "The peasant is a vicious, crafty animal, a ferocious, half-civilized beast; he has no heart, probity, or honor; he would frequently let himself be

---

* The manuscript (fol. 2) adds: "and because the workers applied forms of illegalisms derived from the old illegalism to this wealth thus set out in space. Port of London: the techniques of smuggling that attacked rights, dues, taxes, in short, the *levies of power*, now attack the materiality of bourgeois wealth. Colquhoun, texts on smuggling."

† In the manuscript (fol. 2), this passage, presented in the form of a reply attributed to the bourgeoisie, ends with: "Go, and repent."

carried away by ferocity if the other two estates did not swoop down on him pitilessly and prevent him from being able to carry out the crime he would like to commit."[3]

*   *   *

*In its rural form, lower-class illegalism undergoes the same transformation as urban illegalism. In the eighteenth century it was a functional element of peasant life. A whole series of tolerances permitted the poorest fringe to survive: fallow land, heaths, and communal goods were so many pockets of illegalism at the heart of peasant space. The smuggling of products under State control (salt, tobacco), likewise, had its points of support within peasant society. Rural illegalism, moreover, was connected to and depended upon that of the landowners. Now, in the second half of the eighteenth century we can make out a sort of change of front that is the effect of a slow process consisting in: first, increasing demographic pressure; then, from 1730, an increase in incomes from landed property, which makes land an economically attractive possession; [and] finally, a great demand for estates for investment. Thus, with the Revolution, we arrive at the abolition of feudal rights, at large property transfers. At the end of the eighteenth century landed property is brought under the regime of the simple contract. Now, precisely at the very moment that, through this triumph of the contract, the whole old armature of feudal rights disappears and land enters into the purely contractual system of property, land becomes much less accessible to the peasant mass as it becomes the object of more or less massive purchases, and this new system of juridical appropriation dispossesses and pauperizes even more the day laborers and smallholders who hitherto had been able to live thanks to these pockets of illegalism. In effect, the new property regime brings about the disappearance of community rights, the heaths, and aims at a more intensive exploitation of the land.

The most notable example[†] is the exploitation of forests, which now follows a faster rhythm. The forest, which had been a place of refuge and

---

* Manuscript (fol. 5), subheading: "*Peasant depredation.*"

† The manuscript (fol. 6) notes in first place the example of "the disappearance of land left fallow."

survival, becomes exploitable and so supervised property.* Certainly, unlike industrial wealth, landed wealth does not change location; however, rural space is modified, for all the instruments that ensure its protection multiply as property enters into the regime of contract: prohibitions of passage, enclosures, and so on. In short, the whole space of transit and precarious survival that rural space had been is changed drastically, and this makes all the rural illegalisms impossible and intolerable. We thus see why the entry of bourgeois wealth into the juridical system of the contract brings about illegalism as an immense rebound. There are the great waves of vagrancy at the end of the eighteenth century, the intensification of old peasant illegalisms, the grain riots [Flour War; G.B.], spontaneous taxations to the [advantage] of the poorest peasants, and so on. It is thus the oldest practices of popular illegalism that are reactivated in the years preceding the Revolution. There are also attempts to continue to exploit old customary rights, old tolerances, despite the new legislation. In this way the Revolution was stirred up by these micro-histories. This explosion of illegalism[†] was nothing other than the spontaneous reaction to new juridical forms that made the old illegalisms impossible and also put landed property in close combat, as it were, with those who were excluded from it and no longer had any tolerated rights of community life over it or accepted illegalism. This practice of peasant illegalism animated the Revolution (as the episodes of the Vendée and the Midi show[5]) and brought

---

* The manuscript (fol. 6-7) develops: "The new mode of exploitation of the forests: more intensive due to new needs; installation of glassworks and forges on the edges of or within these forests. The old forest (with an age-old rhythm of exploitation), a place of refuge, toleration, and survival not only for marginals, but also for the poorest inhabitants (who graze, take wood, and poach in it), tends to become exploitable and supervised property. Add to this the phenomena more directly linked to the Revolution: the rise in agricultural prices (which only benefits the peasants well enough off to sell); the mistrust of bad money (which provokes hoarding)."

† The manuscript mentions other examples of this "formidable explosion of peasant illegalism," some "with more violence" like the riots, "spontaneous taxation," and the "looting of hoarders"; others in the form of "attempts to continue to assert customary rights or old tolerances, in the form of voluntary depredations (passage or toll rights; gleaning)"; "direct attacks against the new land grabbers or against their harvests"; and "extreme forms of banditry and the economico-political sedition of the West and South (between [17]93 and [1799)."[4]

The manuscript (fol. 8) adds: "But it [peasant illegalism] framed, animated, and overflowed the Revolution. And if to a certain extent it brought about the Revolution, it was because the bourgeois, urban, juridical revolution was intended to curb it."

it about inasmuch as a good part of the Revolution was directed at controlling this movement.

Let us take some examples of this background noise of peasant illegalism. The intendant of Provence writes to Necker in the Spring of 1789: "I could cite you several communities that the peasant has completely devastated and plundered; he attacks the bourgeois, craftsman, and noble indiscriminately. It is he who reigns and the bandits who direct and are at the head of the mob."[6] In Year III there are plans to modify the 1791 Rural Code when it is realized that it has no real hold on this illegalism; the author of one of these projects writes thus: "It is inconceivable, I say, how many villagers have little respect for estates: the most formal prohibitions do not stop them ... one is plundered, devastated, ruined, usually without knowing who to blame."[7] In Year VI, in the first volume of the *Annales d'agriculture*, we find this: "In the past, excessive greed no doubt made some farmers hateful to the poorer class; today we see men of this poorer class who seek to appropriate what belongs to the farmers. The wrongs of the past do not justify those of today."[8]

So we can see how the wage, the contract, redistributes the interplay of law, illegalism, the individual, and the very substance of wealth. I think the analysis of penality, if done properly, that is to say if related to illegalism, must constantly take account of these four elements that are actually in play in this part of the struggle over illegalism: the law, illegal practice, the individual, the body of wealth. The contract redistributes the interplay between these elements, but more ambiguously than the wage. In fact, after all, the urban populace was constrained to wage-earning, and in the new game established between individuals and the body of wealth, the former were constrained; whereas, although the contract, as juridical form of rural property, does introduce certain constraints, it is at the same time desirable inasmuch as it liberates from old rights and obligations, strips property of all feudal constraints, and, due to this, is desired by the peasantry as the way to acquire property. But at the same time it introduces into the rural world difficulties, risks, defensive reactions, and calculations calling for a new illegalism that will be deployed in this new world of the contract. This will take two forms: an illegalism against the contract, that is to say against property, that practices the pure and simple depredation of goods, of harvests; [and] an illegalism that invests the contract from within and tries to get round it: we enter then the world of challenge and dispute.

This means that, whereas urban illegalism will necessarily be a penal matter, peasant illegalism will, to a large extent, involve civil law, not without difficulties and suffering. Balzac described the suffering caused by marriage and commercial contracts.[9] The sufferings befalling peasant property and investment due to the peasant contract should also be described. Actually, this has been described, by Pierre Rivière for example, who, on the basis of his experience as a small Normandy peasant, recounted the suffering [linked to] this contract:[10] to escape conscription, [his father] married and entered into the marriage contract, and this contract, in itself illegalist since it is a way of getting round the law, proves to be a trap.*

*   *   *

So we can draw out some points. First, bourgeois wealth, as it is being established in its rural as well as industrial and commercial forms, has no sooner escaped feudal predation, thanks to the Revolution, than it comes up against lower-class depredation, the two illegalisms, rural and urban. These are connected to each other through another illegalism, that of the army. The large armies of the end of the eighteenth century are a constant source of renewal of illegalisms and of contact between them, while serving moreover as a brake by absorbing all those who put themselves in the situation of illegality or by repressing the most extreme forms of illegalism.[11] But even more they play a part in accelerating illegalism by assuring impunity for those who become soldiers, giving the habits of pillage and vagabondage to those who join their ranks, and, finally, giving rise to a host of illegalisms, like refusal of conscription, which increase from Year II. They serve, in short, as an exchanger between rural and urban illegalisms, since, through their

* The manuscript (fol. 13) adds: "Pierre Rivière: contract-illegality (to avoid the army); contract booby-trapped within by a range of illegalisms; contract from which one cannot free oneself, or that one cannot recreate by murder. A whole precipitation of little contractual illegalisms into the greatest of crimes."

displacement of populations, they redistribute peasants to the towns and the urban populace into the countryside, through the system of desertion. This is also the problem in England, as Colquhoun says in his *A Treatise on the Police*: "It is indeed true, that during the first three years of the present war, many Convicts and idle and disorderly persons were sent to the Army and Navy ... how necessary is it to be provided with antidotes, previous to the return of peace ...?"[12]

Second, I would like to stress a point on the basis of which we can try to understand the problems I have raised. Pre-revolutionary illegalism is generally seen as the consequence of a series of crises of power, institutions, and legality: the economic upsurge made the old legalities outmoded and, before giving way to the new legality, there would have been this great explosion of illegalism. What I would like to show is that the birth of industrial society overturned not just the order of legalities, but the whole system of both traditional and robust illegalisms that enabled considerable masses of the population to live. At the end of the eighteenth century, the illegalisms thus threatened by the new forms of society began to take the form of revolt. Illegalism is therefore not only the extreme and lower-class form of the revolutionary upsurge; it is what is at stake in this upsurge. All the major movements sought to maintain illegalism as a practice to which one had a right. Consider what took place in the Vendée with the refusal of the new legality.[13] At issue was struggle against a system of appropriation incompatible with the old game of illegalisms, and if the inhabitants of the Vendée appealed to the Ancien Régime, it was doubtless not out of a positive love of the law and the whole regulatory system and game of exactions linked to that regime, but because they wanted to return to a regime that permitted the operation of certain illegalisms necessary for the existence of the peasant community. *In the towns, spontaneous taxations, looting of hoarders, and popular courts were all ways of asserting the old practices of lower-class illegalism in the forms of a new legitimacy.

Third consequence: to this illegalist upsurge, not only in its form but particularly in its aim—since it aims at the preservation of the illegalism that no longer threatens the old structures of feudalism, but the very body of social wealth—the bourgeoisie responds with a

---

* The manuscript (fol. 17) adds: "The opposite example."

gigantic operation of penal and penitentiary encirclement of lower-class illegalism in general.* This was absolutely programmed. Its fundamental formulae are found in texts of the end of the eighteenth and the beginning of the nineteenth century. Thus, there is a network of penal theories and practices that designate the offender as enemy of society in general, and a whole practice of correction that considers the offender less as an enemy than as someone on whom one can act, whom one can morally transform, correct. The junction between the juridico-penal definition of the offender as a social enemy and the definition of the prisoner (*correctionnaire*) as an individual to be transformed takes place in certain discourses that make the great installation of the nineteenth-century penitentiary system theoretically and discursively acceptable. This junction consists, first of all, in asserting that all illegalism is, in a privileged if not exclusive way, the product of a single social class, that of the workers; then, in declaring that this illegalism is the work of this class inasmuch as it is not really integrated into society; finally, in saying that this refusal of the social pact specific to the lowest class is a sort of primary, wild delinquency, peculiar to a stratum of population still close to instinct and the life of nature: these are the enemies of the very body of wealth.†

This description of the class of workers as the privileged object of penitentiary transformation for integration into a social pact constitutes the pre-institutional, ideological join that will make the whole organization of the penal and penitentiary system acceptable. We can refer to several texts. The first [dates from] 1722; a text in which the agents of the *Ferme générale* write to the intendant of Auvergne complaining of the indulgence of the Clermont judges towards smugglers: "they [the judges] should regard contraband salt merchants and smugglers less as intruders who have sought to share out a portion of the profits of the Farm, than as disturbers of the public peace."[14] That is to say, the magistrates saw the latter as intruders who, in the system of feudal predation, take their share of what is levied on wealth, in short, as supplementary tax

---

* The manuscript (fol. 17) indicates with an interlinear addition that this vast operation of the bourgeoisie, which "is to be studied," "is programmed in an ideological operation that exists."

† The manuscript (fol. 18) adds: "We still have savages among us. Turning illegalism into delinquency, social latitude into social danger."

farmers, and, in this sense, not to be treated as criminals: they are only
collectors of illegal taxes. Now, they have to be treated as disturbers of
the public peace, that is to say delinquents who endanger the whole
of society. Such is the program: to transform intruders in the system
of feudal predation into a social enemy. In 1768, in order to cut the
smuggler Montagne off from his popular support, the Auvergne Farm
proposes to print a false fly sheet in which pseudo-crimes of the latter
would be recounted so as to transform his image as a smuggler, which
is positive for the peasants, into the negative image of the criminal:
"This news has been published, some thefts have been put down to
him, the truth of which is, to tell the truth, rather uncertain; Montagne
has been depicted as a wild beast to be hunted down. Given that the
people of Auvergne are naturally hot-headed, the idea has taken hold
and several have said that if Montagne were to pass through their land,
they would kill him like a wild and harmful animal."* We have here
again the transformation of the character of tolerated illegalism into
a character who is already the monstrous delinquent of nineteenth-
century penality, criminology, and psychiatry. This conversion is the
result of an absolutely concerted strategy.

Thirty years later, in 1798, the effects of this operation appear in a
report on banditry in the Midi: "Considering the murders and crimes
no night has yet clothed in darkness, crimes the telling of which would
appall any country at any time; considering cannibals that nature
blushes for having placed in the class of humans."[16] [They also appear
in] a text by Target, an Ancien Régime lawyer, responsible from 1802
to 1804 with developing the first draft of a penal code, which will be
resumed in 1808.[17] In his presentation, most of the real operations that
penal legislation will carry out later are clearly set out: "Imagine a large
country whose immense population is formed, as it were, of various
peoples who have nothing in common but the center of authority, and
is divided into innumerable classes, some enlightened by knowledge,
improved by education, softened by sociability, ennobled by moral
sentiments; others, degraded by poverty, debased by contempt, and
long matured in the habits of crime or sin; every day one will see there
the distressing contrast between the most honorable virtues and lowest

---

* Manuscript (fol. 18): "In 1768: Propaganda bulletin against Montagne."[15]

vices. There, close to the loftiness of courage, generosity, and heroism one will note with disgust egoism, insensitivity, abjection, and atrocity itself. There, hard, dry, inflexible souls, devoid of moral ideas, will obey only their coarse sensations; idleness, debauchery, greed, and envy will show themselves irreconcilable enemies of wisdom and work, of economy and property. There, offenses and crimes of every kind will proliferate, not so much in the mass of the nation as in the dregs of this tribe foreign to the general character, which is formed alongside the true people by the force of circumstances and habits built up over centuries. For such a nation, penalties must almost always be gauged by reference to the nature of this degenerate race, which is the source of crimes, and the regeneration of which can barely be glimpsed, after many years of the wisest government."[18]

In this text we see, first, the assimilation of the illegalist and the new character of the delinquent who, with those around him, form a foreign population. Second, a population that is foreign because wild: it is at the same time debased and primitive, degenerate and close to nature and the instincts. This character of savagery is determined by immorality: the savage, who, in his primitiveness, was the bearer of morality in the pure state, has disappeared, savageness manifesting itself through immorality. Third, political power is defined as an arbiter in relation to these opposed classes. The function of political power is defined with regard to this confrontation between classes and in order to protect one class against another. And finally, the idea of a regeneration of this primitive and degenerate class through the intervention of political power and constant supervision makes it possible to connect up the theory of the delinquent as social enemy and the practice of correction.[*]

I have emphasized this text on the prior ideological operation as condition of acceptability of certain operations for several reasons.[†] In the first place, it is a text of prodigious lucidity. We are forever in the habit of speaking of the "stupidity" of the bourgeoisie. I wonder whether the theme of the stupid bourgeois is not a theme for intellectuals:[‡] those

---

[*] Manuscript (fol. 18) in margin: "Articulation social enemy—correction."

[†] After the last numbered sheet (fol. 18), the manuscript contains three unnumbered sheets, the first of which has "App. c[ours] no. 9." The first line has: "N.B. A text like Target's is worth dwelling on: ..."

[‡] Without the modulation of belief, present in the typescript, the manuscript has: "for artists, for intellectuals, philosophers" (App. cours no. 9, first sheet).

who imagine that merchants are narrow-minded, people with money are mulish, and those with power are blind. Safe from this belief, moreover, the bourgeoisie is remarkably intelligent. The lucidity and intelligence of this class, which has conquered and kept power under conditions we know, produce many effects of stupidity and blindness, but where, if not precisely in the stratum of intellectuals? We may define intellectuals as those on whom the intelligence of the bourgeoisie produces an effect of blindness and stupidity.* And then, everything that takes place in the organization of the penal system was said: is not the principle of an analysis in the form of a search for the unsaid the property of those who cannot see the actual cynicism of the class in power? It does not need the silence of the unsaid for the intelligence, the profundity of the interpreter to rush in and find what the others could not say. Actually, the others have always said [everything]. The problem therefore is not to seek in the lacunae of a text the force or effect of an unsaid.[19] Finally, this entails that this said, this cynicism, this intelligence, is never to be sought in an author's texts or oeuvre.† If the bourgeoisie appears stupid it is because one looks for traces of its intelligence or stupidity in that particularly schooled category of discourse called the works of authors, texts. These categories—authors, writers, works, texts—are what the schooling of society has separated off from the active, strategic mass of discourse. A text is a discourse that has lost its context and strategic

---

* The manuscript adds:

"- As it [the bourgeoisie] holds power, it can be cynical.
- The development of com[mercial] exploitation and the exercise of power creates knowledge. Those who deny this are public entertainers. They fail to recognize the seriousness of the struggle." (App. cours no. 9, first sheet).

† Manuscript: "This is not a question of an author, a work, or a text. To the 'artistic' theme that the bourgeoisie is stupid corresponds the professorial theme that only one thing counts (the author, the writer, the oeuvre, the text), that these are what dominate us and dictate our law; that it is these that engage us. Kant has bound us, and Kierkegaard will liberate us. These notions are the product of a 'schooling' of discourse; of the fabrication of objects intended for academic explanation. It hardly matters whether one places oneself at one or the other end of the series, on the side of the author or of the text, on the side of the expression or of the expert, on the side of [psychology] or of rhetoric, in any case, the entire series is a product of the schooling of discourse. A schooling that makes it possible, on the one hand, to evade all discourses outside the text (*hors text*), and above all to hide the role, position, and function of discourses in strategies and struggles." (App. lecture 9, first and second sheets).

effectiveness. An oeuvre is a discourse attached to an author, on the one hand, and to the implicit meanings of an unsaid, on the other.

"The bourgeoisie is stupid," "things are not said," "works are what matter"—these three propositions* govern textual analysis, which we should discard. To say that things are said is to accept the principle of the bourgeoisie's cynicism and to gauge the full extent of the power against which one is struggling. To accept that discourses are what matters is to situate discourse where it can, in actual fact, be attacked: not in its meaning, not through what it does not say, but at the level of the operation carried out through it, that is to say in its strategic function, in order to dismantle what the discourse has done. So let us disregard works and texts, and study rather discourses in the functions or strategic fields in which they produce their effects.†

---

* Manuscript: "The three propositions are linked:

  - the bourgeoisie is not stupid: principle of struggle;
  - things are absolutely said: principle of cynicism;
  - what matters is not works." (App. lecture 9, second sheet).

† The manuscript ends in the following way: "Because in effect, from the point of view of works, from which it is absent, at least as bourgeoisie, and on first analysis, it is stupid, mute, and stubborn. But if we want to see it at work, in its decisions, in its strategic agility, in the uninterrupted formation of its knowledge (*savoir*), then we have to turn to the outside-the-text (*hors-texte*). It is in the outside-the-text [that] it is decided, it is said, it is seen. In the text it sleeps, it is hidden, it is not said. It is normal for the search for the unsaid to be finally the great mode of textual analysis. [Becoming] finally interpretive. The role of analysis of the outside-the-text (*hors-texte*), on the other hand, is to fix the strategic function and role of discourses in struggles. How are they linked to such operations that they make possible or of which they are a part, or a consequence.

To oppose the series text-unsaid-interpretation and the series *hors-texte*-discursive act-strategy. Which makes it possible to plot the positions, alliances, blockages, points of strength and weakness. In short, to produce a critique that is immediately a part of the struggles. To produce thus a history of morality 'outside the text':[20]

  - trial components
  - [components] of medico-legal expertise
  - matters of conscience
  - police reports
  - proceedings of all the societies of moralization
  - official records of all the [ruling] authorities.

This would be neither the architectonics of systems of morality, nor the doxology of opinions about morality. It would be the history of morality as strategy." (App. lecture no. 9, second and third sheets).

1. See M. Foucault, "À propos de l'enfermement pénitentiaire," *DE*, II, p. 436/"Quarto," I, p. 1304: "Under the Ancien Régime, wealth was basically landed and monetary ... But when bourgeois wealth comes to be invested on a very large scale in an industrial type of economy, that is to say invested in workshops, tools, machines, machine tools, raw materials, and stocks, all of which has been put in the hands of the working class, then the bourgeoisie has literally put its fortune in the hands of the lower strata."

2. P. Colquhoun, *A Treatise on the Police of the Metropolis*, p. 433 [The French translation cited by Foucault has "*un système de pénitence*"; G.B.].

3. In his manuscript, Foucault refers here to an "anonymous pamphlet, 2nd half of the eighteenth century, South of France" (fol. 4), which, the typescript notes (p. 132), is "quoted by Agulhon, *La Vie sociale en Provence*, 1970." Maurice Agulhon, in *La Vie sociale en Provence intérieure au lendemain de la Révolution* [see above, p. 40, note 22] p. 180, quotes this passage; he attributes it to "an anonymous [native of Arles] ... in 1752," and notes its origin: "In a manuscript of the Arles library, cited by G. Valran, *Misère et Charité en Provence au XVIIIᵉ siècle*, p. 29." In the latter work, *Misère et Charité en Provence au XVIIIᵉ siècle. Essai d'histoire sociale* (Paris: Arthur Rousseau, 1899), Gaston Valran attributes this passage to "an anonymous eyewitness, a bourgeois (one presumes), for he is animated by a lively resentment against the nobility and against the peasant" (p. 28).

4. On banditry in general, see M. Agulhon, *La Vie sociale en Provence intérieure*, pp. 367-404.

5. It is possible that Foucault is referring here to the military repression of banditry recounted by Agulhon (ibid.), but the juxtaposition with the Vendée points more towards the federalist insurrection. After the Jacobin forcible takeover against the Girondins at the Convention on 2 June 1793, numerous departmental administrations where the Girondins were well established will oppose Paris. In particular, in the Midi, Lyon, Marseille, Bordeaux, and Toulon become centers of an attempt to reconquer power. The Jacobins and representatives of the Convention are driven out and sometimes executed. Lyon, Marseilles, and then Toulon will be retaken by the revolutionary armies, giving rise to bloody repressions. A decree of 12 October 1793 in article 3 states thus: "The town of Lyon will be destroyed. All that was inhabited by the rich will be demolished." It is at the siege of Toulon that the military genius of Napoléon Bonaparte, then a young artillery officer, becomes famous. See H. Wallon, *La Révolution du 31 mai et le fédéralisme en 1793* (Paris: Hachette & Companie, 1886) 2 volumes; C. Riffaterre, *Le Mouvement antijacobin et antiparisien à Lyon et dans le Rhône-et-Loire en 1793*, 2 volumes (Lyon: A. Rey, 1912 and 1928).

6. This passage is quoted in *La Vie sociale en Provence intérieure*, p. 182. Maurice Agulhon situates it in the following way: "in the Spring of 1789 the struggle between the different 'estates' is signaled many times in the letters of the intendant to Villedeuil and Necker—27 and 30 March." Agulhon gives as his source the Archives départementales des Bouches-du-Rhône, 4110. See M. Cubells, *Les Horizons de la liberté. Naissance de la Révolution en Provence (1787-1789)* (Aix: Édisud, 1987) pp. 92-109.

7. In his manuscript (fol. 9), Foucault refers to an: "Anonymous pamphlet. Year III (shortly before the vote on the decree of 20 Messidor, completing the Rural Code of [17]91." The text comes from a pamphlet of twelve pages by F. L. Lamartine, *Mémoire sur une question d'agriculture et d'économie politique, relative à la cotisation des prairies artificielles et aux moyens de pourvoir à leur conservation* (Dijon: Desay, March 1793), in *L'Esprit des journaux français et étrangers* (Paris: Valade, 1795) vol. V, Sept.-Oct. 1795, pp. 119-120.

8. See H.-A. Tessier, *Annales de l'agriculture française, contenant des observations et des mémoires sur l'agriculture en général* (Paris: Huzard, 1797 [Year VI]) 4 volumes, vol. I, p. 371.

9. See H. de Balzac, *Le Contract de mariage* (1835), *Eugénie Grandet* (1834), and the other texts collected in the "Scènes de la vie de province" of *La Comédie humaine*. In the lecture of 7 March (below, p. 180, note 3), Foucault broaches the theme of the dangerous and laboring

classes—central theme of the historian Louis Chevalier, author of *Classes laborieuses et Classes dangereuses à Paris, pendant la première moitié du XIXe siècle* (Paris: Hachette, 1984 [Plon, 1958]). It is interesting to note and compare Chevalier's treatment of Balzac's work with Foucault's analysis; see L. Chevalier, ibid., pp. 133-150.

10. See M. Foucault, ed., *Moi, Pierre Rivière, ayant égorgé ma mère, ma sœur et mon frère. Un cas de parricide au XIXe siècle* (Paris: Gallimard, "Archives" 49) pp. 73-148 ("La mémoire"); English translation by F. Jellinek, *I, Pierre Rivière, having slaughtered my mother, my sister, and my brother ... A case of parricide in the 19th century* (New York: Pantheon, 1975; Harmondsworth: Peregrine, 1978) pp. 53-121 ("The Memoir").

11. The manuscript mentions: "Vendée, Midi". See above, p. 158 and note 5.

12. P. Colquhoun, *A Treatise on the Police of the Metropolis*, pp. 99-100.

13. There is an extensive and conflicting historiography on the causes of this revolt, which seems to stem from the disappointed hopes of poor regions in which the peasants, not coping with the burden of taxation, did not have the necessary means to benefit from the sale of national goods; from the levy of volunteers for the army; as well as the replacement of refractory clergy in a very Catholic region. See E. Gabory, *Les Guerres de Vendée* (Paris: Robert Laffont, 2009 [1912-1931]); L. Dubreuil, *Histoire des insurrections de l'Ouest* (Paris: Rieder, 2 volumes, 1929-1930); G. Walter, *La Guerre de Vendée* (Paris: Plon, 1953); C. Tilly, *La Vendée. Révolution et contre-révolution* (Paris: Fayard, 1970).

14. *Inventaire sommaire des Archives départementales antérieurs à 1790, Puy-de-Dôme: C 1516 à C 2817*, archivists Michel Cohendy and Gilbert Joseph Rouchon, vol. II (Clermont-Ferrand: Imprimerie et lithographie G. Mont-Louis, 1898) serie C (Intendance d'Auvergne), C 1660 (Liasse), 769-779 ("Smugglers").

15. Foucault mentions this episode in *Surveiller et Punir*, p. 70; *Discipline and Punish*, p. 66, and the reference given is: "Archives du Puy-de-Dôme, cited in M. Juillard, *Le Brigandage et la Contrabande en Haute-Auvergne au XVIIIe siècle* (Aurillac: Imprimerie moderne, 1937) p. 24."

16. Archives départementales, Arrêté of 26 vendémiaire Year VIII, série L, fol. 49-51 sq., quoted in abbé Maurel, *Le Brigandage dans les Basses-Alpes* (Marseille: P. Ruat, 1899) part II, ch. II.

17. Foucault puts Target in the category of great "reformers" alongside figures like Beccaria, Servan, and Duport. In the manuscript for the lecture of 7 March (below, p. 170 sq.), he describes Target as "a jurist of the Ancien Régime, who became a legislator under the Empire" (fol. 1). See *Surveiller et Punir*, p. 77, and also p. 82, p. 84, p. 95, p. 280; *Discipline and Punish*, p. 75, p. 80, p. 81, p. 92, p. 276.

18. Foucault returns to some expressions mentioned in this passage on Target, in particular that of "degenerate race" in *Surveiller et Punir*, p. 280; *Discipline and Punish*, p. 276, and gives as reference (ibid., p. 95; p. 92): "G. Target, *Observations sur le projet du Code pénal*, in Locré, *La Législation de la France*, vol. XXIX, pp. 7-8." See M. Target, "Observations sur le Projet de Code criminel" in Jean-Guillaume Locré, *Législation civile, commerciale et criminelle, ou Commentaire et complément des Codes français* (Brussels: Société typographique belge, 1837) vol. XV, pp. 2-16, esp. p. 5.

19. It is possible that Foucault, through his references to the "unsaid (*non dit*)," is alluding to the analysis put forward by Louis Althusser in "Du 'Capital' à la philosophie de Marx" in L. Althusser, E. Balibar, R. Establet, P. Macherey, and J. Rancière, *Lire Le Capital* (Paris: Maspero, 1968 [1965]) 2 volumes; English translation by Ben Brewster, "From *Capital* to Marx's Philosophy" in L. Althusser and E. Balibar, *Reading Capital* (London: New Left Books, 1970) of Marx's reading of Adam Smith. Inspired by psychoanalysis, the "'*symptomatic*' (*symptomale*)" reading "divulges the undivulged event in the text it reads, and in the same movement relates it to *a different text*, present as a necessary absence in the first" (ibid., vol. 1, pp. 28-29; Eng., p. 28). "Only since Freud have we begun to suspect what listening, and hence what speaking (and keeping silent), *means* (*veut dire*); that this '*meaning*' (*vouloir dire*) of speaking and listening reveals beneath the innocence of speech and hearing the culpable

depth of a second, *quite different* discourse, the discourse of the unconscious" (ibid., pp. 12-13; Eng., p. 16, emphasis in original).

20. Foucault's analysis in terms of *"hors-texte"* was, quite clearly, provoked by Jacques Derrida's work, *De la grammatologie* (Paris: Éditions de Minuit, 1967), p. 227; English translation Gayatri Chakravorty Spivak, *Of Grammatology* (Baltimore and London: The Johns Hopkins University Press, 1998, corrected edition) p. 158; see also, by the same author, *Limited Inc* (Paris: Galilée, 1990), p. 273; English translation Samuel Weber and Jeffrey Mehlman, *Limited Inc* (Evanston, IL: Northwestern University Press, 1988).

ten

7 MARCH 1973

*Analogies between Target and the Quakers. (I) Fear at the start of the nineteenth century: 1. linked to the new modes of production; a fear of the worker, of his desire and his body; 2. grounded in reality; 3. fear of the laboring class; 4. of the fact that "they" do not work enough. Threat to the capitalist apparatus. The penal system is directed at the worker's body, desire, and need. Double requirement: free market and discipline. The worker's record book (*livret*). (II) Penal dualism: the double front of penality. 1. Recodification of crimes and penalties: homogeneous, positive, constraining, representative, effective. 2. Integration of a moral conditioning: aggravating and extenuating circumstances; supervision; reformatories; re-education. ⌒ Law-correction duality. Criminology: a discourse that ensures the transcription of this duality. Monomania. ⌒ Symbiosis of criminology and penal system.*

TARGET'S TEXT[1] DEFINED THE place of political power between two classes, one the bearer of virtues, of the values of the good, and the other characterized by the vices driving it, by its immorality, and by the fact that it was considered to be foreign to the very body of society, as if forming a sort of nation connected up to the real nation from outside. Now, in the image of power as arbiter we have a kind of echo of what was found in the political theory of the Quakers, who presented the State as a sort of indispensable authority for resorbing, for controlling evil in society and putting this on the agenda of the good. In this text we see a division of society into two classes taking shape; an imputation of social dissidence in one of these classes; an accusation of moral weakness in the dissident class; and a social fear against which the author appeals to the authority of the State, which should master and correct this immorality.

*   *   *

I would like to come back to the fear that seems to have played a determinant role in the organization of the nineteenth-century penal system. This social fear is usually described as, first of all, essentially linked to the process of urbanization, that is to say to the arrival in towns of a whole floating population turned out by poverty and the new regime of property, already unemployed, a dangerous, marginal population pitted against the industrious population. We have an image of it in the Paris ragmen who revolt in 1832.[2] We have its theoretical image in Frégier's 1840 book on the dangerous classes,[3] and in Sue, where there is a constant interplay between the virtuous worker and the dangerous classes ([for example, in his novel] *The Wandering Jew*).[4] Then this fear is described as a half-physical, half-political fantasy,[*] more than as fear determined by a lucid perception of social processes. Certainly we find expressions of this, in 1840 for example, in the sermons of the abbé Le Dreuille: the rich have more to fear than they think; "There [among the workers], needs are countless and plans more numerous than needs; dreams of organization are debated in the midst of disorder, vengeance is prepared in the shadows. ... But know therefore: one gets tired of waiting, and, if care is not taken, next year, tomorrow, perhaps, from out of the depths, looking dreadful on the edges of the abyss crossed, shaking off resignation like a vile dust ..., breathing implacable vengeance, the formidable people will appear like the exterminating angel in the midst of your rich mansions, your sumptuous residences."[5]

But if this analysis is applicable to the years 1840-1845, it does not seem to me to be right for the beginning of the century. At that time,

---

[*] Manuscript (fol. 3): "As a mix of physical and political fear. Irruption of the shaggy-haired proletariat who was able to terrorize the bourgeois. A game, an avatar of the literature of terror: the proletarian will be the successor of the ghost of the Château d'Otrante, the damned of Lewis."

the fear we find in those who make the law, and which appears at the level of the discourse that is decisive, is of a different type. First, it is a fear linked less to the process of urbanization than to the new mode of production—that is to say to the accumulation of capital now invested visibly in a tangible and accessible material form, in stocks, machines, raw material, commodities—[and] to wage-earning, which brings the worker, stripped of all property, into contact with this wealth. The fear is connected to this physical presence of the worker's body, of his desire, on the body of wealth itself. And second, this fear is not a fantasy; it is absolutely grounded: bourgeois wealth, thus exposed, faces new risks, from the daily erosion of theft up to great collective machine breakings. The danger represented by the working class in extreme poverty is not fantasy. Third, initially this fear is not addressed to those marginal categories, on the fringes of the town and the law; at the beginning of the nineteenth century, it is less the idle and beggars who are feared than those who work and are in physical contact with this wealth. It is inasmuch as it is industrious that this class is dangerous,[6] and it is only as the effect of a whole procedure of selection, in which the penal system is a cornerstone, that around 1840 we see a whole series of discourses appear that are both the effect of the division and have the function of furthering it. Thus, Frégier's text-fiction constructs the category of dangerous class.[7] Prior to this division, the working class was the dangerous class.[8] [As evidence, there is, for example,] this text from a physician, describing the social classes in Brest in 1830: the class that possesses "delicacy of thought and loftiness of soul"; that of the "intelligent and skilled workers, who are calm, peaceful, and conciliatory"; that of the proletarians, "of a proportionally immense extent, which, apart from a few honorable exceptions, possesses profound ignorance, superstition, ignoble habits, and the moral depravity of wild children. Its triviality, rustic simplicity, improvidence, and extravagance, in the midst of ludicrous pleasures and orgies, cannot be expressed. Its dwellings are old hovels and attics open to the wind, dirty, dilapidated, and cramped, in which, packed in, living from day to day, it proliferates abundantly in shameful nudity, insulting modesty with its cynicism and abandoning thousands of victims of its debauchery or corruption either to public commiseration or to the civil poorhouse."⁹ Fourth, this fear is not just aimed at the great monstrosities, at political agitations, but the heart of the danger falls well short of illegalism: it is not even a matter of infraction. What is dangerous is the worker who does not work hard enough, who is lazy, who gets drunk, that is to say everything by which the worker practices illegalism, not in this case on the body of the employer's wealth, but on his own body, on the labor-power that the employer considers he owns, since he has purchased it with wages and because it is the worker's duty to offer his labor-power on a free market.

Consequently, anything that may affect not only the accumulated capital of bourgeois wealth, but the worker's body itself as labor-power, anything that may steal it from use by capital, will be considered as that infra-legal illegalism, the great immorality, on which capitalism will try to get a hold: an illegalism that is not a breach of the law, but a way of stealing the condition of profit. And at the end of the eighteenth and beginning of the nineteenth century we see the appearance of those singular expressions that a lazy worker "steals."* He steals what he owes the employer, what he could earn for his family. Worker immorality is constituted by all that by which the worker circumvents the law of the job market as capitalism wants to constitute it.

The point of application of the social and daily bourgeois fear as it functions at the start of the nineteenth century—at the time of the organization of the penal system—is less the marginal and dangerous classes, than the class of workers as permanent and daily source of immorality. In the form of the relationship established between the worker's body and wealth, or of the way labor-power can be used to the maximum, ultimately it is always the worker's body in its relationship to wealth, to profit, to the law, that constitutes the major stake around which the penal system will be organized. Hence the need to set up an

---

* Manuscript (fols. 5-6): "Now, with wage-earning and the disappearance of the whole regulatory fabric that surrounded artisan activity, what becomes fearsome is not the breach of the law, but the avoidance of what is presented to the wage-earner as obligatory; and which is simply the employer's requirement, need. Laziness, unpunctuality, leaving work, this is the highly fearsome form of worker illegalism. An illegalism that is not a violation of the law, or a way of getting round it. An illegalism that starts below, before the law. A refusal of adherence at the pre-legal level. Immorality in short, laziness, unpunctuality, dishonesty."

apparatus that is sufficiently discriminating and far-reaching to affect the very source of this illegalism: the worker's body, desire, need.

At the same time that the bourgeoisie is establishing the civil code that is to govern the contract between owners, it defines a Penal Code whose function will be, on the face of things, to sanction violations of the contract, but more profoundly, to reach back as far as possible to this source of immorality that calls into question the worker's body and its relationship to wealth, profit, and the law, and to constitute, no longer a contract, but a habit: to the owner's contract will have to correspond the worker's good habits.*

Now, at the time this plan is emerging so clearly, we can see the difficulty: on the one hand, we have a productive apparatus that incurs a number of risks arising from those in contact with it, and, on the other, with the worker's body, we have productive forces subject to dangers coming from the worker himself. To protect this productive apparatus and enable it to develop, the bourgeoisie provides itself with a strong State. Now, at the same time that this need to protect the apparatus of production appears, in order for it to function, for the formation and growth of profit, the bourgeoisie needs competition between the workers, the free labor market, the possibility of drawing at will from this free breeding-ground of the labor force. It needs the purchase and the use it makes of this labor-power, which it wants to protect however, to be subject to the law of free competition. On the one hand, the legislative deregulation of workers is needed,† the worker

---

* Manuscript (fols. 6-7): "So we have in sum a complex process:

- the recognition of two classes and their confrontation, around, on either side of the apparatus of production;
- the impossibility of allowing proletarian illegalism the margins that were conceded to lower-class illegalism;
- the fear of this illegalism, a fear that initially takes the form of a general accusation of moral incapacity;
- the need, finally, to set up a necessarily highly complex apparatus, multiple in its points of application, which has to ensure, at the same time:

  • protection of the productive apparatus
  • repression of illegalism
  • the moral equipping of the proletariat."

† Manuscript (fol. 7): "The legislative deregulation of workers is necessary to the market economy,

must be at the point of destitution to keep wages as low as possible; on the other hand, property must not be prey to the needs of the worker on the brink of poverty. This is the problem posed to the penal system: a solution is required such that the conditions of use of labor-power are freed from every hindrance and the materiality of the apparatus of production and the vigor of the forces of production are protected.

There is a text of Regnaud de Saint-Jean-d'Angély, a legislator of the Consulate and the Empire, which envisages the means for regaining control of the workers.[10] On the one hand there is the solution of military force,* but it is not a good one; on the other hand, the return to corporations, a way of recoding the worker's life in its most daily framework, but this would go back on the Le Chapelier law[11] and risk disrupting the labor market. The solution recommended is then the record book (*livret*).[12] Thus, in 1803 this text defines the two great limits of the penality of the capitalist regime: the use of military force, which has the advantage of protecting the apparatus of production directly, and corporatism. (The fascist solution uses both). It is between these two limits that the nineteenth century defines a set of solutions that can be characterized by several things.[†]

* * *

The double front of penality:[‡] this is not the typical ambiguity of all penal systems, by which those who make the law do so and make it work in such a way that they can actually evade it, contriving a sort of pocket of statutory illegalism. Thus, in the Penal Code drawn up in 1810, the penalties for coalition [in England: combination; G.B.] are not the same for workers and bosses;[13] likewise, there is a whole interplay between prison and fine.[14] What this means is that there is a double tactical front in the drafting itself of the Penal Code, and independently

---

and to the construction of capitalist profit when its apparatus of production is exposed to illegalism, to worker immorality."

* The manuscript (fol. 8) adds: "protecting the apparatus of production while letting unemployment develop; while allowing conditions of use of labor-power as favorable as possible to the employers."

† The manuscript (fol. 8) adds: "The whole penal apparatus is constructed in order to respond to this double requirement."

‡ Manuscript (fol. 9), subtitle: "*Penal dualism.*"

of the theory/practice distinction. On the one hand, a [sort] of general recodification of the system of crimes and punishments, the function of which is to resorb all the regions in which lower-class illegalism was deployed. It presents several characteristics: it is a set of homogeneous laws that explicitly challenges any reference to a religious, natural, or moral law. There is no question of sanctioning a moral lapse. The first article defines the infraction as that which is punished by the law: the difference between contravention, misdemeanor, and crime does not refer to a natural law: the contravention is that which is punished by a simple police penalty; misdemeanor, by a correctional penalty; and crime, by a penalty involving loss of civil rights. It is therefore the penalty, the actual exercise of penality that defines the nature of the offense. It is a Code in which the judge's arbitrary right to decide is reduced to the minimum. In 1791, the judge could do only one thing: after having established the materiality and imputability of the infraction, he applied the penalty provided for the crime. It is a Code in which one appeals to the participation of the citizen as "representative of society,"[15] for we see precisely that justice is not a power alongside the legislative and executive powers, but the very exercise of society's right to judge each of its members; it is a right of society over itself. Finally, what makes the Code effective must be not the law's severity, but the inevitable character of the penalty once the crime has been committed; the exercise of a judicial police must be added to the Code. In this, the legislation of 1810 is no different in its general principles from what the theorists of the eighteenth century called for when they wanted a penal law* not founded on a natural law, but on the will of society.

But, if it is true that it is not the illegalism directly affected by the laws that is most perilous, but immorality, which concerns the body, need, desire, habit, and will, then a whole system of moral conditioning needs to be incorporated into penality. Thus, when the Code seems to speak only of positive law in its text, we see a certain number of measures appear that will permit moral control and coercion. Not two different apparatuses, but just one is thus hatched: for example, there

---

* Manuscript (fol. 11): "[a] law suited to society; inevitably applied with minimum intervention by the judge; the law does not represent a natural, religious, or moral law, but solely social utility."

are articles of the Penal Code on vagabondage,[*] an offense defined as not having a fixed abode and moving without documents or anyone to vouch for you. We also have elements that indicate the organization of a moral control, a series of measures that take the individual's morality into account.

Thus, if the Code does not allow itself to punish in the name of the moral law, it provides for the possibility of punishing according to morality, which is thus a legal[†] modulation of the law: a second offense is an aggravating circumstance; the introduction of extenuating circumstances will function as a *moralizing modulation* of the penal system.[16] And, apart from the Penal Code, if we look at the way in which penalties should function, we see that their objective is quite different from the penalties of the eighteenth century, or what the theorists of the eighteenth century wanted them to be. Beccaria, for example, says that their sole objective is to prevent crimes, that is to say the penalty must be such that it prevents others from committing the crime: the value of the penalty must be measured by its value as an example, by its deterrent effects.[17] [On the other hand,] in the nineteenth century, we have a penalty that is intended to act on the individual himself and to correct him, its deterrent value being no more than a corollary. Finally, the *Code d'instruction criminelle* provides for the organization of para-penal institutions with a moralizing function: all the systems that follow the sanction, the supervision that must accompany a whole series of penalties, the reformatories, houses of re-education.

So there is a sort of essential duality of the penal system as a whole: on the one hand, the development of Beccaria's theory, a discourse of pure penality, which knows only the positivity of the law and not the immorality of the crime, the universality of the law and not the moralization of individuals, the inevitability of the law and not the correction of individuals; and, on the other hand, mixed with the texts, with the institutions, a kind of research claiming to correct, to regenerate the individual.[‡] These two elements are fundamental in the

---

* The manuscript (fol. 12) adds: "on drunkenness."
† [The French text has "legal," but the sense of the passage suggests this should be "moral"; G.B.]
‡ The manuscript (fol. 13) adds: "a rampant Quakerism (a research, a claim to transform, correct, improve, regenerate, individualize)."

penal system, and at the point of their articulation is the place where the transcription of one into the other takes place, a kind of psycho-juridical discourse* the function of which is to retranscribe the juridical elements of penality in terms of correction, regeneration, and recovery, and, conversely, to recodify moral notions into penal categories.

This strange discourse, which brings with it the code of this transcription, is the discourse of criminology: thanks to its code, criminological discourse assures the juridico-medical† transcription that consists in describing as immature, maladjusted, and primitive the person penal theory described as a social enemy. This discourse also makes it possible to define the offender as aggressive and describe punishment as a process of rehabilitation, of social reintegration. Criminology has, moreover, an opposite function, of medico-judicial‡ codification that consists in representing as socially dangerous, and therefore requiring, if not punishment, at least confinement, the individual who, without having committed any infraction, represents a certain number of dangers due to psychologically or medically defined characteristics.[18] What is called "social dangerousness," the tendency to delinquency, is a way of recoding in penal terms a kind of psychological category that does not come under the courts. The same discourse will ask that punishment no longer be measured in terms of the crime, or of the state of the individual at the time of the crime[19]—for, if it is true that punishment is a recovery, one can put a term to it only with the assurance that recovery has taken place, hence the idea of grading penalties in terms of "progress" of social integration.§

*   *   *

Two comments in conclusion. First, it is strange to witness the historical formation of this criminological discourse, which exists solely to function as the code, with the appearance of the notion of monomania.[20] The object of discussions among doctors and judges

---

* Manuscript (fol. 13): "psycho-sociological."
† Manuscript (fol. 14), in margin: "juridico-psychological."
‡ Manuscript (fol. 14), in margin: "psychologico-judicial."
§ The manuscript (fol. 15) clarifies with regard to "function of transcription ... that assures criminological discourse: it is what accounts for its existence."

around 1815–1850, monomania is an odd notion in that the doctors define homicidal monomania as an illness that consists in presenting no other symptom than that of killing someone. The symptomatology is reduced to what is codified in penal terms as homicide. We have here the simplest degree of the transcription. The crime is nothing other than the illness. And conversely, on condition that the crime is not defined by any assignable motive, with the notion of monomania,* that transcription of the juridical in the medical, which will give rise to the formidable proliferation of criminological discourse, begins to be developed.

Second, and finally, there is no antinomy between criminology and the penal system. It is traditional to present criminology as a sort of science formed outside the penal system and which thus arrives, fully charged with medical or sociological knowledge, to work on the Penal Code and make possible its transformation. Now if the analysis I have made is right, it is not possible to conceive of the penal text as it exists without the set of all the procedures of moralization it brings with it, and without at least the possibility and therefore necessity of a discourse like that of criminology being given. This discourse is an integral part of the whole of the penal system [in force] in 1811. It can therefore only extend the functioning of the penal system. [The juridical and the medical] fit together and in different periods we see either a tendency to return to a purely legislative functioning, or a tendency to adopt a more criminological functioning of the Code. In any case, it is the same penal system at work, with a different accentuation. So we should not expect a recasting of the penal system on the basis of criminological discourse. Indeed, on the contrary, the true dis-functioning of this system is introduced by suppressing the criminological codification and, as the Magistrates' Association[21] tries to do, by applying the law in its universality, its inevitability, that is to say by getting the penal system to work in a Beccarian way, without this kind of corrective-correlative of moralization and criminology.†

---

* Manuscript (fol. 15): "Monomania: illness that consists in one committing a crime; illness that is cured by confinement. This is exactly the matrix of the code of criminological transcription."
† The manuscript (fol. 15) adds: "Paradoxical as it may be, strict application of the Code is more subversive than correction by criminology."

1. See above, lecture of 28 February, p. 163 and p. 172, note 17.

2. In the framework of their struggle against the cholera epidemic that was rampant in Paris from April 1832. See J. Tulard, *La Préfecture de police sous la monarchie de Juillet* (Paris: Imprimerie municipale, 1964) pp. 102-103 and p. 132. The authorities drastically reformed the modalities of refuse collection, disturbing the means of subsistence of the Paris ragmen, who revolt in April. See L. Chevalier, ed., *Choléra: la première* épidémie *du XIXe siècle.* Étude *collective* (La Roche-sur-Yon: Imprimerie de l'Ouest, 1958); P. Delaunay, "Le corps médical et la choléra de 1832," *Médecine internationale illustrée*, October 1931-October 1933, p. 43.

3. See H.-A. Frégier, *Des classes dangereuses de la population dans les grandes villes, et des moyens de les rendre meilleures* (Paris: J.-B. Baillière, 1840) 2 volumes. Foucault returns to this text in *Surveiller et Punir*, p. 286; *Discipline and Punish*, p. 281. Frégier's work, given an award by the Academy of Political and Moral Sciences, proposed a quantitative and qualitative study of "the part of society reputed dangerous for its vices, ignorance, and poverty" (*Des classes dangereuses*, p. 1). Although he notes that "vice appears in every rank of society" (ibid., p. 7), this chief clerk of the Seine Prefecture notes that "the vice-ridden rich or well-off ... inspire pity or disgust, but not fear" (ibid., p. 10). On the other hand, "the poor and vice-ridden classes have always been and will always be the productive breeding-ground for every sort of malefactor; it is these that we will designate more particularly with the title of dangerous classes; for, even if vice is not accompanied by perversity, when it is combined with poverty in the same individual he is a just subject of fear for society, he is dangerous" (ibid., p. 11).

    Louis Chevalier, in his work, "Classes laborieuses et Classes dangereuses à Paris pendant la première moitié du XIXe siècle (see above, p. 168, note 9) sees in Frégier's work, as in Eugène Buret's inquiry, *De la misère des classes laborieuses en Angleterre et en France: de la nature de la misère, de son existence, de ses effets, de ses causes*, which also appeared in 1840 (Paris: Paulin, 2 volumes), the completion of "that difficult transition between dangerous classes and laboring classes." Actually, Chevalier emphasizes "the impossibility of Frégier extricating himself from the confusion between the laboring classes and the dangerous classes: despite his subject, the dangerous classes" (*Classes laborieuses et Classes dangereuses*, p. 159).

4. Foucault is referring here to the serial novels by Eugène Sue (1804-1857) such as *Les Mystères de Paris* (Paris: Gosselin, 1843-1844) 4 volumes; *Le Juif errant* (Paris: Paulin, 1844-1845) 10 volumes; *Les Mystères du peuple, ou Histoire d'une famille de prolétaires à travers les* âges (Paris: 1849-1857) 16 volumes. On Sue and his *Les Mystères du peuple*, Foucault writes in 1978 that readers will find "a whole Alexandre Dumas or Ponson du Terrail side: beyond the striking images and the scenes picked out in direct light, there are subterranean trajectories, dark episodes, death and reunions, adventures"; M. Foucault, "Eugène Sue que j'aime," *Les Nouvelles littéraires*, 56th year, no. 2618, 12 and 19 January 1978, p. 3; *DE*, III, no. 224, pp. 500-502, see p. 500/"Quarto," II, pp. 500-502, see p. 500; see also *Surveiller et Punir*, p. 292; *Discipline and Punish*, p. 286.

    Here, as in the previous lecture (above, lecture of 28 February, p. 160 and p. 167, note 9) regarding Balzac, we find a possible link with Louis Chevalier's *Classes laborieuses et Classes dangereuses* in which, through the works of Balzac, Sue, and Hugo, Chevalier follows the transformations and metamorphoses of the criminal problem into a social problem. The analysis of Sue's *Les Mystères de Paris* is thus central in Chevalier's work: unlike the descriptions by Balzac or Hugo, "Sue's works are less resistant to the expertise of economic history" (*Classes laborieuses et Classes dangereuses*, p. 11). Chevalier writes: "*Les Mystères de Paris* can be considered one of the most important documents we possess concerning that popular mentality for which we have no other means or chance of access. [... And this,] through the work's success, through the adherence of the people to a description that did not concern them, but in which it wanted to recognize itself and that it progressively inflected to the point of making it, through a real collective constraint, its most faithful portrait, of transforming this book about the dangerous classes into a book about the laboring classes" (ibid., p. 510).

5. The sermon referred to here appears in [F.-A. Le Dreuille,] "Discours prononcés aux réunions des ouvriers de la Société de saint François-Xavier, à Paris et en province, par M. l'abbé Françoise-Auguste Le Dreuille, recueillis et publiés par M. l'abbé Faudet" (Paris: Presbytère de Saint-Roch, 1861); reprinted in J.-B. Duroselle, *Les Débuts du catholicisme social en France (1822-1870)* (Paris: PUF, 1951) p. 269. According to a citation which refers to an article of the *Gazette de France*, in 1845, the sermon, called "Discours de Saint-Roch," was delivered on 25 May 1845. The abbé Le Dreuille was one of the main speakers of the Société de saint François-Xavier, a Catholic workers' organization founded around 1837. It was devoted to the improvement of the workers' conditions of life. Expressing himself first of all as a layman, Le Dreuille became a priest in 1845. Journal editor, creator of clubs and employment centers for workers, he was one of the pioneers of social Catholicism. His work and discourse were the object of media and governmental debate; see J.-B. Duroselle, *Les Débuts du catholicisme social*, pp. 262-277.

    In the manuscript (fol. 3) Foucault adds a reference to the serial-novel of Pierre Alexis de Ponson du Terrail, *Rocambole*. This novel, from the years 1857 to 1871, recounts the adventures of Rocambole, from delinquent youth to law-abiding maturity. Foucault establishes a link between Ponson du Terrail, Eugène Sue, and Alexandre Dumas; see "Eugène Sue que j'aime," p. 500/p. 500.

6. In the manuscript, after this phrase Foucault adds (fol. 3) this note: "(Text by Taxil)". Léo Taxil (1854-1907) was an anti-clerical and anti-Masonic free-thinker. After publishing numerous pamphlets mixing free-thought and pornographic libertinage, he made himself famous in 1885 by his fake conversion to Catholicism, which deceived even Pope Leo XIII. His work is entirely directed towards the denunciation of the clergy and free-masons.

7. H.-A. Frégier, *Des classes dangereuses de la population dans les grandes villes.* Foucault's designation of this text as "text-fiction" seems to disqualify the descriptive value of the memoir, which presents itself as "a work of administration and morality" (ibid., p. 2), and claims to have a great empirical ambition (see the presentation of the sources, ibid., pp. 4-5). Chevalier emphasizes also the weakness of the quantitative documentation, but lists the work among the "social enquiries" (*Classes laborieuses et Classes dangereuses*, p. 151).

8. It seems that by this juxtaposition Foucault differentiates himself from the thesis defended by his Collège de France colleague, the historian and demographer, Louis Chevalier (1911-2001), in his work, *Classes laborieuses et Classes dangereuses.* Actually, Chevalier criticized the table drawn up by sociologists of "a town and society in which every problem—even that of rest— would be reducible to a single problem, that of work" (ibid., p. xxviii). To this approach Chevalier opposes what he calls the "biological foundations of social history," that is to say "the influence of the physical characteristics of populations on different aspects of individual and collective existence, without the knowledge of which there could not be any description of societies" (ibid., p. 559). Calling upon both literary works and statistical data, Chevalier presents the transformations of the reality and representations of crime and poverty in the Paris of the start of the century as the consequence of the "volume and rhythm of the growth of population in the big urban areas" (ibid., p. 183).

    In Chevalier we find themes and sources similar to those Foucault takes up, but apprehended from a very different theoretical angle and with very different methodological tools. The divergence of intellectual approach between the two men is coupled with very different positions in the political domain. A conservative historian, close to government, which he advises—in particular as counselor of the Seine Prefect—and teaches—as professor at Institute politique in Paris and at the École nationale d'administration—for a long time Chevalier defended policies inspired by his vision of the necessary unity between a territory and its population, by becoming, for example, the promoter of populating policies rather than of opening up to immigration to resolve problems of labor.

9. It has not been possible to find this text from the pen of a Brest physician in 1830. Consult, however, the work of the physicians Ange Guépin and Eugène Bonamy, *Nantes au XIXe siècle. Statistique topographique, industrielle et morale*, republication preceded by *De l'observation de la ville comme corps social* by P. Le Pichon and A. Supiot (Nantes: Université de Nantes, 1981; http://archive.org/details/nantesauxixesi00guuoft), which describes in particular the population of Nantes in eight classes, including those of the "well-off workers" and "poor workers" (pp. 455-492), providing many details of their habitation and their "physical and moral hygiene."

10. Michel-Louis-Étienne Regnaud de Saint-Jean-d'Angély (1761-1819) was one of Napoleon's closest advisers, who was conspicuous in the course of the campaign in Egypt and assisted him in the coup d'État of 18 Brumaire. Sent by the Third Estate to the Estates-General, he became a member of the Council of State in 1799 and during the Empire exercised numerous political and, to a lesser extent, military functions, which earned him the reputation of being "Napoleon's éminence grise" (O. Blanc, *L'Éminence grise de Napoleon, Regnaud de Saint-Jean d'Angély*, Paris: Pygmalion, 2003). In 1803 he was the rapporteur of the law re-establishing the worker's record book (*livret ouvrier*) (see below, note 12), which he justified by the need to "guarantee workshops against desertion and contracts against violation" (E. Dolléans and G. Dehove, *Histoire du travail en France. Mouvement ouvrier et législation social*, Paris: Domat-Montchrestien, 1953-1955, 2 volumes, vol. I, p. 156). Elected to the French Academy in 1803, Regnaud de Saint-Jean-d'Angély collaborated with André Chénier on the *Journal de Paris*, and then with Bonaparte, at the time of the Italian campaign, in the publication of *La France vue de l'armée d'Italie: 16 thermidor-16 brumaire an V. Journal de politique, d'administration et de littérature françoise et étranger* (18 issues published), no. 1, 16 thermidor an V (3 August 1797). Minister under Napoleon during the One Hundred Days, he was exiled by Louis XVIII and was not allowed to return to France until 1819, the year of his death. See A. Fierro-Domenech, "Regnaud de Saint-Jean-d'Angély" in Jean Tulard, ed., *Dictionnaire Napoléon* (Paris: Fayard, 1987) p. 1449.

11. Voted on 14 June 1791, the Le Chapelier law, following the suppression of corporations three months earlier, declared all worker or employer associations illegal. The first article states: "The suppression of all kinds of corporation being one of the fundamental bases of the French Constitution, it is forbidden to re-establish them on any pretext and in any form" (quoted by A. Soboul, "Le choc révolutionnaire, 1789-1797" in Fernand Braudel and Ernest Labrousse, eds., *Histoire économique et sociale de la France*, Paris: PUF, vol. III, 1976, p. 12). From 20 July 1791, these provisions apply also to campaigns. According to Albert Soboul, "the prohibition of coalition and of the workers' strike ... constitutes one of the cornerstones of the capitalism of free competition: liberalism, founded on the abstraction of egalitarian social individualism, profited the strongest" (ibid.) See also E. Soreau, "La loi Le Chapelier," *Annales historiques de la Révolution française*, 8th year, 1931, pp. 287-314.

12. According to Jacques Lagrange, *Le Pouvoir psychiatrique*, p. 92, n. 14; *Psychiatric Power*, p. 90, n. 14, it is from 1781 that the worker has to be provided with a "*livret*" or "*cahier*" when employed and that he must be able to show to the administrative authorities when he moves. This practice, some traces of which go back to the twelfth century, disappears with the Revolution, before being partially reintroduced, only for paper-making workers whose know-how seems particularly critical with the development of banknotes; see E. Dolléans and G. Dehove, *Histoire du travail en France*, vol. I, p. 155. Generalized to all workers by a law of April 1803 (22 Germinal, Year XI), the worker's record book (*livret ouvrier*) was regulated by the decree of 1 December 1803 (9 Frimaire, Year XII). "Employers were, in fact, prohibited from employing a worker who had not brought his record book, with a certificate of receipt delivered by his old boss ... Now it is quite obvious that the latter would agree to

give it only when he was reimbursed for advances he may have granted the worker" (ibid., p. 156). The worker's record book was finally abolished in 1890. See: M. Sauzet, *Le Livret obligatoire des ouvriers* (Paris: Jouve et Boyer imprimeurs, 1900); G. Bourgin, "Contribution à l'histoire du placement et du livret en France," *Revue politique et parlementaire*, vol. LXXI, January-March 1912, pp. 117-118; S. Kaplan, "Réflexions sur la police du monde du travail (1700-1815)," *Revue historique*, 103rd year, no. 529, January-March 1979, pp. 17-77. For more recent studies of practices related to the worker's record book in the nineteenth century, see also: A. Cottereau, "Droit et bon droit. Un droit des ouvriers instauré, puis évincé par le droit du travail (France, XIXe siècle)," *Annales. Histoire, Sciences sociales*, 57th year, 2002/6, pp. 1521-1557; J.-P. Le Crom, "Le livret ouvrier au XIXe siècle entre assujettissement et reconaissance de soi" in Yvon Le Gall, Dominique Gaurier, and Pierre-Yannick Legal, eds., *Du droit du travail aux droits de l'humanité. Études offertes à Philippe-Jean Hesse* (Rennes: Presses universitaires de Rennes, 2003). Foucault's presentation of the law is very close to that of Édouard Dolléans and Gérard Dehove in their *Histoire du travail en France*.

13. "With regard to coalitions, articles 6, 7, and 8 of the law of Germinal, XI, will confirm their general prohibition, decreed by the Le Chapelier law, while introducing into it a subtle distinction, enabling worker coalitions to be treated more severely than employer coalitions"; E. Dolléans and G. Dehove, *Histoire du travail en France*, vol. I, p. 162. Article 6 punishes seeking to lower wages "abusively" and "unjustly with a fine, and possibly a maximum of a month in prison," while article 7 sanctions "any coalition on the part of workers" in order to "suspend, prevent, or increase the cost of work" (quoted, ibid., pp. 162-163), and provides for penalties of up to three months confinement. The Penal Code of 1810, article 414-416, reinforces this inequality: "The bosses were liable to imprisonment for from 6 days to one month and a fine from 200 to 3,000 francs, but the minimum prison sentence for workers was fixed at one month" (ibid., p. 163). The 1810 Penal Code also contains more severe provisions for the leaders of workers' movements; see: J. Godechot, *Les Institutions de la France sous la Révolution et l'Empire* (Paris: PUF, 1951) pp. 634-636; P. Lascoumes, P. Poncela, and P. Lenoël, *Au nome de l'ordre* (see above, p. 96, note 12); A. Damien, "Code pénal" in J. Tulard, ed., *Dictionnaire Napoléon*, 1989 [1987], pp. 454-455; J.-M. Carbasse, "État autoritaire et justice répressive. L'Évolution de la législation pénale de 1789 au Code pénal de 1810" in *All'ombra dell'aquila imperiale. Trasformazioni e continuità istituzionali nei territori sabaudi in età napoleonica* (Rome: Ministerio per i beni culturali e ambientali, Ufficio centrale per i beni archivistici, 1994) pp. 313-333; J.-M. Carbasse, "Code pénal" in *Dictionnaire de la culture juridique* (Paris: PUF, 2003) pp. 210-216.

14. The 1810 Penal Code, article 15, states in fact: "The execution of sentences to fines, refunds, damages, and costs will be able to be pursued by way of civil imprisonment." Article 53 provides in addition that the imprisoned offender, "for the discharge of these pecuniary sentences," will be able, after a year for crimes and six months for misdemeanors, to obtain his provisional freedom if he can prove his insolvency, and so long as that lasts.

15. The expression "representative of society," which does not figure in the Penal Code, is no doubt a reference to the doctrinal expression used in treatises of criminal law of the time (and still today) to designate the public prosecutor.

16. Foucault will return often to the functioning of extenuating circumstances, introduced into the 1810 Penal Code in 1832; see *Les Anormaux*, lecture of 8 January 1975, pp. 9-10; *Abnormal*, pp. 9-10 (the true objective not being the softening of the penalty, but the prevention of acquittals, "when they [juries] did not want to apply the full rigor of the law"); *Surveiller et Punir*, p. 23; *Discipline and Punish*, pp. 20-21 (through extenuating circumstances, juridical reforms introduced a whole game of knowledge about the criminal who will double the crime as object of judgment).

17. See, C. Beccaria, *Des délits et des peines*, chapter XII, pp. 86-87; *On Crimes and Punishments*, ch. 12, p. 31.

18. Foucault develops this theme in a lecture in 1978, "L'évolution de la notion d'"individu dangereux' dans la psychiatrie légale du XIXe siècle" in *Déviance et Société*, vol. 5 (4), 1981, pp. 403-422; *DE*, III, no. 220, pp. 443-464/"Quarto," II, pp. 443-464; English translation "About the Concept of the 'Dangerous Individual' in Nineteenth-century Legal Psychiatry" in *EW*, 3, pp. 176-200, as well as in *Mal faire, dire vrai*, lecture of 20 May 1981, p. 199 sq.; *Wrong-Doing, Truth-Telling: The Function of Avowal in Justice*, p. 199 sq.

19. In the manuscript (fol. 14), Foucault notes; "Jackson." The reference is to George Jackson (1941-1971), a member of the Black Panther Party, who was incarcerated in San Quentin, California, and killed by bullets coming from the warders-marksmen in the security wing during a rebellion on 21 August 1971. Jackson, imprisoned from the age of eighteen until his death eleven years later, was politicized in prison and founded a Marxist-Maoist group, Black Guerilla Family. See the political letters in *Soledad Brother: The Prison Letters of George Jackson* (Lawrence Hill Books, 1970); see too his conversations collected in the fascicule 3: *L'Assassinat de George Jackson* of the G.I.P. booklet: *Intolérable: les prisons*, with a Preface by Jean Genet (Paris: Gallimard, 1971). In this booklet, which appeared on 10 November 1971, under the names of Catherine von Bülow, Daniel Defert, Gilles Deleuze, Jean Genet, and Michel Foucault, the G.I.P. will write: "The death of George Jackson is not a prison accident. It is a political assassination. In America, assassination has been and remains today a mode of political action" (back cover); see also P. Artières, L. Quéro, and M. Zancarini-Fournel, eds., *Le Groupe d'information sur les prisons. Archives d'une lutte, 1970-1972* [see above, p. 42, note 32] p. 105 sq.

20. Foucault introduces here the notion of monomania, a theme taken up in a number of his writings, notably, in the following years, in *La Pouvoir psychiatrique*, lectures of 9 January 1974, p. 177 and 23 January, p. 249; *Psychiatric Power*, p. 180 and p. 249; *Les Anormaux*, lectures of 29 January 1975, pp. 94-97, 5 February 1975, pp. 102-125, and 12 February, pp. 131-145; *Abnormal*, pp. 101-104, pp. 109-134, and pp. 141-156; and in *Moi, Pierre Rivière; I, Pierre Rivière* (see above, p. 168 note 10). The notion of monomania will play a major role in the sixth lecture given at Louvain on 20 May 1981, in *Mal faire, dire vrai*, pp. 215-219 (see p. 232, n. 14); *Wrong-Doing, Truth-Telling*, pp. 216-220 (p. 232, n. 14), as well as in the lecture on "L'évolution de la notion de d'"individu dangereux' dans la psychiatrie légale du XIXe siècle"; "About the Concept of the "Dangerous Individual" in Nineteenth-Century Legal Psychiatry." Robert Castel will study the notion in "Les médecins et les juges" in *Moi, Pierre Rivière*, pp. 315-331; "The Doctors and Judges" in *I, Pierre Rivière*, pp. 250-269. See also the chapter "Monomania" in J. Goldstein, *Console and Classify: The French Psychiatric Profession in the Nineteenth Century* (Cambridge: Cambridge University Press, 1987) pp. 152-196, as well as the references provided by Jacques Lagrange in *Le Pouvoir psychiatrique*, pp. 264-265; *Psychiatric Power*, pp. 263-264; R. Fontanille, *Aliénation mentale et Criminalité (Historique, expertise médico-légale, internement)* (Grenoble, Allier Frères, 1902); P. Dubuisson and A. Vigouroux, *Responsabilité pénale et Folie*. Étude médico-légale (Paris: Alcan, 1911); A. Fontana, "Les intermittences de la raison" in *Moi, Pierre Rivière*; "The Intermittences of Rationality" in *I, Pierre Rivière*, pp. 269-288.

21. The Magistrates' Association, created in June 1968, but without being a direct consequence of May 1968 (since it was decided to found it in January of 1968), was both a professional and militant organization that devoted a great deal of attention to the problem of white collar criminality and supported some of the objectives of G.I.P. and Foucault. The "red judges" of the Association, according to the expression of *Paris Match* in 1975, combined a "concern for improving the standing and the defense of the profession with more militant and less directly corporatist ambitions of openness to and support of trade union mobilizations, notably in the world of work." See L. Israël, "Un droit de gauche? Rénovation des pratiques professionelles et nouvelles formes de militantisme des juristes engagés dans le années 1970," *Sociétés contemporaines*, no. 73, 2009, p. 59; see also L. Joinet, "Critiques du jugement. Propos

recueillis par Olivier Doubre et Stany Grelet," *Vacarme*, no. 29, 2004; http://www.vacarme. org/article1370.html. Louis Joinet, one of the pioneers of the Magistrates' Association, reports having taken part in the foundation of G.I.P. alongside Foucault. He invited him in 1973 and again in 1977 to take part in the seminar of the Association at Goutelas; see, M. Foucault, "La redéfinition of the judiciable. Intervention au séminaire du Syndicat de la Magistrature, 1977," *Vacarme*, no. 29, 2004. In 1977 the Syndicat committed itself against the extradition of Klaus Croissant, the old lawyer of the "Baader gang"—a battle in which Foucault will also play a prominent role; see M. Foucault, "Va-t-on extrader Klaus Croissant?" in *Le Nouvel Observateur*, no. 679, 14 to 20 November, 1977; *DE*, III, no. 210, pp. 361-365/"Quarto," II, pp. 361-365; see too, L. Israël, "Défendre le défenseur de l'ennemi public. L'affaire Croissant," *Le Mouvement social*, no. 240, 2012-13, pp. 67-84.

(I) New illegalism: from depredation to dissipation. Refusing
one's labor-power. The worker's body as dominant factor:
idleness; refusal to work; irregularity; nomadism; festivity;
refusal of family; debauchery. *(A)* History of laziness.
Classical idleness of seventeenth and eighteenth centuries;
collective and organized refusal in the nineteenth century. *(B)*
Characteristics of this dissipation: reciprocal reinforcement of
illegalisms; collective and easy to spread; infra-legal; profitable
to the bourgeoisie; object of disapproval. The three forms of
dissipation: intemperance, improvidence, disorderliness. The
three institutions of dissipation: festivity, lottery, cohabitation.
(II) Controlling dissipation. Para-penal mechanisms; savings
book; worker's record book. Graduated, continuous, and
accumulative system. *(III)* Continuity and capillarization of
justice in everyday life. General supervision. Examination
form. The supervision-punishment couple. Disciplinary society.

*WHEN I TALKED ABOUT the illegalism of depredation, I talked
about accumulated wealth as if it were made up of goods for consumption,
of elements of wealth to be put into circulation that could be taken

---

* Manuscript (fol. 1) subtitle: "*Short history of laziness.*" In the lecture, Foucault does not take up
the first section of the manuscript (fol. 1), entitled "*Short history of theft*": "- not tied to delinquent
conduct, but to collective practices, to an illegalism of depredation.
Illegalism of depredation
- which is not new to the nineteenth century, but which has new forms."

either for one's own use, or in order to distribute. But this is only an abstraction. This wealth is, above all, an apparatus of production in relation to which the worker's body—now directly in the presence of this wealth that does not belong to him—is no longer merely the locus of desire, but is now the source of labor-power, which must become productive force. It is precisely at this point of the transformation of physical strength into labor-power and its integration into a system of production, which will make it a productive force, that a new illegalism is formed which, like that of depredation, concerns the relationship between the worker's body and the body of wealth, but the point of application of which is no longer the body of wealth as object of possible appropriation, but the worker's body as force of production.

This illegalism essentially consists in refusing to apply this body, this force to the apparatus of production. It may take several forms: 1. the decision of idleness: the refusal to offer these arms, this body, this strength on the labor market; "*stealing*" them from the law of free competition of labor, from the market; 2. worker irregularity:* the refusal to apply one's strength at the proper time and place; this is to *dissipate* one's forces, to decide oneself the time during which one will apply them; 3. festive revelry: not safeguarding everything in this force that is a condition for its effective use, to *waste* it by not taking care of one's body, by falling into disorderliness;† 4. refusal of family: not using one's body in the reproduction of its labor-powers in the form of a family, raising its children and guaranteeing through its care the renewal of labor-powers within the family; this is the refusal of the family in cohabitation, debauchery.

This set of practices is designated and denounced by a whole series of authors who present their discourse as an enterprise of moralization of the working class. Thus, in *De la moralisation des classes laborieuses*, published in 1851, Grün indicates the main defects of the working class:[1] 1. intemperance; 2. improvidence and early marriage: one should marry only if one has the means to maintain a family; purity of morals should be inculcated by entrusting education "to religious instruction, the solicitude of fathers and mothers, and the vigilance of employers";[2]

---

* The manuscript (fol. 2) adds: "nomadism."
† Manuscript (fol. 2): "(drunkenness, disorderliness, ill health)."

3. unruliness, anarchical passions, the refusal to submit to the laws, to settle; 4. lack of economy; 5. refusal to educate oneself, to improve one's labor-power; 6. lack of hygiene: "The laboring classes often fail to understand the rules of good hygiene, abandon their person and their dwellings to dirtiness, and fall into a state of physical degradation in which they lose both their health and their dignity";[3] 7. bad use of leisure activity; employers and the administration should concern themselves with its organization. All this is presented as a plea in favor of what will detach the laboring classes from poverty and make them happier. But this literature also explicitly says that it is in the employer's interest that this labor-power is effectively applied to the apparatus of production. Thus Thouvenin, in 1847, writes in "La santé des populations dans les grands centres manufacturiers," published in the *Annales d'hygiène publique*, that the worker should not give himself up to alcoholism and should have a family and maintain it, for "the worker should think also of the harm he does to the manufacturers, who, having devoted a considerable capital in the construction of buildings, the purchase of machines and raw materials, incurs a great loss as a result of the uncalculated cessation of work by their workers; during this time, the owners are always obliged to pay their taxes, while losing the interest on the money put into their factories."[4]

Thus a figure of illegalism appears that is no longer one of *depredation*, but of *dissipation*: what is at issue is not a relationship of *desire* to the materiality of wealth, but one of *fixing* to the production apparatus. This illegalism takes the form of absenteeism, lateness, laziness, festivity, debauchery, nomadism, in short, everything that smacks of irregularity,* of mobility in space. In a text from 1840, Michel Chevalier declares: "It is just one step from an irregular existence to a disorderly life."[5] Currently the industrial army has the same form of life, the same practices "as the barbarian, undisciplined, ragged, plundering hordes of twelve centuries ago."[6] One day, abandoning this old model of the ragged army, the industrial army will have to be like the modern army, that "regular, well-equipped, well-disciplined body, well provided for in everything ... Here an indefatigable foresight accompanies each man from the day of his entry into military service to the moment of his

---

* Manuscript (fol. 3): "of irregularity in time, mobility in space, and frenzy of the body."

retirement, to that of his death; an inestimable benefit for which our proletarians yearn today, crushed as they are by the weight of their absolute independence!"[7]

Certainly, the nineteenth century did not invent idleness, but one could write a whole history of laziness, that is to say not of leisure activities—which is how idleness has been codified, institutionalized, as a certain way of distributing non-work across the cycles of production, integrating idleness into the economy by taking it up and controlling it within a system of consumption—but of the ways one evades the obligation of work, steals labor-power, and avoids letting oneself be held and pinned down by the production apparatus. Now, if a history of laziness is possible, it is because it is not at issue in the same way in the different struggles that correspond to the different relations of production within which it acts as a disruptive force. There is a classical form of laziness in the seventeenth and eighteenth centuries that is defined by the term idleness. It is located and controlled at two levels: [on the one hand,] it is subject to a local, almost individual pressure, that of the master-craftsman who makes his journeyman work as much as possible. [On the other hand,] at the level of the State, and in a form of economy dominated for a long time by mercantilist themes, it is the obligation to put everyone to work in order to increase production as much as possible—the instruments of this being the police and intendants. Between these two pressures, craft cell and State police, there is a broad space in which idleness may manifest itself. In the nineteenth century, laziness will take another form; to start with because there will be need for the cyclical idle: the unemployed. Hence we see the reproach of idleness leveled against the working class disappear quite quickly. On the other hand, with the birth of industrial centers, of factories as objects of control and pressure, there are all those refusals of work that take on a more or less collective and organized form, including strikes.

This illegalism[*] of dissipation has then a specificity that must now be clarified. First, the relations between the illegalism of dissipation

---

[*] Manuscript (fol. 5): "All those illegalisms that bear on the economy of labor-power, and which can be put under the label, no longer of *idleness*, but of *dissipation*, are therefore new

- in their forms
- in their diffusion

and the illegalism of depredation: one of the great problems of morality, police, and all the instruments of control of the nineteenth century will be to separate these illegalisms and to make depredation subject to a severe penality, as a crime, dissociating it from the soft, everyday, permanent illegalism of dissipation. But the same apparatus, which tries to distinguish the thief from the lazy, at the same time, shows how one passes from one to the other. In fact, behind this effort of severance and junction, there is a different and complex reality. On the one hand, a reciprocal reinforcement of these illegalisms: the more dissipated and mobile the masses, the less they are fixed at precise points of the apparatus of production, the more they are tempted to pass to depredation. And the greater their tendency to depredation, the more they will tend to lead an irregular life, to lapse into nomadism, in order to escape sanctions.* On the other hand, when one tries to control one of these illegalisms, one is led to reinforce the other. In fact, all the heavy controls by which one attempts to supervise populations and check depredation bring about an acceleration of the process of mobility.[8] And the means used to control the illegalism of dissipation, notably the means used to fix workers to their place of work and have them working there when one wants—that is to say, the lowest possible wage and weekly payment to ensure that the worker looks forward to the least money possible—leads to the reinforcement of depredation. Backing him up against destitution, one fastens him to his work, but at the same time one directs him to the possibility of depredation as a way of escaping this poverty. Thus, the two illegalisms mutually reinforce each other, until, towards the middle of the nineteenth century, another means of controlling the illegalism of dissipation is found.†

Second, what makes the illegalism of dissipation more dangerous than depredation is that it can more easily take collective forms: in the first place, it is an illegalism that is easily spread. Whereas to reach a certain

---

- in their effect
- in the struggle engaged regarding them."

* The manuscript (fol. 6) adds: "cf. criminality in the migrant population."

† The manuscript (fol. 7) adds: "And these two mutually reinforcing illegalisms come together in machine breaking, the destruction of accumulated wealth; but inasmuch as it is an apparatus of production; inasmuch as it reduces one to poverty; inasmuch as it subjects one to a form of production."

scale depredation presupposes an organization of receiving, resale, and circuits, dissipation does not presuppose this closed system. It is not even an organization; it is a mode of existence that may reflect a choice, the refusal of industrial labor. There were huge and sometimes collective refusals of Monday work, circuits of nomadism organized according to labor markets, tavern societies,* spontaneous forms of organization of the working class. Thus, while the illegalism of depredation was blocked in a "smuggler" form that forced it into a closed system and found hardly any other outlet than in explosions, types of pillage, the illegalism of dissipation opens onto possibilities of concerted actions that put pressure on the market, against the employers.[9] It will have a far reaching economic and political impact, on the basis of which the absolutely well-ordered strategies of struggle against the employers are developed.†

Third, whereas the first [illegalism] recedes in the nineteenth century, the second, which appeared milder, more quotidian, will have a political destiny and confront bourgeois wealth with more serious dangers. The difficulty of controlling this illegalism is even greater than in the first case: all these irregularities are not infractions and, given the freedom of the labor market necessary to this bourgeois economy,‡ it is impossible to organize its juridical system so that they can all be constituted as infractions; this illegalism takes hold therefore at a new, infra-legal level. Furthermore, to a certain extent, the bourgeoisie basically has an interest in this illegalism: the existence of a mobile work force with no physical resistance or financial advance, and which cannot permit itself the luxury of a strike, is, in a sense, in its interests. Finally, [it] manages to lodge its own illegalism in this illegalism: at the time of the worker's record book, a worker not in order with the employer he is leaving cannot ask for the return of his record book and so cannot present it to his new employer; without his papers in order, he does not

---

* Manuscript (fol. 8): "cafe societies" and "finally collective refusals to work in order to obtain wage increase, or struggle against lowering wages."

† The manuscript (fol. 9) adds: "And, as a result, it will be able to multiply on the basis of itself. Giving rise to a whole political struggle. Anti-legalism, anti-concession, anti-new illegalism legislation. When the employers say: The strikers are lazy, they are putting it in a historical nutshell."

‡ The manuscript (fol. 10) adds: "and that in order to give the employer free rein, he is given the (illusory) form of the free contract."

have the same claim on wages. Thus, non-observance of the decrees on the worker's record book was a standard practice of employers in the nineteenth century.[10]

Fourth, this illegalism was moreover less the object of "fear"—for it did not attack the body of wealth itself but represented simply a lack of earning—than of disapproval. Thus, with reference to workers of the North, Villeneuve-Bargemont, in the *Économie politique chrétienne*, said: "[I]f the destitute portion of the Flemish population have vices that contribute to casting it and keeping it in this hideous state of abjection and poverty, the softness, or, if you like, the lack of vigorous character on the part of the destitute generally keeps them from excess that is harmful to society. They live in the most complete destitution, and yet they are rarely guilty of serious offences against persons and property; they suffer without revolt and almost without murmur, and would be, thus, much more an object of pity than a subject of alarm and mistrust."[11] We could follow the objects, the mechanisms of this disapproval; it would suffice, for example, to study a term like *dissipation*.[12] We find it whenever it is necessary to designate worker immorality. We find it in the seventeenth century in the registers of confinement or the *lettres de cachet*: [at that time] the dissipater was someone opposed or resistant to a certain reasonable way of managing his goods. From the nineteenth century, the dissipater is someone who undermines, not capital, not riches, but his own labor-power: dissipation is no longer a bad way of managing one's capital, but a bad way of managing one's life, time, and body.

This is why dissipation takes three major forms in these analyses: intemperance, as wasting the body; improvidence, as dispersion of time; and disorderliness, as mobility of the individual in relation to the family, to work.[13] The three major institutions in which dissipation will be actualized are: festivity, the lottery—which is precisely the way the individual tries to earn his living without working, the sporadic time and luck of which are opposed to earning money in the rational system of economy, that is to say by continuous work rewarded by an amount fixed in advance—and cohabitation,[14] as modality of sexual satisfaction outside a settled family. The target of these terms is everything that could be called moral nomadism. What was most feared in the classical period was physical nomadism linked to depredation. Now, the circulation of individuals around wealth is still feared, but moral [nomadism] is equally feared: if industrial production no longer has much need for the worker's technical "qualification," it does need a vigorous, intense, continuous labor—in short, the worker's moral quality.

Fifth, the problem is how this irregularity is to be controlled. Such control presupposes first of all the moralization of penality;[15] but it also presupposes a much finer and more far-reaching machine than the penal machine strictly speaking: a mechanism of *penalization of existence*. Existence needed to be framed in a kind of diffuse, everyday penality, with para-penal extensions introduced into the social body itself, prior to the judicial apparatus. There was an attempt to frame popular life in a whole interplay of rewards and punishments; for example, measures to control drunkenness decided at a purely regulatory or factual level: thus a system of punishment was established at Sedan:[16] a worker found drunk in the street was thrown out of his workshop and was re-employed only on swearing never to get drunk again. From 1818 there is also control through savings:[17] the savings book functions as a moral training, a constant interplay of rewards and punishments for the existence of individuals. From 1803, workers without a work record book in which the names of their successive employers were recorded were arrested for vagrancy; now, from 1810, a de facto arrangement with the police meant that a worker without a work record book was not arrested if he possessed a savings bank book. The latter, a guarantee of morality, allowed the worker to escape different police controls; likewise, the preferential hiring of workers with a savings bank book was standard employer practice. So we see a whole series of games of rewards and punishments, a game of infra-judicial penalties, creeping into economic mechanisms.

Now the first characteristic of this extra-judicial punitive system is that it does not fall under the heavy penal machine with its binary system; for this punitive game does not mean that someone is actually sentenced, it does not make someone fall on the other side of the law, into delinquency. It is a game that warns, threatens, [exerts] a sort of constant pressure. It is a graduated, continuous, cumulative system: all these little warnings, all these little punishments, finally, are added up and recorded, either in the employer's memory or in the worker's record book, and accumulating in this way it all tends towards a threshold, exerts an ever greater pressure on the individual, to the point that, finding it increasingly more difficult to find work, he falls into delinquency. Delinquency will become the threshold, as if naturally fixed in advance, of this whole series of little pressures exerted on the individual throughout his life. For example, this is how the extra-penal punitive mechanism functions in the case of the worker's record book: from the application of the Vendémiaire decree of Year XI, a worker has to leave his employer with a record book in which the latter has recorded the work, wages, and dates of employment.[18] Now employers very quickly acquire the habit of recording in the book their evaluation of the worker. In 1809, a circular of the Minister of the Interior, Montalivet, reminds the Prefects that the employers do not have the right to record negative assessments, but only the conditions of employment, and he adds: As it is still permitted to make laudatory annotations, everyone will understand that the absence of such will be equivalent to a pejorative annotation.[19] Thus, conditions of employment are linked to the presence or absence of such assessments; furthermore, the worker's indebtedness forces him to ask for an advance when he is taken on, and this is always [indicated] in the record book. The worker does not have a right to leave his employer without having repaid the advance, in either money or work; if he left before doing so, he could not get his record book back, was arrested for vagrancy, and passed then into the hands of justice. We can see then how this system of micro-punishments ends up making the individual fall into the hands of the judicial apparatus.

*   *   *

I think we have a historically important configuration in these strictly punitive mechanisms that have penetrated the whole social body. It entails, first of all, and for the first time in the history of Western society, the perfect continuity of the punitive and the penal. Henceforth, we will have an uninterrupted web extending justice into daily life; like a capillarization of the instance of judgment, of the to and fro between the punitive and the penal. In the classical period, there was a whole punitive sector assured, on the one hand, by the Church and its system of confession-penance, and, on the other, by a police system allowing punishment outside the law. It had a certain number of links with the penal sector, but, either through the effect of privilege—when it was a matter of the nobility or clergy—or through the effect of hyper-control—as in the case of *lettres de cachet*—the punitive sector was relatively independent of the penal system. Now, [in the nineteenth century,] we have a very subtle system comprising continuity of the punitive and the penal and reliant upon a certain number of laws, measures, and institutions. Thus, the worker's record book is both a contractual act between employer and worker, and a police measure: one must have an economic and moral control over the worker. The worker's record book is one of these, not exactly penal institutions, but one that makes it possible to assure the continuity of the punitive and the penal. The *Conseils de Prud'hommes* [employment tribunals; G.B.] also play this role: intended in principle to regulate employer-worker disputes, they can take a certain number of measures, home visits [for example,] and thus play the role of punitive agencies that, at a certain point, marginalize the individuals punished and push them into delinquency. All the institutions of supervision—homes, poorhouses, and so on—play this role of everyday and marginalizing control.

Subsequently, this continuity that characterizes the punitive society is possible only on condition of a sort of general supervision (*surveillance*), of the organization not only of a check, a perception, but of a knowledge of individuals, such that they are subject to a permanent test, up to the point at which it becomes necessary to make them cross over to the other side and actually subject them to an instance of judgment. Now this kind of permanent subjection to judgment, this instance of rewards and punishments following the individual throughout his existence, does not have the form of the test found in the Greek or Medieval penal system;[20] in that system of the test, [the decision as to guilt is taken] in the course of a confrontation, a joust, and [determines] once and for all whether or not the individual is guilty—a single act, a joust of individual against individual, a trial of strength. It no longer has the form of the inquiry, which is formed at the end of the Middle Ages [and] lasts until the eighteenth century;[21] a form of knowledge that, when an action has taken place, a crime identified, makes it possible to determine who did what and in what circumstances; given the crime, the problem is to find out where the guilty are to be found. We have then an inquisitorial form of knowledge and control.

Now the system of the permanent checking of individuals is neither of the order of the test, nor of the inquiry. Or rather, it is like a permanent test, with no final point. It is an inquiry, but before any offence, apart from any crime. It is an inquiry of a general and *a priori* suspicion of the individual. We can call *examination*[22] this uninterrupted, graduated, and accumulated test that permits a control and pressure at every moment, that makes it possible to follow the individual in each of his steps, to see if he is regular or irregular, orderly or dissipated, normal or abnormal. Effectuating this constant division, the examination authorizes a graduated distribution of individuals up to the judicial limit.* Thus, at this precise point of the relationship of worker body and force of production, we see a form of knowledge arising that is the examination. This society, which has to resolve problems of management, of the control of new forms of illegalisms, becomes a society that is not commanded by the judicial—for, never has the judicial had less power than in this society—but that diffuses the judicial in a daily, complex, deep punitive system that moralizes the judicial, which had never been the case formerly. In short, it is a society that links to this permanent activity of punishment a closely related activity of knowledge, of recording.†

The supervision-punishment couple is imposed as an indispensable power relationship for fixing individuals to the production apparatus, for the formation of productive forces, and characterizes the society that may be called *disciplinary*.[23] We have here a means of ethical and political coercion that is necessary for the body, time, life, and men to be integrated, in the form of labor, in the interplay of productive forces. There will remain one more step to take: how is this supervision-punishment possible? By what instruments was the disciplinary system that is established actually able to be assured?‡

---

* The manuscript (fol. 15) adds: "(with inquiry of investigation and test of the hearing)."
† Manuscript (fol. 15): "leave to one side this new form of knowledge. Keep in mind that we live in a punitive and examining, a *disciplinary* society."
‡ The manuscript (fol. 16) adds:

"- Many means: education; association; consumption (after destitution); housing; but
- a general form: confinement."

1. A. Grün, *De la moralisation des classes laborieuses* (Paris: Guillaumin, 1851). Grün's book, which amounts to no more than 91 pages, devotes 70 of them (pp. 17-91) to the seven moral defects of the laboring classes described by Foucault in his lecture.

2. Ibid., p. 23.

3. Ibid., p. 76.

4. J.-P. Thouvenin, "De l'influence que l'industrie exerce sur la santé des populations dans les grands centres manufacturiers," *Annales d'hygiène publique et de médecine légale*, series 1, no. 36, pp. 16-46, and no. 37, pp. 83-111, especially pp. 84-85 (Paris: Jean-Baptiste Baillière, 1847).

5. Michel Chevalier, *De l'industrie manufacturière en France* (Paris: Jules Renouard et Cie, 1841), p. 38. Louis Reybaud dedicates a chapter to Michel Chevalier in his book, Économistes *modernes* (Paris: Lévy Frères, 1862), pp. 172-243.

6. Ibid., p. 39.

7. Ibid., pp. 39-40 ("absolute independence!"—in accordance with original text).

8. In the margin of a section concerning the relationship between control and mobility: "moving to avoid the bailiff, the creditor, or the employer for whom one has not finished a piece of work," Foucault adds in the manuscript: "domiciliary visits by the *Conseils de Prud'hommes* (industrial tribunal)" (fol. 7); see above, p. 195. These Councils, composed of "half employers and half workers elected by their peers," were intended to "judge disagreements between workers and employers concerning arts and crafts" (Émile Littré, *Dictionnaire de la langue francaise*, vol. 5, p. 5074), or conflicts concerning the right to work. The first jurisdiction of *prud'hommes* was established at Lyon (law of 18 March 1806), the second at Paris (law of 27 December 1844). After many reforms, the laws of 18 January 1979 and 6 May 1982 extended this jurisdiction to the whole of the French territory and professional sectors.

9. Foucault refers in the manuscript margin to "Weitling" (fol. 9): Wilhem Weitling (1808-1871) is seen as a precursor of Marx, although the latter classified him as a "utopian socialist." Of working-class origin, an autodidact, Weitling professed a form of "primitive evangelical communism" (see L. Kolakowski, *Histoire du marxisme*, translation Olivier Masson [Paris: Fayard, 1987] 2 volumes; Volume I, *Les Fondateurs. Marx, Engels et leurs prédécesseurs*, pp. 302-305, see p. 304) calling for violent and collective revolt of the oppressed against the rich. The author of pamphlets widely distributed in Europe, Weitling took part in several illegal communist organizations, including the "Ligue des justes": in 1846, he briefly assisted Marx in the latter's attempt to establish links between the various European communist leagues.

10. With regard to the advantage the bourgeoisie draw from the illegalism of dissipation, Foucault adds in his manuscript: "The bar as example: financial interest, moral and political interest, tolerance of lending" (fol. 10), in reference to the recovery of worker savings by bar managers, which multiply as a result of the law of 17 July 1880, under the Third Republic.

11. A. de Villeneuve-Bargemont, Économie politique *chétienne, ou Recherches sur la nature et les causes du paupérisme, en France et en Europe, et sur les moyens de le soulager et de le prévenir* (Paris: Paulin, 1834 [republished Paris: Hachette, 1971]), 3 volumes, vol. 2, p. 64.

12. In the manuscript Foucault writes: "an example: Madre, *Des ouvriers* (1863)" (fol. 11). See A. de Madre, *Des ouvriers et des moyens d'améliorer leur condition dans les villes* (Paris: Hachette, 1863).

13. In the manuscript, Foucault writes this reference: "Grün (*Moralisation des classes laborieuses*, 1851): the *true* and the *false socialism*" (fol. 11). See, A. Grün, *De la moralisation des classes laborieuses*.

14. In the manuscript Foucault adds the term "Primitivism" and refers to "V. Bargemont" (fol. 11). See A. de Villeneuve-Bargemont, Économie politique *chétienne*.

15. In the manuscript Foucault mentions (fol. 12): the "law on drunkenness" (the law of 23 January 1873 punishing public drunkenness) and "the criminal character of nomadism" (article 270 of the 1810 Penal Code).

16. This practice is reported by Louis-René Villermé in his, *Tableau de l'état physique et moral des ouvriers employés dans les manufactures de coton, de laine et de soie* (Paris: Études et documentations internationales, 1989 [original edition: Paris: Jules Renouard et Cie Librairies, 1840]) p. 391. With regard to the means employed to struggle against worker drunkenness, Villermé writes: "But I have seen better at Sedan. I have learned, not without surprise and satisfaction, that in this town the heads of the leading firms, and most of the others, joined together and agreed among themselves to repress drunkenness ..., and that they were clever and lucky enough to succeed. Their means consists in preventing unemployment as much as they can, keeping jobs for workers who fall ill, in a word treating well those with whom they are happy, becoming attached to them, but also never allowing a drunk into their workshops, dismissing and never re-employing any man seen drunk, and applying the same punishment to those absent from the workshops on Mondays ... The workers are well aware of what they owe to their masters for such a service, and they show their gratitude. It is through them that I was initiated into the good actions of their manufacturers and was able to convince myself of the happy influence of the latter in preventing bad habits" (ibid.). Paul-Leroy-Beaulieu, in *État moral et intellectuel des populations ouvrières* (Paris: Guillaumin et Cie, 1868) also cites Sedan at several points as an example of towns that take measures likely to raise the moral condition of workers: "wherever we see sober workers, at Sedan, at Guebwiller, we find the intelligent initiative of industrialists" (p. 74). (Jacqueline Lalouette notes, at the end of the twentieth century, that no statistics yet enable us to work out alcoholic consumption according to social class; see J. Lalouette, "Alcoolisme et classe ouvrière en France aux alentours de 1900," *Cahiers d'histoire*, vol. 42 (1), 1997, http://ch.revues.org/index11.html.

17. In the manuscript, after "savings," Foucault adds: "Bruno" (fol. 13), no doubt referring to the fictional character invented by Pierre Édouard Lemontey in his *Moyen sûr et agréable de s'enrichir, ou, les Trois Visites de M. Bruno* (Paris: Hacquart, 1818) and taken up in *Suite à la brochure de M. P.-E. Lemontey, intitulée Moyen sûr et agréable de s'enrichir, ou Quatre Nouvelles Visites de M. Bruno. Conseils aux hommes de tous les rangs et toutes les classes, et surtout aux pères de famille, aux capitalistes, aux propriétaires, aux rentiers, aux artistes, aux salariés, etc.,* (Paris: Renard, 1825). Monsieur Bruno, a cabinetmaker retired from business, undertakes to teach workers the benefits of saving. Pierre Édouard Lemontey was president of the Legislative Assembly in 1791 and then, on his return to Lyon, he took part in the insurrection in support of the Girondins and went into exile in Switzerland after the victory of the republicans. On coming back into favor under the Empire and then the Restoration, he was elected in 1819 to the French Academy and died in 1826. See Dr. Robinet, A. Robert, and J. Le Chaplain, *Dictionnaire historique et biographique de la Révolution et de l'Empire 1789-1815* (Évreux: Charles Hérissey, 1898).

18. See above, p. 182, note 12.

19. See [Jean-Pierre Bachasson (1766-1823), comte de Montalivet,] "Circulaire du Ministre de l'intérieur (Comte de Montalivet) aux Préfets, Paris, Novembre 1809, sur les 'Livrets des Ouvriers'" in *Circulaires, Instructions et autres actes émanés du Ministère de l'intérieure, ou, relatifs à ce département: de 1797 à 1821 inclusivement*, 2nd edition (Paris: Ministère de l'Intérieure, 1822) vol. II (1807 to 1815 inclusive) p. 162: "If it is not permitted to write disadvantageous notes in the record book, nothing prevents the issue of favorable leave taking. The silence kept by the manufacturer, in the first case, proves in an indirect way, if not a deficiency of conduct, at least little satisfaction with the worker's services." It is Marthe-Camille Bachasson, comte de Montalivet (1801-1880) who will appear in *Surveiller et Punir*, p. 237; *Discipline and Punish*, p. 234, regarding questionnaires he sent to the directors of State prisons on the question of the solitary confinement of prisoners.

20. The notion of the "test" as form of exercise of power and production of truth, in contrast with other forms like the inquiry or examination, was introduced from 1970-1971 in the first course at the Collège de France; see *Leçons sur la volonté de savoir*, on the subject of the Greek system (lecture of 3 February 1971, pp. 82-83); *Lectures on the Will to Know*, p. 85, and the following year, "Théories et Institutions pénales" (ninth lecture, fols. 3-9, and lecture 13a, fols. 1-6) on the subject of proof by oath, ordeals, and judicial duel in the Middle Ages, between the tenth and the thirteenth centuries. Foucault will continue to develop the notion of test in "La vérité et les formes juridiques," *DE*, II, pp. 555-556/"Quarto," pp. 1423-1424 (in Greek pre-law), pp. 572-577/pp. 1440-1445 (in ancient Germanic law and feudal law); "Truth and Juridical Forms," *EW*, 3, p. 18, pp. 34-40. See too, *Le Pouvoir psychiatrique*, lecture of 23 January 1974, pp. 237-239; *Psychiatric Power*, pp. 237-239; *Surveiller et Punir*, pp. 45-46; *Discipline and Punish*, p. 44; *Mal faire, dire vrai*, lecture of 22 April 1981, p. 20 sq.; *Wrong-Doing, Truth-Telling*, p. 9 sq.

21. The notion of "inquiry" was at the center of the previous years' lecturers. See: "Théories et institutions pénales," course summary, in *DE*, II, no. 115, p. 390/"Quarto," p. 1258; English translation Robert Hurley, "Penal Theories and Institutions" in *EW*, 1, pp. 17-18: "*Measure* was analyzed the previous year as a form of 'power-knowledge' linked to the formation of the Greek city-state. This year the *inquiry* was studied in the same manner as it related to the formation of the medieval state; next year the *examination* will be considered, as a form of power-knowledge linked to systems of control, exclusion, and punishment typical of industrial societies"; "Théories et Institutions pénales," thirteenth lecture, fols. 4-10; *Leçons sur la volonté de savoir*, lecture of 3 February 1971, pp. 84-89; *Lectures on the Will to Know*, pp. 87-92. It will also be taken up and developed in the following years. See: "La vérité et les formes juridiques," pp. 557-570/pp. 1425-1438 (on Sophocles' *Oedipus The King*), pp. 577-588/pp. 1445-1456 (in the Middle Ages); "Truth and Juridical Forms," pp. 19-32, pp. 34-52; *Surveiller et Punir*, pp. 24-25, pp. 226-229; *Discipline and Punish*, pp. 19-20, pp. 225-228; *Mal faire, dire vrai*, lecture of 28 April 1981, p. 47 sq.; *Wrong-Doing, Truth-Telling*, p. 57 sq. For a rather close analysis of the role of the inquiry in Medieval law, see J. R. Strayer, *On the Medieval Origins of the Modern State* (see above, p. 18, note 13) pp. 39-40 (description of the emergence of the jury as a quasi-inquiry method—inquiry no longer based upon testimony but on the knowledge of "neighbors, drawn from the law abiding men of the district").

22. The notion of "examination" plays an important role in Foucault's thought. The notion will be developed in "La vérité et les formes juridiques," pp.594-595/pp. 1462-1463; "Truth and Juridical Forms," pp. 58-59 (in the context of the Panopticon); *Le Pouvoir psychiatrique*, lecture of 21 November 1973, p. 54; *Psychiatric Power*, p. 52; *Surveiller et Punir*, pp. 186-196 and pp. 227-228; *Discipline and Punish*, pp. 184-194 ("*The examination*") and pp. 225-227.

23. The concept of disciplinary power, which is distinct from the power of sovereignty, from bio-power (which appeared in *La Volonté de savoir*, Paris: Gallimard, 1976; English translation, R. Hurley, *The History of Sexuality, volume 1: An Introduction*, New York: Pantheon, 1978, and "*Il faut défendre la société*"; "*Society Must Be Defended*," lecture of 17 March 1976), and from security apparatuses (*dispositifs*) (which will become important in 1978 and 1979 with *Sécurité, Territoire, Population; Security, Territory, Population*, and *Naissance de la biopolitique*; *The Birth of Biopolitics*), will form one of the most important axes of Foucault's thought in the years from 1973 to 1980.

The hypothesis of a disciplinary power, closely linked to the set of practices of control, surveillance, and punishment, will be developed not only in the last lecture of this course, 28 March 1973, but in the lectures and course of the following year; see: "La vérité et les formes juridiques," p. 588 sq./p. 1456 sq. (presentation of disciplinary society); "Truth and Juridical Forms," p. 52 sq; *Le Pouvoir psychiatrique*, lecture of 21 November 1973, pp. 42-59, see p. 42; *Psychiatric Power*, pp. 40-57, p. 40: "I would like to advance the hypothesis that something like disciplinary power exists in our society. By this I mean no more than a particular, as it were, terminal, capillary form of power; a final relay, a particular modality by which political power, power in general, finally reaches the level of bodies and gets a hold on them, taking actions, behavior, habits, and words into account"; see also *Les Anormaux*, lecture of 15 January 1975, pp. 40-45; *Abnormal*, pp. 43-48 (development of the model of the grid-work division and control of plague-stricken towns as opposed to the model of the exclusion of lepers; on p. 50, note 10; English p. 53, note 10 it is pointed out that Foucault questions his own analyses of the forms of punitive tactics that he set out in the lecture of 3 January 1973, but it would seem rather, as Foucault himself indicates in this lecture of 3 January, pp. 2-4, that it is his earlier use of the notion of exclusion that he is criticizing retrospectively); *"Il faut défendre la société,,* lecture of 25 February 1976, pp. 161-166 (recapitulation of disciplinary power) and pp. 219-226 (comparison between discipline and security); *"Society Must Be Defended,"* pp. 181-186 and pp. 246-254; *Sécurité, territoire, population*, lecture of 11 January 1978, pp. 6-25 (more thorough comparison of juridical power, disciplinary power, and security); *Security, Territory, Population*, pp. 4-23. The notion of the power of sovereignty is developed in *Le Pouvoir psychiatrique*, pp. 44-48; *Psychiatric Power*, pp. 42-46; security apparatuses (*dispositifs*) in *Sécurité, territoire, population*, lecture of 18 January 1978, pp. 46-50, and lecture of 1 February 1978, pp. 111-113; *Security, Territory, Population*, pp. 44-49, pp. 108-110.

twelve

21 MARCH 1973

The factory-barracks-convent at Jujurieux. Minutely detailed regulations, employers' Icaria. (I) The institutions of confinement: pedagogical, corrective, therapeutic. Architectural and micro-sociological research. (II) Analysis of these institutions. (A) New form of confinement-sequestration. Three differences from the classical age. 1. Form of hyper-power. 2. Normalization. 3. Intra-State system. (B) The functions of sequestration. The sequestration of time. Subjection of the time of life to the time of production. 2. Direct or indirect control of entire existence. Fabrication of the social. 3. Permanent and uninterrupted judgment. 4. Production of a new type of discursivity: daily moral accounting of entire existence; ordered by reference to the normal and the abnormal.

IMAGINE A SOCIETY OF from three to four hundred unmarried individuals who employ their time in the following way: rise at 5 o'clock, fifty minutes for washing, dressing, and breakfast; workshop from 6.10 until 20.15, with a one hour break for lunch; dinner, prayers, and bed at 21.00.[1] On the subject of Sunday, article 5 of the regulations notes: "Sunday is an exceptional day; we wish to preserve the character it must always have, devoting it to the fulfillment of religious duties and rest. However, as it won't take long for tedium to make Sunday more tiresome than a weekday, exercises will be varied to make this day pass in a Christian and cheerful way."[2] In the morning, religious exercises followed by reading and writing, then recreation; afternoon, catechism and vespers and, at four o'clock, if weather permits, a walk, or else reading together; dinner, prayers, and bed. The religious exercises do not take place in church, but in a chapel inside the buildings.[3] The walks are constantly supervised by a religious employee, who is also responsible for management of the house and control in the workshops.[4] Money earned is held back until departure.[5] In the event that someone of a different sex from the residents is called upon for some service within the establishment, he is to be chosen, the regulation says, "with the greatest care and [these individuals] stay only for a very short time; they must remain silent on pain of dismissal."[6] The general principles of the organization are that no resident is ever alone, that mixing is to be avoided, and that the same spirit must prevail at all times.[7]

What we are dealing with here is not an ideal type of the regulations of a house of confinement in the seventeenth century, but the regulations of a silk mill at Jujurieux in the Ain in 1840.[*] In a sense it is a utopia, the institutionalization of the factory-barracks-convent:[†] a factory without wages, in which the worker's time belongs wholly to the employer, with nothing left over, in which the worker's body is literally bound to the production apparatus. It is the employers' Icaria. Now, there were quite a few of these utopias and, while it is true that they disappeared fairly quickly, around 1860-1870, there were quite a large number of them: around 1860, forty thousand workers were working in these conditions in the Midi.[8] Reybaud similarly describes a wool factory at Villeneuvette, which specialized in clothing for the army: "[T]he village is completely contained in the factory. Civil and industrial life are merged. The church and the town council, like the workshops and workers' houses, constitute a private property subject to an almost military regime. Crenellated ramparts encircle it; reveille is sounded, and in the evening the drawbridge is raised."[9] The regulations are strict: all travelers are excluded; return must take place at fixed

---

* Manuscript (fols. 3-4): "Of what institution are these the regulations? It doesn't matter which institution. For men or women; prison; boarding school; school; reformatory; psychiatric hospital; orphanage; workshop for penitent girls. Brothel. Barracks. And yet this is not a reconstruction, or an ideal type. It is an establishment that really existed—the silk mill of Jujurieux. Why cite this extreme example?"

† Manuscript (fol. 4): "factory-convent, factory-prison."

times; all games and drunkenness are prohibited. The only tavern in the village closes at 21.00; for a seduction not rectified by marriage, the worker was immediately considered to be delinquent and downgraded, and if he refused to marry he was forced into exile.[10] The report concluded: "How did these laboring classes, so intractable to the yoke, come to be here? ... The cause is a means of government that acted on the workers without them knowing it, flattered their vanity, and disarmed their envy."[11]

It is then an extensive phenomenon. In the first half of the nineteenth century there was a whole enterprise of confinement, of lodging the working class in barracks and, apart from the apparatus of production, in a whole series of non-productive institutions such as, for example, pedagogical institutions: crèches, schools, orphanages; correctional institutions: agricultural colonies, reformatories, prisons; therapeutic institutions: homes, asylums. All these institutions could provisionally be grouped together in terms of confinement.[*] To these real institutions we could add all the plans or dreams of confinement: for example, Marquet-Vasselot,[12] director of the Loos prison, imagines a town-refuge for delinquents and the destitute of a whole region of France,[†] or the dream of Villeneuve-Bargemont who, with regard to the problem of marriage and births in the working class, said: "No doubt a day will come ... when governments will be induced, by the force of things and by the greater development of enlightenment and freedom, to authorize the formation"—on the model of monks and priests—"of new celibate associations of work and charity, which will no longer seek opulence, but utility, and the aim of which, in the present state of civilization, will be in conformity with the new needs of society."[13]

---

* The manuscript (fol. 5) presents these examples as "a whole series of mixed institutions, both productive and repressive: agricultural 'colonies'; productive and pedagogical: workshops, homes for children."

† On the subject of this series of dreams and utopias, the manuscript (fol. 6) adds that they: "have the characteristics of:

1. representing adjacencies in relation to existing society; these utopias have to assure existing functions in present society;
2. representing systems of domination. Memorizing certain categories.

Utopias of service and servitude. One dreams of slavery - enclaves of slaves."

A whole activity of research runs through this production of utopias. Architectural research: for resolving the problem of how to construct an establishment such that optimum supervision is assured; architecture of the inverted theater,[14] where the aim is to ensure that the maximum number of people come under the gaze and supervision of the smallest number of people (see the research of Baltard[15]). "Micro-sociological" research:* before the term existed, research on schemas of dependence, authority, and supervision in a limited group. The Mettray agricultural colony,[16] founded around 1841, is a model of this research: the group of colonists was divided into small families, with a double authority, one external, of the overseer, and the other coming from the group itself and in the hands of one the children regarded as elder brother.

*   *   *

†The problem is the status of these strange institutions, some of which have disappeared, like the factories-convents, while others have been preserved and have proliferated, like the prisons. We may in fact wonder to what extent this confinement can be seen as the legacy of seventeenth- and eighteenth-century confinement, that is to say of those more or less widespread controls organized by the State, and of the classical great confinement.[17] One thing is certain: everyone is aware of the proliferation of these institutions. Thus, in the *Habitations ouvrières et agricoles*, published in 1855, Muller writes: "Let's follow the worker from his first days of childhood to those terrible years of old age, when nature makes him physically powerless. Alongside each of his needs, an institution has been created to provide for it ... For childhood, see the crèches and nurseries, which allow the mother to go to the workshop ... As for maturity, ... the State's charity supplements the old resources of monastic charity with hospitals ... [And recently,] the organization of assistance at home [has been invented] ... The worker could be at risk of dissipating in speculative impulses the few funds he has laboriously amassed at the cost of strain and effort. To keep him from this danger,

---

* Manuscript (fol. 6): "'micro-sociological' research: optimum authority. Study of the circulation of orders; forms of grouping and isolation of individuals."

† Manuscript (fol. 7), subtitles: "*Analysis of these institutions*". "A: *Confinement-sequestration.*"

savings banks have been thought up. Suffering and misfortune threaten his old age; our fathers, through the poorhouses, thought only of relieving improvidence: we do more, we facilitate foresight through our private pension funds. Finally workers' housing needed to be improved"[18]—and this is how workers' cities were created. So there is an awareness of the individual's constant framing, from birth to death, by these institutions.

In this text we can identify the crucial differences between confinement in the classical age and what we see in the nineteenth century. In the classical age, individuals are controlled and tied down first of all by their membership of castes, communities, and groups, like the *jurandes*, corporations, guilds, and professional bodies. By belonging to a certain social body, the individual was thereby, first of all, caught up in a set of rules that directed and possibly sanctioned his behavior, and then, in another way, through the group itself, he was caught within an instance of supervision that did not differ from the group in question. In other words, the group, with its rules and the supervision it exercised, was a sort of endogenous instance of control. From the nineteenth century, on the other hand, individuals are tied, externally as it were, to and by apparatuses of which they are not a part. At birth they are placed in a crèche; in childhood they are sent to school; they go to the workshop; during their life they come under a charity office; they must deposit money in a savings bank; they end in a home. In short, throughout their life, people enter into a multiplicity of links with a multiplicity of institutions, none of which represents them exactly, none of which constitutes them as a group—one does not form a group depositing in a savings bank, going through school, whereas in the classical age, control and supervision was organized within and by the fact that one belonged to a group, such as a corporation, and so on. Thus, individuals are fixed as if from outside by these apparatuses with an institutional specificity in relation to those for whom they are made, which have a spatial location, and so on.

In short, at this point we see absolutely new "bodies" emerging in the social space, different from what was formerly understood when one spoke of corporations, of *jurandes*, and so on. What appear with these institutions like crèches, savings banks or contingency funds, and prisons are not social bodies, that is to say membership bodies. Nor are they bodies with a mechanical form, that is to say productive bodies, although there are links between the development of mechanization and these new bodies. They are bodies that function as multipliers of power, as zones in which power is most concentrated and intense. At a certain level, these institutions are indeed only simple relays of the power exercised by one class on another; but when we look more closely at how they work, we see that they establish a real break, and that, in the space and sphere of influence of these institutions, a sort of concentrated and quasi autonomous power with a new force reigns: the power of the boss in the factory, of the foreman in the workshop. This power is not just derived from and directly in line with hierarchies of power from the bottom up. In fact, there is an instance of almost controlled power since, through a certain number of measures—a certain number of dismissals or bad evaluations suffice—the foreman or boss may push the worker into the arms of penal justice.

The most striking example of this discontinuity, of this re-concentration, re-intensification of power within these zones, is the prison. In principle, it should be a place where only what is most legal in institutions is applied, that is to say the decisions of justice. Now, in fact, the prison is something else entirely than a place where decisions of justice made elsewhere, in the courts, are applied. It functions not only as its own power to itself, but also its own justice. Thus, in 1819, Decazes could exclaim that "the law should reign in the prison"[19] and, in 1836, Béranger defined the role of the prison director in this way: "The prison director is a true magistrate called upon to rule sovereignly in the establishment."[20]

These instances of hyper-power are therefore not membership or mechanical bodies, but dynastic bodies. What is more, they were seen in this way at the time. From what we can see through the workers' press, the workers' reaction consisted in talk of a return to feudalism: the factory is designed as a fortified castle, the worker is seen as the lord-employer's serf, correctional establishments are new Bastilles.* And this

---

* Manuscript (fol. 9): "Note the ways they are analyzed or perceived:

 - the 'institutional' analysis, which tries to skirt around them as hyper-power and reduce them to a function, and to integrate them in a legislative or regulatory system;

perception of society is not just the transposition of an old schema that had remained in popular memory; it is the perception of something distinctive: in the capitalist society being established, just as in feudal society, there are zones of power that are not exactly integrated into the State apparatus, not exactly controlled by it, in the territoriality of which reigns a very loose control, but a power in excess of what power would be in a simply hierarchically ordered society. The perception of capitalist power as the resurgence of a feudal grain in society was so strong in the working class that Reybaud himself, in a report of 1865 on the condition of wool workers, speaking of the mill founded by Patrol, writes: "It is a sort of feudalism that has emerged from the completely arbitrary."[21]

Such is the first difference: the instances of control, rather than being immanent to the social body itself, are deported, as it were, towards the outside and are assured by a certain number of regions, institutions of hyper-power.[22] A second transformation with regard to the old system is, in a way, the opposite of the first. In the eighteenth century, alongside the endogenous supervision of the group by itself, one has the great system of confinement, which in itself is marginal in relation to the body of society and targets those who are marginalized either at the individual level, in relation to forms of behavior and the ethical rules of their milieu, or, even more, at the level of the masses marginalized by poverty, unemployment, vagabondage. Those outside the group are confined and thereby placed for a time outside the law. These establishments are therefore, above all, instruments of removal. With the apparatuses that emerge in the nineteenth century, however, confinement no longer appears as so many ways of marginalizing individuals or of removing already marginalized individuals. When a child is placed in an agricultural colony, when a young female worker is put in a factory-convent, when an individual is sent to a prison in which there are workshops, in reality they are fixed to a productive

---

- or, in contrast: a very keen perception of these regions of hyper-power. A quasi-mythical perception retranscribed in a half-political, half-historical vocabulary. They are seen as the resurrection of the Middle Ages, or of the Ancien Régime: factory-fortified castle; the new Bastilles; school-convent."

apparatus. The child sent to school is fixed to an apparatus that transmits knowledge, that normalizes.*

In all these cases, the function of the apparatus in relation to marginality is quite different from the monotonous system of classical confinement: it is not a matter of marginalizing at all, but of fixing within a certain system of the transmission of knowledge, of normalization, of production. Certainly, these apparatuses have a function of marginalization; but they marginalize those who resist.† The school in which children are confined is such that the majority is supposed to connect up to a certain apparatus of the transmission of knowledge, and those who are resistant to this transmission are marginalized. The machine works in order to demarginalize, and marginalization is only a side effect. The most striking example of this is doubtless that of the homes for abandoned children. Around 1840-1845, the one at Lille functioned in the following way: in the first weeks the child is sent to a wet nurse in the country; at twelve years he returns to the home, where he is given a uniform and sent either to school with other children outside the home or to the workshop. Starting from this marginality of the abandoned child—that is to say, illegitimate child, the fruit of a liaison against which the systems of control established by the bourgeoisie struggle—a marginality marked by the uniform, hence the name they are given, "yellow collars," the home's role is to see to it that individuals overcome this marginality by becoming integrated into either the production apparatus or the school apparatus, by connecting up to a certain number of social apparatuses.‡

So what is involved is a confinement for fixing individuals to and distributing them across social apparatuses. These institutions of confinement function, so to speak, adjoined to the apparatuses of production, transmission of knowledge, and repression, and they assure the kind of supplement of power the latter need in order to function. They are no longer institutions of the classical type of confinement, but rather of what we may call *sequestration*, by reference to that kind of arbitral authority that seizes something, withdraws it from free

---

* The manuscript (fol. 10) adds: "or which corrects, cures, rectifies."
† The manuscript (fol. 11) adds: "for example, those who do not adapt to the school, the workshop."
‡ The manuscript (fol. 11) adds: "of sorting, of distribution."

circulation, and keeps it fixed at a certain point, for a certain time, until the court's decision. What is interesting is the position and interplay of these instruments of sequestration in relation to what we usually call the State apparatus. I have picked out a kind of tendency to centralization at the end of the eighteenth century, a tendency of the State to take over the means of control that are at work in society at that time. Now, when we see all these flourishing and proliferating instruments of sequestration, we have the impression that there is, rather, a spreading that in a sense escapes the State. They are often the result of private initiative; and for some of them the State, in the strict sense, only follows initiatives that are not its own. But we should note that most of these establishments take the State structure as their model: they are all little States that are made to function inside the State. They still rely on the State apparatuses for a whole system of referrals and reciprocities: the workshop could not function in the structure of the convent or barracks if there were not the police or the army alongside. All these establishments, whether or not they come directly under the State, still refer, despite everything, to State apparatuses, even though they are not themselves State apparatuses but, rather, relays-multipliers of power within a society in which the State structure remains the condition for the functioning of these institutions.*

*   *   *

†We need to know what precisely the point of this sequestration was, why these supplements of power were needed to fix individuals to social, pedagogical, productive, and other apparatuses. The first thing we should note is this: it is true that the most visible of these sequestration apparatuses—the factory-convent—disappeared fairly early on, around 1870;‡ but, at the very moment of its disappearance and, in truth, throughout its existence from 1830 to 1870, it was

---

* Manuscript (fol. 12): "It is not a State apparatus, it is an apparatus caught up in a state node (*noeud étatique*). An intra-State system."

† Manuscript (fol. 13), subtitle: "B. *The functions of sequestration.*"

‡ The manuscript (fol. 13) adds: "for economic (too rigid) [and] political reasons. But in fact many of its functions were taken up and had moreover been anticipated by a whole series of more diffuse, but also more supple and better adapted institutions: the worker's record book, the savings bank, the provident bank, workers' cities."

preceded and supported by supple, diffuse forms of sequestration. To analyze sequestration in capitalist society, I do not think we have to stick to the spatially isolated forms of sequestration: savings banks, contingency funds, to take Muller's examples, are instances of control just as much as crèches and homes.[23] The function of sequestration should be located not only in those geographically and architecturally isolated establishments, but also in all those diffuse instances that assure control around them or in place of them. Now, there are three major functions of sequestration in capitalist society.

*The first function appears quite clearly in the Jujurieux regulations: the total acquisition of time by the employer. Actually, the latter not only acquires individuals, but also a mass of time that he controls from start to finish. This characterizes the policy of capitalism at the beginning of the nineteenth century: it does not need full employment but a mass of unemployed workers in order to put pressure on wages; on the other hand, to ensure that some workers are not employed, it needs the full employment of time, and work of twelve or fifteen hours is not uncommon. Today, we have discovered the value, not of the full employment of time, but of the full employment of individuals; the full control of time is assured by means of leisure activities, entertainment, consumption, which amounts to reconstituting the full employment of time that was one of the primary concerns of capitalism in the nineteenth century.

All these institutions of sequestration are characterized by the fact that the individuals in them are occupied all the time in either productive, purely disciplinary, or leisure activities. The control of time is one of the fundamental points of the hyper-power organized by capitalism through the State system.[†] Even apart from the institutions of concentrated sequestration, school, factory-prison, reformatory—in which the employment of time is an essential component [...]— the control, management, and organization of the life of individuals [represents] one of the main things established at the beginning of the nineteenth century. It was necessary to control the rhythm at which people wanted to work. When individuals were paid by day, one had

---

* Manuscript (fol. 14), subtitle: "*The sequestration of time.*"
† The manuscript (fol. 15) adds: "but without localizing it in a State apparatus."

to make sure that they did not take their leave when they wanted. It was necessary to hunt down festive revelry, absenteeism, gambling, and notably the lottery as a bad relationship to time in expecting money from the discontinuity of chance rather than from the continuity of work. The worker had to be made to master chance in his life: illness, unemployment.* To make him responsible for himself until death, he had to be taught the quality called foresight by offering him savings banks. Now, all this, which appears in the literature of the time as an apprenticeship in moral qualities, actually signifies the integration of the worker's life into the time of production, on the one hand, and the time of saving, on the other. The time of life, which could be broken up by leisure, pleasure, chance, revelry had to be homogenized so as to be integrated into a time that is no longer the time of individuals, of their pleasures, desires, and bodies, but the time of the continuity of production, of profit.† The time of people's existence had to be fitted and subjected to the temporal system of the cycle of production.‡

Such is the first function of sequestration: to subject the time of life to the time of production. If the problem of feudal society was one of localizing individuals, tying them to an estate over which one could exercise one's sovereignty and from which one could take rent, the problem of capitalist society is not so much to tie individuals down locally, as to capture them in a temporal mesh that ensures that their life is effectively subjected to the time of production and profit. We pass from fixing locally§ to temporal sequestration.

---

* The manuscript (fol. 15) adds in the margin: "contingency fund."

† The manuscript (fol. 16) adds: "What Bouvel did naively at Jujurieux, is done cleverly at Mulhouse."[24]

‡ Manuscript (fol. 16): "In sum, it is a matter of the integration of the time of individuals into the time of capitalization, profit, and production. Integration that takes place in three ways:

α - by a model that homogenizes: you are subject to the same laws and to the same advantages since you also save;

β - by a moralizing schema: you owe and you must. You are in debt. You are caught up in a system of obligation;

γ - by an operation of subjugation. Because actually the full employment of time enables the time of production and profit to establish its norms."

§ Manuscript (fol. 16): "from a local confinement."

*The second function is located in some paradoxes of these institutions of sequestration, whether it be in a concentrated or diffuse and labile form within society. These institutions are seemingly intended to be monofunctional: the school instructs, the factory produces, the prison inflicts a penalty, the hospital gives treatment; and, in principle, why should the school ask the child to do anything more than learn, or the hospital be asked to do anything more than provide treatment, and so on. Now, there is a supplement of constraint that is indispensable to the existence of these institutions. The discourse running through a workshop's regulations is never: "Work and, apart from that, do as you please"; the discourse delivered at school never consists in saying: "Learn to read, write, do sums, and then, don't wash if you don't feel like it."† In fact, these institutions take responsibility for the direct or indirect control of existence. They fix on a certain number of points in existence, which are, generally, the body, sexuality, and relationships between individuals.[25] On these three points they exercise a supplement of control that, at first sight, is absolutely not implied in the major, visible, institutional function of the establishment itself. These institutions of sequestration are, we might say, "indiscreet/indiscrete" (*"in-discrètes"*)‡ insofar as they concern themselves with what does not directly [concern] them. It is part of their function to be indiscreet/indiscrete (*indiscrètes*), syncretic, that is to say to mix a control focused on learning, production, or health, with controls bearing on something else and, in particular on the three points I have mentioned. This is clear in the example of the Jujurieux§ where girls are required to work from 6.00 a.m. to 8.00 p.m. in the silk mill and, in addition, not to go out on Sunday, and not to speak to men who enter the establishment, and so on.

Now, what is found in the concentrated state in the strict institutions of sequestration, is found in a diffuse state in a whole series of measures of sequestration through which the employers' power almost always sought

---

* Manuscript (fol. 17) subtitle: "*Other characteristic of institutions of sequestration.*"

† The manuscript (fol. 17) adds: "I look after you, and you can make love as you like."

‡ [The different meanings of the French *discrète* should, I think, be heard here; hence "*in-discrète*" suggests both *indiscrète* (prying, inquisitive, indiscreet) and, say, "*non-discrète*" (in the sense of not discontinuous, divisible, or divided, as in the English "indiscrete"); G.B.]

§ Manuscript (fol. 17): "the *example-princeps* of Jujurieux. It is clear again in the compact institutions."

to control outside the factory, in everyday life, a number of elements of existence that really had nothing to do with the activity of production itself.* Thus, in 1821, a regulation, cited by Villermé, is [decreed] by the Mayor of Amiens who wants, he says, to prevent "disorders, which have become too scandalous":[26] "Whereas it has been noted that [in the workshops] girls often take boys as assistants, that boys, on the other hand, choose girls for the same purpose; and that it is thus essential and in the interest of good morals to prevent the difficulties resulting from the coming together of the two sexes, especially for the young boys: *Rules the following* ... Men and women are both categorically ordered to have only young people of their own sex as assistants."[27]

The question is what purpose is served by this kind of supplement of control exercised through the institution of sequestration and independently of its major and visible function. In fact, an institution of sequestration isolates individuals from the rest of the population. In doing this it takes two risks: on the one hand, that of forming a foreign population, irreducible to the others, advantaged or disadvantaged in relation to the others; on the other, that of constituting, within the sequestration itself, a group that becomes a [sort] of collective force reliant upon the specific forms of existence it is given. Consequently, a way has to be found, on the one hand, to attach somehow the sequestrated population to society's collective forms of existence, and, on the other, to have at one's disposal a means of supervision enabling one to prevent the formation within the sequestration itself of a kind of counter-force, a counter-collectivity that might threaten the institution itself.

Take the example of sexuality at school. One goes to school to learn reading, writing, and good manners. How is it then that one of the most fundamental bases of all school regulations in the nineteenth century was hinged on sexual "repression"? Actually, the term "repression"

---

* The manuscript (fol. 17) gives two examples here: "worker drunkenness [and] the family." The next two pages (fols. 18 and 19) are missing. Page 20 begins: "Preventing the formation of a real collective; and this by forcibly substituting for it a 'moral universal.' A 'Normality,' something like a social *habitus* and *consensus*. Apparatus to fabricate society as fiction, as norm, as reality." The rest of page 20 and the following sheet (unnumbered, between fol. 20 and fol. 21) are entirely crossed out. They deal with the family and sexuality in the working class, especially with the formation of "monosexual groups, while imposing the norm of heterosexuality," with "the attitude of the working class with regard to the family and homosexuality," and with "the penetration of the bourgeois ideology of the family" in the working class.

seems to me more of a hindrance than exact, because there are two things in this restriction of sexuality within the school. First of all, there is the strict prevention of heterosexuality; the monosexuality of the institution means that it is materially impossible to have a heterosexual relationship. Then, in addition to this, there is something of an entirely different type: the prohibition of homosexuality, a prohibition that no longer has the character of prevention since, on the contrary, the prohibition assumes and can only really function insofar as a latent homosexuality is actually practiced to some extent and in such a way that at any moment it may be the occasion for power to intervene, for judgment and sanction, an occasion for intervention such that a hyper-control is thus exercised on individuals and they may be subject to something like a constant monitoring, a constant supervision that extends to their physical, affective, private life.

Now, from this double system of prevention of heterosexuality and prohibition of homosexuality that characterizes schools, a certain image of society is diffused in which heterosexuality is permitted as reward and in which homosexuality is supposed to not exist or to be a marginal phenomenon, so abnormal that it can concern only a small number of individuals. In short, prohibition of sexuality in school serves, on the one hand, to establish an internal norm, and therefore to give power a hold, and, on the other, to diffuse an external norm: it presents a fictive image of society the function of which is to give individuals both a certain conception of the society in which they live and a certain model for their future behavior [in the society in which they will live].* Thus, on the basis of this double system, we have the creation of a certain social fiction that serves as norm and permits the exercise of powers within the institution and, finally, the projection of what has to become the very reality of society, in which heterosexuality is permitted and homosexuality will no longer exist.

The function of the institution of sequestration in a case like this is to fabricate the social.† Between the classes on which these systems of sequestration work and the State on which they rely, one role,

---

* Typescript (page 189): "when they will be in society."
† The penultimate sentence of the unnumbered sheet (between fol. 20 and fol. 21) is scored out. One can read: "In summary: The apparatuses of sequestration fabricate social normativity."

among others, of these systems is to form an image of society, a social norm. The institutions of sequestration fabricate something that is both prohibition and norm, and that has to become reality: they are institutions of normalization.[28]

For there really to be this fabrication of the social and organization of a homogeneous time of life and production, within these institutions of sequestration there had to be: first, an instance of judgment,[*] a sort of uninterrupted judicature, which means that individuals are always subject to something like a judicial authority that assesses and imposes punishments or gives rewards. Whether it be school, factory, psychiatric hospital, or prison, whether it be compact forms of sequestration or broad forms, like the system of the worker's record book or worker cities, in the background we see a supplementary judicial authority.

[Second, there had to be] a type of discursivity, because to say judgment is to say supervision, assessment, accounting, et cetera. As a result, the behavior of individuals will enter into an absolutely new type of discursivity. Certainly, this is not the first time that individual behavior enters into discourse, and we don't have to wait for these institutions of sequestration for everyday personal existence to be taken up within a system of discursivity. After all, Catholic confession[†] is one of the ways of bringing it into a type of discursivity.[29] But this is characterized by the fact that it is the subject himself who speaks; it never leaves behind an archive; and the discursivity to which confession gives rise is caught up in the framework of something like casuistry.[‡] What we see emerging in the nineteenth century is completely different: it is a discursivity that takes up the quotidian, the individual, the personal, the bodily, and the sexual in a space defined by instances of sequestration. It is always from the point of view of the totality of time that the individual's life will be scoured and dominated. Whereas confession focuses always on a case—what was done in such and such circumstances—the discursivity that arises within these general techniques of sequestration follows the individual from birth to death and is a discursivity of the individual's whole existence. Thus, in

---

* Manuscript (fol. 21): "These institutions always have a third, or rather a third and fourth function. These coupled functions are: 1/ function of permanent judgment."

† The manuscript (fol. 22) characterizes Catholic confession as: "the best known, or rather the most poorly known and the most important" of the "discursivities responsible for recording the behavior of individuals."

‡ The manuscript (fol. 22) adds: "Then police reports: categorization, anecdotes."

the penitentiary colony of Mettray, the boys arrive with a dossier that is supposed to recount their life, the reasons for their arrest, the judgment, their attitude during the investigation and trial; from that point on they are caught in a kind of daily moral accounting. The whole of their time is, in this way, taken up within a discursivity.

[Third,] this discourse not only takes individuals from the beginning to the end of their existence, but it is not produced by the individual, but by an authority hierarchically situated within these systems of sequestration. This discourse is inseparable from a certain situation of power and a certain circuit of individuals in the apparatuses of production, of transmission of knowledge. Finally, this discursivity orders the discourse it produces by reference to normativity.* The individual is always described in terms of his possible or real divergence from something no longer defined as the good, perfection, or virtue, but as the normal. This norm, which we know full well, at this time, is not necessarily the average, is in a way not a notion, but a condition of exercise of this discursivity within which sequestrated individuals are caught. To be sequestrated is to be caught within a discursivity that is at once uninterrupted in time, produced from outside by an authority, and necessarily ordered by reference to the normal and the abnormal.†

---

* Manuscript (fol. 23): "it is ordered by reference to a certain normativity that plays the double role

    - of presenting itself as a collective social fact, about which one can do nothing, and
    - of functioning as a rule in the name of which one punishes and rewards

    according as it is, if not exhaustively produced, at least constantly revived and reactivated by the ceaseless activity of sequestration."

† The manuscript (fols. 23-24) ends in the following way:

    "• The replacement of religious time (exercises, holy days, eternity) by a time geared to the time of production.
    • The formation of a network of normative sociality (both object of study and prescription of behavior), to mask the class relationship ["struggle" crossed out] and the State.
    • The formation of an instance, or rather a whole network of cognitive-punitive epistemological-judicial instances, whose general form of intervention is perpetual examination, and whose diverse regions will be psychology, sociology, criminology, psychiatry, et cetera.
    • The organization, on the borders of the State apparatuses, but often in a very advanced position relative to them, of a whole body of 'agents of social sequestration'—social workers.

These are four correlative phenomena that all have sequestration as their common instrument."

APPENDIX

The manuscript for this lecture is followed by six unnumbered sheets, and then by three sheets entitled "Conclusion," also unnumbered, which would be a sketch, derived from this lecture, of the second part of the fifth lecture Foucault gave at Rio some months later (see "La vérité et les formes juridiques," pp. 612-623/pp. 1480-1491; "Truth and Juridical Forms," pp. 76-87). These nine pages are re-transcribed here:

In a sense, it is indeed

- the legacy of "French" techniques of confinement;
- the legacy of "English" procedures of moral control.

But, in fact, profound transformations.

1. In English control, the individual was supervised by a group insofar as he belonged to the group: religious, social, or work.

Here, the individual is external to the institution that supervises him: the workshop where he works; the school where he studies; the hospital he goes to.

More a "supervision (*surveillance*)" than a "control."[30]

2. In French confinement it was a matter of exclusion: either temporary, as punishment, or an additional exclusion sanctioning an already acquired marginality (the unemployed, vagabonds, beggars).

Now it is an internment that fixes to a process of production, or to a process of training, of the normalization of producers.

It is an inclusion more than an exclusion.

Hence the term "sequestration."

Contrast   Sequestration/confinement
             Inclusion/marginality
             Normalization/exclusion

3. Situation in relation to the State
   - in England, extra-State control

- in France, it was openly Statist. Here there will be an intra–State network.

What is the purpose of these institutions?

1. The control of time

In the feudal system, the control of individuals was linked to their location:

- particulars of such and such a place

   such and such a landowner

   such and such a sovereign

In industrial society it is the individual's time that is controlled:

- time must be put on the market
- it must be transformed into working time.

Hence, in the "compact" forms, time is acquired once and for all:

- the group
- the monastic model.

In diffuse forms:

- festivity
- saving (making sure that he can work after unemployment; that he does not die of hunger. But that he does not use his savings to not work).

In short, it is a matter of transforming time into the object of wages. Bringing into the wage exchange.

2nd function

Not only does sequestration control the individual's time, it imposes a whole series of ancillary controls:

- cleanliness
- drunkenness
- sexuality

These are controls of the body. There is a whole history to be written of controls of the body:

- body as surface of inscription of torture;
- body as element in drill (*dressage*).

What is involved is the transformation of the body into labor-power, just as it was a matter of transforming life into labor-power.

3rd characteristic: establishing a particular type of power

- economic power: giving a wage or asking for one;
- "political" power to give orders, make regulations;
    - judicial power to reward, to punish, to bring to judgment;
    - power to extract knowledge: either from practice
                                         or from individuals

knowledge that, by being redistributed in other forms of power, makes it possible to rationalize them: econ[omic], pol[itical], judicial.

Multiplied, accumulated power: "hyper-power",

But at the same time: "infra-power"

below the great State structures.

Its overall function is to connect up time, the body, the life of individuals, to the process of production and the mechanisms of hyper-profit. Infra-power that leads to hyper-profit; but with margins of uncertainty, of discrepancy.

Conclusion

1. Prison: concentrated form of this infra-power isomorphic with social panopticism.
2. The concrete essence of man is labor: actually man is linked to labor, at the level of his life and body, only through a power relationship.
3. Power is not a way of reproducing relations of production, but of constituting them.
4. Normalizing knowledge, in the form of the examination, which functions
   - not only at the level of the expression of relations of production,
   - not only at the level of the forces of production,
   but at the level of the very organization of the relations of production.

We have seen a knowledge that arose from the shift of the forms of feudal levy.

We have seen one that arises from the power relations inherent in the constitution of relations of production.

Some [contemporaries were aware] of this panopticism.

Julius   • spectacle
          • social community
          • sacrifice
          • supervision
          • individuals
          • the State

Its different manifestations.

History of the whole judicial institution.

Treilhard. Presentation of the Penal Code.

Analyzing it rather from the bottom, and in muted, insidious, everyday forms.

1. Taken from the regulations of the silk mill of Jujurieux in Ain, which dates from 1840 (see below, p. 202). It is likely that Foucault relied on the model of the "Régime et règlement d'un tissage de soies" presented in L. Reybaud, *Étude sur le régime des manufactures. Condition des ouvriers en soie* (Paris: Michel Lévy Frères, 1859), "Note F" to supporting documents, p. 334 sq., as well as on the description of Jujurieux offered by Louis Reybaud in the body of the work (ibid., p. 198 sq.). Reybaud explains that at Jujurieux a rule was established "which, by its severity, comes close to that of religious congregations" (p. 199). On the regime and regulations of Jujurieux, see also: J. Simon, *L'Ouvrière* (Paris: Librairie de L. Hachette & Cie, 1891^9 [1861]), p. 56 sq.; M. Cristal, "De l'éducation professionnelle des filles," *Revue contemporaine*, vol. 83, XIVth year, 2nd series, vol. 48, 15 November 1865 (Paris: Librairie Dentu, 1865) pp. 32-62, especially p. 41 sq. Foucault takes up this example again some months later in his lectures at Rio, "La vérité et les formes juridiques," pp. 609-611/pp. 1477-1479; "Truth and Juridical Forms," pp. 73-75, in this form: "Let me give you a riddle to solve. I'll present the prescribed routine of an institution that actually existed during the years 1840-1850 in France—that is, at the beginning of the period I am analyzing. I'll describe the routine without saying whether it's a factory, a prison, a psychiatric hospital, a convent, a school, or a barracks, and you will guess what institution I have in mind" (p. 609/p.1477; Eng., p. 73); as well as in *Surveiller et Punir, Discipline and Punish* in which he presents it as an extension of "this great carceral network" from the prison to orphanages, establishments for apprentices, and "still farther away the factory-convents, such as La Sauvagère, Tarare, and Jujurieux (where the girl workers entered at about the age of thirteen, lived confined for years and were allowed out only under supervision, received instead of wages pledged payment, which could be increased by bonuses for zeal and good behavior, which they could use only on leaving" (p. 305; Eng., p. 298). For a description of worker accommodation constructed at Lille, Foucault quotes (ibid., n. 2; Eng., p. 324, n. 2) a passage taken from Houzé de l'Aulnay, *Des logements ouvriers à Lille* (1863) pp. 13-15. The notions of the regularization and employment of time, which will be developed in this lecture, emerge as main themes in the introduction and development of *Surveiller et Punir*, pp. 12-13 and pp. 151-153; *Discipline and Punish*, pp. 6-7 and pp. 149-152.

2. Chapter V of the Jujurieux regulations, quoted in J. Simon, *L'Ouvrière*, pp. 56-57, and in *Revue contemporaine*, p. 43. This passage is also found in the anonymous model of the "Régime et règlement d'un tissage de soies" in L. Reybaud, *Étude sur le régime des manufactures*, p. 344.

3. In the manuscript (fol. 2), Foucault retranscribes a passage that comes directly from the *Étude sur le régime des manufactures*, p. 201: "The parish church could have been a point of contact with the world; a chapel was consecrated within the establishment to which the faithful from outside were not admitted."

4. Ibid.: "When workers go out, and only in determinate cases, a nun accompanies them; they go for a walk only under the guide of nuns."

5. In the manuscript (fol. 2), Foucault notes: "No wages. Just pledges (40 to 80 francs a year) kept back until departure; with a bonus system for work well done." See L. Reybaud, Étude, p. 203: "Instead of wages, they receive a pledge that varies between 80 and 150 francs a year, according to the nature of the work and the level of apprenticeship. Some bonuses are attached in addition to good work, and are distributed following a classification made every month"; and p. 204 (concerning the establishment at Tarare, it is written that the pledges vary from 40 to 100 francs a year; the bonuses, from 1 franc to 50 centimes a month).

6. Ibid., p. 201.

7. See ibid.: "Sequestration is therefore as absolute as possible, and time is distributed between work and pious exercises, accompanied by some distractions."

8. In the manuscript, Foucault gives the following examples: "Tarare, Séauve, Bourg-Argental, and La Sauvagère" (fol. 4), and adds (fols. 4-5): "weaving—In Switzerland 'The worker is

a genuine resident; he is housed, fed, dressed; he enters a big family, he does not lack care and attention'; 'The female workers have the right to go out to visit their relatives settled in the neighborhood. Earnings pledges of 50 to 100 francs' // Episode of the young woman with the bold look (Reybaud file). // There are similar factories for men. // In France, Villeneuvette. In America, Lowell." The indications concerning Tarare, as well as the other places mentioned and Switzerland come from L. Reybaud, *Étude sur le régime des manufactures*, p. 197 sq. Louis Reybaud (1799-1879), member of the Institut de France, personally "visited three of these establishments: Jujurieux in Ain, Tarare in Rhône, and La Séauve in Haute-Loire" (ibid., p. 197) and studied the others: Bourg-Argental, La Sauvagère, etc.

9. L. Reybaud, *La Laine. Nouvelle série des* études *sur le régime des manufactures* (Paris: Michel Lévy Frères, 1867), p. 111.

10. Ibid., p. 127.

11. Ibid., pp. 127-128.

12. In the manuscript (fol. 6), Foucault refers to the work of L.-A.-A. Marquet-Vasselot, *La Ville du refuge. Rêve philanthropique* (Paris: Ladvocat, 1832). Marquet-Vasselot was director of the Loos *maison centrale* at Lille. Foucault will return to this work in *Surveiller et Punir*, p. 248, as well as to the author's function as penitentiary director (p. 237, p. 244, p. 256, p. 257); *Discipline and Punish*, p. [235] 318, n. 3, p. [245] 319, n. 11, p. 253.

13. A. de Villeneuve-Bargemont, Économie *politique chrétienne, oi Recherches sur la nature et les causes du paupérisme, en France ou en Europe, et sur les moyens de le soulager et de le prévenir*, vol. I, p. 236 [see above, p. 197 note 11].

14. There is quite clearly an allusion here to the principle of universal supervision developed in the *Leçons sur les prisons* of Julius (see above, lecture of 10 January, p. 23 and p. 38 note 3) and to Bentham's Panopticon (see above, lecture of 24 January p. 64 and p. 77 note 16). It is interesting to note that in his criticism of Foucault, the American sociologist Philip Smith, *Punishment and Culture* (Chicago: University of Chicago Press, 2008) pp. 106-107, suggests that Bentham may have been inspired by the model of the theater rather than the manor; we find here, thirty-five years later, this possible link with the theater. See also below, p. 247 note 26.

15. L.-P. Baltard, *Architectonographie des prisons, ou Parallèle des divers systèmes de distribution dont les prisons sont susceptibles, selon le nombre et la nature de leur population, l'étendue et la forme des terrains* (Paris: the author, 1829). Baltard will be cited in *Surveiller et Punir*, p. 238; *Discipline and Punish*, p. 235.

16. Foucault develops his analysis of Mettray in *Le Pouvoir psychiatrique*, lecture of 28 November 1973, p. 86; *Psychiatric Power*, pp. 84-85, and *Surveiller et Punir*, pp. 300-304; *Discipline and Punish*, pp. 293-296. The Mettray colony was founded near Tours by the magistrate Frédéric-Auguste Demetz (1796-1873). For contemporary references, see: F.-A. Demetz, *Fondation d'une colonie agricole de jeunes détenus à Mettray* (Paris: B. Duprat, 1839); [E. Ducpetiaux,] *Colonies agricoles, écoles rurales et écoles de réforme pour les indigents, les mendiants et les vagabonds et spécialement pour les enfants ... en Suisse, en Allemagne, en France, en Angleterre, dans les Pays-Bas et en Belgique. Rapport adressé à M. Tesch, Ministre de la Justice, par Ed. Ducpetiaux* (Brussels: impr. T. Lesigne, 1851) pp. 50-65; F.-A. Demetz, *La Colonie de Mettray* (Batignolles: De Hennuyer, 1856), and *Notice sur la colonie agricole de Mettray* (Tours: Ladevèze, 1861). Jean Genet describes his experience of living at Mettray from 1926 to 1929 in *Miracle de la Rose* (Paris: Marc Barbezat-L'Arbalète, 1946); English translation Bernard Frechtman, *Miracle of the Rose* (New York: Grove Press, 1966). For a more recent study, see L. Forlivesi, G.-F. Pottier, and S. Chassat, Éduquer *et Punir. La colonie agricole et pénitentiaire de Mettray (1839-1937)* (Rennes: Presses universitaires de Rennes, 2005).

17. See M. Foucault, *Folie et Déraison. Histoire de la folie à l'âge classique*, pp. 54-96: "Le grand renfermement"; *History of Madness*, pp. 44-77: "The great confinement."

18. E. Muller, *Habitations ouvrières et agricoles. Cités, bains et lavoirs, sociétés alimentaires* (Paris: Liobrairie scientifique-industrielle et agricole de Lacroix-Comon, 1856) pp. 6-7.

19. See above, p. 78, note 26.

20. Pierre Jean de Béranger (1780-1857), a French songwriter and poet who was very popular in his time, played a certain political role in the liberal opposition to the Restoration, allying also with the Bonapartists. His writings earned him several prison sentences, notably to the Sainte-Pélagie prison in 1821 and the La Force prison in 1829. Close to Adolphe Thiers, Béranger nonetheless kept his distance from political power after the revolution of 1830. In his abundant correspondence with numerous political, literary, and artistic personalities of the first half of the nineteenth century, see the four volumes of *Correspondance de Béranger*, collected by Paul Boiteau (Paris: Perrotin, 1860), Béranger showed himself particularly sensitive to the fate reserved for political prisoners. In 1836 he writes in particular several times to Adolphe Thiers on the subject of the status of a political prisoner, Ulysse Trélat, and his conditions of incarceration; see D. Halévy, "Lettres inédites de Béranger et de Lamartine à Thiers," *Revue d'histoire littéraire de la France*, 24th year, no. 1, 1917, pp. 133-143. The sentence quoted by Foucault is however not found in this correspondence. (A keyword search in almost the whole of Béranger's oeuvre has not enabled us to identify the source of this quotation.)

21. L. Reybaud, *La Laine*, p. 183.

22. Foucault takes up this notion of "hyper-power" again in *Le Pouvoir psychiatrique*, lecture of 19 December 1973; *Psychiatric Power*, defining psychiatric power as a "surplus-power of reality" (p. 143; p. 143).

23. E. Muller, *Habitations ouvrières et agricoles*.

24. Regarding the worker cities constructed at Mulhouse around 1830-1835, Foucault comes back to it in *Le Pouvoir psychiatrique*, lecture of 28 November 1973, p. 85; *Psychiatric Power*, pp. 83-84, as well as in "L'œil du pouvoir" in J. Bentham, *Le Panoptique*, p. 12; English translation Colin Gordon, "The Eye of Power" in Michel Foucault, *Power/Knowledge. Selected Interviews and Other Writings, 1972-1977*, ed., Colin Gordon (Brighton: The Harvester Press, 1980) p. 162. See too A. Penot, *Les Cités ouvrières de Mulhouse et du département du Haut-Rhin* (Paris: Eugène Lacroix, 1867).

25. See "La vérité et les formes juridiques," pp. 617-618/pp. 1485-1486; "Truth and Juridical Forms," pp. 81-82.

26. L.-R. Villermé, *Tableau de l'état physique et moral des ouvriers employés dans les manufactures de coton, de laine et de soie*, p. 292. Suggesting an interesting parallel between life and work, this illustration is taken up again some years later by Édouard Ducpetiaux in a book dealing with analogous subjects: *De la condition physique et morale des jeunes ouvriers et des moyens de l'améliorer* (Brussels: Meline, Cans et Compagnie, 1843) vol. I, p. 326.

27. Extract from the decree of the Mayor of Amiens, 27 August 1821, reproduced in L.-R. Villermé, *Tableau de l'état physique et moral des ouvriers*, pp. 292-293, n. 1 (the words in brackets added by Foucault).

28. The notion of normalization, associated with disciplinary power is already present in M. Foucault, *Naissance de la clinique*, pp. 56-62 and p. 76; *The Birth of the Clinic*, pp. 57-62 and p. 76 [*normalisés* is here translated as "standardized"; G.B.], and is developed in the course of the following years. See: *Le Pouvoir psychiatrique*, lecture of 21 November 1973, p. 56; *Psychiatric Power*, p. 54: "In short, disciplinary power has this ... property ... of always being normalizing, that is to say, inventing ever new recovery systems, always re-establishing the rule. What characterizes disciplinary systems is the never-ending work of the norm in the anomic"; *Les Anormaux*, lecture of 8 January 1975, p. 24, and 15 January, pp. 45-48; *Abnormal*, pp. 25-26 and pp. 49-52; *Surveiller et Punir*, "La sanction normalisatrice" pp. 180-186; *Discipline and Punish*, "Normalizing judgement" pp. 177-184; *"Il faut défendre la société"* lecture of 14 January 1976, pp. 35-36, and of 17 March 1976, pp. 225-226; *"Society Must Be Defended"* pp. 39-40 and pp. 252-254. Foucault presents the treatment inflicted on the "delinquent individual" as

coming under a "technique of normalization," on the basis of "the emergence of the power of normalization, the way in which it has been formed, the way in which it has established itself ... [and] has extended its sovereignty in our society," *Les Anormaux*, p. 24; *Abnormal*, p. 26; he will question the relations the notion of normalization enters into with the reflections put forward by Georges Canguilhem in the second edition of his works on *Le Normal et le Pathologique* (Paris: PUF, 1966); English translation Carolyn R. Fawcett (Dordrecht/Boston/London: D. Reidel, 1978); see *Les Anormaux*, pp. 45-48; *Abnormal*, pp. 49-52; and develops the theme of the productive power of the "discipline-normalization" system (ibid., p. 48; Eng., p. 52; see too *Surveiller et Punir*, p. 186 and p. 196; *Discipline and Punish*, p. 184 and p. 193).

29. Already present in the previous year's course, "Penal Theories and Institutions," thirteenth lecture, fols. 1-6, Foucault will develop this theme of avowal and confession as mode of discursivity inherent to subjectivity in *La Volonté de savoir*, p. 79 sq.; *The History of Sexuality. Volume 1: An Introduction*, p. 58 sq. See also: *Du gouvernement des vivants. Cours au Collège de France, 1979-1980*, ed., M. Senellart (Paris: Gallimard-Seuil, coll. "Hautes Études"), 2012, p. 80 *et passim*; English translation Graham Burchell, *On the Government of the Living. Lectures at the Collège de France, 1979-1980*, English series editor, Arnold I. Davidson (Basingstoke: Palgrave Macmillan, 2014) p. 82 *et passim*; *Surveiller et Punir*, pp. 47-48, p. 72, p. 99; *Discipline and Punish*, pp. 46-47, p. 69, p. 97; as well as his study of the function of confession or avowal (*aveu*) in justice, *Mal faire, dire vrai*; *Wrong-doing, Truth-telling*.

30. Gilles Deleuze will later contrast Foucault's "surveillance (*surveillance*)" with the idea of a "society of control" corresponding to our present societies; see G. Deleuze, "Post-scriptum sur les sociétés de contrôle" in G. Deleuze, *Pourparlers 1972-1990* (Paris: Éditions de Minuit, 1990) pp. 240-247; "Postscript on Control Societies" in G. Deleuze, *Negotiations 1972-1990*, trans. Martin Jouhin (New York: Columbia University Press, 1995); "Qu'est-ce qu'un dispositif?" in *Deux Régimes de fous* (Paris: Éditions de Minuit, 2003) pp. 316-325, spec. p. 323; English translation "What is a *Dispositif*?" in G. Deleuze, *Two Regimes of Madness: Texts and Interviews 1975-1995*, ed., David Lapoujade (New York: Semiotext(e), 2007). Foucault here clarifies clearly the difference he introduces between the two concepts.

thirteen

28 MARCH 1973

Theme of the lectures: the prison-form as social form; a
knowledge-power. (I) General analysis of power. Four
schemas to be rejected. 1. Appropriation: power is not possessed,
it is exercised. The case of worker saving. 2. Localization:
power is not strictly localized in the State apparatuses,
but is much more deep rooted. The case of police in the
eighteenth century and of the penal in the nineteenth century.
3. Subordination: power does not guarantee, but constitutes
modes of production. The case of sequestration. 4. Ideology: the
exercise of power is not the site of the formation of ideology,
but of knowledge; all knowledge makes possible the exercise of
*a power. The case of administrative survey (*surveillance*).*
(II) Analysis of disciplinary power: normalization, habit,
discipline. ∽ Comparison of the use of the term "habit" in
the philosophy of the eighteenth and nineteenth centuries.
Comparison of power-sovereignty in the eighteenth century and
power-normalization in the nineteenth century. ∽ Sequestration
produces the norm and produces normal individuals. New type
of discourses: the human sciences.

TO CONCLUDE WHAT I have said this year I am going to try to
bring to the fore what I have kept at the back of my mind while I have
been talking. Basically, the point of departure was this: why this strange
institution, the prison? The question is justified on several counts. In

the first place, it is justified historically by the fact that the prison as a penal instrument was, after all, a radical innovation at the beginning of the nineteenth century. Suddenly, all the old forms of punishment, all that marvelous and shimmering folklore of classical punishments—the stocks, quartering, hanging, burning at the stake, and so on—gave way to this monotonous function of confinement. Historically, then, it is something new. Moreover, theoretically, I do not think the necessity of imprisonment can be deduced from the penal theories formulated in the second half of the eighteenth century, it cannot be deduced as a system of punishment coherent with these new theories. Theoretically it is a foreign element. Finally, for a functional reason:[*] the prison was dysfunctional from the start. First it was realized that the new system of penality did not bring about any reduction in the number of criminals, and then that it led to recidivism; that it quite perceptibly reinforced the cohesion of the group formed by delinquents.

So the problem I posed was this: why the prison one hundred and fifty years ago, and for one hundred and fifty years? To answer this, I picked up the track of the text by Julius in which he speaks of particular architectural features of the prison, saying that these are not characteristic of the prison alone, but of a whole form of society linked to the development of the State.[1] It seemed to me that this point of departure was actually important. There is a certain spatial form of the prison: that of the star,[†] with a center that is the point of constant and universal surveillance, in every direction and at every moment; around the center are wings in which the life, the work of the prisoners takes place; and, constructed on the central point, a tower, which is the heart of the edifice in which authority is established, from which orders are transmitted and to which information flows in from the whole. This is an exact diagram of order as command and regularity; the architectural problems of the theater, but reversed: showing everything, to a single individual; of the fortress, but reversed: for the latter defined a place that shields you and allows you to see everything happening outside, whereas with the prison it is a case of seeing everything taking place

---

* Manuscript (1st fol.): "economically or politically/functionally." The manuscript for this lecture is not numbered and consists of 26 sheets.
† The manuscript (2nd fol.) adds: "Bentham → Petite Roquette."[2]

inside without one being able to see in from the outside, and, at the same time, of the holder of power inside the prison being shielded from the very ones he sees.

Now, this prison-form is much more than an architectural form; it is a social form.[3] With a great deal of speculation we might go so far as to say that if the Greek city state invented a certain social space, the *agora*, which was the institutional condition of possibility of the *logos*, the form of the star, of the power of surveillance, gives rise to a new type of knowledge. Such was the point of my remarks: the prison as social form, that is to say as form according to which power is exercised within a society—the way in which power extracts the knowledge it needs in order to be exercised and the form in which, on the basis of this knowledge, it distributes orders, prescriptions.[*] We could thus try to identify the image in which the form of power is symbolized; we would have the medieval image of the throne, the seat from which one listens and judges: this is the magisterial form of power. We then have the absolutist image of the head that commands the body, which comes to a head: this is the capital form of power as it figures on the title page of *Leviathan*.[4] Finally, we would have the modern image of the center from which the watchful and controlling gaze radiates, where a whole series of flows of knowledge end up and from which a whole flow of decisions issues: this is the central form of power.[†] It seemed to me that, in order really to understand this institution of the prison, we had to study it against this background, that is to say not so much on the basis of penal theories or conceptions of law, nor on the basis of a historical sociology of delinquency, but by putting the question: in what system of power does the prison function?

*   *   *

It is now time to talk about this power.[5] To situate the problem, I would like to note four [types] of theoretical schemas that seem to

---

[*] The manuscript (3rd fol.) adds: "This starred form is a form of knowledge-power."

[†] The manuscript (4th fol.) adds: "Now this form, still according to Julius, was linked to the birth of an industrial society [and] to the development of the State. In fact, this need for surveillance is linked to the threat of a class that was immediately seen as numerous; foreign; on the verge of indigence; dangerous."

me to govern [...] analyses of power—and from which I would like to distinguish myself.

First, the theoretical schema of the appropriation of power, that is to say the idea that power is something one possesses, something in a society that some possess and others do not. There is a class that possesses power: the bourgeoisie. Certainly, the formula: "such a class has power" has its political value, but it cannot be used for a historical analysis. In fact, power is not possessed for several reasons. First of all, power is exercised in all the depth, over the whole surface of the social field, according to a whole system of relays, connections, points of support, of things as tenuous as the family, sexual relationships, housing, and so on. However finely we penetrate the social network, we find power, not as something someone possesses, but as something that takes place, is effectuated, exercised. And then, power may or may not succeed in being exerted: it is therefore always a certain form of momentary and continually renewed strategic confrontations between a certain number of individuals. It is not possessed because it is in play, it is risked. At the heart of power is a warlike relation therefore, and not a relation of appropriation. Finally, power is never entirely on one side. There are not those who have power and who apply it brutally to those who have no power at all. The power relationship does not conform to the monotonous and definitive schema of oppression. Of course, in this kind of general war through which power is exercised, there is a social class that occupies a privileged position and may thereby impose its strategy, carry off a certain number of victories, accumulate them, and obtain the advantage of an effect of hyper-power, but this effect is not of the order of total possession. Power is not monolithic. It is never entirely controlled from a certain point of view by a certain number of people. At every moment it is in play in little singular struggles, with local reversals, regional defeats and victories, provisional revenges.

To take some examples, I will refer to the problem of worker saving: how is it played out? In the nineteenth century it is the site of a battle of powers, with a whole series of opposed strategies, of victories and defeats that depend upon each other. This saving stems from the need felt by the employers to fix the working class to an apparatus of production, to avoid worker nomadism, and it fixed the working class in space by fixing it in time: by depositing in such and such a place something that assures the future. But, at the same time, this saving, imposed by the employers' strategy, produces the counter effect of the worker now having funds available to him for certain freedoms, including that of going on strike. So that the strike as instrument of retaliation against the employers is inscribed in the very measure by which the employers thought to control the working class. Hence, in return, a new employers' measure: control this saving and impose the presence of employer representatives in the provident banks. Hence, from the second half of the nineteenth century, the struggles over the direction and control of these funds. We thus see how, within a general strategy of worker sequestration by the employers, a whole series of struggles are played out, how a whole series of victories and defeats are set off one after the other, or one on top of the other.

So the power relationship is never stable, suffered definitively, but is always in this kind of mobility. So we cannot say power and profit as if they were analogous. Power should not be assimilated to a wealth possessed by some; it is a permanent strategy that should be thought of against the background of civil war. Similarly, we should abandon the schema according to which power, through a commercial kind of contract, would be conferred on some by the will of all—a contract that would mean that those who break it fall outside society and resume the war of all against all. Power, the legality it makes use of, and the illegalisms it carefully manages, or against which it struggles, should be understood as a certain way of conducting civil war.

Second, the schema of the localization of power: political power is always located in a society in a certain number of elements, essentially in State apparatuses.[6] So there is a match of forms of power and political structures. Now I do not think that power can adequately be described as something located in State apparatuses. Maybe it is not even sufficient to say that the State apparatuses are the stake of an internal or external struggle. It seems to me rather that the State apparatus is a concentrated form, or even a support structure, of a system of power that goes much further and deeper. Which means, practically, that neither control nor destruction of the State apparatus may suffice to transform or get rid of a certain type of power, the one in which it functioned.

I have tried to give some examples of this relationship between State apparatuses and the system of power within which they function. Let's take the police apparatus of the eighteenth-century French monarchy, a very new type of State apparatus. The apparatus was not externally laid on those who are subject to it; it is profoundly bound up with a system of power running through the whole of the social body. It could only function engaged with, linked, to powers distributed in families (paternal authority), religious communities, professional groups, and so on. And it is because there were these micro-instances of power in society that something like this new State apparatus was actually able to function. Similarly, the penal apparatus of the nineteenth century is not some kind of great isolated edifice. It functions in constant collaboration* with something that is not just its ancillary field, but its condition of possibility: the whole punitive system, whose agents are employers, landlords, and contractors who constitute so many instances of power enabling the penal apparatus to function, since it is bit by bit, through an accumulation of punitive mechanisms foreign to the State apparatus, that individuals are ultimately pushed into the penal system and actually become its objects.

So we should distinguish not only systems of power from State apparatuses, but even, more generally, systems of power from political structures. In fact, the way in which power is exercised in a society is not adequately described by political structures like the constitutional regime† or by the representation of economic interests in the State apparatus. There are systems of power that are much more extensive than political power in its strict functioning: a whole set of sources of power that may be sexual relations, the family, employment, accommodation. And the problem is not so much whether these other instances of power repeat the structure of the State. Really, it matters little whether the family reproduces the State or the other way round. The family and the State function in relation to each other, by relying on each other, possibly confronting each other, in a system of power that, in a society like ours, may be characterized as disciplinary in a

---

* Manuscript (8th fol.): "in collaboration with a disciplinary system, a punitive system in which the employer, the foreman, the landlord, the supplier constitute instances of power."

† The manuscript (9th fol.) adds: "the recruitment of the political class."

homogeneous way, that is to say [where] the disciplinary system is the general form in which power is inserted, whether located in a State apparatus or diffused in a general system.

Third, the schema of subordination according to which power is a certain way of maintaining or reproducing a mode of production: power is always subordinate, then, to a mode of production that is, if not historically, at least analytically prior to it. If we give power the extension I have been talking about, we are led to locate its functioning at a very deep level. Power, therefore, can no longer be understood solely as the guarantee of a mode of production, as that which allows the formation of a mode of production. Power is, in fact, one of the constitutive elements of the mode of production and functions at its heart. This is what I wanted to show when I talked about all those apparatuses of sequestration, which are not all linked to a State apparatus, far from it, but which all, whether provident banks, factories-prisons, or reformatories, function at a certain level that is not that of the guarantee given to the mode of production, but rather of its constitution.

What in fact is the point of this sequestration? Its basic aim is the subjection of individual time to the system of production and, quite precisely, to three of its elements. The time of life must be subjected to the temporal mechanisms, the temporal processes of production. Individuals must be tied to a production apparatus according to a certain use of time that continues hour by hour and fixes the individual to the chronological course of the productive mechanism. This excludes all irregularities like absence, debauchery, revelry, and so on. Individuals must be subjected not only to the chronology of production, but also to the cycles of productive activity. Although they do not possess any means of production, they must be able to withstand periods of unemployment, crises, reduced activity. This implies the coercive prescription of saving; saving will thus be a means of plugging into and submitting to the great cycles of productive activity. Saving—which means exclusion of all useless expenditure, gambling, and dissipation. The individual's time must be subject to the time of profit, that is to say that labor-power must be put to use for at least as much time as is needed for the investment to become profitable. For this, individuals must be fixed to a certain apparatus of production for a certain length of time, which entails all the controls tying workers down locally, the system of debt,* for example.

A system of power like *sequestration* goes far beyond the guarantee of the mode of production; it is constitutive of it. We could say: the problem of feudal society was to assure the extraction of rent through the exercise of a sovereignty that was, above all, territorial; the problem of industrial society is to see to it that the individual's time, which is purchased with wages, can be integrated into the production apparatus in the forms of labor-power. It is necessary to ensure that what the employer buys is not empty time, but indeed labor-power. In other words, it is a matter of constituting the individual's time of life into labor-power.[7] Which leads to this conclusion: if it is true that the economic structure, characterized by the accumulation of capital, has the property of transforming individuals' labor-power into productive force, the aim of the structure of power which takes the form of sequestration is, prior to that stage, to transform the time of life into labor-power. People must be able to bring onto the market something that is labor-power, which is secured by this system of power that is sequestration, the correlative, in terms of power, of the accumulation of capital in economic terms. Capitalism, in fact, does not simply encounter labor-power, just like that.†

It is false to say, with certain famous post-Hegelians, that labor is man's concrete existence.[8] The time and life of man are not *labor*‡ by nature; they are pleasure, discontinuity, festivity, rest, need, moments, chance, violence, and so on. Now, it is all this explosive energy that needs to be transformed into a continuous labor-power continually offered on the market. Life must be synthesized into labor-power, which involves the coercion of this system of sequestration. For exercising this coercion that transforms the time of life into labor-power, the clever ploy§ of industrial society was to take up the old technique¶ of the confinement of the poor, which, in the classical age, was a way of fixing and, at the same time, suppressing those who through idleness, vagabondage, or

---

* Manuscript (11th fol.): "the pressure of indigence is a system of indebtedness."
† Manuscript (13th fol.): "as immediate and concrete form of human existence."
‡ Manuscript (14th fol.): "continuous *labor*."
§ Manuscript (14th fol.): "stroke of genius."
¶ Manuscript (14th fol.) adds: "apparently much depreciated."

revolt had escaped all the geographical fixations in which the exercise of sovereignty was carried out. This institution will have to be generalized and utilized, in contrast, to connect up individuals to the social apparatuses; it will be specified in accordance with a whole series of apparatuses from the factory-prison to the prison, passing through poorhouses, schools, and reformatories. Reutilized to this end, all this old system of confinement will make possible sequestration, which is actually constitutive of modes of production.*

Fourth, the schema of ideology† according to which power can produce only ideological effects in the realm of knowledge (*connaissance*), that is to say power either functions in the silent fashion of violence, or in the discursive and wordy fashion of ideology.‡ Now power is not caught in this alternative of either being exercised purely and simply through violent imposition,§ or hiding itself and getting itself accepted by holding the wordy discourse of ideology.9 Actually, every point at which a power is exercised is, at the same time, a site of formation, not of ideology, but of knowledge (*savoir*); and, on the other hand, every knowledge formed enables and assures the exercise of a power. In other words, there is no opposition between what is done and what is said, between the silence of force and the prattle¶ of ideology. It is necessary to show how knowledge and power are effectively bound up with each other, not in the mode of identity—knowledge is power, or the other way round—but in an absolutely specific fashion and according to a complex interplay.

Let's take the example of the administrative survey (*surveillance*) of populations, which is a requirement of any power. In the seventeenth to eighteenth centuries, the administrative survey is a function of power assured by a number of people: intendants, police apparatus, and so on. Now this power, with its specific instruments, gives rise to a number of forms of knowledge.

---

* The manuscript (15th fol.): "Dismantling or not dismantling a type of power is therefore essential to the very existence of a mode of production."

† Manuscript (5th fol.): "that of ideological production."

‡ The manuscript (5th fol.) adds: "It needs an ideology. And it fabricates ideology."

§ Manuscript (15th fol.): "threat, violence, terror."

¶ Manuscript (15th fol.): "and the chatter (even persuasion) of ideological discourse."

1. A *management knowledge*: those who manage the State apparatus, either directly on behalf of the political power, or indirectly by a system of farming out, form at the same time a certain knowledge, which they accumulate and use. Thus, after inquiry, they know how they must tax, how to calculate the taxes, who can pay them, who in particular must be watched so that they pay their taxes, and on what products customs duties need to be levied.*

2. On the fringes of this knowledge of management, we see the emergence of a *knowledge of inquiry*: there are people who generally are not linked directly to the State apparatus or responsible for managing it, but who conduct inquiries into the wealth of a nation, the demographic movement of a region, the craft techniques employed in a particular country, and the state of health of populations. From the second half of the eighteenth century, these inquiries conducted, originally at least, on private initiative, begin to be taken over by the State. Thus, the Société royale de médecine, founded in 1776, will codify and take over responsibility for inquiries on the state of health;[10] similarly, inquiries into craft techniques will be taken back under State control and in the form of a State apparatus in the nineteenth century.[11]

3. A *police inquisition knowledge*: consigning someone to a place of detention is thus accompanied by a report on his behavior, his motives. From the nineteenth century, all the forms and techniques of this survey knowledge will be taken up again and, at the same time, founded in a new way, and this takes place in terms of two great principles that are crucial in the history of knowledge.

First, the principle we see emerging under the Revolution that is systematized, notably by Chaptal,[12] and at the time of the Consulate:[13] henceforth, every agent of power will be at the same time an agent of the formation of knowledge. Every agent† must provide information on both the effects of, and the consequent necessary corrective changes to be made to, actions ordered by the authorities. From the end of the

---

* The manuscript (16th fol.) adds: "from what population to recruit soldiers."

† Manuscript (16th fol.): "Every agent of power must report back knowledge correlative to the power it exercises (which enables its conditions and effects to be determined: possible corrections): Prefects; public prosecutors."

In the margin: "We enter the era of the report. As important in [industrial] society as *feed back* [English in original; G.B.] in modern technology, as double-entry book-keeping in the economy."

eighteenth century, prefects, public prosecutors, police functionaries, and so on, are bound to this fundamental obligation of the report. We are entering the era of the report as the fundamental form of the relations between knowledge and power. Certainly, this was not invented in the eighteenth century, but the systematization of what, for example, in the seventeenth century were only sporadic actions in the relations between intendants and ministers, the institutionalization of every agent having to report particular kinds of knowledge to his superior is an essential phenomenon.

In close connection with this introduction of reporting knowledge to the origin of power, there is the setting up of a whole series of specific instruments of abstraction, generalization, and quantitative assessment. This can be brought out if we compare several strata of documents. The reports produced by Sartine,[14] one of the last lieutenants of police of the Ancien Régime: the way in which he monitors the population, and the sporadic, individual kind of information given to his minister. The reports of Fouché,[15] which are already a kind of synthesis and integration, but of what is supposed to represent the state of the political opposition, of delinquency, and the constant state of the latter in France. The annual reports of the minister of Justice, published from 1826,[16] in which there is the same type of information as at the beginning, but treated, filtered by a knowledge machine and a number of techniques of abstraction and statistical quantification. A history of this State knowledge could be written, that is to say the history of the administrative extraction of knowledge.[17]

Second, the other phenomenon, opposite to the previous one, is the opening of apparatuses of power to autonomous sources of knowledge.* Certainly, one didn't have to wait for the nineteenth century for power to be enlightened by the advice and knowledge (*connaissances*) of a number of supposedly competent people; but, from the nineteenth century, knowledge (*savoir*) as such is statutorily endowed with a certain power. The nineteenth century brought something new, which is that knowledge must function in society as endowed with a certain quantity of power. School, grades, the way in which degrees of knowledge are

---

* The manuscript (17th fol.): "Up to the eighteenth century, this took place in the form of advice or pedagogy, kings [listening] to the philosophers, the learned and the wise."

actually calculated, measured, and authenticated by all the apparatuses of training, all this is both a factor and the expression of the fundamental phenomenon that knowledge has the right to exercise a power. Thus, the character of the scholar who exercised no other power in society than that of speaking the truth, of giving advice, gives way to a character, a laboratory director, a professor, whose knowledge is immediately authenticated by the power he exercises. This goes for the economist, for example: who were economists in the eighteenth century? Vauban, someone who is out of favor and takes up economics after losing power.[18] Quesnay, who wants, but does not have power.[19] At this point those in power have only an administrative knowledge. Economic theory does not arise within the power apparatus. The clearest case is that of the physician who, from the nineteenth century, inasmuch as he is the master of the normal and the pathological, thereby exercises a certain power not just on his client, but on groups, on society. Similarly, the psychiatrist has a power institutionalized by the 1838 law which, by turning him into an expert who has to be consulted for any action of confinement, gives the [doctor-]psychiatrist and psychiatric knowledge (*savoir*) a certain power.[20]

It is necessary here to reply to an objection: does not speaking of strategy, calculation, defeat, and victory get rid of all opacity of the social field? In a sense, yes. I think in fact that we too readily endow the social field with opacity, envisaging in it only production and desire, the economy and the unconscious; there is in fact a whole margin that is transparent to analysis and that can be discovered if we study the strategies of power. Where sociologists see only the silent or unconscious system of rules, where epistemologists see only poorly controlled ideological effects, I think it possible to see perfectly calculated, controlled strategies of power. The penal system is a privileged example of this. It is clear that if we pose the problem of the penal system in terms of economy, it appears opaque and even obscure, because no analysis of the economic role of the prison, of the population marginalized by this penal system, can account for its existence.[21] In terms of ideology, it is not just opaque, but completely muddled, the system having been so covered over with varied ideological themes.* On the other hand, if one

---

* The manuscript (19th fol.) adds: "It collects them all, from the social enemy to the neurosis

poses the problem in terms of power and of the way in which power has actually been exercised within a society, it seems to me that the penal system becomes much clearer. Which does not mean that the social field is entirely transparent, but that it should not be given facile opacities.

*   *   *

Where was I wanting to go? I wanted to analyze a certain system of power: disciplinary power.* It seemed to me, in fact, that we live in a society of disciplinary power, that is to say a society equipped with apparatuses whose form is sequestration, whose purpose is the formation of a labor force, and whose instrument is the acquisition of disciplines or habits. It seems to me that since the eighteenth century there has been a constant multiplication, refinement, and specification of apparatuses for manufacturing disciplines, for imposing coercions, and for instilling habits. This year I wanted to do the very first history of the power of habits, the archeology of those apparatuses of power that serve as the base for the acquisition of habits as social norms.

Let's consider this notion of *habit*. If we look at it in eighteenth-century political philosophy, habit has a primarily critical use. This notion makes it possible to analyze law, institutions, and authority. The notion of habit is used for knowing the extent to which something that appears as an institution or authority can be founded. To everything appearing thus founded, the following question is put: You claim to be founded by the divine word or by the sovereign's authority, but are you not [quite simply] a habit? This is how Humean criticism works, using the notion of habit as a critical, reductive instrument, because habit, on the one hand, is only ever a result and not an original datum—there is something irreducibly artificial in it—and, on the other hand, while unable to lay claim to originality, it is not founded by something like a transcendence: habit always comes from nature,

---

of confession, by way of debauchery, the primitive, the degenerate, the perverse. If one poses the problem in economic terms, the penal system loses all utility. [If one poses the problem in] ideological [terms], it loses all specificity. It is rationalized if one studies it in the form of power in which it works."

* Manuscript (20th fol.): "the analysis of a form of power I have called punitive, which it would be better to call disciplinary."

since in human nature there is the habit of contracting habits. Habit is both nature and artifice.[22] And if this notion was used in the political and moral philosophy of the eighteenth century, it was in order to get away from anything of the order of traditional obligations founded on a transcendence, and to replace these obligations with the pure and simple obligation of the contract; in order to replace these traditional obligations, which are shown to be only the effects of habit, with a game of obligations in which the will of each will be voluntarily bound and actualized in the contract. To criticize tradition through habit in order to contractualize social bonds, such is the essence of this use of the notion of habit.

Now it seems to me that the use of the term habit in the nineteenth century is different. In political literature, it ceases being regularly used in a critical way. On the other hand, it is used prescriptively: habit is what people must submit to. There is a whole ethics founded on habit. Far from habit limiting the sphere of morality, of ethics, a whole politics of habit is formed that is transmitted by very different sorts of writing—writings of popular moralization or tracts of social economy.[23] Habit is always given as something positive, something to be acquired. Now, in this position, it does not have the same relation to the contract that habit had in the eighteenth century: in the eighteenth century, one scoured tradition with criticism of habit so as to give way to the *contract*, which replaced habit, [whereas] in the nineteenth century habit is conceptualized as complementary to the contract. In the political thought of the nineteenth century, the contract is the juridical form that binds property owners to each other. It is the juridical form that guarantees the property of each. It is what gives a juridical form to exchange. Finally, it is through the contract that individuals form alliances on the basis of their property. In other words, the contract is the link between individuals and their property, or the link between individuals through their property. Habit, on the other hand, is what links individuals, not to their property, since this is the role of the contract, but to the production apparatus. It is what binds those who are not property owners to an apparatus they do not own; it is what links them to each other as members, not of a class, but of society as a whole. Habit, therefore, is not what links one to a partner at the level of property, but what links one to an order of things, to an order of time and to a political order. Habit is the complement of the contract for those who are not linked through their property.

We can say then how the apparatus of sequestration can effectively fix individuals to the production apparatus: it fixes them by forming habits through a play of coercion and punishment, apprenticeship and chastisement. It produces a fabric of habits through which the social membership of individuals to society is defined. It produces something like the norm; the norm is the instrument by which individuals are tied to the apparatuses of production. Whereas classical confinement ejected individuals outside the norms, whereas by confining the poor, vagabonds, and the mad it produced, hid, and sometimes displayed monsters, modern sequestration produced the *norm** and its function is to produce the normal.[24] And so we have a series that characterizes modern society: formation of labor-power—apparatus of sequestration—permanent function of normalization.†

In conclusion, if one wanted to characterize the system of power in which the prison functions and of which it is, at the same time, a symbol, a concentrate, but also a strategic functional component, we could say the following. Up to the eighteenth century, we had a society in which power took the visual, solemn, and ritual form of hierarchy and sovereignty. This power carried out its operations through a set of marks, of ceremonies that designated it as sovereign. To this sovereignty, thus made visible in the ritual of the ceremony, corresponded a certain type of historical narrative still close to the heroic narrative and, thereby, still fairly close to mythical effectiveness; a historical narrative whose function was to recount the sovereign's past, to reactualize the past of sovereignty in order to reinforce power. Historiography, as supplementary form of discourse of this power in the form of sovereignty, was a supplementary function of power; and, even though in the eighteenth century we witness its critical reversal, with Voltaire,

---

* The manuscript (24th fol.) adds: "Its medium is normalization."

† The manuscript (24th fol.) presents this series in the following way: "Apparatus of sequestration. Formation of a labor force. Disciplinary society. Permanent function of normalization/normativity."

Saint-Simon, Dupin, and so on, this discourse is always formed in the region of power, either in order to reinforce it or to undermine it.[25]

In the nineteenth century, power is no longer effectuated through that solemn, visible, ritual form of sovereignty, but through the habit imposed on some, or on all, but in order that, first of all, fundamentally, some are obliged to yield to it. On these conditions, power may well abandon all that visible, ritual magnificence, all its drapery and marks. It will take the insidious, quotidian, habitual form of the norm, and in this way it is hidden as power and passes for society. The role of the ceremony of power in the seventeenth century[26] is now taken over by what is called social consciousness. This is precisely where Durkheim will find the object of sociology. We should re-read what he says in *Suicide* regarding anomy: what characterizes the social as such, in contrast with the political, which is the level of decisions, and the economic, which is the level of determinations, is nothing other than the system of disciplines, of constraints.[27] Power is exercised through the medium of the system of disciplines, but so that it is concealed and appears as that reality called society, the object of sociology that is now to be described, to be known. Society, Durkheim said, is the system of the disciplines; but what he did not say is that this system must be analyzed within strategies specific to a system of power.[*]

If in fact power now no longer manifests itself through the violence of its ceremony, but is exercised through normalization, habit, and discipline, we will see the formation of a new type of discourse. The discourse that will now accompany disciplinary power can no longer be the mythical or heroic discourse that recounted the birth of power and whose function was to reinforce it. It is a discourse that will describe, analyze, and found[†] the norm and make it prescriptible, persuasive. In other words, the discourse that speaks of the king and founds his kingship can disappear and give way to the discourse of the master, that is to say to the discourse of he who supervises, states the norm, makes the division between normal and abnormal,[28] evaluates, judges, decides: discourse of the schoolmaster, the judge, the doctor, the psychiatrist. Linked to the exercise of power, we thus see the appearance of a

---

* Manuscript (26th fol.): "Durkheim will find in our habits the very sign of the social."
† Manuscript (26th fol.): "found in reason."

discourse that takes over from the mythical discourse on the origins of power—which periodically recounted the genealogy of the king and his ancestors—this is the normalizing discourse of the human sciences.[29],*

---

* The manuscript (26th fol.) ends in the following way: "In the Assyrian Empire, there was a mythical discourse profoundly connected to the exercise of power.[30] A discourse of origins. There is currently another type of discourse connected to the exercise of power, inseparable from it; but which is connected to it in a different way; which is delivered from a completely different place, and by completely different people. But which, in a certain way and while standing back, has taken over from these discourses of power. These are those 'normalizing' discourses of the human sciences."

1. N. H. Julius, *Leçons sur les prisons* [see above, p. 37 note 2], p. 384 sq.
2. The "Petite Roquette" mentioned in the manuscript (fol. 2) refers to the prison originally built for young offenders in the 11th arrondissement of Paris, in 1827, based on plans inspired by Bentham's *Panopticon*; at the time of the G.I.P., the Petite Roquette was a women's prison. It was destroyed at the end of the 1970s. As Jacques Lagrange points out in *Le Pouvoir psychiatrique*, p. 92, n. 18; *Psychiatric Power*, p. 90, n. 18, according to the terms of the circular of 24 February 1825, the architectural project of the model-prison had to have an arrangement "such that, with the aid of a central point or internal gallery, the whole of the prison can be supervised by one, or at the most two people." See also: C. Lucas, *Du système pénitentiaire en Europe et aux États-Unis* [see above, p. 78 note 25], vol. I, p. cxiii; M. Foucault, *Surveiller et Punir*, p. 276; *Discipline and Punish*, p. 271.
3. In his manuscript, (2nd fol.), Foucault adds this sentence: "Now this architectural form is at the same time a general social form that extends far beyond the prison. Should we say: *agora-logos* // prison-surveillance?" The theme of social surveillance and the punitive society, central in this course and treated in *Surveiller et Punir*, for example, p. 196, p. 209, and p. 211; *Discipline and Punish*, p. 189, pp. 202-203, and p. 206, did not, on the book's reception, capture the attention of the readership a great deal, which focused on panopticism as describing a penitentiary rather than a social form, in other words, on the theme of the prison, rather than on the more general theme of the punitive society. Now, in Foucault's conception, as Daniel Defert confirms, *Surveiller et Punir* is in continuity with this course on a problem of society.
4. Allusion to the famous frontispiece of Hobbes' *Leviathan*, p. III.
5. An analysis developed in *Surveiller et Punir*, pp. 31-33; *Discipline and Punish*, pp. 26-28, and in *"Il faut défendre la société"* lecture of 7 January 1976, pp. 15-19; *"Society Must Be Defended"* pp. 14-18.
6. As Jacques Lagrange points out in *Le Pouvoir psychiatrique*, p. 20, n. 21; *Psychiatric Power*, p. 18, n. 21, it may be that this criticism is directed at Louis Althusser, who deals with the concept of "State apparatus" in his article: "Idéologie et appareils idéologiques d'État. (Note pour une recherche)," *La Pensée. Revue du rationalisme moderne*, no. 151, June 1970, pp. 3-38; reprinted in L. Althusser, *Positions* (Paris: Éditions Sociales, 1976) pp. 79-137; English translation Ben Brewster, "Ideology and Ideological State Apparatuses," in L. Althusser, *Lenin and Philosophy* (London: New Left Books, 1971). On Foucault's argument, see below, "Course context," pp. 272-273 and pp. 288-289. In *Le Pouvoir psychiatrique; Psychiatric Power*, Foucault offers the following analysis: "Rather, therefore, than speak of violence, I would prefer to speak of a micro-physics of power; rather than speak of the institution, I would much prefer to try to see what tactics are put to work in these forces which confront each other; rather than speak of the family model or 'State apparatus,' I would like to try to see the strategy of these relations of power and confrontations which unfold within psychiatric practice" (lecture of 7 November 1973, Fr., p. 18; Eng., p. 16); "Methodologically this entails leaving the problem of the State, of the State apparatus, to one side and dispensing with the psycho-sociological notion of authority" (lecture of 21 November 1973, Fr., p. 42, fn.*; Eng., p. 40, fn.*). Note that the manuscript of *The Punitive Society*, in this passage, as after (8th and 9th sheets), has "State apparatus" in the singular, although it appears that Foucault speaks in the plural (typescript, pp. 197-199).
7. On this theme see *Les Anormaux*, the schematic summary in the lecture of 29 January 1975, pp. 80-81; *Abnormal*, pp. 87-88, and *Surveiller et Punir*, p. 30; *Discipline and Punish*, pp. 25-26: "This political investment of the body is bound up, in accordance with complex reciprocal relations, with its economic use; it is largely as a force of production that the body is invested with relations of power and domination; but, on the other hand, its constitution as labour power is possible only if it is caught up in a system of subjection (in which need is also a

political instrument meticulously prepared, calculated and used); the body becomes a useful force only if it is both a productive body and a subjected body"; see also ibid., p. 147 and pp. 222-223; Eng., pp. 137-138 and pp. 220-221.

8. The point is taken up in May 1973 in "La vérité et les formes juridiques," pp. 621-622/ pp. 1489-1490; "Truth and Juridical Forms," p.86: "What I would like to show is that, in point of fact, labor is absolutely not man's concrete essence or man's existence in its concrete form ... It needs the operation or synthesis carried out by a political power for man's essence to appear as being labor" [translation slightly amended; G.B.].

9. With this juxtaposition of the coercive and the ideological it is clear that Foucault is addressing Althusser with regard to his article of 1970 (see above, note 6, and below, "Course context," pp. 284-286).

10. In 1776, Turgot created a Commission of medicine responsible for studying epidemics, which, under Necker, took the name of Société royale de médecine. Its members, largely drawn from the Academy of Sciences, were responsible for: "a) inquiring into epidemics; b) discussing and interpreting them; c) prescribing the most suitable curative methods" (J.-P. Peter, "Une enquête de la Société royale de médecine: malades et maladies à la fin du XVIIIe siècle," *Annales. Économies, Sociétés, Civilisations*, 22nd Year, no. 4, 1967, p. 713). Dependent upon the Finance minister, the Société royale is widely thought to be the first State health body. See: *Histoire et mémoires de la Société Royale de Médecine et de Physique, tirés des registres de cette société* (Paris: Didot, 1776-1779); C. Hannaway, "The Société royale de médecine and epidemics in the Ancien Régime," *Bulletin of the History of Medicine*, 46, 1972, p. 257; J.-P. Desaive et al., *Médecins, climat et épidémies à la fin du XVIIIe siècle* (Paris: Éditions de l'EHESS, 1972). For a more recent analysis of the place of the Société royale de médecine in the formation of an administrative science of health, see V. Tournay, "'Le concept de police médicale.' D'une aspiration militante à la production d'une objectivité administrative," *Politix*, 2007/1, no. 77, pp. 173-199; see also M. Foucault, *Naissance de la clinique*, ch. II, especially pp. 49-56; *The Birth of the Clinic*, pp. 26-31.

11. This could refer to the chambers of commerce, as well as, from the Consulate, the consultative chamber of Arts and Manufactures, "assembly of the principal industrialists responsible for enlightening the government about the needs of industry" (A. Chéruel, *Dictionnaire historique des institutions, mœurs et coutumes de la France*, first part, Paris: Librairie Hachette et Cie, 1899, p. 123). This would justify, notably, the use of the verb "*taken back*," since these institutions, officially established in 1701, were suppressed by the Revolution in 1791 and then re-established in 1802 with the mission of "presenting views on the means of increasing the prosperity of commerce, of making known to the government the causes that check its progress, of indicating the resources that may be obtained ..." (Decree of 3 Nivôse Year XI/24 December 1802, quoted by B. Magliulo, *Les Chambres de commerce et d'industrie*, Paris: PUF, 1980, p. 31). Chaptal, Minister of the Interior, presented the reasons for this re-establishment in these terms: "The action of government on commerce can be enlightened only by the faithful account of the condition and needs of commerce at every point of the Republic" (quoted, ibid., p. 32). However, the notion of inquiry, and a fortiori of inquiry into craft techniques, does not appear directly in these activities. For an extensive bibliography on the subject, see E. Pendleton Herring, "Chambres de Commerce: Their Legal Status and Political Significance," *The American Political Science Review*, vol. 25(3), August 1931, pp. 691-692; see also A. Conquet, *Napoléon [III] et les chambres de commerce*, APPCI, 1978.

12. Foucault also refers to Chaptal's inquiry in *Surveiller et Punir*, p. 236; *Discipline and Punish*, p. 234: "that [inquiry] of Chaptal in 1810 (whose task it was to discover what could be used to introduce the carceral apparatus into France)" [translation slightly modified; G.B.].

13. In the manuscript (16th fol.), Foucault draws up a list which mentions: "Revolution; Consulate; Empire." See the list of inquiries in *Surveiller et Punir*, pp. 236-237; *Discipline and Punish*, p. 234: "that of Decazes in 1819, Villermé's work published in 1820, the report

on the *maisons centrales* drawn up by Martignac in 1829, the inquiries carried out in the United States by Beaumont and Tocqueville in 1831, by Demetz and Blouet in 1835, the questionnaires addressed by Monalivet to the directors of the *maisons centrales* and to the general councils of the *départements* during the debate on solitary confinement."

14.   See A. de Sartine, *Journal des inspecteurs de M. de Sartines, 1ʳᵉ partie, 1761-1764* (Brussels: Ernest Parent, 1863). Antoine de Sartine, Count of Alby (1729-1801), politician, was criminal lieutenant at Le Chatelet in Paris, lieutenant general of police (1759-1774), and Naval Minister under Louis XVI.

15.   See J. Fouché, *Rapport fait aux consuls par le ministre de la Police sur l'infâme complot tendant à assassiner les consuls, leurs familles, les ministres et les principaux membres du gouvernement* (Paris: impr. Cornu, no date); *Rapport du ministre de la Police générale concernant l'attentat commis contre le 1ʳᵉ consul Bonaparte, le 3 nivôse* [14 nivôse, Year IX]. *Arrêté des consuls, qui ordonne la déportation de 131 individus. Arrêté du Sénat conservateur, qui approuve cette mesure* (Paris: impr. Marchant, no date). Joseph Fouché (1759-1820) was Police minister under the Directory and the Empire.

16.   Foucault is referring here to the *Compte général de l'administration de la justice criminelle*, which appeared for the first time in 1827, based on the figures of the year 1825. "The *Compte générale* has an annual periodicity (except for war years) with recapitulatory volumes in 1850, 1880, and 1900. It was produced with the help of statistical tables sent to the courts ... The detailed facts and figures, abundant in the nineteenth century, tend to decrease from the years 1920-1930. The most numerous tables concern the accused, details of civil status, profession, and place of residence being taken into account only at the beginning of the twentieth century" (J.-C. Farcy, *Guide des archives judiciaires et pénitentiaires 1800-1948* (Paris: CNRS Éditions, 1992, p. 228). Following this mode a *Compte général de l'administration de la justice civile et commerciale* (1831), a *Compte générale de l'administration de la justice militaire* (1832), and a *Compte générale de l'administration de la justice dans la colonies* (1834) were created successively. They all appear as "a series of statistical tables preceded by a more or less lengthy introduction produced by the minister responsible for the statistical account, which comments on the facts and figures from an official point of view" (ibid.). See: M. Perrot, "Premières mesures des faits sociaux: les débuts de la statistique criminelle en France 1780-1830," in [collective,] *Pour une histoire de la statistique*, vol. I: *Contributions/Journées d'études sur l'histoire de la statistique* (*Vaucresson, 1976*) (Paris: INSEE, 1977) pp. 125-177; Ministère de la Justice, *Compte générale de l'administration de la justice criminelle en France pendant l'année 1880 et Rapport relatif aux années 1826 à 1880*, published with a commentary by Michelle Perrot and Philippe Robert (Geneva and Paris: Slatkine Reprints, 1989).

17.   In the manuscript (16th fol.), Foucault adds: "Statistics as science of State," then writes (17th fol.): "The philosophical critique of abstraction, of the evolution of the experimental method, has been made 1000 times, [but] never the history of State knowledge, of the administrative extraction of knowledge." In *"Il faut défendre la société,"* lecture of 11 February 1976, p. 120; *"Society Must Be Defended,"* p. 138, he says: "Between the knowledge (*savoir*) of the prince and the knowledge (*connnaissances*) of his administration, a ministry of history was created, which, between the king and his administration, had to establish, in a controlled way, the uninterrupted tradition of the monarchy" [translation slightly amended; G.B.]. This connects with the subject of Daniel Defert's thesis on the development of statistics as administrative knowledge of the State in German universities in the eighteenth century, titled, "Le Savoir du Prince et les ci-devant secrets" (under the direction of Raymond Aron).

18.   Sébastien Le Prestre de Vauban (1633-1707), better known for his essential role as general superintendent of fortification, from 1695, addresses several memoranda to the king developing "the idea of reducing the numerous taxes then existing and replacing them by capitation. The aim of this capitation was to levy a tax at fifteen denier on the clergy, salaries, pledges, and pensions of all the civil and military officers of the realm, the King's household, the troops of land and sea, 'without excepting any of those who can support it'" (G. Michel

and A. Liesse, *Vauban économiste*, Paris: E. Plon, Nourrit et Cie, 1891, p. 17). Forced by illness to retire from his military functions, Vauban appointed Marshal of France in 1703, progressively lost royal favor. The work in which he set out his project, *La Dîme royale*, was published in 1707 without authorization and quickly became the object of an interdiction. Vauban died some weeks later. The book opens with a justification of the author's intentions: "I say therefore with the best faith in the world, that it was not the wish to delude myself, or to earn new considerations for myself, which made me undertake this Work. I am neither a man of letters nor a man of Finance, and it would be wrong of me to seek glory and advantage through things which are not part of my profession" (Vauban, *Le Dîme royale*, presented by Emmanuel Le Roy Ladurie, Paris: Imprimerie nationale, 1992 [1897], p. 57). See also A. Rebelliau, *Vauban* [published by Jacques Lovie] (Paris: Club des libraires de France, 1962).

19. François Quesnay (see above, p. 56 note 3), due to his status as King's surgeon and Madame de Pompadour's physician, as well as his desire to live in the mezzanine of the Versailles château so as to encourage the visits of influential personages, exercised a certain influence at court. Many accused him of having political pretentions; see G. Weulersse, *Le Mouvement physiocratique en France de 1756 à 1770* [above p. 56 note 3], vol. 2, pp. 626-682.

20. Foucault describes and analyzes the 1838 law in *Le Pouvoir psychiatrique*, lecture of 5 December 1973, pp. 97-99; *Psychiatric Power*, pp. 94-97, and *Les Anormaux*, lecture of 12 February 1975, pp. 130-141; *Abnormal*, pp. 140-151. It seems that Foucault wrote "Castel" in the margin of the manuscript (17th fol.), no doubt referring to the works of Robert Castel on the history of psychiatry; see Robert Castel, "Le traitement moral. Thérapeutique mentale et contrôle social au XIXe siècle," *Topique*, no. 2, 1970, pp. 109-129. In *Le Pouvoir psychiatrique*, p. 88, footnote*; *Psychiatric Power*, p. 87, footnote * (which refers to the manuscript for the course), Foucault refers explicitly to Castel's 1973 work, *Le Psychanalysme* (Paris: Maspero, 1973), about which he says: "This is a radical book because, for the first time, psychoanalysis is situated solely within psychiatric practice and power" (ibid., Fr., p. 198, n. 41; Eng., p. 199, n. 41). And the following year, in *Surveiller et Punir*, p. 29, n. 1; *Discipline and Punish*, p. 309, n. 2: "I should also have quoted a number of pages from R. Castel's *Psychanalysme*." See too, Robert Castel's book, published in 1976, *L'Ordre psychiatrique. L'âge d'or de l'aliénisme* (Paris: Éditions de Minuit); English translation W. D. Halls, *The Regulation of Madness: The Origins of Incarceration in France* (Berkeley: University of California Press, 1988).

21. On this subject, see G. Rusche and O. Kirchheimer, *Punishment and Social Structure* (New York: Columbia University Press, 1939). In *Surveiller et Punir*, p. 29; *Discipline and Punish*, p. 24, Foucault notes that: "Rusche and Kirchheimer's great work, *Punishment and Social Structure*, provides a number of essential reference points" and he borrows their notion of political economy of punishment in order to develop his idea of a "'political economy' of the body" (ibid., p. 30).

22. See D. Hume, *A Treatise of Human Nature*, ed., L. A. Selby-Bigge (Oxford: Clarendon Press, 1978 [1739]) Book I, Part III, Section XVI, p. 179: "Nature may certainly produce whatever can arise from habit: Nay, habit is nothing but one of the principles of nature, and derives all its force from that origin." Hume not only places custom or habit at the heart of the explanation of probable reasoning, but he describes them as both natural *and* artificial. It is habit that "determine[s] us to make the past a standard for the future" and "the supposition *that the future will resemble the past* is not founded on arguments of any kind, but is derived entirely from habit" (*Treatise*, Book I, Part III, Section XII, pp. 133-134, Hume's emphasis). When habit is the product of a constant past experience, it is "full and perfect" and "we make the transition without any reflection, and interpose not a moment's delay betwixt the view of one object and the belief of that which is often found to attend it" (ibid.). In other words, it is habit, without any reflection, and without any reference to the supposition according to which the future resembles the past, that assures the transition between the experience of the perception of an object and the belief in that which is usually associated with it. What

then is involved is a natural production of belief, but which is only produced in the presence of a full and perfect habit, itself the consequence of a constant past experience. On the other hand, in the more common case where past experience is mixed, the "reasonings of this kind arise not *directly*, but in an *oblique* manner" (ibid., Hume's emphasis). At another point in the text, Hume also speaks of an "oblique and artificial manner" (p. 104). In such cases, we consciously consider the supposition according to which the future will resemble the past, and it is this consideration that produces belief. The latter is therefore an artificial human product, from the point of view reference to the supposition that the future resembles the past, which "has establish'd itself by a sufficient custom" (p. 105). For further clarifications, see D. Owen, *Hume's Reason* (Oxford: Oxford University Press, 1999) ch. 7, pp. 147-174.

23. Foucault notes two examples in the manuscript. "Discussion of [M.] Bruno; *Traité d'économie sociale*" (22nd fol.). On M. Bruno, see above, p. 198 note 17. Furthermore, Foucault refers here to the work of the doctor Ange Guépin (1805-1873), *Traité d'économie sociale* (Paris: De Lacombe, 1833). Philanthropic physician and theorist of socialism inspired by Saint-Simon and Fouriér, Ange Guépin played a central role in the political life of nineteenth-century Nantes. He applied himself in particular to measuring the poverty of Nantes workers and to putting forward solutions to combat it; see A. Guépin and E. Bonamy, *Nantes au XIXᵉ siècle* (see above, p. 182 note 9). In his *Traité d'économie social* (pp. 82-83), doctor Guépin, starting from the example of print workers, develops the idea of industry associations allowing in particular the socialization of risks of accident or inactivity as well as the cost of retirement, and the final aim of which would be to enable the workers to buy out the printing works themselves; see J. Maitron, ed., *Dictionnaire biographique du mouvement ouvrier français. Première partie: 1789-1864. De la Révolution française à la fondation de la Première Internationale* (Paris: Les Éditions ouvrières, 1865) 3 volumes, vol. II, pp. 309-311.

24. See *Surveiller et Punir*, pp. 104-105; *Discipline and Punish*, pp. 102-103.

25. In the manuscript Foucault notes: "its critical reversal (Saint-Simon or Voltaire) only apparently removes it from this primary function" (25th fol.). In his *Mémoires*, Louis de Rouvroy, duc de Saint-Simon (1675-1755), distances himself from the adulation of Louis XIV practiced by the official history of his time, and, in a series of portraits and accounts of historical episodes, describes something like an underside of the monarchy; see M. Stefanovska, *Saint-Simon, un historien dans les marges* (Paris: Honoré Champion, 1998) p. 29. In the "Considérations préliminaires" of his work, Saint-Simon notes: "The account of events must discover their origins, causes, and consequences, and the connections between them, which can be done only through the exposition of the actions of the characters who took part in these things ..., what involved them in the part they have played in the facts one recounts, and the relationship of union or opposition that existed between them." Louis XIV nevertheless always occupies a symbolically central position in the exposition of the facts. On the importance of ceremony in Saint-Simonian history, see M. Stefanovska, pp. 59-65.

Claude Dupinde Chenonceaux (1686-1769), financier and tax farmer-general, was a precursor of physiocratic thought. In *Œonomiques* (Paris: Marcel Rivière et Companie, 1913 [1745]), Claude Dupin set out the economic organization of France and advanced various means of improving it. The third volume of the work puts forward a history of taxation, in which the author describes the evolution of royal taxation policies. Claude Dupin is, however, better known for his opposition, in two successive works, to *L'Esprit des lois* (*Observations sur un ouvrage intitulé "L'Esprit des lois"* was prohibited by the censor) and to Montesquieu's questioning of the system of the *Ferme générale*. From 1745 to 1751, Jean-Jacques Rousseau was the private secretary of Claude Dupin's wife, Louise-Marie-Madeleine Fontaine.

As for Voltaire, he is widely considered to be one of the fathers of modern historiography. He devoted several works to history and the philosophy of history, including the *Nouvelles Considérations sur l'histoire* (1744) and *Le Siècle de Louis XIV* (1751), in which he writes: "It is not just the life of Louis XIV that we aspire to write; we set ourselves a larger object. We wish to depict for posterity, not the actions of a single man, but the spirit of men in the most enlightened century there has ever been" ("Introduction" to *Siècle de Louis XIV*, in Voltaire, *Œuvres avec préface, avertissements, notes, etc., par M. Beuchot,* Paris: Lefèvre, 1830, vol. 19, p. 237). In the *Nouvelles Considérations sur l'histoire,* Voltaire contrasts "the history of men," which he hopes and prays for, with "the history of kings and courts" (*Œuvres historiques,* Paris: Gallimard, 1987 [1744], pp. 47-48).

26. On this theme Foucault gives a lecture entitled "Cérémonie, théâtre et politique au XVIIe siècle" at the University of Minnesota, Minneapolis, in April 1972, as a contribution to the Fourth Annual Conference on 17th-Century French Literature, summarized in English by Stephen Davidson in Armand Renaud, ed., *Proceedings of the Fourth Annual Conference of XVIIth-Century French Literature, with programs and brief account of the first, second, third conference* (Minneapolis, MN: 1972), pp. 22-23.

27. See E. Durkheim, *Le Suicide. Étude de sociologie* (Paris: Felix Alcan, 1897); English translation by John A. Spalding and George Simpson, *Suicide. A Study in Sociology* (Glencoe, IL: The Free Press, 1952). Regarding the declassification produced for certain individuals by economic disasters, Durkheim writes notably: "All the advantages of social influence are lost so far as they are concerned; their moral education has to be recommenced. But society cannot adjust them instantaneously and teach to practice the increased self-repression to which they are unaccustomed ... The state of de-regulation or anomy is thus further heightened by passions being less disciplined, precisely when they need more disciplining" (pp. 252-253). However, in Durkheim, the notion of discipline is necessarily founded in justice, and cannot confine itself to force or habit: "But ... this discipline can be useful only if considered just by the people subject to it. When it is maintained only by custom and force, peace and harmony are illusory ...; appetites superficially restrained are ready to revolt" (ibid., p. 251).

28. This theme is taken up again in *Les Anormaux*; *Abnormal.* In his manuscript, Foucault adds to the abnormal, the "deviant" and the "sick" (26th fol.).

29. This critique of the human sciences, the first formulations of which are found in the "Préface" to the *Anthropologie* of Kant, in *Folie et Déraison. Histoire de la folie*; *History of Madness,* and in *Les Mots et les Choses*; *The Order of Things,* will be developed subsequently. See: "La vérité et les formes juridiques," pp. 622-623/pp. 1490-1491; "Truth and Juridical Forms," p. 87; *Le Pouvoir psychiatrique,* lecture of 21 November 1973, pp. 58-60; *Psychiatric Power,* pp. 56-58; *Surveiller et Punir,* pp. 28-29 and p. 315; *Discipline and Punish,* pp. 23 and p. 308.

30. On the reference to the Assyrian Empire, locus of a mythical discourse connected to the exercise of power, see, *Leçons sur la volonté de savoir,* lecture of 10 February 1971, pp. 106-107; *Lectures on the Will to Know,* pp. 111-112.

COURSE SUMMARY[*]

IN THE PENAL REGIME of the classical age we can find, mixed together, four major forms of punitive tactics—four forms with different historical origins and each of which has played, in different societies and periods, if not an exclusive, then at least a privileged role.

1. To exile, drive out, banish, expel beyond the borders, ban from certain places, to destroy the home, obliterate the place of birth, confiscate goods and property.
2. To organize a compensation, impose a redemption, converting damage caused into a debt to be repaid, converting the crime into a financial obligation.
3. To expose, mark, wound, amputate, scar, to leave a sign on the face or shoulder, to fix an artificial and visible reduction, to torture; in short, seizing hold of the body and inscribing on it the marks of power.
4. To confine.

As a hypothesis, can we distinguish societies according to the types of punishment they privileged: banishment societies (Greek society), redemption societies (Germanic societies), marking societies (Western

* Published in the *Annuaire du Collège de France, 73ᵉ année, Histoire des systèmes de pensée, année 1972-1973*, 1980, pp. 255-267, and in *Dits et* Écrits, *1954-1988*, ed. D. Defert and F. Ewald, with the collaboration of J. Lagrange (Paris: Gallimard, 1994) vol. 2, no. 131, pp. 456-470; "Quarto" ed., vol. 1, pp. 1324-1338. An earlier translation of this summary by Robert Hurley appears with the title "The Punitive Society" in M. Foucault, *The Essential Works of Michel Foucault, 1954-1984, Vol. 1: Ethics: subjectivity and truth*, ed. Paul Rabinow, trans. Robert Hurley and others (New York: New Press, 1997), pp. 23-37.

societies at the end of the Middle Ages), and societies that confine,
our own?

Ours, but only since the end of the eighteenth century. For one thing is
certain: detention and imprisonment are not part of the European penal
system before the great reforms of the years 1780-1820. Eighteenth-
century jurists are unanimous on this point: "Prison is not regarded as
a penalty in our civil law ... although Princes are sometimes inclined to
inflict this penalty for reasons of State, they are exceptional executive
measures, and ordinary justice makes no use of this kind of sentence."[1]
But already we can say that such insistence on *denying* that imprisonment
has any penal character indicates a growing uncertainty. In any case,
the confinements practiced in the seventeenth and eighteenth centuries
remain outside the penal system, even if they are very close to it, and
constantly getting closer.

- security-confinement, practiced by the law during the investigation
  of a criminal matter, by a creditor until repayment of the debt,
  or by royal power when it fears an enemy. It is less a matter of
  punishing an offense than of apprehending someone as security;
- substitute-confinement, imposed on someone who does not come
  under criminal justice (either because of the nature of his offenses,
  which are only matters of morality or conduct; or as a result of
  a privilege of status: the ecclesiastical courts, which, since 1629,
  no longer have the right to pass prison sentences in the strict
  sense, may order the culprit to withdraw to a monastery; the *lettre
  de cachet* is often a means whereby the privileged escape criminal
  justice; women are sent to *maisons de force* for offenses that men
  will pay for on the galleys).

It should be noted that, apart from the last case, this substitute-
imprisonment is generally characterized by the fact that it is not decided
by the judicial power, that its duration is not fixed definitively, and
that it depends on a hypothetical end: correction. Punishment rather
than penalty.

Now, about fifty years after the great monuments of classical criminal law (Serpillon, Jousse,[2] Muyart de Vouglans[3]), prison has become the general form of penality.

In 1831, in a speech in the Chamber, Rémusat said: "What penal system does the new law authorize? It is incarceration in all its forms. Compare in fact the four main penalties that remain in the Penal Code. Forced labor ... is a form of incarceration. The penal colony is an open-air prison. In a way, detention, reclusion, and correctional imprisonment are only different names for the same punishment."[4] And Van Meenen, opening the Second Penitentiary Congress at Brussels, recalled the time of his youth when the land was still covered "with wheels, gibbets, gallows, and pillories," with "hideously stretched out skeletons."[5] It is as if at the end of the eighteenth century, the prison, a parapenal punishment, had entered the penal system and very quickly occupied its whole space. The Austrian Criminal Code, drawn up under Joseph II, gives the most manifest evidence of this immediate triumphant invasion.

The organization of a penality of confinement is not just recent; it is enigmatic.

It was the object of fierce criticism at the very moment it was being planned; criticisms expressed in terms of basic principles, but also with reference to all the dysfunctions that prison might give rise to in the penal system and in society generally.

1. Prison prevents judicial power from checking and verifying the application of penalties. The law does not penetrate the prisons, said Decazes in 1819.

2. By mixing together both different and isolated convicts, prison forms a homogeneous community of criminals who establish a solidarity in confinement that will continue to exist on the outside. Prison produces a veritable army of internal enemies.

3. By providing convicts with shelter, food, clothing, and sometimes work, prison offers them a condition that is sometimes preferable to that of workers. Not only can it have no deterrent effect, it encourages delinquency.

4. Those leaving prison are condemned to a life of crime by the habits they have acquired and the infamy with which they are stamped.

So, prison is denounced straightaway as an instrument that, on the fringes of justice, manufactures those whom that justice will send or return to prison. The carceral circle is clearly denounced from the years 1815-1830. The three successive responses to these criticisms were:

- to devise an alternative to the prison that retains its positive effects (the segregation of criminals, removing them from circulation in society) and suppresses its dangerous consequences (their return to circulation). To this end, the old system of transportation, which the British had suspended at the time of the War of Independence and reinstated to Australia after 1790, was taken up again. The big debates about Botany Bay took place in France around the years 1824-1830. In actual fact, deportation-colonization never replaces imprisonment; in the period of the great colonial conquests it plays a complex role in the controlled circuits of delinquency. In the course of the nineteenth century a whole ensemble formed by groups of more or less voluntary colonists, colonial regiments, African battalions, the Foreign Legion, and the penal colony of Cayenne came to function in correlation with what remained an essentially carceral penality;
- to reform the prison's internal system in such a way that it ceases to manufacture that army of internal dangers. This is the goal that throughout Europe was referred to as "penitentiary reform." Its chronological markers can be given as the *Leçons sur les prisons* by Julius (1828),[6] on the one hand, and the 1847 Brussels Congress, on the other. This reform has three main aspects: complete or partial isolation of those held in prison (debate on the Auburn and Pennsylvania systems); moralization of convicts through work, education, religion, rewards, reduction of sentence; development of parapenal institutions of prevention, rehabilitation, or control. Now these reforms, which the revolutions of 1848 brought to an end, did not alter in any way the prison dysfunctions denounced in the previous period;

- finally, to give an anthropological status to the carceral circle; to replace the old project of Julius and Charles Lucas[7] of founding a "science of prisons" that can provide the architectural, administrative, and pedagogical principles of an institution that "corrects," with a "science of criminals" that would be able to describe them in their specificity and define the modes of social reaction suited to their case. The class of delinquents, whose autonomy was at least partially due to the carceral circuit, which ensured both its isolation and sealing off, appears then as psycho-sociological deviation. Deviation that is a matter for "scientific" discourse (which psycho-pathological, psychiatric, psychoanalytic, and sociological analyses will rush to occupy); deviation with regard to which it will be wondered whether prison really is an answer or appropriate treatment.

What prison was criticized for at the beginning of the nineteenth century, and using other words—forming a "marginal" population of "delinquents"—is now seen as inevitable. Not only is it accepted as a fact, but it is constituted as a fundamental given. The "delinquency" effect produced by the prison becomes the problem of delinquency to which prison has to provide a suitable response. A criminological turn of the carceral circle.

*   *   *

We have to ask ourselves how such a turnaround was possible; how effects that were denounced and criticized could, in the end, be taken as fundamental givens for a scientific analysis of criminality; how the prison, a recent, fragile, criticizable and criticized institution, could become so deeply embedded in the institutional field that the mechanism of its effects could be passed off as an anthropological constant; what ultimately is the prison's raison d'être; to what functional requirement was it found to respond?

It is all the more necessary to pose the question, and especially more difficult to give an answer, as it is hard to see the "ideological" genesis of the institution. It might be thought that the prison was indeed denounced, and early on, for its practical consequences, but that it was so strongly linked with the new penal theory (the theory that presided over the drafting of the nineteenth-century code) that it had to be accepted along with it; or that the theory would have to be completely revised if one wanted a radical policy for the prison.

Now, from this point of view, an examination of penal theories from the second half of the eighteenth century produces some rather surprising results. None of the great reformers—whether theorists like Beccaria, jurists like Servan, legislators like Le Peletier de Saint-Fargeau, or all three like Brissot—proposed the prison as a universal or even major penalty. In all these projects the criminal is generally defined as the enemy of society. In this respect, the reformers take up and transform the result of a whole political and institutional evolution since the Middle Ages: the replacement of settlement through litigation by public prosecution. By his intervention, the king's prosecutor designates the infraction as not only an offense against a person or private interest, but as an attack on the king's sovereignty. Commenting on English laws, Blackstone said that the public prosecutor defends both the king's sovereignty and the interests of society.[8] In short, a large majority of the reformers, starting with Beccaria, sought to define the notion of crime, the role of the public party, and the necessity of punishment, solely on the basis of the interest of society or the need to protect society. First and foremost, the criminal harms society; breaking the social pact, he constitutes himself in society as an enemy within. A number of consequences derive from this general principle.

1. Each society will have to adjust the scale of penalties according to its own needs. Since the punishment does not derive from the offense itself, but from the harm it does society or the danger to which it exposes it, a weaker society will have to be better protected and show itself to be more severe. So, there is no universal model of penality and an essential relativity of penalties.
2. If the penalty were expiation, there would be nothing wrong in it being too harsh; in any case, it would be difficult to establish a just proportion between crime and penalty. But if it is a question of protecting society, the penalty can be calculated to ensure that

it performs this function exactly: anything more than this, all supplementary severity, becomes an abuse of power. The justice of the penalty is in its economy.
3. The role of the penalty is directed entirely towards the outside and the future: to prevent the crime from being repeated. In the final analysis, a crime that one knew with certainty to be the last would not have to be punished. So, to render the guilty harmless and dissuade the innocent from any similar infraction. Here, the effectiveness of the penalty is due more to its inevitability than to its severity.

Now, what actually takes place in penal practice, namely the universalization of the prison as the general form of punishment, cannot be deduced from these principles. On the contrary, we see the emergence of very different punitive models:

- one is organized by reference to infamy, that is to say, to the effects of public opinion. Infamy is a perfect penalty since it is the immediate and spontaneous reaction of society itself: it varies with every society; it is graduated according to the harmfulness of each crime; it may be revoked by public rehabilitation; finally, it affects only the guilty. Thus it is a penalty adjusted to the crime without having to pass through a code, without having to be applied by a court, and without risking abuse by a political power. It exactly fits the principles of penality. "The triumph of a good legislation is when public opinion is strong enough on its own to punish offenses ... Happy the people in whom the sense of honor can be the only law! It has almost no need of legislation: infamy, there is its penal code";[9]
- another model used in the reform projects is that of talion. By condemning the guilty person to a punishment of the same type and gravity as the crime, one is sure to obtain a penality that is both graduated and exactly proportional. The penalty takes the form of a counter-attack. And, on condition that it is swift and inevitable, it nullifies almost automatically the advantages expected by the offender, making the crime pointless. The benefit of the crime

is brutally reduced to zero. The model of talion was, no doubt, never proposed in a detailed form; but it often allowed types of punishment to be defined. Beccaria, for example: "Attacks against persons should be punished by corporal penalties"; "personal injuries to honor should be pecuniary."* It is also found in the form of a "moral talion"): not punishing the crime by reversing its effects, but by returning to the start and the vices that cause it.[10] Le Peletier de Saint-Fargeau proposed to the National Assembly (23 May 1791): physical pain to punish atrocious crimes; hard labor to punish crimes arising from idleness; infamy to punish crimes inspired by an "abject and degraded" soul;[11]

- finally, a third model of enslavement for the benefit of society. This kind of penalty may be graduated, in both intensity and duration, according to the harm done to the community. It is linked to the offense through the interest damaged. Regarding theft, Beccaria says: "Temporary slavery puts the work and person of the criminal at the service of society so that, through this state of total dependence, he makes up for the unjust despotism he exercised by violating the social pact."[12] Brissot: "What should replace the death penalty ...? Slavery, which will prevent the criminal from harming society; work, which will make him useful; long and continuous suffering, which will frighten those who might be tempted to imitate him."[13]

Of course, in all these projects, the prison often figures as one of the possible penalties: either as a condition of forced labor, or as a retaliatory penalty for those who have violated the liberty of others. But it does not appear as the general form of penality, nor as the precondition for a psychological and moral transformation of the delinquent.

---

* [Something appears to have gone wrong here, probably a line left out in transcription. The second example here ("personal injuries to honor should be pecuniary") simply does not make sense and cannot be reconstructed as a single example consistent with Foucault's argument. In the lecture referenced in endnote 10 (below p. 264) there are three examples: attacks on persons punished with corporal penalties; personal offenses contrary to honor punished with infamy; and theft not accompanied by violence should be punished with a pecuniary sanction (see above lecture of 24 January 1973, p. 69); G.B.]

It is in the first years of the nineteenth century that we see theorists giving the prison this role. "Prison is the penalty par excellence in civilized societies. It has a moral tenor when accompanied by the obligation to work."[14] But at this time the prison already exists as a major instrument of penality. Prison as a place of improvement is a reinterpretation of a practice of imprisonment that had become widespread in the previous years.

*   *   *

So prison practice was not implied in penal theory. It arose elsewhere and was formed for other reasons. And in a way it was imposed on penal theory from outside, and penal theory was obliged to justify it after the fact, as Livingstone, for example, does in 1820 when he says that prison punishment has the quadruple advantage of being divisible into as many degrees as there are degrees of seriousness in crimes; of preventing repetition of the offense; of enabling correction; and of being sufficiently mild for juries not to hesitate to punish and the people not to revolt against the law.[15]

To understand how prison really functioned, behind its apparent dysfunction, and how successful it was, behind its surface failures, we no doubt need to go back to those instances of parapenal control in which it figured, as we have seen, in the seventeenth and especially the eighteenth century.

In these instances, confinement plays a role that includes three distinct characteristics:

-   it intervenes in the spatial distribution of individuals through the temporary imprisonment of beggars and vagabonds. Doubtless, at the end of the seventeenth and in the eighteenth century, ordinances sentence them to the galleys, at least in the event of a second offense. But imprisonment remains the most frequent punishment in fact. Now, if they are confined, it is not so much in order to fix them where they are held as to move them: to forbid them entry to towns, to send them back to the countryside, or again, to prevent them from wandering about a region, to force

them to go where they can be given work. This is at least a negative
way of controlling their location in relation to the apparatus of
agricultural or manufacturing production; a way of acting on the
population flow by taking the needs of both production and the
job market into account;

- confinement also intervenes at the level of individual conduct. It
  is an infrapenal sanction for ways of living, types of discourse,
  political plans or intentions, forms of sexual behavior, rejections
  of authority, defiance of public opinion, violence, and so on. In
  short, it intervenes less in the name of the law than on behalf of
  order and regularity. The objects of confinement are the irregular,
  the unsettled, the dangerous, and the infamous. Whereas
  penality punishes the infraction, confinement is the sanction for
  disorderliness;

- finally, if it is true that confinement is in the hands of political
  power, that it wholly or partially escapes the control of regular
  justice (in France, it is almost always decided by the king,
  ministers, intendants, or subdelegates), it is far from being the
  instrument of arbitrariness and absolutism. The study of *lettres
  de cachet* (of both how they functioned and their motivation)
  shows that in the great majority of cases they were solicited by
  fathers, minor notables, and by local religious and professional
  communities against individuals who are for them the cause of
  difficulties and disorder. The *lettre de cachet* comes from below (in
  the form of a request) before coming back down the apparatus
  of power in the form of an order bearing the royal seal. It is the
  instrument of a local and, so to speak, capillary control.

We could make the same kind of analysis of societies found in England
from the end of the seventeenth century. Often led by "dissidents," they
set out to denounce, exclude, and take measures against individuals
for breach of conduct, refusal to work, and everyday disorders. There
are clearly enormous differences between this form of control and that
ensured by *lettres de cachet*, to speak only of the fact that the English
societies (at least in the first half of the eighteenth century) are
independent of any State apparatus: moreover, recruiting from lower

classes, they generally attack the immorality of the rich and powerful; finally, the strictness they demonstrate towards their own members is no doubt a way of enabling these members to escape an extremely strict penal justice (English penal law, a "bloody chaos," included more capital cases than any other European code). In France, in contrast, forms of control were closely connected with a State apparatus that had organized the first great system of police in Europe, imitated by the Austria of Joseph II, and then by England. With regard to England, it should be noted that in the last years of the eighteenth century, basically after the Gordon Riots, and at the time of the big popular movements roughly contemporaneous with the French Revolution, new societies of moral reform appeared, with a much more aristocratic membership (some of them militarily equipped): they called for intervention by royal power, new laws, and the organization of a police force. Colquhoun, through his work and as a figure, was central to this process.

It was the adaptation of the judicial system to a mechanism of supervision (*surveillance*) and control that transformed penality at the turn of the century: it was their integration in a centralized State apparatus, but also the establishment and development of a whole series of parapenal and sometimes non-penal institutions, that provided the main apparatus with points of support, forward positions, or limited forms. A general system of supervision-confinement penetrates society in depth, taking forms that go from the big prisons built on the model of the Panopticon to charitable societies, and that apply themselves not only to delinquents, but also to abandoned children, orphans, apprentices, high school students, workers, and so on. In his *Leçons sur les prisons*, Julius contrasted civilizations of the spectacle (civilizations of sacrifice and ritual where all are to be given the spectacle of a unique event and the main architectural form is the theater) with civilizations of supervision (where the few are to be assured uninterrupted control over the majority, with its privileged architectural form, the prison). And he added that European society, which had replaced religion with the State, was the first example of a civilization of supervision (*surveillance*).[16]

The nineteenth century founded the age of panopticism.

*   *   *

To what needs was this transformation a response?

Probably to new forms and a new game in the practice of illegalism. To new threats, above all.

The example of the French Revolution (but also of many other movements in the last twenty years of the eighteenth century) shows that the political apparatus of a nation is within reach of popular revolts. A food riot, a revolt against taxes or fees, the refusal of conscription are no longer localized and limited movements that may well affect (and physically) the representative of political power, but leave its structures and distribution out of reach. They may challenge the possession and exercise of political power. But, on the other hand, and maybe especially, the development of industry puts the apparatus of production, on a massive scale, in direct contact with those who have to make it work. Small craft units, factories with limited and relatively simple equipment, and warehouses with limited capacity serving local markets provided little purchase for wholesale depredation or destruction. But mechanization, the organization of large factories with significant stocks of raw materials, the globalization of the market, and the appearance of great centers for the redistribution of goods, put wealth within reach of incessant attack. And these attacks do not come from outside, from the deprived or poorly integrated in beggar's or vagabond's rags who provoked such fear in the eighteenth century, but from within, as it were, from the very ones who have to handle this wealth in order to make it productive. From the daily plunder of stored products to great collective machine breaking, the wealth invested in the apparatus of production is threatened by a constant danger. A whole series of measures taken at the end of the eighteenth and the beginning of the nineteenth century to protect the London ports, docks and arsenals, and to dismantle the network of black market dealers, can serve as an example.

In the countryside, an apparently opposite situation produces analogous effects. The dividing up of rural property, the more or less complete disappearance of the commons, and the working of fallow land solidify appropriation and make rural society intolerant of a whole set of minor illegalisms that, like it or not, had to be accepted in the regime of large, under-exploited estates. The margins, in which the poorest and most mobile could subsist, profiting from tolerance, neglect, forgotten regulations, or accepted states of affairs, disappear. The tightening of property ties, or rather the new status of landed property and its new exploitation, transform many established illegalisms into crimes. The importance, more political than economic, of rural crimes in France of the Directory and the Consulate (crimes connected either to struggles in the form of civil wars or to resistance to conscription); the importance also of resistance in Europe to the different forest codes at the beginning of the nineteenth century.

But maybe the most important form of the new illegalism is elsewhere. It concerns less the body of the apparatus of production, or landed property, than the very body of the worker and the way in which it is applied to the apparatuses of production. Inadequate wages, the disqualification of labor by the machine, excessive hours of work, the multiplicity of regional or local crises, the banning of associations, and the mechanism of debt all lead workers to forms of conduct such as absenteeism, breaking the "hire contract," migration, and an "irregular" life. The problem is then to fix workers to the production apparatus, to establish them in one place or move them to another where they are needed, to subject them to its rhythm, to impose on them the constancy or regularity it requires, in short, to form them as a labor force. Hence legislation creating new offenses (obligation of the worker's record book, law on drinking places, prohibition of the lottery); hence, a whole series of measures that, while not being absolutely constraining, establish a division between the good and the bad worker and seek to ensure a training of behavior (the savings bank, encouragement of marriage, and later, workers' cities); hence the appearance of organizations of control or pressure (philanthropic associations, youth fellowships); hence, finally, a huge campaign of worker moralization. This campaign defines what it wants to keep at bay as "dissipation," and what it wants to establish as "regularity": a concentrated, applied worker's body adjusted to the time of production, and supplying the exact force required. It points to delinquency as the inevitable outcome of irregularity, thus giving the status of a psychological and moral consequence to the marginalizing effect of the mechanisms of control.

*   *   *

We can draw a certain number of conclusions from this.

1. The forms of penality we see appearing between 1760 and 1840 are not linked to a renewal of moral perception. The basic nature of the infractions defined by the code hardly changed (however, we can note the gradual or sudden disappearance of religious offenses, and the appearance of certain economic or professional types of offense); and if the regime of penalties became considerably milder, the infractions themselves remained almost identical. What activated the great renewal of the epoch was a problem of bodies and materiality, it was a question of physics: a new form of materiality taken by the apparatus of production, a new type of contact between this apparatus and those who make it function; new requirements imposed on individuals as productive forces. The history of penality at the beginning of the nineteenth century is not essentially a matter of a history of moral ideas; it is a chapter in the history of the body. Or let's say, putting it differently, that by interrogating moral ideas on the basis of penal practice and institutions we discover that the evolution of morality is, above all, the history of the body, the history of *bodies*. On that basis we can understand:

- that the prison became the general form of punishment and replaced torture. The body no longer has to be marked; it has to be trained and re-trained; its time has to be measured and fully utilized; its forces have to be continually applied to labor. The prison-form of penality corresponds to the wage-form of labor;
- that medicine, as science of the normality of bodies, took a place at the heart of penal practice (the penalty must aim to cure).

2. The transformation of penality does not belong just to a history of bodies; it belongs more precisely to a history of the relations between political power and bodies. The constraint on bodies, their control, their subjection, the way in which this power is directly or indirectly

exerted on them, the way in which it bends, fixes, and uses them are at the source of the change studied. It would be necessary to write a *Physics* of power, and to show how much that physics was modified at the beginning of the nineteenth century, at the time of the development of State structures, in relation to its earlier forms.

A new *optics*, first of all: an organ of generalized and constant surveillance; everything must be observed, seen, and transmitted: organization of a police force; creation of a system of records (with individual files); establishment of a *panopticism*.

A new *mechanics*: the isolation and regrouping of individuals; location of bodies; optimal utilization of forces; control and improvement of output; in short, the organization of a whole *discipline* of life, time, and energies.

A new *physiology*: the definition of norms, the exclusion and rejection of what does not conform to them, and a mechanism to re-establish them through corrective interventions that are ambiguously therapeutic and punitive.

3. Delinquency plays an important role in this "physics." But this term delinquency needs to be understood. It is not a matter of delinquents, of a sort of psychological or social mutant, who would be the object of penal repression. By delinquency, we should understand rather the coupled penality-delinquent system. The penal institution, with the prison at its center, produces a category of individuals who enter into a circuit with it: the prison does not correct; it ceaselessly recalls the same ones; it gradually forms a marginalized population that is used to put pressure on the "irregularities" or "illegalisms" that cannot be tolerated. And it exerts this pressure on illegalisms through the medium of delinquency in three ways: by gradually leading the irregularity or illegalism to the infraction, thanks to a whole interplay of exclusions and parapenal sanctions (a mechanism that may be called "indiscipline leads to the scaffold"); by integrating delinquents into its own instruments for supervising illegalism (the recruitment of provocateurs, informers, police officers; a mechanism that may be called "every thief can become a Vidocq"); by channeling the infractions of delinquents towards the populations over which it is most important to

keep watch (the principle: "It is always easier to rob a poor person than someone who is rich").

So, to return to the question we asked at the start: "Why this strange institution of the prison, why this choice of a penality whose dysfunctional character was denounced so early on?" We should perhaps seek an answer in these terms: prison has the advantage that it produces delinquency, an instrument for controlling and putting pressure on illegalism, a not insignificant component in the exercise of power on bodies, an element of that physics of power that gave rise to the psychology of the subject.

*   *   *

The seminar this year was devoted to preparing the dossier on the Pierre Rivière case for publication.

1. F. Serpillon, *Code criminel, ou Commentaire sur l'ordonnance de 1670* (Lyon: Périsse, 1767), vol. 2, third part, title XXV: "Des sentences, jugements et arrêts," art. XIII, §33, p. 1095.

2. D. Jousse, *Traité de la justice criminelle de France* (Paris: Debure, 1771) 4 volumes.

3. P.-F. Muyart de Vouglans, *Institutes au droit criminel, ou Princeps généraux en ces matières* (Paris: Le Breton, 1757).

4. C. de Rémusat, "Discussion du projet de loi relatif à des réformes dans la législation pénale," Chamber of Deputies, 1 December 1831, *Archives parlementaires de 1787 à 1860. Recueil complet des débats législatifs et politiques des Chambres françaises*, second series (Paris: Pual Dupont, 1889) vol. LXXII, p. 185, col. 2.

5. P.-F. Van Meenen, Presiding Judge of the Brussels Court of Appeal, "Discours d'ouverture du IIᵉ Congrès international pénitentiaire," 20-23 September 1847, Brussels, in *Débats du Congrès pénitentiaire de Bruxelles* (Brussels: Deltombe, 1847) p. 20.

6. N. H. Julius, *Vorselungen über die Gefängnisskunde ...* (Berlin: Stuhr, 1828) 2 volumes; French translation (volume 1) by H. Lagarmitte, *Leçons sur les prisons, présentées en forme de cours au public de Berlin en l'année 1827* (Paris: F. G. Levrault, 1831).

7. C. Lucas, *De la réforme des prisons, ou De la théorie de l'emprisonnnement, de ses principes, de ses moyens et de ses conditions pratiques* (Paris: Legrand et Bergounioux, 1836-1838), 3 volumes.

8. W. Blackstone, *Commentaries on the Laws of England* (Oxford: Clarendon Press, 1758).

9. J. P. Brissot de Warville, *Théorie des loix criminelles* (Berlin: 1781), 2 volumes: vol. I, ch. II, section II, p. 187.

10. C. Beccaria, *Dei delitti e delle pene* (Milan: 1764); French translation by J.-A.-S. Collin de Plancy, *Traité des délits et des peines* (Paris: Flammarion, coll. "Champs," 1979) ch. XXVII, p. 118; ch. XXVIII, p. 121; and ch. XXX, p. 125; English translation Richard Davies with Virginia Cox and Richard Bellamy, *On Crimes and Punishments* in Beccaria, *On Crimes and Punishments and Other Writings*, ed., Richard Bellamy (Cambridge: Cambridge University Press, 1995) ch. 20, p. 50 (corporal punishment), ch. 22, p. 53 (fines) and ch. 23, p. 54 (public disgrace) [See my footnote * above, p. 255; GB].

11. L.-M. Le Peletier de Saint-Fargeau, "Rapport sur le projet du Code pénal," National Assembly, 23 May 1791, *Archives parlementaires de 1787 à 1860. Recueil complet de débats législatifs et politiques des Chambres françaises*, first series (Paris: Paul Dupont, 1887) vol. XXVI, p. 322, col. 1.

12. C. Beccaria, *Traité des délits et des peines*, p. 125; *On Crimes and Punishments*, p. 53: "the most fitting punishment shall be the only sort of slavery which can be called just, namely the temporary enslavement of the labor and person of the criminal to society, so that he may redress his unjust despotism against the social contract by a period of complete personal subjection."

13. J. P. Brissot de Warville, *Théorie des loix criminelles*, vol. 1, p. 147.

14. P. L. Rossi, *Traité de droit pénal*, Book III, chapter VIII: "De l'emprisonnement" (Paris: A. Sautelet, 1829) p. 169.

15. E. Livingstone, *Introductory Report to the System of Penal Law Prepared for the State of Louisiana* (New Orleans: 1820); *Rapport fait à l'Assemblée générale de l'État de la Louisiana sur le projet d'un code pénal* (New Orleans: B. Levy, 1822).

16. N. H. Julius, *Leçons sur les prisons*, pp. 384-386.

COURSE CONTEXT

Bernard E. Harcourt[*]

AT THE PEAK OF one of his most politically engaged periods regarding matters of punishment and penal law in France, and following the 1971-1972 lectures devoted to the repressive dimension of penality, Foucault turns his attention in January 1973 to a broader object. Beyond repression, he devotes himself not only to the productive dimension of penality, but to the more general question of the emergence of what he will call a "disciplinary" power throughout society in the nineteenth century—at the birth of contemporary society, which Foucault would describe as

> a society of disciplinary power, that is to say a society equipped with apparatuses whose form is sequestration, whose purpose is the formation of a labor force (*force de travail*), and whose instrument is the acquisition of disciplines or habits.[1]

A month earlier, the *Groupe d'information sur les prisons*, (G.I.P.), of which Foucault was one of the co-founders in 1971, decides to dissolve.[2] The ambition of the G.I.P.—"Let the prisoners speak (*La parole aux détenus*)!" in Foucault's words[3]—had been satisfied: the first prisoners' organization in France, the *Comité d'action des prisonniers*,

* Bernard E. Harcourt is Isidor and Seville Sulzbacher Professor of Law and Director of the Columbia Center for Contemporary Critical Thought at Columbia University, and *Directeur d'études* at the École des Hautes Études en Sciences Sociales in Paris. His most recent book is *Exposed: Desire and Disobedience in the Digital Age* (Cambridge, MA: Harvard University Press, 2015).

had been formed by the prisoners themselves.[4] Foucault will support the creation of an association for the defense of prisoners' rights; but henceforth, for the latter: "Autonomy of speech has been achieved."[5] In the same month, December 1972, Foucault writes to Daniel Defert that he is beginning to analyze power relations on the basis of "the most criticized of all wars: not Hobbes, nor Clausewitz, nor class struggle, but civil war."[6] This notion of civil war, and the associated figure of the "criminal-social enemy," come to the forefront.[7] A few weeks later, at the beginning of January 1973, Foucault begins his course of lectures on "the punitive society;" thirteen lectures that link political economy and genealogy of morals to describe the emergence of a new form of power throughout society—inseparably wage-form and prison-form—as well as the organization of panoptic relations that subject the whole life time to the cycles of capitalist production.

Situated in the trajectory of the research project established in his first year at the Collège de France—which was focused on the historical analysis of juridical and political forms that produce effects of truth[8]— and in furtherance of his longstanding interest in forms of knowledge associated with "dividing" techniques,[9] *The Punitive Society* offers a first outline of the regime of truth associated with generalized confinement and emphasizes its centrality throughout contemporary society. At issue, in fact, is more the study of that juridical and political form than the prison itself: "this prison-form," Foucault stresses, "is much more than an architectural form; it is a social form."[10]

Two years earlier, in his *Lectures on The Will to Know*, Foucault had begun to analyze the relationship between truth and juridical forms, studying the test as mode of veridiction in the agonistic battle between Antilochos and Menelaos in Book XXIII of Homer's *Iliad*; the inquiry in the case of Sophocles' *Oedipus the King*; and finally the question of money as measure of truth. In his first lecture at the Collège de France, 9 December 1970, Foucault explained that the theme of his research seminar would be the question of truth in the context of nineteenth-century penality: "The precise point of the analysis will be the insertion of a discourse claiming scientific status (medicine, psychiatry, psychopathology, sociology) within a system—the penal system— which had previously been entirely prescriptive."[11] The following year's lectures, *Penal Theories and Institutions*, were to pursue the analysis of other juridical forms, notably that of the inquiry as it related to the establishment of the State in the Middle Ages and the "new forms of social controls" in sixteenth- and seventeenth-century France.[12] So it is in 1973, in *The Punitive Society*, that Foucault broaches in depth, for the first time, the juridical and social specificity of the prison-form, and directly targets penality in the nineteenth century. "Such was the point of my remarks," he says then,

> the prison as social form, that is to say as form according to which power is exercised within a society—the way in which power extracts the knowledge it needs in order to be exercised and the form in which, on the basis of this knowledge, it distributes orders, prescriptions.[13]

Foucault would set out the complete scheme of this research project in his lectures at the Pontifical Catholic University of Rio de Janeiro a few months later, in May 1973. Then, in 1975, came the publication of *Discipline and Punish*, which, in the light of his first courses at the Collège de France, may be read—or re-read—as a *case study* of the juridical form of the examination in the nineteenth century, of the production of the scientific and juridical truth of the subject in industrial society.[14] The question at the center of *Discipline and Punish*—why confinement? or more precisely: "Why did the physical exercise of punishment (which is not torture) replace, with the prison that is its institutional support, the social play of the signs of punishment and the prolix festival that circulated them?"[15]—should be understood in this light: it is not just a question of the predominance of an institution, but, more precisely, of the production of a truth and a knowledge throughout the whole of society. In this sense, the 1973 lectures elaborate the way in which imprisonment was imposed and generalized as a punitive tactic, and in doing so offer us the possibility of re-reading *Discipline and Punish* not just in terms of power, but as a continuation of the problem of truth.

These 1973 lectures also mark a break with certain previous analyses—notably those that deploy the notions of repression, exclusion, and transgression—and a turn to an exploration of the productive functions of penality. Foucault begins to move in this direction some months earlier, in April 1972, when he visits Attica prison in New York State—direct access to a prison, an experience which he describes as "overwhelming."[16] Upset and "undermined" by this visit, Foucault begins an analytical transition towards the "positive functions" of the penal system: "the question that I ask myself now is the reverse," he explains.

> The problem is, then, to find out what role capitalist society has its penal system play, what is the aim that is sought, and what effects are produced by all these procedures for punishment and exclusion. What is their place in the economic process, what is their importance in the maintenance and exercise of power? What is their role in the class struggle?[17]

It is precisely this turn to the positive functions of penality that will lead Foucault to an analysis of political economy—not only in the sense of that "political economy" of the body[18] that would motivate *Discipline and Punish*, but more traditionally, in the manner of a classical study. In 1973, through the prism of civil war, Foucault combines a classical study of political economy with a Nietzschean genealogy of morals focused on the Quakers and other English dissidents of the eighteenth century. The latter, who play a much more important role in the 1973 lectures than in *Discipline and Punish*, are placed at the heart of the historical movement that would give rise to the prison-form. Thus Foucault seeks to understand—a fundamental question—"[h]ow these little men [in] black, who did not take off their hats, can be seen as ancestors in the genealogy of our morality."[19] These Quaker ancestors—these little men in black—would bring about a conversion of penality into ascesis, a moralization of criminality, and a penitential model of confinement, which would then be taken up by the privileged classes to organize an industrial society.

The thesis is radical and committed. And it reflects well that these 1973 lectures crown one of the most active periods of Foucault's political life, during a period that Foucault himself experienced as highly repressive in France. "[T]oday, for reasons I do not really understand," Foucault pointed out, "we are returning to a sort of general, undifferentiated confinement."[20] Some months before, Foucault had given unreserved support to the prisoners who had revolted in many prisons and jails across France, including the Ney prison of Toul in December 1971, the Charles-III jail of Nancy 15 January 1972, and the prisons of Nîmes, Amiens, Loos, and Fleury-Mérogis among others.[21] After the revolt at Toul, on 5 January 1972, in a joint press conference of the G.I.P. and the *Comité Vérité Toul*, Foucault declares that "what took place at Toul is the start of a new process: the first phase of a political struggle directed against the entire penitentiary system by the social strata that is its primary victim."[22] Two weeks later, on 18 January, with Deleuze, Sartre, and about forty others, Foucault organizes a "sit-in" at the Ministry of Justice.[23] Demonstrations, press conferences, inquiries—the inquiries: "*Intolérable*"—and pamphlets of the G.I.P., reports of the new Agence de Presse Libération/APL, columns in *Le Monde* and in other newspapers multiply.[24]

Returning from his visit to the Attica prison—where, seven months before, a general revolt of the prisoners had led to a military assault on the prison and the death of twenty-nine prisoners and ten warders—Foucault already points to the "function of massive elimination in the American prison,"[25] although the expression "mass incarceration" only begins to be employed in the United States twenty years later. From 1973, in fact, the number incarcerated in American prisons begins to explode and it is not long before it reaches the "more than one million prisoners"[26] that Foucault announces. (Today the figure is more than 2.2 million). With prescience, Foucault describes the new "radical concentration"[27] developing in the United States, and adopts towards it a position that is itself quite radical: "The only way for prisoners to escape from this system of training (*dressage*) is collective action, political organization, rebellion," he says when leaving Attica. "It appears that the American prison, much more easily than European prisons, can be a place for political action."[28] Involved in this struggle at a distance, Foucault and the G.I.P. circulate a leaflet after the death—or rather, they assert, the murder—of George Jackson, a member of the Black Panther Party, incarcerated in San Quentin, California, and killed by warders during a revolt in or near the prison's security wing on 21 August 1971.[29] Likewise in France, Foucault emphasizes "an enormous carceral organization" in which "*grosso modo*, 300,000 pass through the prisons or return to them."[30] The situation is such that Foucault declares, in an interview published in March 1972:

> If I concern myself with the G.I.P., it is precisely because I prefer effective work to university chattering and scribbling books. To write today a sequel to my *Histoire de la folie* … has no interest for me. On the other hand, a concrete political action in favor of prisoners seems to me charged with meaning.[31]

This commitment can be felt while reading *The Punitive Society*. The 1973 lectures are driven by indignation, almost anger, against those who misjudge the stakes of the political struggle:

> We are forever in the habit of speaking of the "stupidity" of the bourgeoisie. I wonder whether the theme of the stupid bourgeois is not a theme for intellectuals: those who imagine that merchants are narrow-minded, people with money are mulish, and those with power are blind. Safe from this belief, moreover, the bourgeoisie is remarkably intelligent. The lucidity and intelligence of this class, which has conquered and kept power under conditions we know, produce many effects of stupidity and blindness, but where, if not precisely in the stratum of intellectuals? We may define intellectuals as those on whom the intelligence of the bourgeoisie produces an effect of blindness and stupidity.[32]

And Foucault adds, in the margin of his manuscript: "*Those who deny this are public entertainers. They fail to recognize the seriousness of the struggle.*"[33]

This indignation fosters a militancy that is expressed throughout the 1973 lectures and is found again a few months later in his lectures at Rio de Janeiro on "Truth and Juridical Forms"—lectures that also reflect well Foucault's imbrication of theoretical and political commitments. At Rio, this theme of the blindness of intellectuals will be directly linked to what he will call the great Western myth of the antinomy of knowledge and power, and more broadly to the question of truth. "This great myth needs to be scrapped," Foucault declares in May 1973. "It is this myth that Nietzsche began to demolish by showing … that, behind all knowledge-*savoir*, behind all knowledge-*connaissance*, what is at stake is a power struggle. Political power is not absent from knowledge, it is interwoven with it."[34] These are strong words—"scrapped," "demolish"—that raise a number of questions about the effects of blindness, how they relate to truth, and the intellectual's important but delicate role. In a conversation with Deleuze, 4 March 1972, Foucault makes clear that "the intellectual's role ... is ... to struggle against the forms of power in which he is both its object and its instrument: in the sphere of 'knowledge,' 'truth,' 'consciousness,' and 'discourse'."[35] And so, to dismantle the great Western myth, to scrap this illusion, Foucault sets out in his 1973 lectures to make a detailed analysis of the production of the regime of truth—prison-form, wage-form—at the heart of disciplinary society.

THE INTELLECTUAL CONTEXT

"Not Hobbes, nor Clausewitz, nor class struggle":[36] the key notion of civil war that drives *The Punitive Society* is situated in a space delimited by these three vanishing points—three dimensions that reflect three particularly fraught debates in the post-May 1968 period, a time during which, in Foucault's words, "the problem of repression and legal pursuits became increasingly acute."[37]

First dimension, Hobbes and the conceptualization of State power: How is the relation between the State—the Commonwealth of Hobbes— and the subject to be understood, or more precisely, how are we to think about political power after May 1968? This first dimension leads Foucault to develop a new way of conceptualizing power, as well as to identify a new form of power, which will be aimed not only at Hobbes, but also, implicitly, at Althusser. Explicitly, Foucault's intervention is addressed to Hobbes: it is a criticism of the Hobbesian analysis in which civil war is subsumed under the notion of the war of all against all. His theoretical effort consists in reintegrating the notion of civil war within the Commonwealth. For Foucault, civil war is not the end of the political condition and does not plunge us back into a state of nature; it is not merely an illustration of that original condition of the war of all against all. Civil war is not the opposite of political power, it constitutes and reconstitutes it: it is "a matrix within which elements of power come to function, are reactivated, break up."[38] It is the quasi permanent condition of the constitution and reconstitution of groups, communities, and politics. And so power itself should be analyzed through the prism of civil war: "What is important for an analysis of penality is seeing that power is not what suppresses civil war, but what conducts and continues it."[39] Or, as Foucault declares on 10 January 1973: "we have to reject the image Hobbes [proposed] in which, with the appearance of the exercise of sovereign [power], war is expelled from [the sovereign power's] space."[40]

But his analysis of power is aimed, implicitly, at Althusser, who had published in 1970 research notes with the title "Ideology and the Ideological State Apparatuses." Foucault's intervention in 1973 may be read as a rejoinder to Althusser's main concern, namely the Althusserian division between, on one side, a State power expressed through violence and coercion and, on the other, a State power that acts through ideology.[41] The thesis according to which the analysis of penality would be situated entirely, or almost entirely, on the side of an analysis of the repressive State apparatus[42]—without much need, according to a bifurcation that Foucault himself challenges, of tools for an analysis of the ideological apparatuses—will serve Foucault as a recurrent theoretical foil. To be sure, Althusser evinces a sharp sensitivity to the subjective dimension of ideology and to the importance of subjection (*assujettissement*) by the interpellation of the subject through ideological forms—themes in which Foucault was already interested from his first works on madness and Kant's *Anthropology*, and to which he will return in his last courses. However, the formulations "State apparatus" and "ideological apparatuses" do not offer Foucault the possibility of thinking about penality or the prison outside of State repression, that is to say, outside the domain, in Althusser's words, "of the 'bad subjects' who on occasion provoke the intervention of one of the detachments of the (Repressive) State Apparatus."[43]

Foucault never explicitly refers to Althusser in his lectures, but he does address him:

Now I do not think that power can adequately be described as something located in State apparatuses. Maybe it is not even sufficient to say that the State apparatuses are the stake of an internal or external struggle. It seems to me rather that the State apparatus is a concentrated form, or even a support structure, of a system of power that goes much further and deeper.[44]

Foucault proposes a more fluid conception to the model of State apparatus: the example of a sequestration of private origin or initiative (for instance, the factory-convent of Jujurieux) that does not derive directly from the State but that gestures to the State apparatus, or "rather [to] relays-multipliers of power within a society in which the State structure remains the condition for the functioning of these institutions."[45] In his manuscript, Foucault notes, as if speaking directly to Althusser: "It is not a State apparatus, it is an apparatus caught up in a state node. An intra-state system."[46]

In *The Punitive Society*, these oppositions to Hobbes and Althusser produce a new theorization of power. The latter cannot be understood as located in the State, or possessed, or subordinate to a mode of production, and certainly not as an ideology.[47] Power has to be thought of as a constitutive factor: by mastering time, power creates subjects who submit to industrialization and capitalism, and, in that sense, disciplinary power relations are in fact constitutive elements of capitalism, not simple instruments or purely coercion. This necessarily implies that the question of power runs through the whole of society— or, as Foucault will explain the following year in *Psychiatric Power* (1974), "[m]ethodologically this entails leaving the problem of the State, of the State apparatus, to one side and dispensing with the psycho-sociological notion of authority."[48]

Second dimension, Clausewitz and war as the continuation of politics by "other means":[49] How are the practices and institutions of war to be understood in relation to ordinary politics? Or, more precisely, in the context of Foucault's 1973 lectures, how can we best understand the relationship between institutions of confinement—which are, in effect, instruments of civil war—and the other social institutions of work, education, religion, and so on? Establishing the relationship between them is obviously necessary: "if it is true that external war is the continuation of politics, we must say, reciprocally, that politics is the continuation of civil war."[50] But how is this relationship to be understood? Are institutions of confinement simply "other means"? Is there continuity, or instead a sharp break between them and other social institutions? Foucault sketches an answer gradually in these lectures: institutions of confinement cannot be strictly differentiated from the others, but neither are they merely "other means."

Foucault delivered his lectures on the punitive society in an intellectually productive period, in France and abroad, regarding this theme of the relationship between institutions of confinement and society in general. In the United States, the sociologist and ethnographer, Erving Goffman, had forged the expression "total institutions"—those social structures characterized by a "barrier to social intercourse with the outside"[51]—and published his signature work, *Asylums*, the same year as *Folie et Déraison* appeared (1961). The two works echo each other on a number of points. Goffman's ethnographic study traces the development of "a sociological version of the structure of the self."[52] His attention to the patients in these total institutions offers a lens to describe various forms of "mortification of the self."[53] These are all very Foucauldian themes. Goffman also attributes an important role to discipline in these establishments. He makes it clear that the use of time is "tightly scheduled"[54] and describes in detail the role of "surveillance" in these institutions, where "one person's infraction is likely to stand out in relief against the visible, constantly examined compliance of the others."[55] Goffman also describes and studies closely the control of time: the way in which time is productively used to "disculturate" the inmate and assure his "civil death" in relation to the world outside.[56] "This time," Goffman writes, "is something its doers have bracketed off for constant conscious consideration in a way not quite found on the outside."[57] And, vice versa, Foucault's analysis of the power relations within these institutions—between prisoners and warders—offers strong parallels with the process Goffman describes between "inmates and staff."[58]

But although there are numerous parallels, their analyses of the relationship between total and other institutions are radically different.

For Goffman, the prison, asylum, and other closed establishments are clearly distinguished from other social institutions. They are demarcated from the rest of society. Likewise, for the historian of medicine, David Rothman, who published his work, *The Discovery of the Asylum*,[59] in 1971, penitentiaries, asylums, orphanages, sanatoria, homes for the poor, in short, closed institutions, are all presented under the same aspect, but differentiated from society at large. They arise from a common movement, but their specificity is strictly intrinsic. For Rothman, they are the common fruit of a desire to restore order to a period—the beginning of the nineteenth century, under the Presidency of Andrew Jackson—that imagined it was on the verge of a breakdown of social order, of family relations, of community and religious ties;[60] but they are distinct from the surrounding society and its ordinary institutions.

For Foucault, on the other hand, it is the features *common to all* social institutions that are important: the common characteristics regarding the control and planning of time, the hold on the body, the similarity between the prison-form and the wage-form of labor. These commonalities are what need to be studied,[61] not the fact of having or not having "locked doors, high walls, barbed wire, cliffs, water, forests, or moors."[62] The common form prevails over the difference. Confinement needs to be thought *together with*, and not in contrast to, these other social and economic institutions.

"[T]hroughout their life, people enter into a multiplicity of links with a multiplicity of institutions,"[63] Foucault observes. It is precisely the multiplicity of institutions that sheds light, most productively, on the central aim of these lectures. For Foucault, the emergent disciplinary power is not a feature common only to "total" institutions. The prison does not distinguish itself neatly from the social sphere. Nor does it represent an "other means" in the Clausewitzian sense. Prison and wages have "the *same* form,"[64] they are "historically twin."[65] They share control over the time of life and its transformation into labor-power. "The prison-form of penality corresponds to the wage-form of labor."[66] One might almost say that, for Foucault, society as a whole is a Goffmanesque "totalizing" institution—or, in Foucault's words: "The penitentiary element, of which the prison is just one expression, is a feature of the whole of society."[67]

In this, the 1973 lectures offer an essential hermeneutics for understanding the book that will follow, *Discipline and Punish*. More clearly perhaps than that work—so often read as a history of the prison, in line with its sub-title—*The Punitive Society*, in line with its title, represents a broader intervention, heralding a new form of power. The panopticism of Julius and Bentham infiltrates all the machinery of the social and is not reducible to an architectural innovation, any more than it is tied exclusively to the prison, the hospital, or even to the factory or convent. The focus is widened, and the object of analysis is henceforth situated at the level of the harnessing and sequestration of time, of the subjection of the entire time of life to the cycles of industrial and capitalist production, of the permanent control (direct and indirect) of each moment of existence, of "a daily, complex, deep punitive system that moralizes the judicial,"[68] of the pervasive formation of an image for society and of a social norm—in short of the production and fabrication of the social.[69] It is indeed disciplinary *society* that Foucault analyzes in his 1973 lectures, not merely penitentiary confinement, nor simply the birth of the prison.

In this respect Foucault's lectures are much closer to the works of Castel and Deleuze and Guattari, than to those of Goffman or Rothman. In the same year, 1973, Castel publishes *Le Psychanalysme. L'Ordre psychanalytique et le pouvoir*, and is working on the themes of *L'Ordre psychiatrique. L'âge d'or de l'aliénisme*, which will appear three years later.[70] Gilles Deleuze and Félix Guattari had just published their *Anti-Œdipe. Capitalisme et schizophrénie* the year before, in 1972.[71] Foucault himself would acknowledge the influence of these two lines of research on his thought.[72] Castel's project in particular seems to share a common dynamic with Foucault's approach: a fairly similar sensibility, an attention to new forms of knowledge, new institutional structures, and new agents, a similar interest in the 1838 Law on the insane, and a common project of analyzing "a new structure of domination" in the nineteenth century and "a totalitarian Utopia ... that might be said to be capillary"[73] in contemporary mental medicine.

The third dimension: Marx and the class struggle. How are civil war and class conflict linked, or must they be distinguished? Or more precisely, in the context of these 1973 lectures, how should we rethink the penal repression of sedition and popular movements in connection with the birth, not only of institutions of confinement, but also of a generalized punitive power? On this question, the 1973 lectures may be read in silent dialog with English Marxist historians, and in particular with the signature work of Edward P. Thompson, *The Making of the English Working Class* (1963).[74] The theme of "making," of course, echoes the genealogical method. And the principal characters—John Wesley, the Methodists and Quakers, the "Society for the Suppression of Vice and Encouragement of Religion," John Howard and Jonas Hanway, Patrick Colquhoun and Edmund Burke, William Wilberforce, the Luddites, the Gordon Riots, and so on—are found on both sides of the conversation. But even more, the central notion of "popular illegalisms," which Foucault develops here, may be read as a response to Thompson and the English Marxist historians.

Thompson's intervention—which builds on the work of George Rudé and other historians who had already rethought and broadened the notion of "mob" (*plèbe*)—consists in part in enriching the notion of "riot." According to Thompson, the riot should not be thought of as a spontaneous, spasmodic, convulsive, or irregular movement, but rather as having a coherence, a logic, and as being in continuity with other instances of resistance.[75] In fact, for Thompson, the riot does not reflect an irrational or temporary reaction responding to a single stimulus (hunger, scarcity, and so on); rather, it expresses a social ethic, or more exactly, in the eighteenth century, a concerted political and moral opposition to the emergence of *laissez-faire*. This, he says, would explain the Luddite movement: "Luddism must be seen as arising at the crisis-point in the abrogation of paternalist legislation, and in the imposition of the political economy of *laissez-faire* upon, and against the will and conscience of, the working people."[76] At the same time, it is the repression of seditious acts that would give rise to a whole bloody penal and repressive system. So the penitentiary system would be the product of repression, for Thompson; and the economic development of the second half of the eighteenth century would take place "in the shadow" of this repressive system—not as the productive effect, nor by means of a *common* form of power: "The commercial expansion, the enclosure movement, the early years of the Industrial Revolution," Thompson maintains, "all took place within the shadow of the gallows."[77]

Foucault came close to Thompson's thesis,[78] but in February 1973 he distances himself from it—and one can read him here in direct conversation with Thompson, precisely on the relationship between popular resistance and repression. To the question: "Why did the State itself become the great 'penitentiary (*pénitentier*)'?" Foucault observes: "for some time I thought [the problem] could be solved in two words"[79]—these "two words" being "seditious mobs" and their repression according to Thompson.[80] "Now," Foucault says,

> I am not sure I am right in using the term "seditious mobs (*plèbe séditieuse*)." Actually, it seems to me that the mechanism that brought about the formation of this punitive system is, in a sense, deeper and broader than that of the simple control of the seditious mobs.[81]

For Foucault, then, the punitive society would not draw its source from repressive fear and reaction to popular movements in the eighteenth century. The dynamic would not boil down to the triptych: change of political economy—moral economy of resistance—repression by the dominant class. Rather, Foucault would develop his thesis of "*popular illegalism*"—a phenomenon that he would describe as "deeper and more constant" and "of which sedition is only a particular case."[82] A key theme of the 1973 lectures, the theory of illegalisms,[83] will form the basis of a political economy that will become central in Foucault's approach to the penal system, and that will be developed in the following months and, subsequently, in *Discipline and Punish*.

Due to this silent dialog with Thompson, as well as with Althusser, the 1973 lectures are far more "Marxist"-sounding than other of Foucault's writings, while formulating clear lines of demarcation, maybe even the clearest he drew, between Marx and himself. Foucault develops a political economy, a history of capitalism, on the basis of a struggle that at times resembles a class struggle—which makes this text so *Marxisant*—but that is ultimately a very different struggle: a generalized civil war involving the "criminal-social enemy" that produces a disciplinary power permeating society and transforming the time of life into a productive force. The 1973 lectures read like a challenge to the great texts on the history of capitalism. To those who think that morality is not indispensable to capitalism, Foucault seems to say: there was actually nothing natural in surplus value, nor in "necessary labor"; it required a multitude of moral battles targeting the lower (*populaires*) classes, a multitude of ethical battles at every level, for the bourgeoisie to become the master of illegalisms. In this, these 1973 lectures articulate a relationship to Marx better than any other of Foucault's engagements, and they propose an analysis of the relations between morality and economy that challenges Max Weber's *The Protestant Ethic and the Spirit of Capitalism.*

THE STRUCTURE OF THE ARGUMENT

The lectures are thus situated at the intersection of three dimensions— Hobbes/Althusser, Clausewitz/Goffman, and Marx/Thompson—and the argument is structured around five main theses: first, a turn to the analysis of the productive aspects of repression; second, the development of a political economy and a theory of illegalisms; third, a differentiation with regard to Marxism and the analysis of ideologies; fourth, a genealogy of penitential morality; which leads, finally, to the couple "*surveil*-punish (*surveiller-punir*)"

From the repressive to the productive

The previous year's lectures, *Penal Theories and Institutions*, were centered on repression and coercion, detailing the different repressive aspects of embryonic State forms from the Middle Ages and the seventeenth century. The aim was to study the formation of the State, not merely with reference to the fiscal dimension of the exercise of justice, or with reference to the army, but by identifying the beginnings of a purely repressive function.[84] The focus was prescient, insofar as the notion of *repression* would be one of the negative cornerstones necessary for the construction of the Foucauldian project on penality. In the 1972 lectures, the penal system is primarily described as one of the emerging modalities implemented in response to sedition in the seventeenth century, as a reaction against the "seditious mobs": "all the major phases of evolution of the penal system, of the repressive system, are ways of responding to forms of popular struggles,"[85] Foucault asserted in 1972. This is precisely what motivates the central thesis of the 1972 lectures: "The penal system-delinquency couple is an effect of the couple repressive system-sedition. An effect in the sense that it is a product, a condition of maintenance, a displacement, and an occultation."[86]

In contrast, from the very first lecture in 1973, Foucault orientates himself towards the *productive* aspects of the penal. From the start, Foucault takes up the positive functioning of transgressions: "we cannot understand the operation of a penal system, a system of laws and prohibitions, if we do not examine the positive functioning of illegalisms."[87] This represents a double distancing with regard to traditional sociology, to what Foucault calls "sociology of the Durkheimian type."[88] First differentiation: whereas Durkheimian sociology posed the question of how society creates moral cohesion—to which Durkheim famously replies, in part, by morally condemning and excluding the offender—Foucault initially endeavored to explore *different forms* of the punitive. This would produce, in *Penal Theories and Institutions*, an analysis of different modes of repression (towards the *Nu-pieds*, the Luddite movement, and so on), and in the first passages of *The Punitive Society*, the analysis of different modes of punishment. But in 1973, there is a second, more radical departure, namely to no longer focus on repression or exclusion: "[P]rison is an organization that is too complex to be reduced to purely negative functions of exclusion."[89] His inquiry is re-orientated and focuses on the positive effects of a specific penal system, that is to say, not on how society functions in general, or on raw moral cohesion, but on the effects on modern capitalist society and, more profoundly, on "the exercise and maintenance of power"[90] in such a society. In other words, what is involved is the exploration of the effects of power of *different* penal systems, in such a way that one does not see just a punitive softening, nor an individualization of penalties independent of power relations, but that one clearly distinguishes the constitutive processes of power relations specific to a given period and a given economic form of organization. This theme will be taken up again in 1975.[91] This methodological turn, which had already begun after his visit to Attica in 1972,[92] would give rise to one of the main assertions of *Discipline and Punish*:

> We must cease once and for all to describe the effects of power in negative terms: it "excludes," it "represses," it "censors," it "abstracts," it "masks," it "conceals." In fact, power produces; it produces reality; it produces domains of objects and rituals of truth. The individual and the knowledge that may be gained of him belong to this production.[93]

A political economy of illegalisms

A methodological turn, then, to the question of the productivity of penality. But productivity regarding what? In 1973, Foucault elaborates a political economy of capitalism at the beginning of the nineteenth century, on the basis of a generalized social struggle, in which the disciplining of the labor force occupies the foreground. As we have seen, the analysis is the result, in part, of the exchange with E. P. Thompson and his work, *The Making of the English Working Class*—Foucault's rejoinder aiming to go beyond the description of the penal system as repression of the "seditious mobs"—but also of his engagement, the previous year, with the Marxist theses of the Soviet historian, Boris Porchnev, in his work, *Les Soulèvements populaires en France au XVIIe siècle*.[94] The focal point of Foucault's reflection is a theory of *illegalisms*: the idea is to situate confinement in the broader economic production of a labor force, a movement by which the "bourgeoisie" would seek to control the behavior of workers precisely by managing what Foucault refers to as "popular illegalisms." The notion of illegalisms rests on the idea that law is a constant contestation over its own boundaries and serves primarily to manage the margins of legality—that law is a management tool.

In *The Punitive Society*, Foucault elaborates a theory of illegalisms in three stages. In the first stage, he develops the thesis that illegalisms are generalized. Throughout society, different social strata practice strategic games in relation to the law, to norms, order, deviance, and disorder. "[I]n every regime, different social groups, classes, and castes each have their illegalism,"[95] he explains. In the seventeenth century, for example, Foucault identifies not only the popular illegalisms, but also the illegalisms of merchants and business, as well as "the illegalism of the privileged, who evade the law through status, tolerance, or exception,"[96] and even the illegalisms of entrenched power—of the intendants, police lieutenants, and so on. These illegalisms of the different social strata are intertwined; they are often in conflict with each other, though often work in tandem with each other. They function together. One could say that they have a symbiotic relationship. The privileged in the eighteenth century, for example, tolerated popular illegalisms, for it too engaged in illegalist practices, and the relationship between all these illegalisms was necessary for the good functioning of the economic system and nascent capitalism: "It seems to me that until the end of the eighteenth century," Foucault lectures in February 1973, "a certain popular illegalism was not only *compatible* with, but *useful* to the development of the bourgeois economy; a point arrived when this illegalism that functioned enmeshed in the development of the economy, became incompatible with it."[97]

Second, then, Foucault identifies a break. Whereas the illegalisms of different classes were intertwined under the Ancien Régime, with the approach of the nineteenth century popular illegalisms are seen as a threat, as a danger, by merchants, aristocrats, and the bourgeoisie in France, as in England, Russia, and elsewhere. The new accumulation and transformation of wealth, the existence of new, more material and mobile forms of property, the marketing of goods, the abundance of commodities—in short, the wealth of movable goods, much more than landed property—is exposed to workers who are in direct contact with this new commercial fortune. These new forms of accumulation and disposability render popular illegalisms useless—indeed dangerous— to the interests of the bourgeoisie. Foucault develops the framework of this historical transformation in his lectures of 21 and 28 February 1973, as well as in an interview given some months later, "À propos de l'enfermement pénitentiaire."[98] In the lectures he explains:

[A]t a certain point, this illegalism was no longer tolerable to the class that had just taken power, because wealth, in its materiality, is spatialized in new forms and runs the risk of being attacked frontally by a popular illegalism that, henceforth, would not clash with the system of the laws and regulations of power, but with its goods themselves in their materiality.[99]

Third, and finally, Foucault detects a turn to the penal.[100] At the end of the eighteenth century, the bourgeoisie takes hold of the judicial system in order to put an end to these popular illegalisms, that is to say: to put an end to not only the "depredation" of material property, but also the "dissipation" of the time and strength of the workers themselves—of human capital, in effect. This dissipation takes "the form of absenteeism, lateness, laziness, festive revelry, debauchery, nomadism."[101] The tolerance of popular illegalisms "became literally impossible: all the lower strata effectively had to be put under generalized surveillance."[102] The bourgeoisie would take hold of the administrative and police apparatus towards the end of the eighteenth century and transform it "into a judicial apparatus responsible precisely for getting rid of popular illegalism. Taking power, the bourgeoisie will lay its hands on this apparatus ... and make it responsible for getting its legality applied."[103] So it is the accumulation of material wealth that motivates the movement towards surveillance, permanent control, the examination. The result is the "penitentiary,"[104] a notion which, as Frédéric Gros puts it well, represents "the idea of a confinement that sanctions less the breach of a law than irregularity of behavior."[105] Foucault explains: "This is how the penitentiary element, which I think functioned in the network of the non-legal, is taken over and integrated into the system of justice, precisely when the bourgeoisie is no longer able to tolerate popular illegalism."[106] In parallel with a movement towards the moralization of workers (we will come to this in a moment), the penitentiary becomes "a political instrument of the control and maintenance of relations of production."[107] On Foucault's account, it is the bourgeoisie's need to bring popular illegalisms under control that puts in gear the new punitive system.

Beyond Marx and Marxism

"[I]t is in this class relationship between the bourgeoisie and the proletariat that the condensed and remodeled penitentiary system begins to function":[108] *The Punitive Society* is tinged with a strong Marxist-sounding tonality. However, it is in no way a Marxist text. First of all, as we have seen, Foucault displaces the notion of "seditious mobs" with that of "popular illegalism," which he describes as "more operational."[109] Then, Foucault replaces the notion of class struggle with that of civil war. To be sure, he sometimes reverts to a reflexive use of the expression "class struggle"; for example, in the interview he gives after his visit to Attica prison in 1972,[110] and in his debate with Noam Chomsky the same year.[111] But in 1973 there is an explicit attempt to go beyond this notion. Henceforth, Foucault will correct himself. Thus, in the manuscript for the lecture of 21 March 1973, he writes "class struggle" and then crosses it out and replaces it with "class relationship."[112] For Foucault, civil war is not reducible to oppression by a dominant class, which he clearly explains:

> Of course, in this kind of general war through which power is exercised, there is a social class that occupies a privileged position and that may thereby impose its strategy, carry off a certain number of victories, accumulate them, and obtain the advantage of an effect of hyper-power, but this effect is not of the order of total possession. Power is not monolithic. It is never entirely controlled from a certain point of view by a certain number of people. At every moment it is in play in little singular struggles, with local reversals, regional defeats and victories, provisional revenges.[113]

The model of civil war should replace the model founded on the existence of a dominant class.

But in addition to these two interventions, the 1973 lectures operate other important displacements vis-à-vis Marx and the Althusserian tendency that dominated the interpretation of Marx in France at the time. Three in particular.

First displacement: with civil war in the foreground, it becomes necessary to study "the *theoretical-political* effect of this principle of the criminal-social enemy."[114] In this regard, Foucault expressly sets himself in opposition to Althusser, while taking up—precisely, strategically, and silently—one of the basic texts that the latter taught dogmatically from

October 1948 on, as tutor to students of the École normale supérieure (including the young Foucault, who was admitted to the École in July 1946): the writings of the young Marx regarding the "Debates on the Law on Thefts of Wood" published in the *Rheinische Zeitung* in October and November 1842.[115]

Althusser had given a reading of these early writings of Marx emphasizing, first, the oppressive ideology that suffocated Marx's thought—"the enslaved thought of the Young Marx"[116]—then, second, the discovery, by the young Marx, of material interests: "Marx at last discovered the reality of the ideological opacity which had blinded him," Althusser noted.[117] Althusser interpreted these texts through the prism of a logic of "escape (*délivrance*) from illusions."[118] According to Althusser, these texts from 1842 were captive to the dominant juris-prudential ideology of the time, but they also revealed how Marx freed himself from that ideology. The movement of his thought and of his writing, at both the intellectual and practical levels—by means of his confrontation with the material interests of the peasants—perfectly reflected the development of Marx's materialist conception of history. Thus, in his reading of these writings, Althusser saw reflected "a logic of *the irruption of real history in ideology itself*":[119] "If 'Marx's path' is an example to us," Althusser emphasized, "it is not because of his origins and circumstances but because of his ferocious insistence on freeing himself from the myths which presented themselves to him as the *truth*, and because of the role of the experience of real history which elbowed these myths aside."[120] As Althusser would write ten years later, in 1970—so at the time of Foucault's first lectures at the Collège de France—his own analysis focused on the question of the "*ideologico-polit-ical* struggle conducted by Marx as early as his articles in the *Rheinische Zeitung* [which] inevitably and quickly brought him face to face with this reality and forced him to take his earliest intuitions [concerning the nature of ideology] further."[121]

In contrast, referring to the very same texts of the young Marx, Foucault deliberately privileges the notion of "*theoretical-political effect*" where Althusser had spoken precisely of "*ideologico-political struggle*." And Foucault makes quite clear that his method "would, for example, have to take into account what Marx wrote regarding the discussion of the theft of wood."[122] Foucault's objective is to shift the analysis of "the ideologico–political struggle" towards the study of "the theoretical-political effect" of a discourse, that is to say, to produce an "analysis of a theoretical–political discussion," and, on the basis of this model, to "see how to analyze political discussions, oppositions, and struggles of discourse within a given political situation."[123] Once again, Foucault does not mention Althusser out loud, but the remarkable parallel of his neologism with Althusser's, and the juxtaposition of the analyses of the text on the theft of wood, are clear indications.

In this, Foucault places himself alongside Deleuze and Guattari—or vice versa—who declare in 1972 in *Anti-Oedipus* that "the concept of ideology is an execrable concept that hides the real problems, which are always of an organizational nature."[124] At the time, Foucault viewed Deleuze as one of the rare philosophical thinkers who could see beyond the old transcendental philosophy.[125] Now Deleuze and Guattari, as we know well, would head in the direction of desire: "Reich is at his profoundest as a thinker when he refuses to accept ignorance or illusion on the part of the masses as an explanation of fascism, and demands an explanation by reference to desire, in terms of desire: no, the masses were not fooled, at a certain moment, under a certain set of conditions, they desired fascism, and it is this perversion of herd desire that needs to be accounted for."[126] In 1973 Foucault will agree with them, at least in part.[127] But he will also move in another direction, not contenting himself merely with displacing the question of ideology, nor merely of distinguishing himself from Althusser. "I will shift the analysis by no longer taking penal theory and practice as the target, but the relationship between the latter and the effective tactic of punishment in the same period," he explained.[128] Doing this "we observe a remarkable phenomenon: in the same period as the principle of the criminal-social enemy is being formulated and put into practice within penal institutions, a new punitive tactic appears: imprisonment."[129] So, for Foucault, imprisonment has to be understood on the basis of the study of strategies, tactics, and relations of force: "we cannot derive the system of imprisonment from a sort of theoretical model based on the penal theory of criminal-social enemy."[130] It has to be understood, rather, on the basis of "the game of power carried out in it."[131]

Second displacement vis-à-vis Marx, or rather, vis-à-vis a certain university Marxism: the need to rethink the subject and what characterizes it. Foucault takes particular aim at the theory, which could be attributed to Marx,[132] according to which labor is the concrete essence of man and the dispossession of his labor is the source of alienation. For Foucault, this is a myth: labor is absolutely not man's essence, but is produced as such—and this entails an entirely different conception of power. The criticism of labor as essence will also be elaborated in his lectures at Rio a few months later, but it is already present in the 1973 lectures: "It is false to say, with certain famous post-Hegelians, that labor is man's concrete existence. The time and life of man are not *labor* by nature; they are pleasure, discontinuity, festivity (*fête*), rest, need, moments, chance, violence, and so on. Now, it is all this explosive energy that needs to be transformed into a continuous labor-power continually offered on the market."[133] Foucault will build on this argument a few months later, suggesting that the theory itself—namely, that labor is the concrete essence of man—is the product of practices intimately connected to capitalist relations of production.[134] These are the practices, Foucault will argue, that render the workers' bodies docile. He will refer to them as an "infra-power," "a set of political techniques, techniques of power ... by which people's bodies and their time become labor time and labor-power, and may be effectively used so as to be transformed into hyper-profit," as a "web of microscopic, capillary political power,"[135]—as opposed to "a state apparatus" or a "class in power."[136]

On Foucault's reading, the Marxist theory of the accumulation of capital depends on disciplinary techniques (themselves intimately connected to capitalist production) intended to fashion "productive bodies."[137] Foucault will develop these ideas two years later in *Discipline and Punish*, in which, citing Marx's *Capital* in particular (vol. I, ch. XIII), he will maintain that the economic revolutions that made possible the accumulation of capital in the nineteenth century are inseparable from the production of docile bodies—what he designates as "the methods for managing the accumulation of men."[138] These methods are precisely the disciplinary techniques at the heart of *Discipline and Punish*: "time-tables, collective training, exercises, total and detailed surveillance";[139] techniques that have replaced the more traditional and ritual methods of violence and force. For Foucault, these techniques are just as important for capitalist production and the exploitation of surplus value as the means of production themselves. "[T]he two processes—the accumulation of men and the accumulation of capital—cannot be separated ... [T]he technological mutations of the apparatus of production, the division of labor and the elaboration of disciplinary processes sustained a set of very close relations."[140]

This reversal produces—third and final displacement—a different conception of power. It is not just that power under capitalism guarantees a mode of production. The control of time is itself essential to capitalism. Power is thus not conceivable as an instrument, as something possessed, nor as an ideological apparatus, but must be thought of as a primary and constitutive factor.[141] Once again, it is in conversation with Althusser that Foucault develops his own conception of power. First of all, by rejecting the idea that power is something that is possessed; one might detect here an allusion to Althusser who had written, in 1970, on the question of State power: "The whole of the political class struggle revolves around the State. By which I mean around the *possession*, i.e., *the seizure and conservation* of State power by a certain class or by an alliance between classes or class fractions."[142] Second, by rejecting the characterization of power as either violence or ideology. One can detect here too a reference to Althusser's work on the ideological state apparatuses, in which he develops a distinction—with, of course, some subsequent qualifications, but a distinction nonetheless—between "the Repressive State Apparatus" which "'functions' ... by violence" and "the Ideological State Apparatuses" which "'function' ... by ideology."[143]

These three displacements will have three important implications. The first is that, for Foucault, there is no dominant class in power that uses confinement to repress the laboring class. There is no way to comprehend power through a conspiracy theory.[144] Second, just as there is no conspiracy, there is no "unsaid." Everything is always said. There is no point in delving into the unconscious or engaging in an occult hermeneutics, one just has to read and re-read, look closely in the archives, listen, rediscover. This can be seen clearly in the manuscript for 10 January 1973, in the passage where Foucault dissects the figure of the criminal-social enemy as "exchanger." This figure, he tells us, is not hidden; on the contrary, "[i]t is what is always said.—Always said: it is said, and explicitly, in the texts, laws, and theories. It is presupposed in practices, decisions, and institutions. It is connoted in literary images. It is not the unsaid; it is the more-than-said. The excessively said."[145] There is no need of any mysterious or esoteric interpretive method. Of course, this does not mean that there is no complexity or opacity. The study of discourse—of the set of discourses uttered—involves both a certain transparency and certain forms of exclusion. The two are integral parts of the analysis, and transparency may be so transparent that it obscures. Discussing his archeological method in 1969, Foucault explained:

> What I look for are not secret, hidden relations that are more silent or more profound than the consciousness of people. I try rather to define relations that are on the surface of discourse; I try to make visible what is invisible only because it is too much on the surface of things.[146]

Invisibility may thus come from the fact that all is too easily, too often said and heard.[147] In sum, everything is already said, but this does not mean that everything is heard. Third and final implication: from the methodological point of view one must focus on discourse. Foucault underscores this concisely in his lecture of 28 February 1973: "So let us disregard works and texts, and study rather discourses in the functions or strategic fields in which they produce their effects."[148]

A genealogy of morals

To read, listen to, and study discourses is precisely what Foucault undertakes in *The Punitive Society*, deploying his method to analyze the discourse of the Quakers and English dissidents—a moralizing discourse that will introduce the idea of the penitentiary into the penal sphere, and whose echoes will reverberate in the discourse of the bourgeoisie at the beginning of the nineteenth century. This provides another cornerstone of these lectures, in particular the way in which certain social strata in England and France used the notions of moral fault and penance to facilitate the construction of the capitalist edifice. The moralization and Christianization of criminality and punishment are accompanied by elements of rectification, re-education, and redemption through penance—by the idea of individual salvation that we encounter as well in the discourse of the Enlightenment, and that produces a conversion of punishment into ascesis.

In this respect, the 1973 lectures are underpinned by a genealogy of morals: it is through value judgments that the bourgeoisie succeeds in transforming behavior that was previously tolerated, and even encouraged, into illegal acts. This transformation of illegalisms into illegalities is facilitated by converting marginal behaviors into morally blameworthy acts, into acts that merit penance and expressions of moral fault. Foucault explains,

> The lower (*populaire*) strata transfer the techniques of the old illegalism to the very body of wealth, and they can reply to the bourgeoisie: did we not violate the law and plunder wealth together? To which, the bourgeoisie replies that it had been rules, laws, and unjustifiable abuses that were attacked under the Ancien Régime, and that it had been a question of power, and so of politics; whereas now, it is things, property, and so common law, natural law that is being attacked. Previously, abuses of power were attacked; now, violating the law displays a lack of morality.[149]

Foucault presents this passage as a rejoinder of the bourgeoisie and ends it on this exclamation: "Go, and repent."[150]

"Go, and repent": we pass here from archeology to genealogy. For Foucault, the prison cannot be derived in an archeological manner from the penal theories of the great eighteenth-century reformers.[151] Their theories were incompatible with a universal model like the prison; essentially, they advocated an "essential relativity of penalties," modulation, marginal deterrence, and did not propose the prison as universal solution.[152] The archeological derivation does not spring "from [their] principles": "[W]hat will actually take place in penal practice, namely the universalization of the prison as the general form of punishment, cannot be deduced from these principles."[153] For Foucault, there is complete "heterogeneity":[154] "So prison practice was not implied in penal theory. It arose elsewhere and was formed for other reasons."[155] This "elsewhere" must be sought out, using another method.

Here, then, is the origin of the genealogical analysis of the prison-form: it is a genealogy from below of ascetic Quaker thought, that turns the unruly body (*indocile*) into labor-power, that deploys pervasively the idea of fault and sin, and that gives rise to the first mention of the term "penitentiary (*pénitentier*)"[156]—"an incredible term," Foucault says.[157] It is "the first real transplant of Christian morality into the criminal justice system."[158] This first transplant, linked to the notion of penance among the Quakers, gives rise to the penitentiary system, to the criminal record, to the "criminal as object of knowledge," to criminological and psychopathological sciences, and to the insertion of priests into the prison.[159] In sum, as Foucault explains in the lecture of 31 January: "[I]f it is true that the prison-form, as institution and practice, cannot be derived from the penal theories of Beccaria, Brissot, and so on, it can be derived from the Quaker conception of religion, morality, and power."[160]

This first transplant will be stabilized, later, by means of the moralization of the daily living habits of the laboring class by the bourgeoisie in the nineteenth century. The practice of surveillance and control by the bourgeoisie will amount, in effect, to the "junction of the moral and the penal."[161] "[A] whole practice of surveillance" is deployed "that attempts to re-moralize penality and invest it in a kind of moral atmosphere, in short, that seeks to establish continuity between moral control and repression on the one hand, and the penal sanction on the other. So what we see is a moralization of the penal system, despite the practice and discourse of this system."[162] This moralization will extend to institutions like the police and other authorities that supervise and target the lower strata of society.[163] According to Foucault, it is this element of penance that, integrated into the penal system through the moralization of criminality and punishment, will make the prison tolerable and make possible its propagation. The coercive element of morality and penance is "the condition of the prison's acceptability."[164]

The objective of this moralization: the control of working-class illegalisms and the production of more effective workers—docile bodies.

Moralization is thus inscribed in an economic process. Illegalisms must be prevented from attacking the material property, the commodities, and the interests of the bourgeoisie—including, here, the workers themselves, their labor-power belonging to the capitalist bourgeoisie:

> [T]he bourgeoisie wanted to insert something that is more than just the negative law of "this is not yours" between the worker and the production apparatus he had in his hands. A supplementary code was needed that complements this law and gets it to work: the worker himself had to be moralized.[165]

This involved taking hold of time in order to master and form bodies.

Methodologically, therefore, this development reflects a transition towards the approach that Foucault at first calls "dynastic,"[166] but which is very quickly re-described as genealogical. The question is how these new forms of truth—the wage-form, the prison-form—arise, become acceptable, and are generalized.[167] This genealogical method is well summarized by the question: What are "the power relationships that made the historical emergence of something like the prison possible"?[168] Foucault had already invoked the genealogical method in his inaugural lecture at the Collège de France in 1970;[169] he develops it in 1973 and the following years,[170] and will put it to work in *Discipline and Punish*.[171] But the point of departure for this trajectory is outlined in *The Punitive Society*:

> Until now, we have been studying the threads of possible derivations: for example, how ideas and institutions join up with each other within the theoretical and practical penal system ... After an archeological type of analysis, it is a matter of undertaking a dynastic, genealogical type of analysis, focusing on filiations on the basis of power relationships.[172]

Theoretically, this development is a source of ambiguities and conflicts that make any thought of a structural reading problematic. At the heart of the analysis, there is a tension between the moralizing initiative, economic needs, and discursive strategies: at the precise moment when the dominant classes deploy the force of the State to moralize, culpabilize, and punish popular illegalisms, they simultaneously have to develop free competition among workers for contracts and open up the free market. This double movement is the origin of a central paradox in liberalism: a strong and heavily moralizing, coercive, and centralized State confronting an economic theory of liberalization and "freedom of the labor market":[173] "To protect this productive apparatus, to enable it to develop, the bourgeoisie provides itself with a strong State," Foucault explains.

> Now, at the same time that this need to protect the apparatus of production appears, in order for it to function, for the formation and growth of profit, the bourgeoisie needs competition between the workers, the free labor market, the possibility of drawing at will from this free breeding-ground of the labor force.[174]

This creates an acute problem for the coherence of the system, a dissonance that will produce what could be called "the illusion of free markets":[175] "in order to give the employer free rein, he is given the (illusory) form of the free contract."[176]

Politically, this development implies a subtle analysis of the conditions that make a repressive apparatus acceptable and tolerated. Foucault identifies two "great mechanisms"[177] for rendering the coercive tolerable: the first, that of fascism and Nazism, but also of the Second Empire, consists in transferring the functions of the repressive apparatus to marginalized social strata or groups; the second, that of the Ancien Régime, consists in acting in such a way that the repressive apparatuses, concentrated in the hands of the "ruling class," serve the lateral interests of other members of society. It is this second mechanism that Foucault sees at work in eighteenth-century France, with, for evidence, the practice of *lettres de cachet*. These must be understood as having been initiated by the lower strata and serving their interests,[178] rather than as an exercise of arbitrary monarchical power. In this respect, they are entirely at the service of the moralization of the penal system: "All the nineteenth-century moralization and psychologization of the penalty will enter through this orientation."[179]

Panoptic society

These four elements, together, produce a vision of a society having the characteristics of full panopticism: a "punitive" or, in the end, "disciplinary" society.[180] The major theme of the 1973 lectures is not—or not solely—that modern panopticism, imagined by Julius and developed by Bentham,[181] gave birth to the prison; it is much rather the extensive application of this architectural concept to the whole of space-time and not only to the prison sector. In his final lecture Foucault explains that panopticism is "a general social form that extends far beyond the prison."[182] The prison is only one place among others, not even a privileged place, to observe the emergence of the control of time and life. The defining feature of our society is easily seen in the industrial techniques of production, since the cycles of capitalist production depend upon the control of time. These techniques have truth effects that can then be identified in the very formation of the carceral system: we observe

> the introduction inside the prison of the general principles governing the economics and politics of work [outside] ... What we see appearing, through these two forms [the wage-form and the prison-form], is the introduction of *time* into the capitalist system of power and into the system of penality.[183]

The analysis extends well beyond penality, and the generalizability of the thesis is an essential dimension of the lectures—which was less well perceived on the reception of *Discipline and Punish*, but strongly emphasized in the Course Summary that synthesizes the thirteen lectures of 1973: what Foucault discovers is precisely "the first example of a civilization of surveillance."[184]

"The nineteenth century founded the age of panopticism":[185] while other thinkers, such as Guy Debord,[186] describe the birth of a society of the spectacle, Foucault takes the opposite view. In Antiquity, our ancestors may well have governed themselves through the spectacle, but contemporary society is governed by its inverse, surveillance. Thus Foucault declares: "This is precisely what takes place in the modern epoch: this inversion of the spectacle into surveillance."[187]

THE SURVEIL-PUNISH COUPLE

In 1973 we see the first sign of the *"surveiller-punir"* couple that will occupy center stage two years later: "The *surveil*-punish couple is imposed as a power relationship indispensable for fixing individuals to the production apparatus, for the formation of productive forces, and characterizes the society that can be called *disciplinary*."[188] It is quite remarkable to witness the birth of this conceptual couple in these 1973 lectures, as well as the figure of Damiens,[189] the timetable in the factory-barracks-convent,[190] the Mettray agricultural colony,[191] and the very idea of disciplinary power—distinct from the power of sovereignty, from bio-power that appears with *The History of Sexuality. An Introduction* and *"Society must be Defended,"* and from the security apparatuses (*dispositifs*) developed in *Security, Territory, Population* and *The Birth of Biopolitics* some years later. What, then, are the important developments and differences from the famous book to which the 1973 lectures open the way?

First, the role of moralizing tendencies in eighteenth-century power relations is more pronounced in *The Punitive Society* than in *Discipline and Punish*, in which the political dimension is slightly more prominent. In this respect, the 1973 lectures are not just preparatory work for the 1975 book, but may be read as a complete text. The Quakers and English dissidents, for example, who form the keystone of the genealogy of the prison-form in the 1973 lectures, will be accorded a minor place in *Discipline and Punish*, even though they are present in that text.[192]

By the same token, the moralization of criminality will be replaced, in 1975, by the more political theme of the production of the delinquent. Certainly, the figure of the delinquent is already present in 1973;[193] however, there is an inversion in 1975, and the discussion relating to moralization loses the dominant place it occupied earlier. In 1973: "the working class must be 'regenerated,' 'moralized'";[194] what the penal laws targeted at the beginning of the nineteenth century was "immorality, which concerns the body, need, desire, habit, and will, ... [and] a whole system of moral conditioning will need to be incorporated into penality";[195] and the Penal Code resulting from this, Foucault stressed in 1973, organized a whole moral control of vagabondage, drunkenness, and a whole procedural apparatus, in particular through the system of mitigating and aggravating circumstances, which functions as a "*moralizing modulation* of the penal system."[196] Thus, in the 1973 lectures, Foucault talks at length about Colquhoun's *Treatise on the Police of the Metropolis*, presenting it as exemplary of this "moralization of penality": "We have an example of this movement in the figure of Colquhoun,"[197] Foucault announced on 7 February 1973, before launching into a detailed reading of his work. Regarding Colquhoun, he goes so far as to say: "unfortunately, when we teach morality, when we study the history of morality, we always analyze the *Groundwork of the Metaphysics of Morals*, and we do not read this character who is fundamental for our morality."[198] By contrast, even though Colquhoun appears at several points in *Discipline and Punish*,[199] Foucault no longer elaborates the moral aspect of his work.

This shift has important effects on the theory of popular illegalisms. In 1973, the bourgeoisie transforms popular illegalisms precisely through moralization. Foucault gives lengthy consideration to those "societies of moralization."[200] In fact, in 1973, the moralization of the penal represents one of the three forms of penality: (1) the strict and juridical penality of Beccaria; (2) the moralization of criminality; and (3) the criminological and scientific discourse of the penal. By contrast, in 1975, the variation of the penal extends only from Beccaria to criminology.[201] The theme of moralization is replaced by "the political dimension of popular illegalisms."[202] In 1975 the accent is more on social struggles "in a general political outlook."[203] The exposition takes up penality rather from the angle of the production of the delinquent and the notion of dangerousness, a notion, of course, that intersects with morality, but in which moralization nevertheless plays a slightly reduced role. Thus, Foucault turns to the question of dangerousness, which is not as present in 1973, but will become a central theme of future research, in particular in the lecture he gives in 1978, "About the Concept of the 'Dangerous Individual' in 19th Century Legal Psychiatry."[204]

In sum, Foucault's theory of illegalisms changes. Whereas in *The Punitive Society* the accent is put on the Quaker injunction: "Go, and repent," in *Discipline and Punish*, the title of the relevant chapter will be "Illegalisms and delinquency," and the delinquent, rather than moralization, will occupy center stage.[205] Moralization, indexed to the juridical and tied to the binary opposition of the permitted and the prohibited, is somewhat effaced, to be replaced by normalization, which becomes far more important in 1975.[206]

Next, one clearly senses, in reading the two texts, the transition from a period of methodological innovation and evolution, in 1973, to one of methodological consolidation, in 1975. In *The Punitive Society*, Foucault is still discovering the inadequacy of a purely archeological approach. This is precisely what accounts for his analysis, sometimes in a stark way: it is not just that the prison cannot be derived from the penal theories of the second half of the eighteenth century, but, even more, "in a way it was imposed on penal theory from outside, and penal theory was obliged to justify it after the fact."[207] With *Discipline and Punish*, the genealogical approach is in place, it is established, and does not need to be justified. We are in full genealogy: Foucault has almost no need to motivate his approach by reference to any weakness of archeological derivation.

Hence, a certain openness to rethink the penal reformers and theories of the eighteenth century. In 1973, the analysis of the latter focuses on the protection of society, the social enemy, and deterrence; two years later, what stands out is a whole dramatization of the penalty. Theater, representation, and the sign come to the fore. "At the crossroads, in the gardens, at the side of roads being repaired or bridges built, in workshops open to all, in the depths of mines that may be visited, will be hundreds of tiny theatres of punishment" with "notices, caps, posters, placards, symbols, texts read or printed."[208] Moreover, one might detect a slight difference in the exact relationship between the great reformers and the penitentiary system of the nineteenth century—as if a fragment of doubt had entered regarding their total incompatibility. In 1975, a small echo of disciplinary power is almost heard in Foucault's description of the grand reformers: "a tendency towards a more finely tuned justice, towards a closer penal mapping (*quadrillage*) of the social body";[209] "the rearrangement of the power to punish, according to modalities that render it more regular, more effective, more constant and more detailed in its effects";[210] "to make of the punishment and repression of illegalisms a regular function, coextensive with society; not to punish less, but to punish better; to punish with an attenuated severity perhaps, but in order to punish with more universality and necessity; to insert the power to punish more deeply into the social body."[211] This is, after all, how discipline in the nineteenth century will be evoked. Not that a radical revision is involved,[212] but one senses a slightly different evaluation of the eighteenth-century reformers.

And then, Hobbes and Clausewitz[213] disappear, essentially, from *Discipline and Punish*—and the notion of civil war becomes less marked, although Foucault takes up this theme again in the 1976 lectures, *"Society Must Be Defended."*[214] Civil war, so operational in the 1973 analysis of Le Trosne's text, for example, as well as in the logic of Maoist militants in the 1970s—this notion of civil war, which "is the matrix of all struggles of power, of all strategies of power, and, consequently ... also the matrix of all the struggles regarding and against power,"[215]—no longer appears as central in *Discipline and Punish* (with the exception, perhaps, of the very last sentence of the original French edition). Maybe it is because in the nineteenth century, the various discourses—including Marxist discourse on the *Lumpenproletariat*—no longer focus on civil war and the social enemy, but on the delinquent. This transition—from the social fact to the psychosocial case, from the collective to the individual, from society to the individuals who compose it, in conjunction with new criteria of morality produced by the effects of capitalist development—will push the analysis of civil war towards the question of racism, eugenics, and bio-power, themes that Foucault will develop in the 1976 lectures and in those of 1975, *Abnormal*.

Finally, the 1973 lectures elaborate the main elements of the exchange with Marxist historians and theorists—for example, popular illegalisms, the notion of the coercive—and develop them "with great conceptual clarity" and "great force," as Frédéric Gros writes.[216] The confrontation with Marx is, of course, found in some passages of *Discipline and Punish*,[217] but it is clearer and more direct in 1973.

CONCLUSION

According to Daniel Defert, Foucault wrote his books in three stages.[218] The first: a complete manuscript, which he threw in the bin, saying that he had simply written what he thought spontaneously about a subject before doing any research in the archives. The second: again, a whole manuscript, which he had transcribed in order to use the typescript as support for the third and final stage, writing the manuscript that would be published. The first mention of *Discipline and Punish* that we can find in the Foucault archives—as far as we know at least—is from September 1972 when, in a letter to Daniel Defert, Foucault writes that he is working on his "book on punishments."[219] And we know that in April 1973, Foucault "[e]nds a first draft of the book on prisons (*Discipline and Punish*)."[220] The lectures making up *The Punitive Society* were transcribed in the following months, and, according to Alessandro Fontana, would have been read and consulted by Foucault. Maybe they correspond then to the second stage of the process of writing. But this is only speculation, and it will be for the reader to decide, by juxtaposing a reading of the 1973 lectures and *Discipline and Punish*. Whatever the case, *The Punitive Society* quite clearly represents a foundation for the future work, and at the same time reads like a complete text.

NOTE ON ESTABLISHING THE TEXT

Foucault gave the thirteen lectures of *The Punitive Society* from manuscript notes which, from 2013, have been kept at the Bibliothèque nationale de France. All of the lectures were recorded on cassettes by Gilbert Burlet with Foucault's consent; the recordings were then transcribed by Jacqueline Germé, who prepared a typescript of 213 pages. According to Alessandro Fontana, the transcription was made at Foucault's request in order to produce a typed version of the text; Foucault would have received this transcription, made corrections, and then consulted the typescript. After Foucault's death in 1984, Burlet deposited all his archives of the courses—recordings and typescripts—at the Collège de France, nine cassettes of which were labeled "1973." These archives were kept in the Michel Foucault collection at the Collège de France. However, the recordings of the 1973 lectures have at some time or other been erased by the recording or copying of the 1974 lectures on the same tapes. This was first discovered by an American researcher, Richard A. Lynch, who deposited a memorandum, dated 12 January 1999, in the Collège de France dossier; it was also confirmed by another researcher, Márcio Alves Da Fonseca, who also left a memorandum to this effect in the Michel Foucault collection on 31 January 2000. Further research in September 2010 confirmed that no recording of the 1973 lectures exists at the Collège de France. Lengthy efforts to find copies of the recordings have been unsuccessful.[221] Consequently, there does not exist, to this day, any audio trace of *The Punitive Society*.

The text was therefore established on the basis of Jacqueline Germé's 1973 transcription, apparently corrected by Foucault, of the now lost recordings made by Gilbert Burlet. The text has been fully checked and corrected against Foucault's manuscript notes. Important passages that were not identical to those in the typescript, as well as additions in relation to the typescript, are indicated in notes at the bottom of the page. In the absence of access to the recordings, we have not in every case reproduced the emphases adopted by the typescript, except where the word or expression was also underlined in the manuscript; on the other hand, we have copied the emphases of the manuscript even when they do not appear in the typescript, thinking that the manuscript—in Foucault's hand—was necessarily more faithful to his expression. We have also added, without comment, the quotation marks present in the manuscript.

My thanks to Daniel Defert and François Ewald, to the members of the editorial committee, Henri-Paul Fruchaud, Frédéric Gros and Michel Senellart, as well as to Corentin Durand.

1. Lecture of 28 March 1973 above, p. 237.
2. D. Defert, "Chronologie" in M. Foucault, *DE*, I, p. 42/"Quarto," I, p. 57.
3. M. Foucault, "Le grand enfermement" (interview with M. Meienberg, *Tages Anzeiger Magazin*, 12, 25 March 1972, p. 15, p. 17, p. 20, and p. 37, trans. J. Chavy), *DE*, II, no. 105, p. 304/"Quarto," vol. I, p. 1172.
4. See D. Defert, "L'émergence d'un nouveau front: les prisons," in Le Groupe d'information sur les prisons. Archives d'une lutte, 1970-1972, documents collected and presented by Philippe Artières, Laurent Quéro, and Michelle Zancarini-Fournel (Éditions de l'IMEC, 2003) pp. 315-326; A. Kiéfer, Michel Foucault: le G.I.P., l'histoire et l'action, philosophy thesis (November 2006), University of Picardy Jules Verne of Amiens, 2009; F. Brion and B. E. Harcourt, "Situation du cours" in M. Foucault, *Mal faire, dire vrai. Fonction de l'aveu en justice* (Louvain: Presses universitaires de Louvain, 2012) pp. 267-276; English translation by Stephen W. Sawyer, "The Louvain Lectures in Context," in *Wrong-Doing, Truth-Telling. The Function of Avowal in Justice* (Chicago: The University of Chicago Press, 2014), pp. 274-283.
5. D. Defert, "Chronologie," p. 42/p. 57.
6. Ibid.
7. See the lecture of 3 January 1973 above, p. 13: "So it is the notion of *civil war* that must be put at the heart of all these analyses of penality."
8. See M. Foucault, *Leçons sur la volonté de savoir. Cours au Collège de France 1970-1971*, ed., D. Defert (Paris: Gallimard-Seuil, coll. "Hautes Études", 2011) pp. 4-6; English translation by Graham Burchell, *Lectures on The Will to Know. Lectures at the Collège de France 1970-1971*, English series editor, Arnold I. Davidson (London: Palgrave Macmillan, 2013) pp. 2-5; M. Foucault, "Théories et institutions pénales," *DE*, II, no. 115, p. 389/"Quarto," I, p. 1257; English translation by Robert Hurley, "Penal Theories and Institutions" in Michel Foucault, *EW*, 1, p. 17 (in which Foucault describes his "broader project, outlined the previous year: to trace the formation of certain types of knowledge [*savoir*] out of the juridico-political matrices that gave birth to them and act as their support").
9. See M. Foucault, *Folie et Déraison. Histoire de la folie à l'age classique* (Paris: Plon, 1961); English translation by Jonathan Murphy and Jean Khalfa, *History of Madness* (London and New York: Routledge, 2006); "Un problème m'interesse depuis longtemps, c'est celui du système pénal" (interview with J. Hafsia, *La Presse de Tunisie*, 12 August 1971, p. 3), *DE*, II, no. 95, p. 206/"Quarto," I, p. 1074; F. Brion and B. E. Harcourt, "Situation du cours," *Mal faire, dire vrai*, pp. 267-273; "The Louvain Lectures in Context," *Doing-Wrong, Truth-Telling*, pp. 274-280.
10. Lecture of 28 March 1973 above, p. 227, and p. 242 note 3; see the lecture of 31 January, 1973 above, p. 84: "So where does this form come from?"
11. M. Foucault, *Leçons sur la volonté de savoir*, p. 4; *Lectures on The Will to Know*, p. 2.
12. M. Foucault, "Théories et institutions pénales," p. 392/p. 1260; "Penal Theories and Institutions," p. 20.
13. Lecture of 28 March 1973 above, p. 227.
14. See "Théories et institutions pénales," p. 390/p. 1258; "Penal Theories and Institutions," p. 18: "next year the *examination* will be considered as a form of power-knowledge linked to systems of control, exclusion, and punishment characteristic of industrial societies."
15. M. Foucault, *Surveiller et Punir. Naissance de la prison* (Paris: Gallimard, 1975), p. 134; English translation by Alan Sheridan, *Discipline and Punish: The Birth of the Prison* (London: Allen Lane, 1977) p. 131.
16. John K. Simon, "Michel Foucault on Attica: An Interview" (translated and edited from a taped conversation), *Social Justice*, vol. 18, no. 3, 1991 (reprinted from *Telos*, no. 19, Spring 1974), p. 26; translated into French by F. Durand-Bogaert as, M. Foucault, "À propos de

la prison d'Attica" (interview with J. K. Simon), *DE*, II, no. 137, p. 526/"Quarto," vol. I, p. 1394.

17. Ibid., p. 28; p. 528/p. 1396.

18. *Surveiller et Punir*, p. 30; *Discipline and Punish*, p. 25.

19. Lecture of 7 February 1973 above, pp. 101-102 footnote ‡ (manuscript, fol. 3).

20. "Le grand enfermement," pp. 298-299/pp. 1166-1167.

21. See *La Révolte de la prison de Nancy. 15 January 1972. Documents et propos de Michel Foucault, Jean-Paul Sartre et de militants du Groupe d'information sur les prisons* (Paris: Le Point du jour, 2013). Foucault gave his unreserved support to political prisoners and common law prisoners without distinction. As he elaborated the notion of "civil war," the very distinction—political prisoner and common law prisoner—no longer had any sense. This is an important aspect, both theoretical and practical, of Foucault's intervention at this time. See M. Foucault, "Sur la justice populaire. Débat avec les maos" (interview with Gilles et Victor, 5 February 1972, *Les Temps modernes*, no. 310 bis, pp. 355-366), *DE*, II, no. 108, pp. 340-369/"Quarto," vol. I, pp. 1208-1237; English translation by John Mepham, "On Popular Justice: A Discussion with Maoists" in Michel Foucault, *Power/Knowledge: Selected Interviews and Other Writings 1972-1977*, ed., Colin Gordon (Brighton: The Harvester Press, 1980).

22. *La Révolte de la prison de Nancy*, p. 19 (reproduction of the manuscript page).

23. See D. Defert, "Chronologie," p. 40/p. 54.

24. See ibid.; *La Révolte de la prison de Nancy*.

25. "Michel Foucault on Attica: An Interview," p. 29; "À propos de la prison d'Attica," p. 530/p. 1398.

26. Ibid., p. 29; p. 529/p. 1397.

27. Ibid., p. 29; p. 530/p. 1398.

28. Ibid., p. 29; p. 529/p. 1397.

29. The event is referred to in the manuscript of *The Punitive Society*; see the lecture of 7 March 1973 above, p. 184, note 19. One year before, in 1970, Jean Genet had written an introduction to the prison letters of George Jackson and this gave rise to a meeting of Foucault with Genet; see G. Jackson, *Soledad Brother: The Prison Letters of George Jackson*, with an Introduction by Jean Genet (New York: Coward-McCann, 1970); D. Defert, "Chronologie," p. 39/p. 52.

30. M. Foucault, "Le grand enfermement," p. 300/p. 1168.

31. Ibid., p. 301/p. 1169.

32. Lecture of 28 February 1973 above, pp. 164-165.

33. Ibid., p. 165 note * (Appendix to lecture 9, first sheet).

34. M. Foucault, "La vérité et les formes juridiques" (Lectures at the Pontifical University of Rio de Janeiro, 21 to 25 May, 1973, *Cadernas da P.U.C.*, no. 16, June 1974, pp. 5-133; trans. J.W. Prado, Jnr.), *DE*, II, no. 139, p. 570/"Quarto," vol. I, p. 1438; English translation by Robert Hurley, "Truth and Juridical Forms" in *EW*, 3, p. 32 [translation slightly modified; G.B.].

35. M. Foucault, "Les intellectuels et le pouvoir" (conversation with Gilles Deleuze, *L'Arc*, no. 49: *Gilles Deleuze*, 2nd quarter 1972, pp. 3-10), *DE*, II, no. 106, p. 308/"Quarto," I, p. 1176; English translation by Donald F. Bouchard and Sherry Simon, "Intellectuals and Power" in M. Foucault, *Language, Counter-Memory, Practice. Selected Essays and Interviews*, ed., Donal F. Bouchard (Oxford: Basil Blackwell, 1977), pp. 207-208.

36. D. Defert, "Chronologie," p. 42/p. 57.

37. M. Foucault, "Le grand enfermement," p. 298/p. 1166.

38. Lecture of 10 January 1973 above, p. 31.

39. Ibid., p. 32.

40. Ibid.

41. See L. Althusser, "Idéologie et appareils idéologiques d'État. (Note pour une recherche)," *La Pensée. Revue du rationalisme moderne*, no. 51, June 1970, pp. 3–38, republished in L. Althusser, *Positions* (Paris: Éditions Sociales, 1976) pp. 79–137; English translation by Ben Brewster, "Ideology and Ideological Apparatuses" in L. Althusser, *Lenin and Philosophy* (London: New Left Books, 1971).

42. See ibid. (1970) p. 13 and p. 17; English, p. 136: "in Marxist theory, the State Apparatus (SA) contains: the Government, the Administration, the Army, the Police, the Courts, the Prisons, etc., which constitute what I shall in future call the Repressive State Apparatus," and p. 142: "the State apparatus secures by repression (from the most brutal physical force, via administrative commands and interdictions, to open and tacit censorship) the political conditions for the action of the Ideological State Apparatuses."

43. Ibid., p. 35; English, p. 134.

44. Lecture of 28 March 1973 above, p. 229. Foucault will draw from this the consequence: "Which means, practically, that neither control nor destruction of the State apparatus may suffice to transform or get rid of a certain type of power, the one in which it functioned" (ibid.).

45. Lecture 21 March 1973 above, p. 209.

46. Ibid., note * (ms. fol. 12).

47. See lecture of 28 March 1973 above, pp. 227-233; an important passage in which Foucault proposes and rejects four theoretical schemas of power.

48. M. Foucault, *Le Pouvoir psychiatrique. Cours au Collège de France, 1973-1974*, ed. J. Lagrange (Paris: Gallimard-Seuil, "Hautes Études," 2003) p. 42, n*; English translation by Graham Burchell, *Psychiatric Power. Lectures at the Collège de France 1973-1974*, English series editor Arnold I. Davidson (London: Palgrave Macmillan, 2006) p. 40, n*. Foucault had declared in the previous week's lecture: "Let's be really anti-institutionalist. What I propose to bring to light this year is, before analysis of the institution, the microphysics of power" (ibid., Fr., p. 34; Eng., p. 33). See Michel Foucault, *La Volonté de savoir* (Paris: Gallimard, "Tel," 1976) p. 117; English translation by Robert Hurley, *The History of Sexuality. Volume 1: An Introduction* (London: Allen Lane, 1979) pp. 88-89.

49. According to Daniel Defert, this expression of Clausewitz was very fashionable among Maoist militants at the time, which might situate Foucault's interest in this second dimension.

50. Lecture 10 January 1973 above, p. 32. See *Surveiller et Punir*, p. 170; *Discipline and Punish*, p. 168; M. Foucault, *"Il faut défendre la société." Cours au Collège de France, 1975-1976*, ed., M. Bertani and A. Fontana (Paris: Gallimard-Seuil, "Hautes Études," 1997), lecture of 7 January 1976, p. 16, and 21 January, p. 41; English translation by David Macey, *"Society Must Be Defended." Lectures at the Collège de France 1975-1976*, English series editor Arnold I. Davidson (New York: Picador, 2003) p. 15 and p. 48.

51. E. Goffman, *Asylums: Essays on the Social Situation of Mental Patients and Other Inmates* (New York: Doubleday, "Anchor Books," 1961) p. 4. For a joint reading of Foucault and Goffman, see Ian Hacking, "Between Michel Foucault and Erving Goffman: Between Discourse in the Abstract and Face-to-Face Interaction," *Economy and Society*, vol. 33 (3), August 2004, pp. 277-302.

52. E. Goffman, *Asylums*, p. xiii and p. 319.

53. Ibid., p. 23, p. 46, p. 48.

54. Ibid., p. 6, p. 290.

55. Ibid., p. 7.

56. Ibid., pp. 13-14, pp. 38-39, pp. 46-48.

57. Ibid., p. 68.

58. Thus this analysis by Foucault could be applied to Goffman's total institution; "in the space and sphere of influence of these institutions, a sort of concentrated and quasi autonomous

304 THE PUNITIVE SOCIETY

power with a new force reigns: the power of the boss in the factory, of the foreman in the workshop" (lecture of 21 March 1973 above, p. 206). We see this parallel also in the definition Foucault gives of sequestration; see ibid. above, p. 216: "To be sequestrated is to be caught within a discursivity at once uninterrupted in time, produced from outside by an authority, and necessarily ordered by reference to the normal and the abnormal."

59. D. Rothman, The Discovery of the Asylum: Social Order and Disorder in the New Republic (Boston, MA: Little Brown, 1971).

60. See M. Foucault, "La vérité et les formes juridiques," pp. 611-612/pp. 1479-1480; "Truth and Juridical Forms," p. 76; the reference here to "an American historian" who "tried to show how those buildings and institutions which spread across Western society appeared in the United States" is to the historian David Rothman who analyzes precisely this question in his book, The Discovery of the Asylum.

61. See "Course Summary," above, pp. 261-262.

62. E. Goffman, Asylums, p. 4 and p. 220.

63. Lecture of 21 March 1973 above, p. 205.

64. Lecture of 31 January 1973 above, p. 83.

65. Lecture of 24 January 1973 above, p. 71.

66. "Course Summary," p. 261.

67. Lecture of 7 February 1973 above, p. 100.

68. Lecture of 14 March 1973 above, p. 196.

69. See the lecture of 21 March 1973, p. 215.

70. R. Castel, Le Psychanalysme. L'ordre psychanalytique et le pouvoir (Paris: Maspero, 1973); L'Ordre psychiatrique. L'âge d'or de l'aliénisme (Paris: Éditions de Minuit, 1976); English translation by W. D. Halls as The Regulation of Madness, the Origins of Incarceration in France (Berkeley and Los Angeles: The University of California Press, 1988).

71. G. Deleuze and F. Guattari, Anti-Œdipe. Capitalisme et schizophrénie (Paris: Éditions de Minuit, 1972); English translation by Robert Hurley, Mark Seem, and Helen R. Lane, Anti-Oedipus. Capitalism and Schizophrenia (New York: The Viking Press, 1977).

72. See Surveiller et Punir, p. 29 n. 1; Discipline and Punish, p. 309 n. 2: "In any case, I could give no notion by references or quotations what this book owes to Gilles Deleuze and the work he is undertaking with Félix Guattari. I should also have quoted a number of pages from R. Castell's Psychanalysme and say how much I am indebted to Pierre Nora."

73. R. Castel, L'Ordre psychiatrique, p. 11.

74. One might perhaps also discern the beginning of a dialog with Thompson the previous year in "Penal Theories and Institutions"; but in 1972, Foucault is much more concerned with the works of the Soviet historian, Boris Porchnev, who drew his sources from the archives of the Séguier collection in Leningrad and who, in a detailed study published in Russian in 1948, interpreted the popular revolts of the seventeenth century in France through the prism of the class struggles. See B. Porchnev, Les Soulèvements populaires en France de 1623 à 1648 (Paris: SEVPEN, 1963; republished, Paris: Flammarion, 1972).

75. See E. P. Thompson, The Making of the English Working Class (London: Victor Gollancz, 1963) pp. 59-71; "The Moral Economy of the English Crowd in the Eighteenth Century," Past and Present, no. 50, February 1971, pp. 76-79, see pp. 78-79: "The food riot in eighteenth-century England was a highly complex form of direct popular action, disciplined and with clear objectives ... This in its turn was grounded upon a consistent traditional view of social norms and obligations, of the proper economic functions of several parties within the community, which, taken together, can be said to constitute the moral economy of the poor"; see also G. Rudé, The Crowd in History: A Study of Popular Disturbances in France and England, 1730-1848 (New York: Wiley, 1964).

76. E. P. Thompson, The Making of the English Working Class, p. 543.

77. Ibid., p. 61. The question of the severity of penalties and of the use of the death penalty in England in the eighteenth century will give rise to important debates among historians. See D. Hay, "Property, Authority and the Criminal Law" in Douglas Hay, Peter Linebaugh, and E. P. Thompson, *Albion's Fatal Tree: Crime and Society in Eighteenth Century England* (New York: Doubleday/Pantheon Books, 1975); J. H. Langbien, "Albion's Fatal Flaws," *Past and Present*, no. 98 (1), 1983, pp. 96-120, republished in David Sugarman, ed., *Law in History: Histories of Law and Society* (New York: New York University Press, 1996) vol. 1.

78. Lecture of 10 January 1973 above, p. 30: "A riot therefore consisted less in destroying the elements of power than in taking them over and using them."

79. Lecture of 21 February 1973 above, p. 140.

80. Foucault explains these "few words" in the following way: "corresponding to the rise of capitalism there would have been a whole series of movements of popular sedition to which the power of the bourgeoisie responded with a new judicial and penitentiary system" (ibid.).

81. Ibid.

82. Ibid. See F. Gros, "Foucault et 'la société punitive'," *Pouvoirs*, no. 136, 2010/4, pp. 5-14, see pp. 10-11.

83. See below, pp. 281-283.

84. See the lecture of 3 January 1973 above, p. 18, note 13; see too the lecture of 14 February 1973 above, p. 123.

85. M. Foucault, "Théories et Institutions pénales. Cours au Collège de France, 1971-1972," seventh lecture, ms. fol. 2 [p. 68]; See "Sur la justice populaire. Débat avec les maos," *DE*, II, p. 351/"Quarto," I, p. 1219; "On Popular Justice," p. 15.

86. "Théories et Institutions penales," ms. fol. 3 [p. 68].

87. Lecture of 21 February 1973 above, p. 145.

88. "Michel Foucault on Attica: An Interview," p. 28; "À propos de la prison d'Attica," p. 527/p. 1395.

89. Ibid.

90. Ibid.

91. See *Surveiller et Punir*, p. 28; *Discipline and Punish*, p. 23.

92. See "Michel Foucault on Attica: An Interview," p. 28; "À propos de la prison d'Attica," p. 528/p. 1396.

93. *Surveiller et Punir*, p. 196; *Discipline and Punish*, p. 194. Which will give, two years after *The Punitive Society*, the methodological imperative: "Do not focus the study of punitive mechanism on their 'repressive' effects alone, on their 'penalty' aspect alone, but situate them in a whole series of their possible positive effects, even if these seem marginal at first sight" (ibid., Fr., p. 28; Eng., p. 23 [translation slightly modified; G.B.].

94. See above, note 74.

95. M. Foucault, "À propos de l'enfermement pénitentiaire" (interview with A. Krywin and F. Ringelheim, *Pro Justitia. Revue politique de droit*, vol. I, no. 3-4: *La Prison*, October 1973, pp. 5-14), *DE*, II, no. 127, p. 435/"Quarto," I, p. 1303.

96. Lecture of 21 February 1973 above, p. 142.

97. Ibid., pp. 140-141.

98. Cited above, note 95. See the lecture of 21 February 1973 above, p. 140 and p. 152, note 2.

99. Lecture of 28 February 1973 above, pp. 155-156.

100. See the lecture of 21 February 1973 above, pp. 139-140; see too M. Foucault, "Le grand enfermement," p. 297/p. 1165; "Sur la justice populaire," p. 357/p. 1225/ "On Popular Justice," pp. 22-23.

101. Lecture of 14 March, 1973 above, p. 181.

102. M. Foucault, "À propos de l'enfermement pénitentiaire," p. 436/p. 1304; see also *Surveiller et Punir*, pp. 84-91 and pp. 277-282; *Discipline and Punish*, pp. 82-89 and pp. 272-277.

103. Lecture of 21 February 1973 above, p. 146.
104. See the lecture of 7 February 1973 above, p. 99 sq., especially p. 101, note *, and the lecture of 21 February above, p. 140 and note *.
105. F. Gros, "Foucault et 'la société punitive'," p. 9.
106. Lecture of 21 February 1973, above, p. 146.
107. Ibid., p. 149.
108. Ibid.
109. Lecture of 28 February 1973 above, p. 155.
110. See "Michel Foucault on Attica: An Interview," p. 28; "À propos de la prison d'Attica," p. 528/p. 1396: "what is their [procedures for punishment] role in the class struggle?"
111. See the Chomsky-Foucault debate, "Human Nature: Justice vs. Power," recorded in November 2011at the Eindhoven École *Supérieur de technologie*, published in Noam Chomsky and Michel Foucault, *The Chomsky-Foucault Debate: On Human Nature* (New York: The New Press, 2006).
112. Lecture of 21 March 1973 above, p. 216, note †.
113. Lecture of 28 March 1973 above, p. 228.
114. Lecture of 24 January 1973, above, p. 62 [my emphasis; B.E.H.].
115. Karl Marx, "Proceedings of the Sixth Rhine Province Assembly, Third Article Debates on the Law on Thefts of Wood" in K. Marx, *Collected Works*, Volume 1 (New York: International Publishers, 1975). For a discussion of this text, see above, p. 74, note 5 (lecture of 24 January 1973); as well as P. Lascoumes and H. Zander, *Marx: du "vol de bois" à la critique du droit. Karl Marx à la "Gazette rhénane", naissance d'une méthode* (Paris: Presses universitaires de France, 1984); and M. Xifaras, "Marx, justice et jurisprudence. Une lecture des 'vols de bois'," *Revue française d'histoire des idées politiques*, no. 15, April 2002.
116. L. Althusser, "Sur le jeune Marx: questions de théorie" in *Pour Marx* (Paris: Maspero, 1968), p. 81; English translation by Ben Brewster, "On the Young Marx" in *For Marx* (London: Allen Lane, 1969) p. 83.
117. Ibid., Fr., p. 79; Eng., p. 82.
118. Ibid., Fr., p. 81; Eng., p. 82.
119. Fr., ibid.; Eng., p. 82 (emphasis in the text). It is important in particular to measure "the *contingent beginnings* (in respect of his birth) that he had to start from and *the gigantic layer of illusions he had to break through before he could even see it*" (p. 83, emphasis in the text).
120. Fr., ibid.; Eng., p. 84 (emphasis in the text).
121. L. Althusser, "Idéologie et appareils idéologiques d'État," p. 22; "Ideology and the Ideological State Apparatuses," p. 149 [my emphasis; B.E.H.].
122. Lecture of 24 January 1973 above, p. 62.
123. Ibid.
124. G. Deleuze and F. Guattari, *Anti-Œdipe*, p. 416; *Anti-Oedipus*, p. 344.
125. See "Michel Foucault explique son dernier livre" (interview with J.-J. Brochier, *Magazine littéraire*, no. 28, April-May 1969, pp. 23-25), *DE*, I, no. 66, p. 775/"Quarto," vol. I, p. 803.
126. G. Deleuze and F. Guattari, *Anti-Œdipe*, p. 39; *Anti-Oedipus*, p. 29 [translation modified; G.B.].
127. See the lecture of 14 February 1973 above, p. 133 (on the origin of "the present theory of desire").
128. Lecture of 24 January 1973 above, p. 63.
129. Ibid.
130. Ibid., p. 67.
131. Ibid., p. 66, note † (ms. fol. 7).
132. Although Foucault does not refer to them, we could evoke here the *Economic and Philosophic Manuscripts of 1844*, trans., Martin Milligan (Moscow: Progress Publishers, 1959) in which Marx defines the essence and specificity of man by contrast to those of the animal: man is

able to supply a freely granted and productive labor, whereas the animal functions primarily by "eating, drinking, and procreating." The alienation of labor, when the latter becomes a mere means of survival, thus reduces man to the animal state: "What is animal becomes human and what is human becomes animal." See R. L. Tucker, *Philosophy and Myth in Karl Marx.*

133. Lecture of 28 March 1973 above, p. 232.

134. See M. Foucault, "La vérité et les formes juridiques," p. 622/p. 1490; "Truth and Juridical Forms," p. 86.

135. Ibid. [translation slightly modified; G.B.].

136. Ibid.

137. Lecture of 21 March above, p. 206.

138. *Surveiller et Punir*, p. 222; *Discipline and Punish*, p. 220.

139. Ibid., p. 221; p. 220.

140. Ibid., p. 222; p. 221 [translation slightly modified; G.B.]. See *Le Pouvoir psychiatrique*, lecture of 28 November 1973, p. 73; *Psychiatric Power*, pp. 71-72.

141. See above p. 273.

142. L. Althusser, "Idéologie et appareils idéologiques d'État," p. 11; "Ideology and Ideological State Apparatuses," p. 134 [my emphasis; B.E.H.]; see too, Fr., p. 15; Eng., p. 139: "*no class can hold State power over a long period without at the same time exercising its hegemony over and in the State Ideological Apparatuses*" (emphasis in the text).

143. Ibid., p. 14; p. 141.

144. See the lecture of 28 March 1973 above, p. 228.

145. Lecture of 10 January 1973 above, p. 36, note *.

146. M. Foucault, "Michel Foucault explique son dernier livre," p. 772/p. 800.

147. See too, M. Foucault, "Les intellectuels et le pouvoir," p. 313/p. 1181; "Intellectuals and Power," p. 214: "A whole series of misunderstandings relates to the 'hidden,' 'repressed,' and 'unsaid'; and they permit the cheap 'psychoanalysis' of what should be the object of struggle. The secret is perhaps more difficult to flush out than the unconscious" [translation slightly modified; G.B.].

148. Lecture of 28 February 1973 above, p. 166.

149. Ibid., p. 156.

150. Ibid., note *.

151. See above, pp. 286-287 and p. 306 note 130.

152. "Course Summary," pp. 253-254.

153. Ibid.; see the lecture of 7 February 1973 above, pp. 108-109 and p. 113.

154. Lecture of 31 January 1973 above, p. 89; see also the lecture of 24 January, p. 65.

155. "Course Summary," p. 256; see the lecture of 31 January 1973 above, p. 84.

156. In his lecture, Foucault lays stress on this old spelling; see the lecture of 31 January 1973, above pp. 89-90, and the lecture of 21 February, 1973 p. 140, footnote *.

157. Lecture of 31 January 1973 above, p. 89.

158. Ibid.

159. See ibid., pp. 90-92.

160. Ibid., p. 87.

161. Lecture of 7 February 1973 above, p. 107.

162. Ibid.

163. See ibid., pp. 108-109.

164. Ibid., p. 111. On the *coercive* in general, see, ibid., pp. 111-112.

165. Lecture of 21 February 1973, above p. 149.

166. See M. Foucault, "De l'archéologie à la dynastique" (interview with S. Hasumi, Paris, 27 September 1972, *Umi*, March 1973, pp. 182-206), *DE*, II, no. 119, p. 406/ "Quarto," I, p. 1273.

167. See the lecture of 31 January 1973 above, pp. 83-84; lecture of 7 February 1973 above, p. 113.

168. Lecture of 31 January 1973 above, p. 84.

169. See M. Foucault, *L'Ordre du discours* (Paris: Gallimard, 1971) p. 62 and p. 68; English translation by Ian MacLeod, "The Order of Discourse," in Robert Young, ed., *Untying the Text* (London: Routledge and Kegan Paul, 1981) p. 71 and p. 77.

170. See M. Foucault, *Le Pouvoir psychiatrique*, p. 14; *Psychiatric Power*, p. 13; "La vérité et les formes juridiques," p. 554 and pp. 643-644/p. 1422 and pp. 1511-1512; "Truth and Juridical Forms," p. 17; *"Il faut défendre la société,"* lecture of 7 January 1976, p. 11; *"Society Must be Defended,"* p. 8; "Dialogue sur le pouvoir" (interview with students of Los Angeles, in S. Wade, ed., *Chez Foucault*, Los Angeles: Circabook, 1978, pp. 4-22); French translation by F. Durand-Bogaert, *DE*, III, no. 221, pp. 468-469/"Quarto," vol. II, pp. 468-469; "Structuralisme et poststructuralisme" (interview with G. Raulet, *Telos*, vol. XVI, no. 55, Spring 1983, pp. 195-211); *DE*, IV, no. 330, p. 443/"Quarto," II, p. 1262; English translation by Jeremy Harding, "Structuralism and Post-Structuralism" in James Faubion, ed., *Essential Works of Foucault 1954-1984. Volume Two: Aesthetics, Method, and Epistemology* (New York: New Press, 1998), p. 445. For a more recent discussion, see A. Davidson, "On Epistemology and Archeology: From Canguilhem to Foucault" in *The Emergence of Sexuality: Historical Epistemology and the Formation of Concepts* (Cambridge, MA: Harvard University Press, 2004) pp. 192-206.

171. See *Surveiller et Punir*, p. 27; *Discipline and Punish*, p. 23.

172. Lecture of 31 January 1973 above, pp. 83-84, and see pp. 93-94, note 2.

173. Lecture of 14 March 1973 above, p. 191.

174. Lecture of 7 March 1973 above, p. 174.

175. See B. E. Harcourt, *The Illusion of Free Markets: Punishment and the Myth of Natural Order* (Cambridge, MA: Harvard University Press, 2011). I regret not having had the opportunity to integrate this discussion of Foucault's lectures in my previous work, published before the preparation of this volume.

176. Lecture of 14 March 1973 above, p. 191, note † (ms. fol. 10).

177. Lecture of 14 February 1973, above pp. 125-126.

178. Ibid., p. 136, note 3.

179. Lecture of 14 February, 1973 above, p. 130.

180. Foucault initially gave the lectures the title: "The disciplinary society"; see D. Defert, "Chronologie," p. 43/p. 58. In his last lecture Foucault will say clearly: "Where was I wanting to go? I wanted to make the analysis of a certain ... form of power that I have called punitive, that it would be better to call disciplinary" (lecture of 28 March 1973 above, p. 237 and note * [ms. 20th fol.]).

181. Lecture of 10 January 1973, above pp. 37-38, note 2, and lecture of 24 January, p. 77, note 16.

182. Lecture of 28 March 1973 above, p. 242, note 3 (ms. 2nd fol.).

183. Lecture of 24 January 1973 above, p. 72.

184. "Course Summary," p. 258, and p. 264, note 16.

185. Ibid., p. 258.

186. Guy Debord, *La société du spectacle* (Paris: Buchet/Chastel, 1967).

187. Lecture of 10 January 1973 above, p. 23.

188. Lecture of 14 March 1973 above, p. 196.

189. See the lecture of 3 January 1973 above, p. 11.

190. See the lecture of 21 March 1973 above, p. 202.

191. Ibid., p. 204.

192. See *Surveiller et Punir*, p. 126, p. 241, p. 242; *Discipline and Punish*, p. 124, p. 239.

193. See the lecture of 21 February 1973 above, p. 150 (regarding the ideological exploitation of the theory of the delinquent as social enemy).

194. Ibid., p. 149.

195. Lecture of 7 March 1973 above, p. 176.
196. Ibid., p. 177.
197. Lecture of 7 February 1973 above, p. 108.
198. Ibid.; note also this passage: "to understand the system of morality of a society we have to ask the question: Where is the wealth? The history of morality should be organized entirely by this question of the location and movement of wealth" (ibid.).
199. See *Surveiller et Punir*, p. 88, p. 199 n. 3, p. 291 n. 1; *Discipline and Punish*, p. 85, p. 313 n. 3.
200. Referred to as such in the lectures of 21 February 1973 above, p. 139, and 28 February above, p. 166, footnote †.
201. One might add another form of penality on the basis of the 1979 lectures, *Naissance de la biopolitique. Cours au Collège de France, 1978-1979*, ed., M. Senellart (Paris: Gallimard-Seuil, "Hautes Études," 2004; English translation by Graham Burchell, *The Birth of Biopolitics. Lectures at the Collège de France 1978-1979*, English series editor Arnold I. Davidson (London: Palgrave Macmillan, 2008) on American neoliberalism: Gary Becker's economic conception of crime and punishment (lecture of 21 March 1979, Fr., pp. 253-254; Eng., pp. 252-252). See G. Becker, F. Ewald, and B. E. Harcourt, "'Becker on Ewald on Foucault on Becker': American Neoliberalism and Foucault's 1979 *Birth of Biopolitics*," *Carceral Notebooks*, vol. 7, 2011, pp. 1-35.
202. *Surveiller et Punir*, p. 278; *Discipline and Punish*, p. 273 [translation modified; G.B.]
203. Ibid., Fr. p. 280; Eng., p. 275.
204. M. Foucault, "About the Concept of the 'Dangerous Individual' in 19th Century Legal Psychiatry," *Journal of Law and Psychiatry*, Vol. 1, 1978, pp. 1-18; republished in *Essential Works of Foucault 1954-1984. Vol. 3: Power*, pp. 176-200. See also *Mal faire, dire vrai*, lecture of 20 May 1981, pp. 199-233, especially p. 223; *Wrong-Doing, Truth-Telling*, pp. 199-229, especially p. 224. The notion of dangerousness is certainly not absent from the 1973 lectures (see above, lecture of 3 January 1973, p. 2; lecture of 7 February 1973, p. 115; and lecture of 14 February 1973, p. 124 and p. 127; lecture of 7 March 1973, p. 178 and p. 184 note 18) but it is not central.
205. *Surveiller et Punir*, pp. 261-299; *Discipline and Punish*, pp. 257-292.
206. On the notion of normalization in *The Punitive Society*, see the lecture of 21 March 1973 above, p. 208 and p. 213 and footnote *, pp. 213-216 and footnote *, pp. 217-220 (appendix); and the lecture of 28 March, p. 237.
207. "Course Summary," above, p. 256.
208. *Surveiller et Punir*, p. 115; *Discipline and Punish*, p. 113.
209. Ibid., Fr., p. 80; Eng., p. 78.
210. Ibid., Fr., p. 83; Eng., p. 80.
211. Ibid., Fr., p. 84; Eng., p. 82 [translation slightly modified; G.B.].
212. See ibid., Fr., p. 116; Eng., pp. 114-115: "All in all, prison is incompatible with this whole technique of penalty-effect, penalty-representation, penalty-general function, penalty-sign and discourse" [translation slightly modified; G.B.].
213. There is a vague reference to the citation on p. 170, *Surveiller et Punir*; p. 168, *Discipline and Punish*.
214. See M. Foucault, *"Il faut défendre la société,"* the lecture of 14 January 1976, pp. 26-27, and above all in the lecture of 4 February 1976, p. 77 sq.; *"Society Must Be Defended,"* pp. 28-30, and p. 89 sq.
215. Lecture of 3 January 1973 above, p. 13.
216. F. Gros, "Foucault et 'la société punitive'," pp. 5-14, see p. 13.
217. See *Surveiller et Punir*, p. 166, p. 171, p. 177, pp. 222-224, p. 286; *Discipline and Punish*, p. 163, p. 169, p. 175, pp. 220-222, and p. 280.

218. Conversation with Daniel Defert; see also D. Defert, "I Believe in Time ...," interviews with Guillaume Bellon, *Recto/Verso*, no. 6: *Genèse de la pensée*, II: *Cheminements et Procédures*, September 2010 http://www.revuerectoverso.com/spip.php?article186.

219. This is *Surveiller et Punir; Discipline and Punish*; see D. Defert, "Chronologie," p. 42/p. 56. Foucault had spoken to Jalila Hafsia about it in August 1971: "if I am still alive and have not been put in prison, well, I will write the book ..." ("Un problème m'intéresse depuis longtemps, c'est celui du système pénal," p. 209/p. 1077.

220. See D. Defert, "Chronologie," p. 43/p. 58.

221. Gilbert Burlet greatly assisted the search for these cassettes, and I am immensely grateful to him. To know more about his contributions to the Foucault scene, as well as about those of Jacqueline Germé, see D. Defert, "Course Context," in *Lectures on The Will to Know*, p. 285, note 66.

INDEX OF CONCEPTS AND NOTIONS

Compiled by Sue Carlton

Page numbers followed by n refer to end of chapter notes

INDEX OF NAMES

Compiled by Sue Carlton

Page numbers followed by n refer to end of chapter notes